PPL Q & A

EASA Private Pilot Exam Questions

Includes Helicopters and IMC Rating

Phil Croucher

CONTENTS

© *Phil Croucher, 2016*

This book contains questions for the EASA Private Pilot's Licence, but it could be valid for almost any country, making due allowance for air law, meteorology and various maps. Indeed, we have included exercises and questions that will suit others, where applicable.

There is a trend to get a sneak peek of the questions, and this is what many publications seek to achieve*. This one doesn't! The questions inside follow the same *style* as those found in the PPL exams, but they are not the exact ones you will find in them. This is because, as a pilot, you are meant to think for yourself! In this respect, this book is very well suited for people intending to take their flying forward to a professional career.

For people intending to fly commercially, the contents of this book represent the minimum knowledge required by anybody starting a modular distance learning course, for which the PPL is a minimum requirement.

*In the UK, the professional pilot licences will be going online, and the PPL questions may join them. In other words, they will not be looked after by the flight schools, so nobody should get to know what they are.

ABOUT THE QUESTIONS

There are separate chapters for each subject involved. Answers (some with explanations**) are given at the end of the book. There is an Appendix containing various pictures, graphs, etc. for use in the questions.

Repetitive questions have been eliminated to make room for others, where the answer is obvious. For example, a question about what happens to Lift when density decreases does not have another that asks what happens when density increases!

These are abridged from my Private Pilot syllabus books, where full explanations can be found. All books are available from **www.electrocution.com/aviation.

REQUIREMENTS

In addition to this book, you will need a flight computer (we recommend the Jeppesen CR 3), a navigation ruler, a protractor, and a CAA 500,000 map.

If this page is a photocopy, it is not authorised!

UNITED KINGDOM CIVIL AVIATION AUTHORITY

CERTIFICATE OF REGISTRATION

This certificate is issued to:

CALEDONIAN ADVANCED PILOT TRAINING LIMITED

Number: OCP2310

Registered with the UK CAA to conduct the course(s) listed below in accordance with JAR-FCL and the Air Navigation Order 2009:

Private Pilot Licence (Aeroplane) Theoretical Knowledge
Private Pilot Licence (Helicopter) Theoretical Knowledge

Validity

This certificate remains valid until

- the EASA Rules for the conduct of PPL training take effect for existing training providers

or

- the Authority is informed by the operator that PPL training is to cease or the Authority establishes that training is not being carried out safely and/or in compliance with JAR-FCL. In both of these situations the registration of the facility will be revoked.

Conditions

Any changes to the information entered on the registration form shall be communicated to the Authority.

Date of issue: 21 August 2012

S E James
For the Civil Aviation Authority

European Union
United Kingdom Civil Aviation Authority

APPROVED TRAINING ORGANISATION CERTIFICATE

GBR.ATO.0129

Pursuant to Commission Regulation (EU) No 1178/2011 and subject to the conditions specified below, the UK Civil Aviation Authority hereby certifies

CALEDONIAN ADVANCED PILOT TRAINING LIMITED

Wycombe Air Centre Building
Wycombe Air Park
SL7 3DP

C/O Helicentre Aviation
Leicester Airport
Gartree Road
Leicester
LE2 2FG

as an Approved Training Organisation with the privilege to provide Part-FCL training courses, including the use of FSTDs, as listed in the attached course approval.

CONDITIONS:

1. This certificate is limited to the privileges and the scope of providing the training courses, including the use of FSTDs, as listed in the attached training course approval.

2. This certificate is valid whilst the approved organisation remains in compliance with Part-ORA, Part-FCL and other applicable regulations.

3. Subject to compliance with the foregoing conditions, this certificate shall remain valid unless the certificate has been surrendered, superseded, limited, suspended or revoked.

Date of issue: 15 February 2013

Signed
For the UK Civil Aviation Authority

EASA FORM 143 Issue 1 – page 1/2

APPROVED TRAINING ORGANISATION CERTIFICATE

Training Course Approval

Attachment to ATO Certificate Number:

GBR.ATO.0129

CALEDONIAN ADVANCED PILOT TRAINING LIMITED

has obtained the privilege to provide and conduct the following training courses and to use the following FSTD:

Training Course	Used FSTD(s)
ATPL (Aeroplanes) Modular Theoretical Knowledge (Distance Learning)	Nil
ATPL (Helicopter) Modular Theoretical Knowledge (Distance Learning)	Nil
ATPL (Helicopter) VFR Modular Theoretical Knowledge (Distance Learning)	Nil
CPL (Aeroplanes) Modular Theoretical Knowledge (Distance Learning)	Nil
CPL (Helicopters) Modular Theoretical Knowledge (Distance Learning)	Nil
IR (Aeroplanes) Modular Theoretical Knowledge (Distance Learning)	Nil
IR (Helicopters) Modular Theoretical Knowledge (Distance Learning)	Nil
No Further Entries	

This training course approval is valid as long as:

(a)   the ATO certificate has not been surrendered, superseded, limited, suspended or revoked, and

(b)   all operations are conducted in compliance with Part-ORA, Part-FCL, other regulations, and, when relevant, with the procedures in the organisation's documentation as required by Part-ORA.

Date of issue: 15 February 2013

Signed

For the Civil Aviation Authority.

EASA FORM 143 Issue 1 – page 2/2

HUMAN PERFORMANCE & LIMITATIONS

1

GENERAL

1. What might an early symptom of carbon monoxide poisoning be?

   (a) Vertigo

   (b) Euphoria

   (c) Disorientation

   (d) Headache

2. What are the initial and progressive stages of carbon monoxide poisoning?

   (a) Euphoria: sleepiness

   (b) Relaxed lethargy, warmness: euphoria

   (c) Blurred thought, inability to concentrate, dizziness, headache, unconsciousness

   (d) Lethargy, warmness and headache, ringing in the ears, dizziness

3. What should you do if you get carbon monoxide poisoning in flight?

   (a) Land

   (b) See a doctor

   (c) Descend

   (d) Turn off the cabin heat, open fresh air vents

4. How long can it take to rid the body of CO?

   (a) Several days

   (b) Several weeks

   (c) Several hours

   (d) Recovery is immediate once the source of the gas is removed

5. Which factors help contribute to reduced night vision?

   (a) Drugs and fatigue

   (b) Smoking and alcohol

   (c) Hypoxia and carbon monoxide poisoning

   (d) All the above

6. After stopping a turn in low visibility conditions, with no natural horizon, what is your initial sensation?

   (a) A turn in the other direction

   (b) Starting a climb

   (c) Starting a descent

   (d) A and B

7. How can you help fight fatigue on long flights?

   (a) Relax when possible and rest your eyes by closing them once in a while

   (b) Drink more coffee

   (c) Use another pilot to share the duties

   (d) Keep alert by performing as many duties as possible

8. After donating blood, for how long might your circulation be upset?

   (a) Several days

   (b) Several hours

   (c) 2 weeks

   (d) One month

If this page is a photocopy, it is not authorised!

9. With alcohol in your system, how will a climb up to 6,000 feet affect you?

(a) There will be no effect

(b) There will be a minor increase to the effect

(c) The effect will decrease

(d) The effect will feel like twice what you drank

10. What are the physical properties of carbon monoxide?

(a) There is no danger

(b) It has no colour or smell, or taste

(c) It has a pleasant smell and makes you feel happy

(d) It makes you feel relaxed and carefree

11. After scuba diving involving decompression stops, or in excess of 30 feet (10 m), or flight above 8,000 feet after any diving, for long should you avoid flight?

(a) 48 hours

(b) 4 hours

(c) 24 hours

(d) 8 hours

12. What are the symptoms of decompression sickness?

(a) A dull, sickening pain followed by chest pain and/or collapse

(b) Blurred thinking, headache and reduced night vision

(c) Euphoria, light-headedness then unconsciousness

(d) Dizziness, feeling cold, tingling in the hands and feet

13. Of the following choices, which does *not* adversely affect vision?

(a) Wearing sunglasses during the day

(b) Bright sunlight

(c) Carbon monoxide, hypoxia, or smoking cigarettes

(d) Fatigue, drugs or alcohol

14. Which of the following is a poor technique for scanning the horizon for traffic in flight?

(a) Frequently focussing on one particular object on the horizon while scanning

(b) Staring fixedly ahead

(c) Constantly sweeping the eyes back and forth across the sky

(d) Scan the sky in sections while briefly focusing on distant objects

15. What can cause you to become disorientated?

(a) Aero sinusitis

(b) Flying with the sun glaring through the main rotor or propeller into the cabin

(c) Flying in light fog with a strobe light flashing

(d) B and C

16. What is one major early symptom of hypoxia?

(a) Drowsiness

(b) Hyperventilating

(c) Euphoria

(d) Dizziness

17. What factors contribute to early hypoxia?

(a) Fatigue and/or poor physical condition

(b) Heavy smoking

(c) Alcohol or certain drugs

(d) All the above

18. A person who smokes is:

1. More likely to develop coronary heart disease

2. Has an increased physiological altitude

3. More likely to develop lung cancer

(a) 3 only

(b) 1 & 2 only

(c) 1 & 3 only

(d) 1, 2 & 3

19. Possible symptoms & remedies for hyperventilation:

   (a) Symptom: Dizziness Remedy: Intermittently hold the breath to slow down the breathing

   (b) Symptom: Euphoria Remedy: Apply oxygen

   (c) Symptom: Fatigue Remedy: Bed rest

   (d) Symptom: Hypocapnia Remedy: General Anesthetic

20. What are the main hazards of flight at higher altitudes?

   (a) Hyperventilation, fatigue and sinus discomfort

   (b) Hypoxia, hyperventilation, carbon monoxide poisoning

   (c) Hypoxia, hyperventilation, decompression sickness

   (d) Hyperventilation, fatigue and disorientation

21. A seat with a Design Eye Reference Point should be:

   (a) Adjusted correctly for takeoff and landing

   (b) Adjusted for the cruise

   (c) Adjusted for the lenses in your spectacles

   (d) Adjusted before flight so that your eyes are in the proper position for all phases of flight

22. Boyle's Law has a role to play in:

   (a) Hypoxia with increased altitude

   (b) DCS

   (c) Gastro-Intestinal Tract Barotrauma

   (d) Night vision

23. A pilot flying with a bad cold could suffer from:

   (a) The chokes

   (b) The bends

   (c) Sinus pain

   (d) Blurred vision

24. What chemical substance in tobacco causes addiction?

   (a) Tar and nicotine

   (b) Tar and carbon monoxide

   (c) Nicotine and carbon monoxide

   (d) Nicotine

25. Out of the following choices, accidents are mainly caused by lack of:

   (a) Physical skills

   (b) Good judgment

   (c) Interpersonal relations

   (d) Good maintenance of aircraft

26. After being exposed to exhaust gases in the cockpit for some time, how long would it take to be fit to fly again?

   (a) About two hours

   (b) 5 hours

   (c) 24 hours

   (d) Several days

27. How is respiration regulated?

   (a) The amount of oxygen in the blood against haemoglobin

   (b) Changes in air pressure

   (c) The amount of carbon dioxide in the blood

   (d) The partial pressure of nitrogen

28. When the aircraft is where the pilot thinks it is, the pilot could be said to be:

   (a) Situationally aware

   (b) Correctly orientated

   (c) Spatially orientated

   (d) Grounded

29. Which symptom does not belong to the following list:

   (a) Leans

   (b) Bends

   (c) Chokes

   (d) Creeps

30. On finals in bad weather, you feel dizzy, get tingling sensations in your hands and a rapid heart rate. These symptoms could indicate:

   (a) Hyperventilation

   (b) Disorientation

   (c) Hypoxia

   (d) Carbon monoxide poisoning

31. Coriolis illusion, causing spatial disorientation is the result of:

(a) Undergoing positive G

(b) Gazing in the direction of a flashing light

(c) Normal deterioration of the semicircular canals with age

(d) Simultaneous head movements during aircraft manoeuvres

32. Carbon Monoxide:

(a) Can have a severe effect on your ability after a short time

(b) Does not have an effect when the body becomes used to the gas over a long period of time

(c) Has no effect on the human body

(d) Is not toxic

33. When does short-term memory impairment occur?

(a) 8,000 ft

(b) 12,000 ft

(c) 15,000 ft

(d) 18,000 ft

34. The body loses water via:

1. the skin and the lungs

2. the kidneys

(a) 1 is right and 2 is wrong

(b) 1 is wrong and 2 is right

(c) Both are wrong

(d) Both are right

35. You should be safe from hypoxia up to and including an altitude of;

(a) 8 000 feet

(b) 10 000 feet

(c) 12 000 feet

(d) 14 000 feet

36. The proportion of oxygen throughout the atmosphere:

(a) Decreases with altitude

(b) Increase with altitude

(c) Remains the same

(d) Varies in proportion to the other gases

37. Respiration is regulated by the brain's sensitivity to:

(a) Alcohol

(b) Atmospheric pressure

(c) Haemoglobin

(d) The CO_2 level in the blood

38. Why is there a reduced amount of oxygen available to the body with an increase in altitude?

(a) Increased partial pressure of oxygen

(b) Decreased proportion of oxygen

(c) Decreased atmospheric pressure

(d) Decreased temperature

39.What is the name of the condition where the body does not have enough oxygen?

(a) Hyperactivity

(b) Hyperventilation

(c) Hypoxia

(d) Hypovigilance

40. What is the Time of Useful Consciousness (TUC)?

(a) The time from when there is no breathable oxygen

(b) The time between the onset of hypoxia to unconsciousness

(c) The time from when there is not enough oxygen in the air to keep you conscious during which you can function relatively normally until at time after hypoxia sets in

(d) The time between hypoxia and hyperventilation

41. Compared to non-smokers, tobacco smokers are more likely to experience hypoxia symptoms at:

(a) The same altitude

(b) A lower altitude

(c) A higher altitude

(d) Pressure altitude

42. How might carbon monoxide get into the cockpit?

(a) cigarette smoke, leaking exhaust

(b) Flying through smoke

(c) Flying through industrial haze

(d) No cockpit ventilation

43. For how long after you ware exposed to prolonged amounts of exhaust gases should you not fly?

(a) After 1 or 2 hours

(b) After 2 -5 hours

(c) After 12 hours

(d) After several days

44. To what gas is haemoglobin most readily attracted to?

(a) Nitrogen

(b) Oxygen

(c) Carbon Dioxide

(d) Carbon Monoxide

45. What would be one remedy for hyperventilation?

(a) Liquids

(b) A cold compress on the forehead

(c) Breathing oxygen until the condition subsides

(d) Relaxation and breathing in and out of a bag

46. A person showing the symptoms of hypoxia, but at low altitudes where hypoxia would not normally be expected is most likely to be:

(a) Hyperventilating

(b) Hyperactive

(c) Hypoglycaemic

(d) None of the above

47. What type of systems are *peripheral*, *autonomic* and *central*?

(a) Circulatory

(b) Nervous

(c) Cardiac

(d) Digestive

48. What gas coming out of solution in the body tissues causes decompression sickness?

(a) Nitrogen

(b) Oxygen

(c) Carbon Dioxide

(d) Carbon Monoxide

49. How long does it take to eliminate one unit of alcohol* from the blood?

(a) One hour

(b) Two hours

(c) Three hours

(d) Four hours

*Half a pint of beer, one glass of wine or measure of spirit

50. For how long after blood donation should you not fly?

(a) 2 hours

(b) 4 hours

(c) 12 hours

(d) 24 hours

51. The effects of alcohol are:

(a) Increased with altitude

(b) Decreased with altitude

(c) Remain the same at whatever altitude

(d) Reduced inversely with black coffee

52. Disorientation is best cured by:

(a) Flying by the seat of the pants

(b) Trusting the flight instruments

(c) Holding the nose and swallowing

(d) Holding the head still

53. What could one primary contribution to motion sickness be?

(a) Fluid motion in the semicircular canals

(b) Fluid motion in the stomach

(c) A mismatch between what the vestibular and visual systems are telling the brain

(d) Change of thinking caused by motion

54. How do you maintain situational awareness?

(a) Scanning

(b) Obtaining new data

(c) Constantly confirming your position

(d) Gathering and considering available data while updating the situation and planning ahead

55. What illusion might be caused by accelerating?

    (a) Pitching nose-up

    (b) Pitching nose-down

    (c) Spinning

    (d) Rolling

56. What is the best source of information to avoid sensory confusion?

    (a) Ears

    (b) Eyes

    (c) Seat of the pants

    (d) Semicircular canals

57. How may a runway that is smaller than expected may be perceived as being?

    (a) Nearer than it actually is

    (b) Where it should be

    (c) Further away than it actually is

    (d) Longer than it actually is

58. What might happen if you approach a runway with very bright lighting in an area without other lighting?

    (a) Descending early for a low final approach

    (b) Flying a 3° flight path

    (c) Descending too late for a very steep final approach path

    (d) Distraction from the intensity of the lighting

59. A visual approach to an unfamiliar aerodrome with a downsloping runway without visual glide slope aids may result in what?

    (a) A steeper approach than intended

    (b) An approach quite close to the intended path

    (c) A more shallow approach than intended

    (d) An approach that varies considerably from the intended path

60. A visual approach to an unfamiliar aerodrome that has an upsloping runway without visual aids may result in:

    (a) A steeper approach than intended

    (b) An approach quite close to the intended path

    (c) A more shallow approach than intended

    (d) An approach that varies considerably from the intended path

61. In haze, external objects may appear to be:

    (a) Larger

    (b) Closer

    (c) Further away

    (d) Dimmer

62. What should a less-experienced pilot do if a more experienced one in the same cockpit decides to do something rather silly?

    (a) Immediately express any doubts

    (b) Question the other pilot's judgement

    (c) Accept the course of action in order to keep the atmosphere in the cockpit benign

    (d) Be assertive and be prepared to take control

63. How could you alleviate the effects of helicopter rotor blades or propellers creating a flickering light in bright sunshine?

    (a) Ignore them

    (b) Cover the relevant window or wear sunglasses

    (c) Keep out of the shade

    (d) Slow the rotor blades down

64. What may a prominent cloud layer sloping across a flight path result in?

    (a) A tendency to bank the opposite way

    (b) Disorientation

    (c) Reduction of speed

    (d) Increasing speed

65. A military fast jet and a light aircraft are on a head-on collision course with a rapid closing speed. How does the military aircraft appear to the light aircraft pilot?

(a) In the initial stages the growth of its image is slow, but in the final stages its grows rapidly

(b) The rapid growth is in the initial stages

(c) The image grows quickly but at a constant rate

(d) The image is stationary at first, but grows quickly in the last stages

66. A military fast jet and a light aircraft are on a head-on collision course with a rapid closing speed of 600 kts in 5 km visibility. How much time is there for any avoiding action if visual contact is made at maximum range?

(a) About 10 seconds

(b) About 17 seconds

(c) About 25 seconds

(d) About 35 seconds

67. Two aircraft flying at 120 and 380 kts are approaching head on in 5 nm visibility. How long will it be before they can see each other?

(a) 20 - 30 seconds

(b) 30 - 40 seconds

(c) 40 - 50 seconds

(d) 50 - 60 seconds

68. Which part of the eye is light sensitive?

(a) The lens

(b) The retina

(c) The pupil

(d) The cornea

69. How long does it normally take to adapt to night vision?

(a) About 5 minutes

(b) 10 - 20 minutes

(c) 20 - 30 minutes

(d) 30 - 40 minutes

70. Of the following choices, what is the most efficient scanning method?

(a) A series of short, regularly spaced eye movements across the field of view

(b) Slow sweeping movements from top to bottom

(c) Selection of the most likely spots

(d) Staring out to the horizon

71. What does the Eustachian tube do?

(a) It drains the middle ear

(b) It connects the inner ear to the semicircular canals, allowing the inner ear to equalise with the ambient pressure

(c) It allows the middle ear to equalise with ambient pressure

(d) It drains the sinuses

72. At night, what is the best way to look at an object?

(a) Directly

(b) To the extreme side

(c) Slightly to one side

(d) It depends on which eye is the Master

73. An aircraft has a constant relative bearing with your aircraft. How is it detectable?

(a) The same as any other aircraft

(b) It is easier to detect

(c) It is undetectable

(d) It is harder to detect

74. With an empty visual field, the eyes will:

(a) tend to focus around 1 - 2 metres away

(b) naturally focus at the correct distance

(c) tend to focus on infinity

(d) not focus on anything

75. If the pilot's seat is too low, during an approach:

(a) There will be no difference

(b) The view ahead will be greater

(c) The view of the runway will be better

(d) The approach area under the nose will be less

76. What is the range of human hearing?

    (a)   1 - 5 000 Hz

    (b)   5 - 10 000 Hz

    (c)   10 - 15 KHz

    (d)   20 - 20 KHz

77. What happens when adrenaline is released into the bloodstream?

    (a)   The pulse rate decreases

    (b)   The pulse rate increases

    (c)   Breathing reduces

    (d)   Breathing stabilises

78. Gastro-enteritis makes a pilot:

    (a)   Fit to fly

    (b)   Fit to fly with medication

    (c)   Unfit to fly

    (d)   Fit to fly with CAA permission

79. The three needle altimeter (see right) works properly, but:

    (a)   It can easily be misread

    (a)   It cannot be misread

    (a)   It can be misread by dyslexic pilots

    (a)   It must be caged during manoeuvres

80. A runway that is narrower than expected may result in:

    (a)   A high approach with a possible overshoot

    (b)   A high approach with a possible undershoot

    (c)   A normal approach

    (d)   A low approach with a possible undershoot

81. With regard to over-the-counter medications, which statement is correct?

    (a)   Any side effects are minor and may be ignored

    (b)   Check for side effects before going flying

    (c)   Professional advice should be sought from an authorised medical examiner

    (d)   They may be combined as necessary

82. How might spatial disorientation be dealt with?

    (a)   Close your eyes and shake your head gently

    (b)   Use the seat-of-the-pants sense

    (c)   Use and trust the aircraft instruments

    (d)   Use an external reference

83. What illusion does acceleration give?

    (a)   Nose-down pitching

    (b)   Nose-up pitching

    (c)   A right turn

    (d)   A left roll

84. Controls that operate different systems should:

    (a)   Look and feel different

    (b)   Look the same but feel different

    (c)   Feel the same and look different

    (d)   Look and feel the same

85. What system moves blood around the body?

    (a)   Respiratory

    (b)   Lymph

    (c)   Circulatory

    (d)   Nervous

86. Which of the following might represent an upslope?

    (a)   The one on the left

    (b)   The one in the middle

    (c)   The one on the right

    (d)   None of the above

87. Why should you not fly when you have a cold?

    (a)   The pressure between the inner and middle parts of the ear may not equalise

    (b)   The pressure between the middle part of the ear and the atmosphere may not equalise

    (c)   The pressure between the inner part of the ear and the atmosphere may not equalise

    (d)   The pressure between the lungs and the atmosphere may not equalise

88. Equalising the air pressure between the outer and the middle ear is:

   (a) difficult when pressure changes are at a low rate

   (b) impossible in descent because the pressure in the middle ear is higher than it is in ambient air

   (c) important to prevent pain and loss of hearing during flight

   (d) more important during a climb because the lower pressure in the middle air can damage the tympanic membrane

89. With the illusion of tumbling backwards after a rapid change from climbing to level flight, you should:

   (a) pay most attention to, and trust, the aircraft instruments

   (b) rely on seat of the pants information

   (c) close your eyes to stop the illusion

   (d) move the control column forward

90. Decision-making can be influenced by what factors?

   1. The outcome of previous situations that are similar

   2. Peer pressure or conformity

   3. The tendency to select data that meets your expectations (confirmation bias)

   4. The suitability of the cockpit design

   (a) 1, 2 and 3

   (b) 3 and 4

   (c) 1, 3 and 4

   (d) 1 and 4

91. Non verbal communication between two people:

   (a) is not possible with high workloads

   (b) accounts for around 15% of normal human communication

   (c) accounts for the majority of normal human communication

   (d) is not possible in an aircraft, due to the seating arrangements

92. Which statement is correct?

   1. Stress can be caused by noise, high or low temperatures and vibration

   2. An increase in arousal always improves human performance

   (a) 1 - incorrect, 2 - correct

   (b) 1 - correct, 2 - correct

   (c) 1 - correct, 2 - incorrect

   (d) 1 - incorrect, 2 - incorrect

93. What is true about divided attention?

   (a) It concerns the ability to perform one task at a time, in rapid succession

   (b) Your ability to perform consecutive tasks reduces as their difficulty increases, but is not affected by similarity

   (c) The similarity between tasks increases your ability to divide your attention between them

   (d) Practice can improve your ability to perform multiple tasks simultaneously

94. How does the blood mainly carry oxygen?

   (a) With haemoglobin in the red blood cells

   (b) With haemoglobin in the white blood cells

   (c) With haemoglobin in the plasma

   (d) With haemoglobin in the platelets

95. To avoid Hypoglycemia (low blood/sugar levels):

   (a) Don't eat sugar or sweet things

   (b) E eat regularly with a balanced diet

   (c) Nuts are recommended for their high energy value

   (d) Do not take snacks between meals

96. When is spatial disorientation most likely to occur?

   (a) when flying in and out of clouds while maintaining an instrument scan

   (b) in light rain below a cloud layer

   (c) when the brain receives conflicting information and you rely on the senses rather than the instruments

   (d) in bright sunlight above a cloud layer

97. A pilot accelerating in straight and level flight may experience what illusory perception?

   (a) pitching nose down

   (b) pitching nose up

   (c) rolling

   (d) turning to the right

98. Perception is based upon:

   (a) past experience and knowledge

   (b) information received as well as past experience and knowledge

   (c) information received

   (d) technical ability

99. Non verbal communication:

   (a) has no meaning in the cockpit

   (b) is always used intentionally

   (c) should be avoided in the cockpit

   (d) supports verbal communication

100. A set of controls that operate different systems should, ideally:

   (a) both look and feel different

   (b) look the same but feel different

   (c) look and feel identical

   (d) be similar and easy to use

101. What does the respiratory process consist mainly of?

   (a) The diffusion of oxygen through the respiratory membranes into the blood, transportation to the cells, diffusion into the cells and elimination of carbon dioxide from the body

   (b) The transportation of oxygen to the cells and the elimination of carbon monoxide

   (c) The transportation of oxygen to the cells and the elimination of nitrogen

   (d) The transportation of carbon monoxide to the cells and elimination of oxygen

102. The eye can fully adjust to:

   (a) High levels of illumination in 10 minutes and darkness in 30 minutes

   (b) High levels of illumination in 20 minutes and darkness in 10 minutes

   (c) High levels of illumination in 10 seconds and darkness in 30 seconds

   (d) High levels of illumination in 10 seconds and darkness in 30 minutes

103. Dizziness, tingling fingers and lips, anxiety and visual disturbances below FL 100 indicate the possibility of:

   (a) Hypervigilance

   (b) Hypothermia

   (c) Hyperventilation

   (d) Hypoxia

104. Regarding the eye and vision:

   (a) The cones detect colour and are highly sensitive to hypoxia

   (b) rods are centrally located and increase visual acuity

   (c) cones are less sensitive in good light

   (d) cones are less sensitive in poor light

105. Which signs and symptoms are associated with hypoxia?

   1. Personality changes

   2. Impaired judgment

   3. Impaired muscle movement

   4. Short-term memory loss

   5. Sensory loss

   6. Loss of consciousness

   7. Blueness

   (a) 1, 2, 3, 4, 5, 6, 7

   (b) 1, 2, 3, 5

   (c) 1 and 4

   (d) 2, 4, 6, 7

106. When might anticipation be hazardous?

(a) mishearing a reply from ATC regarding a non-standard procedure when a standard procedure was expected

(b) expecting the weather to get worse

(c) mishearing a reply from ATC regarding a standard procedure when a non-standard procedure was expected

(d) reading ahead on a checklist

107. Which systems are involved in motion sickness?

1. Hearing

2. Sight

3. The seat of the pants

4. The vestibular system

(a) 1 and 2

(b) 2, 3, 4

(c) 3 and 4

(d) 1, 3, 4

108. Through which part of the ear does pressure equalise when you change altitude?

(a) Eustachian tube

(b) The ossicles

(c) Semicircular canals

(d) ear lobe

109. Which statement is correct about alcohol consumption?

(a) As transport legislation tends to follow the Road Acts, being within the current driving limits is acceptable

(b) the ratio of error to skill increases significantly

(c) it depends how much alcohol was consumed with what type of food

(d) alcohol increases performance up to a point

110. What is peripheral vision useful for?

(a) the field of vision

(b) the detection of moving objects

(c) colour vision

(d) monocular vision

111. What role should automation play with respect to flight safety?

(a) Automation should be used only when pilots have to make decisions and flying the aircraft should be compulsory in good weather

(b) Automation should be used as much as possible to replace the pilot who will inevitably make mistakes

(c) Automation should be used as an aid to the pilot and not have full authority

(d) Automation should only be used in IMC to achieve flight safety

112. With in flight fires, what are most fatalities caused by?

(a) Burns

(b) Suffocation from fumes caused by aircraft furnishings and electrical wiring

(c) Inhalation of carbon dioxide fumes

(d) Cardiac arrest caused by stress, fear and heat exhaustion

113. If AVGAS gets on the skin, the affected area should be:

(a) Bandaged after a skin salve has been applied to avoid blistering

(b) Initially washed with soap and hot water

(c) Initially washed copiously with water, but without soap

(d) Immediately exposed to ambient air to allow the fuel to vaporate as quickly as possible

114. High levels of arousal lead to:

(a) Faster but less accurate responses

(b) Slower but more accurate responses

(c) Slower but less accurate responses

(d) Faster and more accurate responses

115. A heart attack (myocardial infarction) is:

    (a) Becoming less common as smoking has become less acceptable

    (b) Always followed by chest pains and Angina

    (c) The most common cause of death in men over the age of 40

    (d) Only curable by ventricular fibrillation

116. What may cause spatial disorientation?

    (a) Flying in clear daylight conditions

    (b) Reference to an external visual cue such as a true or artificial horizon

    (c) A false perception of orientation with respect to spatial references

    (d) Damage to the hair-like cells in the eyes

117. Automation helps to conserve resources but may result in:

    (a) Routine errors and passive monitoring

    (b) Errors of commision

    (c) Errors in the selection of an appropriate plan of action

    (d) Errors involving decision-making

118. Which statement is correct?

1. A person experiencing sleep loss may not be aware of personal performance degradation

2. Performance degradation may be present for more than 20 minutes after waking from a short sleep (nap)

    (a) 1 is false and 2 is correct

    (b) 1 and 2 are false

    (c) 1 is correct and 2 is false

    (d) 1 and 2 are correct

119. Divided attention is the ability to:

1. Carry out several mental activities at almost the same time, as when switching attention from outside the aircraft to the ASI on the instrument panel

2. Monitor the progress of a motor program, as when flying or taxying on a relatively straight heading while making a radio call at the same time

3. Select information and check if it is relevant to the task in hand, during which time no other operation can be performed.

4. Delegate tasks to passengers while concentrating on procedures

    (a) 3 is false

    (b) 1, 2 and 3 are correct. 4 is false

    (c) 1 and 3 are correct 2 and 4 are false

    (d) 1 and 2 are correct. 3 and 4 are false

120. Which statement is correct?

    (a) The majority of oxygen is carried in the plasma

    (b) The diffusion gradient (differential pressure) is higher at altitude than at sea level

    (c) Oxygen diffusion from the lungs into the blood does not depend on an oxygen pressure gradient

    (d) Oxygen diffusion from the lungs into the blood depends on the oxygen pressure gradient

PRINCIPLES OF FLIGHT & AIRCRAFT GEN.

2

GENERAL

1. What properties of the atmosphere affect performance?

    (a)   Temperature, pressure and humidity

    (b)   Pressure, humidity and oxygen

    (c)   Temperature, pressure, density and humidity

    (d)   Temperature, pressure, density, humidity and oxygen

2. If the temperature at 10 000 ft AMSL is -10°C, what is its relation to ISA conditions?

    (a)   ISA +5

    (b)   ISA -5

    (c)   ISA +10

    (d)   ISA -10

3. What happens to ambient temperature in the standard atmosphere?

    (a)   It increases with height

    (b)   It decreases with height

    (c)   It stays constant until higher up, then decreases

    (d)   It stays constant until higher up, then increases

4. Which statement is true for handling aviation fuel?

    (a)   You should not use low octane fuel in an engine that requires high octane fuel

    (b)   Use of fuels other than those specified in the flight manual for that engine is not approved

    (c)   All fuelling equipment, and the aircraft being fuelled, must be bonded (grounded) before fuelling takes place

    (d)   All are correct

5. How would you describe a monocoque structure?

    (a)   A structure where all loads are carried by the skin

    (b)   A structure where some loads are carried by the skin which is reinforced from underneath

    (c)   A structure where no load is carried by the skin

    (d)   A structure where some loads are carried by the internal structure, and the remainder by the skin

6. Why would an engine miss and overheat?

    (a)   Fouled plugs

    (b)   Fuel mixture is too rich

    (c)   Fuel mixture is too lean

    (d)   Carburettor icing

7. Extended idling of an engine might cause what?

    (a)   Burned ignition plugs

    (b)   Detonation

    (c)   Fouled plugs

    (d)   Backfiring in the induction system

8. What are the main constituents of air?

    (a)   Oxygen, nitrogen, carbon dioxide

    (b)   Oxygen, nitrogen, ozone

    (c)   Oxygen, nitrogen, water vapour

    (d)   Oxygen, water vapour, carbon dioxide

9. Aside from eliminating carburettor icing, advantages of fuel injection include…

    (a)   Simpler mechanics

    (b)   There is only one input to the pump, the throttle

    (c)   Fuel consumption is improved by up to 35%

    (d)   Uniform fuel distribution, more power & efficiency, better cooling

10. What is Pressure Altitude?

    (a) The height at which a pressure of 1013 exists

    (b) The height indicated by an altimeter set to QFE

    (c) The height indicated by a pressure altimeter with its subscale set to 1013.25 hPa or 29.92 inches

    (d) The height indicated by a pressure altimeter with its subscale set to Regional QNH

11. Why is a venturi required in a float-type carburettor?

    (a) To prevent backfiring through the carburettor

    (b) To increase manifold pressure

    (c) To reduce the risk of carburettor icing

    (d) To create a differential pressure to draw fuel into the main jets

12. Application of carburettor heat will…

    (a) Decrease manifold pressure and enrich the mixture

    (b) Increase the manifold pressure and lean the mixture

    (c) Decrease manifold pressure and lean the mixture

    (d) Increase manifold pressure and enrich the mixture

13. What conditions are most likely to cause carb icing?

    (a) -5 to -30°C, high humidity

    (b) -5 to +30°C, high humidity

    (c) Zero to +10°C in low humidity

    (d) +20 to +30°C in low humidity

14. Carb icing is most likely when you combine the following air temp, humidity, and engine RPM…

    (a) -10°C, high humidity, low cruise

    (b) +10°C, high humidity, idle

    (c) +10°C, high humidity, high cruise

    (d) +10°C, low humidity, idle

15. At constant pressure and temperature, what effect will an increase in humidity have on density?

    (a) Increase it

    (b) Nothing

    (c) Decrease it

    (d) It depends on the altitude

16. The fins around an air-cooled engine…

    (a) Stop foreign materials from entering the manifold

    (b) Retain heat for the run-up

    (c) Increase the engine's surface area for better cooling

    (d) Give the piston added strength, for better combustion

17. The magneto is there to…

    (a) Improve safety

    (b) Supply high tension current to the spark plugs

    (c) Check the function of the engine during run-up

    (d) Improve performance

18. If you see no RPM drop during a magneto check:

    (a) The engine may be running hot

    (b) The magnetos are performing correctly

    (c) The magneto ground should be checked

    (d) This is normal

19. What does a turbocharger do?

    (a) Provide a more immediate engine response

    (b) Boost power during takeoff

    (c) Eliminate carb icing

    (d) Allow the engine to produce rated power at higher altitudes

20. What is the correct fuel/air mixture for a four stroke light aircraft engine?

    (a) 1 lb fuel to 12 lbs of air

    (b) 1 Gallon fuel to 12 cubic feet of air

    (c) 10 Gallons of fuel to 1500 lbs of air

    (d) 12 lbs of fuel to 1 lb of air

21. If you use fuel with a lower octane level than what is needed for your engine, what will be the result?

    (a) Decreased power and a lower CHT

    (b) Detonation, overheating and possible destruction of the engine

    (c) Fouling of the spark plugs

    (d) The engine won't run at all

22. When an aerofoil stalls:

    (a) Lift and drag decrease

    (b) Lift and drag increase

    (c) Drag increases while lift decreases

    (d) Drag increases, lift increases

23. Yaw is motion about what axis?

    (a) Normal axis

    (b) Lateral axis

    (c) Horizontal Axis

    (d) Longitudinal Axis

24. What is movement about the longitudinal axis called?

    (a) Yaw

    (b) Roll

    (c) Pitch

    (d) Bank

25. Why does air density fall with altitude?

    (a) The fall in pressure

    (b) The amount of water vapour

    (c) The oxygen content

    (d) The increase in humidity

26. Which factors combine to give the coefficient of lift?

    1. Wing surface area

    2. Camber

    3. Freestream air velocity

    4. Air density

    5. Angle of attack

    (a) 1, 4

    (b) 2, 5

    (c) 2, 4

    (d) 3, 4

27. What is the angle between the chord line of an aerofoil and the relative airflow called?

    (a) The gliding angle

    (b) The flapping angle

    (c) The angle of attack

    (d) The angle of coning

28. A directionally statically stable aircraft does what after a disturbance?

    (a) Oscillates around the original attitude

    (b) Tends to return to the original heading

    (c) Tends to move away from the original heading

    (d) Stays where it is

29. Where does the VSI get its pressure information from?

    (a) The pitot source

    (b) The static source

    (c) The dynamic source

    (d) The pitot-static system

30. What does the ball of a turn and slip indicator rely on?

    (a) Battery power to indicate a slip, skid or balanced flight

    (b) Gyroscopes to indicate a balanced turn

    (c) No external power to indicate a slip, skid or balanced flight

    (d) Battery power to indicate a balanced turn

31. In the Northern hemisphere, when turning through South, how will the direct reading magnetic compass act?

    (a) It will indicate correctly

    (b) It will over-indicate

    (c) It will under-indicate

    (d) It will not work at all due to excessive dip

32. What is a busbar?

    (a) An earth return

    (b) Two or more switches joined together

    (c) A distribution point for electrical power

    (d) A dipole battery

33. The accuracy of fuel gauges:

    (a) Should be checked every year by an engineer

    (b) Are set to under-read so you always have fuel

    (c) Should be confirmed by checking the tank contents

    (d) Can always be relied upon

If this page is a photocopy, it is not authorised!

34. If a hand-held BCF extinguisher is used in a cockpit:

    (a) You should open a window first

    (b) You should increase speed first for ventilation

    (c) You should open a window or panel afterwards

    (d) You should turn the electrics off first

35. Minor maintenance carried out by a private pilot:

    (a) Does not need to be recorded

    (b) Must be recorded by an engineer

    (c) Must be countersigned by an engineer

    (d) Must be recorded in the log book concerned and signed by the pilot

36. Who may carry out a duplicate inspection away from base?

    (a) Any engineer

    (b) A qualified pilot

    (c) Any pilot

    (d) All of the above

37. Why does the engine slow down when carburettor heat is applied?

    (a) Airflow in the manifold is restricted

    (b) A gear is engaged

    (c) Fuel flow is reduced

    (d) The warmed air is less dense

38. What does the crankshaft do?

    (a) Open and closes the inlet and exhaust valves

    (b) Convert reciprocating motion into rotary motion

    (c) Spin the magneto

    (d) Switch on the capacitor

39. What does the ignition switch control?

    (a) The current to the coils

    (b) The earthing of the primary windings in the magneto

    (c) The earthing of the secondary windings in the magneto

    (d) The battery supply to the starter

40. Why should prolonged ground running of a piston engine be avoided?

    (a) The engine gets too cold

    (b) The engine gets too hot

    (c) The valves will overheat

    (d) The plugs will get fouled

41. What values do sea level pressure and temperature have in the International Standard Atmosphere (ISA)?

    (a) 1013 hPa, 15°C

    (b) 1013.25 hPa, 59°F

    (c) 29.92 hPa, 15°C

    (d) 29.92 inches, 12°C

42. A fuel contents gauge must accurately indicate:

    (a) Fuel contents when the aircraft is on the ground

    (b) Fuel contents when the aircraft is in the cruise

    (c) Fuel tank contents with a 10% margin for safety

    (d) Usable fuel remaining in level cruising flight

43. If the static source becomes blocked during a climb, what will the altimeter do?

    (a) Over-read

    (b) Under-read

    (c) Stay at the altitude when the blockage occurred

    (d) Nothing

44. If using the cabin heat in flight:

    (a) The vents should be closed to keep the heat in

    (b) The vents should be opened to stop carbon monoxide from building up

    (c) The vents should be opened to stop carbon dioxide from building up

    (d) Its operation should be restricted to stop carbon monoxide from building up

45. Carbon monoxide fumes:

    (a) Look like thin smoke

    (b) Smell like coal burning

    (c) Are invisible and are hard to detect by smell

    (d) Are harmless

46. If the static source is partially blocked, the air speed indicator will:

(a) Return to zero

(b) Over-read in a climb

(c) Over-read in a descent

(d) Read the same in all conditions

47. As an aircraft climbs, TAS for any given IAS will:

(a) Increase

(b) Stay the same

(c) Decrease

(d) Vary as the square root of the OAT

48. What does the ASI compare?

(a) Static and atmospheric pressures

(b) Standard and pilot pressures

(c) Dynamic and pitot pressures

(d) Static and dynamic pressures

49. What instruments are connected to the static source?

(a) VSI, Altimeter

(b) ASI, VSI, Altimeter

(c) Altimeter, VSI and Gyros

(d) VSI, ASI, Altimeter and Turn/Slip

50. An aircraft with an altimeter set to 1015 is flying towards an area of low pressure. If the instrument is not reset, what will happen?

(a) It will read low

(b) It will read high

(c) It will cease to function

(d) The error in the altimeter will decrease as you fly closer to the centre of the low

51. When will the altimeter read the elevation of an airport when set to 29.92 inches or 1013 hPa?

(a) Never

(b) Only on a standard day

(c) When the airport is at sea level

(d) When the barometric pressure is 29.92/1013

52. In conditions far colder than standard, what will the altimeter do?

(a) Lag

(b) Over read

(c) Under read

(d) Be accurate

53. What formula converts temperature from Fahrenheit to Celsius?

(a) $°C = (°F - 32) \times {}^5/_9$

(b) $°F = (°C - 32) \times {}^5/_9$

(c) $°C = (°F - {}^5/_9) \times 32$

(d) $°C = (°F - 32) \times {}^9/_5$

54. What does dry air consist of?

(a) 23% oxygen, 23% nitrogen, carbon dioxide and others 55%

(b) 21% oxygen, 78% nitrogen, others 1%

(c) 78% oxygen, 21% nitrogen, others 1%

(d) 78% oxygen, 21% nitrogen, carbon dioxide1%

55. If the static source becomes blocked, what does the VSI do?

(a) Read correctly

(b) Reads zero

(c) Reads high

(d) reads low

56. What does a blocked filter in an air-driven instrument cause?

(a) Low airflow with a low vacuum gauge reading

(b) High airflow with a low vacuum gauge reading

(c) Low airflow with a high vacuum gauge reading

(d) High airflow with a high vacuum gauge reading

57. What does a pressure maintaining valve in a hydraulic system do?

(a) It ensures that adequate hydraulic pressure is available for emergencies

(b) It keeps a reserve available for pressure surges

(c) It conserves hydraulic pressure for essential services

(d) It conserves hydraulic pressure for vital services

58. What is the most common type of portable fire extinguisher found in an aircraft?

    (a) Foam

    (b) Carbon dioxide

    (c) Water

    (d) Dry powder

59. Why are water checks on the fuel system so important?

    (a) The water may cause carb icing

    (b) The water may stop the engine working

    (c) Water is heavier than fuel

    (d) The water will not lubricate the fuel pumps

60. When should a Check A be carried out?

    (a) Every day, by an engineer

    (b) Before the first flight of the day, to the satisfaction of the pilot

    (c) Before each flight, to the satisfaction of the pilot

    (d) Before each flight, to the satisfaction of the owner

61. What is the definition of relative humidity?

    (a) The percentage of air that is actually water vapour

    (b) The amount of water vapour in the air compared to the maximum amount that it could hold at the same temperature, expressed as a percentage

    (c) The ratio of water vapour in the air at any time

    (d) The ratio of water vapour in the air when saturated

62. What does the reading on the oil pressure gauge represent?

    (a) The pressure on the inlet side of the pump

    (b) The pressure on the outlet side of the pump

    (c) The average system pressure

    (d) The total system pressure

63. A dry sump engine lubrication system:

    (a) Has oil collected from the sump by a scavenge pump which is returned to the reservoir

    (b) Does not use oil

    (c) Has the oil collecting in the sump for a minimal period before being splashed around the inside

    (d) Has all of its oil contained in the cylinders

64. The bypass valve relating to an oil cooler depends on:

    (a) Pressure

    (b) Temperature

    (c) Humidity

    (d) Air density

65. What is a wet sump lubrication system? One where:

    (a) The oil is contained in a sump, topped up as required from a reservoir

    (b) All the oil is contained in a sump within the engine

    (c) Oil is not used

    (d) Water is mixed with the oil

66. How is excessive oil pressure prevented?

    (a) With a shuttle valve

    (b) With a pressure relief valve

    (c) With a non-return valve

    (d) With a shimmy valve

67. Where is oil temperature sensed?

    (a) In the cylinder

    (b) Before the oil cooler

    (c) In the reservoir

    (d) In between the oil cooler and the engine

68. What would you do if the engine oil pressure was indicating lower than normal with a temperature higher than normal?

    (a) Land as soon as possible

    (b) Increase speed to reduce the temperature with increased airflow

    (c) Increase engine RPM to boost the pressure

    (d) Stop the engine immediately and carry out a forced landing

69. What is the sequence of events in the Otto cycle?

(a) Induction, Compression, Power and Exhaust

(b) Induction, Compression, Ignition, Power and Exhaust

(c) Induction, Conduction, Power and Exhaust

(d) Induction, Compression, Priming and Exhaust

70. Two 24 volt 20-ampere/hour batteries connected in parallel are equivalent to a:

(a) 48 volt battery supplying 40 ampere/hours

(b) 48 volt battery supplying 20 ampere/hours

(c) 24 volt battery supplying 40 ampere/hours

(d) 24 volt battery supplying 20 ampere/hours

71. For how long should a 50 ampere battery supply a current of 25 amps for?

(a) 2 hours

(b) 25 hours

(c) 4 hours

(d) 50 hours

72. The picture on the right is of a centre reading ammeter. Where should the needle be in normal circumstances?

(a) In the middle

(b) To the left

(c) To the right

(d) Slightly right of centre

73. What should you do if the starter light remains on after the engine starts.

(a) Shut down if the light has not gone out after 30 seconds

(b) Shut down immediately

(c) Push the starter button again

(d) Keep the engine running and call an engineer

74. With a 24 volt ground supply being used for starting:

(a) A 28 volt supply would cause the starter fuse to blow

(b) A 24 volt supply would match the helicopter

(c) At least a 115v AC supply is required

(d) A 28 volt supply is acceptable

75. What is disc loading?

(a) The total weight of the helicopter divided by the blade area

(b) The total weight of the helicopter divided by the disc area

(c) The total weight of the helicopter multiplied by the blade area

(d) The total weight of the helicopter multiplied by the disc area

76. If you set the altimeter to QFE at one aerodrome, then fly to another one with the same elevation, what happens to the altimeter on landing?

(a) The altimeter will read the height above sea level without needing to be reset

(b) The subscale might need to be reset

(c) The altimeter will over-read

(d) The altimeter will under-read

77. A trip-free circuit breaker will:

(a) Reset when held in

(b) Does not trip, but resets automatically

(c) Restore power when held in

(d) Not restore power when held in

78. A hydraulic system:

(a) Can use any fluid

(b) Needs the fluid specified in the flight manual

(c) Needs fluid from one manufacturer only

(d) Any fluid meeting certain specifications

79. What is the camber of an aerofoil?

(a) The line between the leading and trailing edges

(b) The maximum distance between the chord and mean camber lines

(c) The curvature over the top

(d) A line between the upper and lower surfaces

80. The valve that allows oil to bypass an engine oil cooler:

  (a) Is pressure sensitive

  (b) Is temperature sensitive

  (c) Is density sensitive

  (d) Is humidity sensitive

81. Where, on a conventional low speed aerofoil, will flow separation normally start as the angle of attack increases?

  (a) On the upper surface nearer the leading edge

  (b) On the upper surface nearer the trailing edge

  (c) On the lower surface nearer the leading edge

  (d) On the upper surface nearer the trailing edge

82. The air over the top of an aerofoil, compared to the free stream airflow, will have:

  (a) reduced speed

  (b) increased speed

  (c) the same speed

  (d) increased static pressure

83. As the angle of attack increases, relative to the leading edge, the stagnation point of an aerofoil will move (1) and the point of lowest pressure will move (2):

  (a) (1) up (2) aft

  (b) (1) down (2) forwards

  (c) (1) up (2) forwards

  (d) (1) down (2) aft

84. For the flow in a venturi:

  (a) static pressure is greatest at the throat

  (b) dynamic pressure increases as the venturi diverges

  (c) total pressure is lowest in the throat

  (d) static pressure reduces as the venturi converges

85. Static stability is the ability of an aircraft to:

  (a) stay in the new position

  (b) go further away from the original position

  (c) return to the original position

  (d) overshoot the original position

86. A semi-monocoque structure consists of:

  (a) light trellissed framework covered with fabric

  (b) heavy duty framework covered with fabric

  (c) light framework covered with a strength bearing skin, usually aluminium

  (d) heavy duty framework covered with a skin, usually aluminium

87. The accelerator pump in a carburettor:

  (a) stops too much fuel being sent to the cylinders

  (b) is fitted before the butterfly valve

  (c) is a small plunger within the float chamber that is connected to the throttle linkage

  (d) supplies more fuel when the throttle is opened slowly

88. After starting a cold engine, if the oil pressure does not rise within around 30 seconds:

  (a) increase the engine RPM to see if there is any movement of the needle

  (b) it can be ignored if there was enough fuel when you did the preflight

  (c) the engine should be warmed up at idle speed

  (d) stop the engine immediately to prevent damage

89. For the best fuel/air mixture altitude, the mixture is leaned until:

  (a) the engine speed drops, then the ICO should be moved to the rich side of peak RPM

  (b) the engine speed increases

  (c) the engine speed drops by around 50 RPM

  (d) the engine speed increases, then the ICO should be moved to the lean side of peak RPM

90. If an AC or DC generator fails in flight:

  (a) electrical loads should be reduced and the flight continued

  (b) electrical loads should be reduced to minimum and a landing made as soon as practicable

  (c) the master switch should be turned off and the flight continued

  (d) the battery will take over so the flight can continue

If this page is a photocopy, it is not authorised!

91. When performing a battery condition check with the aircraft voltmeter:

  (a) the battery does not need to be loaded because that would reduce the voltage reading

  (b) the condition of the load is not important

  (c) the battery should be isolated

  (d) the battery must be loaded to give a better idea of its working condition

92. Alternate static pressure is:

  (a) lower than the main sensed static pressure

  (b) the same as the main sensed static pressure

  (c) higher than the main sensed static pressure

  (d) a separate system from the main sensed static pressure

93. What does the green arc on an airspeed indicator denote?

  (a) The caution range

  (b) the normal operating range

  (c) the never exceed range

  (d) the maximum operating range

94. What does the rigidity of a gyroscope depend on?

  1. rotor mass

  2. rotor speed of rotation

  3. the radius at which the mass is concentrated

  (a) 1, 2

  (b) 1, 2, 3

  (c) 2, 3

  (d) 3

95. The gyroscope in a turn coordinator has a gimbal axis that is:

  (a) horizontal

  (b) vertical

  (c) tilted around 30° to the horizontal

  (d) tilted around 30° to the vertical

96. The altimeter:

  (a) compares static pressure against a reference pressure set on the subscale and displays the difference in terms of height or altitude above ground

  (b) compares the pitot and static pressures and displays the difference in terms of height or altitude above ground

  (c) compares pitot pressure against a reference pressure set on the subscale and displays the difference in terms of height or altitude above ground

  (d) displays the static pressure in terms of height or altitude above ground

97. Why are compass deviation cards required?

  (a) to indicate the difference between compass and true headings

  (b) to correct compass readings when loads change

  (c) to show the corrections to be made to magnetic headings to obtain true headings

  (d) to show the corrections to be made to compass readings to obtain magnetic headings

98. What is the compression ratio of an engine?

  (a) The ratio of the total cylinder volume to its volume when the piston is at Bottom Dead Centre (BDC)

  (b) The ratio of the total cylinder volume to the swept volume

  (c) The ratio of the cylinder volume when the piston is at Top Dead Centre (TDC) to that at Bottom Dead Centre (BDC)

  (d) The ratio of the cylinder volume when the piston is at Bottom Dead Centre (BDC) to that at Top Dead Centre (TDC)

99. Where does a magneto get the current for its primary circuit from?

  (a) It has a self contained electromagnetic induction system

  (b) The aircraft battery

  (c) The generator

  (d) A separate battery

100. Why might you get detonation?

    (a) using a grade of fuel that is too high for the engine

    (b) Using a manifold pressure that is too low

    (c) Using a mixture that is too weak

    (d) Using a mixture that is too rich

101. What does the Idle Cut Off valve in a piston engine do?

    (a) It keeps the engine turning over at idle RPM

    (b) It increases the fuel flow during engine acceleration

    (c) It decreases the fuel flow during engine acceleration

    (d) It stops the flow of fuel from the discharge nozzle

102. How can you stop the spark plugs from fouling?

    (a) By not idling the engine at low RPM for long periods

    (b) By idling the engine at low RPM for long periods

    (c) By applying short bursts of power when taxying

    (d) By keeping the engine RPM just below the red line on the RPM gauge

103. If the static source becomes blocked during descent:

    (a) The ASI and altimeter will over-read

    (b) The ASI and altimeter will under-read

    (c) The ASI will over-read and the altimeter will under-read

    (d) The ASI will under-read and the altimeter will over-read

104. How does the altimeter work?

    (a) Static pressure is connected to an aneroid capsule and pitot pressure is connected to the case.

    (b) As you climb or descend, a suitable linkage transmits the expansion or contraction of an aneroid capsule to the dial

    (c) As you descend, a suitable linkage transmits the expansion of an aneroid capsule to the dial

    (d) Pitot pressure is connected to an aneroid capsule and static pressure is connected to the case.

105. The VSI converts a rate of change of what type of pressure to a rate of change of altitude?

    (a) Static

    (b) Dynamic

    (c) Total

    (d) Pitot

106. What instruments use gyros?

    (a) Turn coordinator, ASI, attitude indicator

    (b) Attitude indicator, altimeter, DGI

    (c) Turn coordinator, attitude indicator, DGI

    (d) ASI, altimeter, DGI

107. What condition must be satisfied before realigning the DGI with the compass?

    (a) It must be done in a steady turn

    (b) It must be done in level, unaccelerated flight

    (c) It may be done in a shallow climb or descent

    (d) It must be done in a rate 1 turn

108. When does ignition occur in the cylinders of a four stroke engine?

    (a) Before TDC at every second revolution of the crankshaft

    (b) Before TDC at every revolution of the crankshaft

    (c) After TDC at every revolution of the crankshaft

    (d) After TDC at every second revolution of the crankshaft

109. What is the primary colour for an avgas 100LL label, and the colour of the fuel?

    (a) Black, Red

    (b) Blue, Blue

    (c) Black, Straw

    (d) Red, Blue

110. What happens when a magneto is switched off?

    (a) The primary circuit is open and grounded

    (b) The primary circuit is open and not grounded

    (c) The primary circuit is closed and grounded

    (d) The primary circuit is closed and not grounded

111. At high power settings (over 75%) a rich mixture:

(a) reduces the mass of fuel in the charge

(b) helps cool the engine

(c) prevents a weak cut in severe manoeuvres

(d) causes detonation

112. The idling jet in a carburettor:

(a) reduces the fuel flow to prevent weak cuts

(b) premixes fuel with air

(c) stops the main jet providing too much fuel when the throttle is opened

(d) provides enough fuel to keep the engine idling at low RPM

113. What is the difference between a fuse and a circuit breaker?

(a) A fuse can be used for high loads

(b) A circuit breaker is resettable

(c) A circuit breaker melts to break the circuit

(d) A fuse does not melt

114. For how long can a 200 amp/hour battery supply a current of 50 amps?

(a) 15 minutes

(b) 8 hours

(c) 4 hours

(d) 2 hours

115. What pressure is sensed by the pitot tube?

(a) Total pressure

(b) Dynamic pressure

(c) Static pressure

(d) Pitot pressure

116. What type of gyro does the attitude indicator use?

(a) A space gyro rotating in the vertical plane about the lateral axis

(b) An earth gyro rotating in the horizontal plane about a vertical axis

(c) A tied gyro rotating in the vertical plane about a horizontal axis

(d) An earth gyro rotating in the vertical plane about a axis

117. True airspeed is determined by correcting:

(a) Calibrated airspeed for nonstandard temperature and altitude

(b) Indicated airspeed for density altitude

(c) Calibrated airspeed for pressure altitude

(d) Equivalent airspeed for the air density variation from the standard value at sea level

AEROPLANES

1. What happens at the stall?

(a) The nose pitches up and the aircraft sinks

(b) The nose pitches up and a wing drops

(c) The nose pitches down and a wing drops

(d) The nose pitches down and the aircraft sinks

2. How does the pressure of air under a wing compare with that flowing over the wing in straight and level flight?

(a) It is lower

(b) It is higher

(c) It is the same

(d) It depends on the airspeed

3. When does the coefficient of lift reach its maximum value?

(a) At around 5°

(b) At or just before the stall

(c) At minimum drag speed

(d) At V_{NO} when clean

4. What is the effect of washout on a wing?

(a) It causes the outboard section of the wind to stall first

(b) It causes the inboard section of the wind to stall first

(c) It makes sure that the whole wing stalls at the same time

(d) It reduces tip vortices

5. What does the green band on the ASI mean?

    (a) Normal operating speed (V_{NO})

    (b) Minimum flap speed

    (c) Caution

    (d) The gear must be up

6. What is the worst combination for wake turbulence?

    (a) Heavy aircraft, dirty configuration, slow speed

    (b) Light aircraft, dirty configuration, slow speed

    (c) Heavy aircraft, clean configuration, slow speed

    (d) Heavy aircraft, clean configuration, fast speed

7. An overstressed aircraft:

    (a) Must be inspected by an engineer

    (b) Must be inspected by at least two pilots

    (c) Must be inspected by an engineer before the next flight

    (d) Must be inspected by two engineers

8. What will an increase in aircraft weight do?

    (a) Decrease the stalling speed

    (b) Have no effect

    (c) Increase the stalling speed

    (d) Increase the stalling speed with flaps down

9. A wing will stall at a given:

    (a) Angle of incidence

    (b) Angle of attack

    (c) Dihedral

    (d) Anhedral

10. Why is the stalling angle of attack increased by slots?

    (a) They allow higher pressure through from underneath the wing

    (b) They decrease the effective upper surface area

    (c) They delay the breaking up of the smooth airflow over the wing

    (d) They increase the effective upper surface area

11. What happens when the C of G is at or near its aft limit?

    (a) Decreased stalling speed

    (b) Increased stalling speed

    (c) Greater rudder force is required

    (d) Greatly reduced elevator force during the flare

12. As TAS increases:

    (a) Parasite drag decreases and induced drag increases

    (b) Parasite drag increases and induced drag decreases

    (c) Parasite drag decreases and induced drag decreases

    (d) Parasite drag increases and induced drag increases

13. Induced drag:

    (a) Does not depend on airspeed

    (b) Increases as airspeed decreases

    (c) Increases as airspeed increases

    (d) Decreases as airspeed increases

14. A fixed trim tab:

    (a) is set by the manufacturer and should not be touched

    (b) is set by an engineer and should not be touched

    (c) is adjusted on the ground after a flight test to keep the wings level

    (d) is adjusted on the ground after a flight test to keep the nose up

15. What is the purpose of an anti-balance tab?

    (a) To stop the Centre of Pressure moving

    (b) To help the pilot move the control surface

    (c) To make the pilot's control load increase with control surface deflection

    (d) To make the pilot's control load decrease with control surface deflection

16. Once a trim has been set, what happens when you move the flying controls?

   (a) The trim tab's position relative to the control surface changes

   (b) The trim tab's position relative to the control surface stays the same

   (c) The trim tab's position relative to the airflow stays the same

   (d) The trim tab moves in the opposite direction to the control surface

17. What factor determines an aeroplane's stalling speed for a given weight?

   (a) The square of the load factor

   (b) The square root of the load factor

   (c) The square of the airspeed

   (d) The square root of the airspeed

18. In straight and level flight, the airflow over the upper surface of a wing compared to the free stream will be:

   (a) Faster

   (b) Slower

   (c) The same

   (d) Nearly the same

19. The stalling angle of attack will be _____ with trailing flaps extended:

   (a) The same

   (b) Less

   (c) Greater

   (d) Reversed

20. What gives an aeroplane directional stability?

   (a) The keel area

   (b) The fin

   (c) The rudder

   (d) The pedals

21. What is movement around the normal axis called?

   (a) Pitch

   (b) Roll

   (c) Yaw

   (d) Spin

22. Forward movement of the left pedal will move a balance tab in which direction?

   (a) Right and the rudder to the left

   (b) Left and the rudder to the left

   (c) Left and the rudder to the right

   (d) Right and the rudder to the right

23. What does mass balance on a control surface do?

   (a) It stops flutter at high speeds

   (b) It stops shimmy at high speeds

   (c) It makes the control easier to move

   (d) It makes the control harder to move

24. Where is a mass or aerodynamic balance fitted?

   (a) Aft of the hinge

   (b) On the hinge

   (c) Forward of the hinge

   (d) Either side of the hinge

25. What does differential aileron help to counteract?

   (a) Momentum

   (b) Adverse aileron drag

   (c) Positive static stability

   (d) Instability

26. The Centre of Pressure's position behind the Centre of Gravity is balanced in straight and level flight by what?

   (a) The tailplane's upward force

   (b) The tailplane's downward force

   (c) The couple formed by Lift and Weight

   (d) The couple formed by Thrust and Drag

27. What does a flying control lock do?

   (a) It stops the controls from moving around when you are changing a radio frequency

   (b) It keeps the trim tabs at the same setting

   (c) It stops the controls from moving around on the ground in gusty conditions

   (d) It keeps the autopilot steady

28. What happens when the C of G is at or near its forward limit?

    (a) Decreased stalling speed

    (b) Increased stalling speed

    (c) Greater rudder force is required

    (d) High elevator forces needed during the flare

29. A propeller blade that is twisted along its length:

    (a) Has less drag at the tips

    (b) Has less drag at the root

    (c) Has a more even distribution of lift along its length because the blade angle becomes smaller from root to tip

    (d) Has the same angle of attack along its length

30. During acceleration at a constant power setting in an aeroplane with a fixed pitch propeller, what happens to engine RPM?

    (a) It decreases

    (b) It remains the same

    (c) It increases

    (d) It depends on the air density

31. What is the result of the torque reaction from the propeller on takeoff, if it is turning clockwise when viewed from the rear?

    (a) The tail will rise

    (b) The tail will fall

    (c) The left wing will descend

    (d) The right wing will descend

32. What is the result of using takeoff flap?

    (a) Greater lifting capacity

    (b) A longer takeoff run

    (c) A shorter takeoff run

    (d) Less turbulence

33. By what margin is Takeoff Safety Speed greater than the stall speed?

    (a) 10%

    (b) 15%

    (c) 20%

    (d) 25%

34. What would mainly cause nose wheel shimmy?

    (a) Failure of the torque link

    (b) Weak shimmy damper (if fitted)

    (c) Not enough pressure in the tyre

    (d) Bad ground

35. An aircraft in the normal or utility categories has load factor limits that are _____ an aircraft in the aerobatic category:

    (a) The same as

    (b) Much greater than

    (c) A little greater than

    (d) Less than

36. In the picture below, what are the items at A & B?

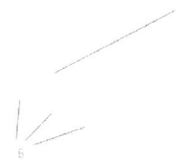

    (a) Spanner, Formers

    (b) Spar, Ribs

    (c) Longeron, Wideron

    (d) Spar, Formers

37. What is the device in the picture below?

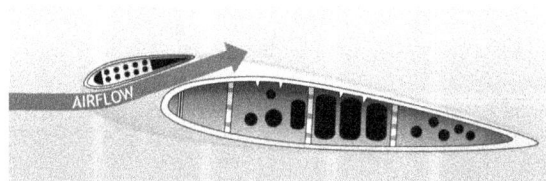

    (a) Slat

    (b) Slipway

    (c) Slot

    (d) Flap

38. On a tyre, what items should be looked for before flying?

(a) Creep

(b) Creep, flat spots and skidding damage

(c) Tread pattern

(d) Valve position

39. Why are baffles fitted in an engine cowling?

(a) To stop the cowling fluttering at high speeds

(b) To make the cowling stronger

(c) To direct the flow of cooling air around the cylinders evenly

(d) Take the heat away from the cooling fins

40. Why is there a cowling around an engine?

(a) To provide streamlining (the engine is quite lumpy)

(b) To catch any leaking oil

(c) To force cooling air around the engine

(d) To ensure that cylinder head temperatures are even

41. If the basic stalling speed of an aeroplane is 90 knots, what will it be in a level turn with a 60° angle of bank?

(a) 127 kts

(b) 110 kts

(c) 175 kts

(d) 99 kts

42. Why might an up-going aileron move through a larger angle than a down-going one?

(a) To counteract adverse aileron yaw

(b) To counteract aileron reversal

(c) To counteract negative stability

(d) To counteract negative inertia

43. Which value shows the lift produced for a level turn?

(a) A

(b) B

(c) C

(d) D

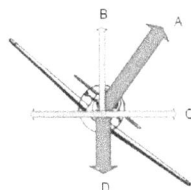

44. A slat:

(a) increases the camber of an aerofoil and diverts the airflow around the sharp leading edge

(b) increases lift by increasing the wing area and the camber of the aft portion of the wing

(c) delays the stall to a higher angle of attack

(d) increases drag to allow a steeper descent path at the same speed

45. Which part of an aeroplane has the greatest effect on induced drag?

(a) The wing tip

(b) The engine cowling

(c) The junction of the wing root with the fuselage

(d) The empennage

46. If an aeroplane that has strong directional stability (with a large fin) and weak lateral stability (no dihedral) is hit by a gust that causes a sidesip, what is the effect?

(a) spiral instability

(b) adverse yaw

(c) dutch roll

(d) flutter

47. Which part of an aeroplane contributes the most to static longitudinal stability?

(a) The fin

(b) The wing

(c) The horizontal tailplane

(d) The fairings

48. What is the manoeuvring load factor for an aeroplane in the utility category in the clean configuration?

(a) 6.0

(b) 3.8

(c) 2.4

(d) 4.4

49. What is the still air glide range for an aeroplane that is 6 000 feet AGL with a L/D ratio of 6:1?

(a) 5.9 nm

(b) 3.8 nm

(c) 4.4 nm

(d) 6 nm

50. What is the result of the torque reaction from the propeller during the initial steady climb after takeoff, if it is turning clockwise when viewed from the rear?

    (a) Right yaw

    (b) None

    (c) Left yaw

    (d) Left roll

51. If you fly 6 000 feet higher, the stalling IAS:

    (a) is 10% higher

    (b) is 10% lower

    (c) is the same

    (d) changes according to air density

52. To remain trimmed in straight and level flight, as speed is increased:

    (a) the trim tab and elevator are deflected further downwards

    (b) the trim tab and elevator do not move

    (c) the trim tab is deflected further downwards and the elevator further upwards

    (d) the trim tab is deflected further upwards and the elevator further downwards

53. Which value shows the load factor for this level turn?

    (a) A/D

    (b) B/D

    (c) C/B

    (d) D/B

54. Which part of an aeroplane contributes the most to static directional stability?

    (a) The fin

    (b) The wing

    (c) The horizontal tailplane

    (d) The fairings

55. What is angular movement of an aeroplane about its lateral axis?

    (a) Yawing

    (b) Rolling

    (c) Pitching

    (d) Sideslip

56. In a steady, straight climb:

    (a) Thrust is greater than drag and lift is greater than weight

    (b) Thrust is greater than drag and lift is less than weight

    (c) Thrust is greater than drag and lift equals weight

    (d) Thrust equals drag and lift equals weight

57. What does using a small flap setting for takeoff and initial climb result in?

    (a) A longer ground run and steeper climb angle

    (b) A shorter ground run and shallower climb angle

    (c) A shorter ground run and steeper climb angle

    (d) A longer ground run and shallower climb angle

58. Which combination increases stall speed?

    (a) An increase in load factor and power

    (b) An increase in weight and power

    (c) An increased angle of bank in a turn, ice on the wing

    (d) An increase in load factor and flap setting

59. What are the primary and secondary effects of using the ailerons and elevator?

    (a) Roll, then yaw; pitch, with no secondary effect

    (b) Yaw, then roll; roll then yaw

    (c) Roll, then pitch; pitch then roll

    (d) Roll then yaw; yaw then roll

60. An aeroplane has neutral dynamic stability if, when it is disturbed, it:

    (a) returns and overshoots the original position before coming back to it

    (b) oscillates with a constant period and amplitude

    (c) continues to move away from its original position

    (d) returns to the original position without overshooting

61. What will applying full rearward control column movement abruptly when above the manoeuvring speed (V_A) most likely lead to?

    (a) A stall

    (b) A zoom climb

    (c) An incipient spin

    (d) Structural damage

62. A low wing aeroplane is affected:

    (a) more by ground effect and will gain a greater increase in lift and reduction in drag during the final approach to land

    (b) less by ground effect and will tend to float and use more runway when landing

    (c) more by ground effect and will experience a reduction in drag and increase in lift when leaving ground effect

    (d) less by ground effect and will tend to balloon on landing

63. Where is the value of the coefficient of lift at its maximum?

    (a) at around the stalling angle of attack

    (b) at the IAS for minimum drag

    (c) at around 4° angle of attack

    (d) at a negative angle of attack

64. As speed is increased in straight and level flight:

    (a) induced and parasite drag decrease

    (b) induced drag decreases and parasite drag increases

    (c) induced drag increases and parasite drag decreases

    (d) induced and parasite drag increase

65. What is the approximate angle of attack for the maximum lift/drag ratio of a conventional aerofoil?

    (a) 0°

    (b) -4°

    (c) 4°

    (d) 15°

66. If the flaps are extended at a constant angle of attack, what will an aeroplane initially do?

    (a) yaw

    (b) bank

    (c) descend

    (d) climb

67. Trailing edge flaps, when extended, will give:

    (a) an increase in stalling angle of attack

    (b) a reduction in stalling angle of attack

    (c) the same stalling angle of attack

    (d) a change in optimum angle of attack

68. How can flutter be overcome?

    (a) Making control surfaces more rigid and using a mass balance

    (b) Using anti-balance tabs

    (c) Using balance tabs

    (d) Using servo tabs

69. With no wind, the maximum gliding distance is achieved at what speed?

    (a) just above stalling speed

    (b) that for minimum drag

    (c) V_{MO}

    (d) V_{NE}

70. The stalling IAS reduces when the:

    (a) pitch reduces and the flap setting increases

    (b) aircraft weight reduces

    (c) angle of bank in a turn increases together with a reduction in power

    (d) wing loading increases and power reduces

71. What is the maximum speed at which full application of the primary controls will not cause structural damage?

    (a) V_{MO}

    (b) V_{NO}

    (c) V_{MCA}

    (d) V_A

72. What are the effects when an aeroplane leaves ground effect after taking off if pitch and thrust remain the same?

    (a) Decreased C_L, decreased induced drag, increased airspeed

    (b) Increased C_L, increased induced drag, decreased airspeed

    (c) Decreased C_L, increased induced drag, decreased airspeed

    (d) Increased C_L, decreased induced drag, increased airspeed

73. On a non-stressed skin type of wing, what elements take up the vertical bending moments?

    (a) spars

    (b) longerons

    (c) ribs

    (d) formers

74. The ability to steer with the nosewheel on light aircraft is mostly made possible by:

    (a) an electric motor

    (b) an electro-mechanical device

    (c) a hydro-mechanical device

    (d) push-pull rods connected to the pivoting section of an oleo-pneumatic strut

75. An under-inflated tyre will:

    (a) Wear more at the shoulders

    (b) increase the risk of hydroplaning

    (c) have a greater tendency to creep

    (d) cause a shimmy

76. What is the purpose of a trim tab?

    (a) To trim the aircraft during low speed flight

    (b) To reduce or cancel out control forces

    (c) To lower control forces

    (d) To trim the aircraft during high speed flight

77. If the suction gauge reads zero but the instruments otherwise appear to be working normally, what can you conclude?

    (a) Nothing

    (b) The air filter is blocked

    (c) The gauge isn't working

    (d) The vacuum pump has failed

78. What should be checked with regard to tyres on a preflight check?

    (a) Creep, inflation pressure, colour

    (b) Creep, inflation pressure, tyre size

    (c) Creep, inflation pressure, wheel tracking

    (d) Creep, inflation pressure, flat spots from skidding and damage to the sidewall

79. If the suction gauge reads lower than normal:

    (a) Nothing

    (b) The air filter is blocked

    (c) The gauge isn't working

    (d) The vacuum pump has failed

80. What does the white arc on an ASI represent?

    (a) $V_{NO}-V_{NE}$

    (b) $V_{S1}-V_{NO}$

    (c) $V_{S0}-V_{FE}$

    (d) $V_{S0}-V_{MCA}$

HELICOPTERS

1. If a rotor blade has a constant blade pitch angle throughout its span, each element of the blade produces a different value of rotor thrust. This is offset by:

   (a) A pre-set coning angle

   (b) Washin

   (c) Washout

   (d) Combination of washout and pre-set coning angle

2. In forward flight, if the rotor RPM increase above those specified:

   (a) The increase in blade drag will automatically cause the RPM to decay to their original level

   (b) The increase in centrifugal force will decrease blade coning and reduce RPM to original levels

   (c) The large centrifugal forces impose severe and possibly excessive loads on the hub

   (d) It will induce retreating blade stall at a reduced forward speed

3. Max rotor RPM in powered flight are governed by:

   (a) Engine and hub limitations

   (b) Retreating blade stall

   (c) Compressibility

   (d) Limit of forward cyclic

4. The pitch angle of the blade sections:

   (a) Varies with the twist of the blade

   (b) Is constant throughout the span of the blade

   (c) Is regarded as constant along the blade

   (d) Is conserved during a rotation

5. Blade sailing is a condition which may occur:

   (a) During starting or stopping the main rotors in strong winds

   (b) During a vertical autorotation

   (c) At the onset of retreating blade stall

   (d) At the onset of vortex ring (settling with power)

6. If the helicopter is affected by a strong gust of headwind whilst the rotor RPM is low:

   (a) Cyclic control will be effective in keeping the disc level

   (b) Groundcrew, standing in front of the helicopter, are in danger from a blade strike

   (c) The effect on the rotor blades will depend on the direction of rotation

   (d) There is a danger of the main rotor blades striking the tail boom

7. To minimise the dangers of blade sailing:

   (a) The start-up and shut-down should be carried out facing directly into wind

   (b) Flapping restrictors, if fitted, should be withdrawn before start-up or shut-down

   (c) Rotor RPM during start-up or shut-down should be increased or decreased as slowly as possible

   (d) The start-up and shut-down should be carried out facing slightly out of wind

8. If you don't change the lift force, an increase of the speed of the rotor:

   (a) Increases conicity

   (b) Causes onset of blade stalling in forward flight

   (c) Increases the stresses in the blade fasteners

   (d) Decreases control surface efficiency

9. Flapping is the:

   (a) Movement, in the plane of rotation, of a rotor blade from its neutral position

   (b) Trimming of a rotor blade to ensure accurate and consistent tracking

   (c) Angular movement of a blade, about its root, in the vertical plane

   (d) Flexing of a blade along its length as a result of turbulence

10. One requirement for a main rotor blade section is that:

(a) Pitch changes produce large changes in the position of the centre of pressure to minimise control forces

(b) The centre of pressure moves rapidly forward as the angle of attack is increased to ensure correct blade flapping

(c) Its induced drag characteristics are insignificant compared with profile drag

(d) Changes in angle of attack produce minimum centre of pressure movement

11. Coriolis effect:

(a) Is basically the movement of the blade to reposition itself relative to the other blades on the cone of the disc when cyclic stick is applied

(b) Causes rotor RPM to stabilise after disturbance from a wind gust

(c) Tends to accelerate or decelerate a blade as it flaps up or down

(d) Only noticeable with helicopters with a semi-articulated head

12. What is the main purpose for a free-wheeling unit in a piston powered helicopter?

(a) It transmits engine power to the main rotor, tail rotor, generator/alternator and other accessories

(b) It provides speed reduction between the engine, and the main and tail rotors

(c) It provides disengagement of the engine from the rotor system for autorotation purposes

(d) This allows the engine to be started without driving the main rotor system

13. The main advantage of using symmetrical aerofoils for rotor blades is that the centre of pressure…

(a) Has relatively little movement with changes in flight conditions

(b) Moves rearwards with an increase to the angle of attack

(c) Moves forward when the aerofoil stalls

(d) Moves along the span of the blade only, and not the chord

14. Why do main rotor blades operate more efficiently in translation than in a hover?

(a) Indicated airflow is reduced to zero

(b) Their angle of attack is reduced

(c) Their pitch angle is reduced in translation

(d) Their angle of attack is increased

15. When the tail rotor is counteracting the torque force, it causes:

(a) The nose to tend to pitch up

(b) The tail boom to swing upwards

(c) A translating tendency in the direction which the anti-torque force acts

(d) A translating tendency in the opposite direction to the anti-torque force

16. A helicopter is most likely to enter a vortex ring state under which conditions?

(a) Zero airspeed, partial power, rate of descent less than 200 fpm

(b) Low airspeed, partial power, rate of descent greater than 300 fpm

(c) Low airspeed in autorotation, rate of descent greater than 300 fpm

(d) Cruise speed, partial power, rate of descent less than 200 fpm

17. Ground effect is most noticeable when hovering at zero airspeed over…

(a) Sloping ground

(b) Tall grass

(c) Rough water

(d) A smooth, hard surface

18. How is flapback corrected?

(a) An automatic aerodynamic change in the pitch angle of the blades as the rotor disc tips forwards

(b) An automatic aerodynamic change in the angle of attack as the rotor disk flaps backwards

(c) Positive movement of the cyclic in the direction of flight

(d) Rotating weights or auxiliary aerofoils mechanically change the pitch of the blades

19. What is Dissymmetry of Lift caused by?

    (a) The tilting of the rotor disk

    (b) The difference in airflow over the advancing and retreating blades

    (c) Improper use of the collective

    (d) No correlation between throttle and collective

20. The purpose of the lead-lag (drag) hinge in a 3 bladed fully articulated system is to compensate for geometric imbalance caused by:

    (a) Coriolis effect

    (b) Dissymmetry of lift

    (c) Gyroscopic precession

    (d) Later instability during autorotation

21. Lift created by an aerofoil varies:

    (a) At ½ the air density

    (b) At the square of the air density

    (c) Inversely with air density

    (d) Directly with air density

22. Induced drag on a main rotor is greatest when?

    (a) During a slow hover-taxi

    (b) In autorotation

    (c) During retreating blade stall

    (d) When over-pitched

23. How does a helicopter develop forward thrust? By:

    (a) Raising the collective

    (b) Increasing engine power

    (c) Tilting the total lift reaction of the rotor disk

    (d) All the above

24. Coning is caused by the combined forces of

    (a) Gravity and thrust

    (b) Weight and centrifugal force

    (c) Drag, weight and gravity

    (d) Lift and centrifugal force

25. Which of the following applies only to a change in helicopter flight speed?

    (a) Translation

    (b) Transition

    (c) Transverse flow

    (d) Translating effect

26. When a fully articulated rotor is tilted for forward flight, the centre of mass of each blade is allowed to rotate about the new axis of rotation without excessive blade fatigue and vibration by the:

    (a) Flapping hinges

    (b) Drag hinges

    (c) Blade washout

    (d) Blade flexibility

27. The main blades in a fully articulated system can

    (a) Flap and feather as a unit

    (b) Flap, drag and feather

    (c) Feather, but cannot flap or drag

    (d) Flap and drag, but can feather collectively only

28. The main blades in a semi-rigid system can:

    (a) Drag and feather, but not flap

    (b) Flap, drag and feather independently

    (c) Feather independently, but not flap or drag

    (d) Flap and drag independently, but feather collectively only

29. How does the Delta-Three flapping hinge improve rotor stability?

    (a) Allowing pilot control of pitch change more easily

    (b) Changing the angle of attack of a blade as it flaps

    (c) Preventing flapping of the blades

    (d) Increasing flapping of the blades

30. Why should an excessively steep approach angle with a slower than normal closing speed be avoided during the approach to the hover?

    (a) The ASI is unreliable

    (b) You could enter vortex ring

    (c) A go-around would be hard to accomplish

    (d) High cylinder head and oil temps may occur

31. Ground resonance is most likely to develop when a helicopter is in contact with the ground and:

   (a) Initial ground contact is made with high gross weight and low RRPM

   (b) There is a sudden change in the blade velocity in the plane of rotation

   (c) The main rotor becomes unbalanced

   (d) There is a combination of a decrease in the angle of attack on the advancing blade side and increase in the angle of attack on the retreating blade side

32. In what type of helicopter is ground resonance most likely to occur?

   (a) Rigid rotor systems

   (b) Fully articulated systems

   (c) Wheeled landing gear instead of skids

   (d) Semi rigid systems

33. What combination of weather conditions will reduce a helicopter's takeoff and climb performance?

   (a) Low temperature, low relative humidity and low density altitude

   (b) High temperature, low relative humidity and low density altitude

   (c) High temperature, high relative humidity and high density altitude

   (d) Low temperature, high relative humidity and high density altitude

34. Helicopter climb performance is most adversely affected by what?

   (a) Lower than standard temperature and low relative humidity

   (b) Higher than standard temperature and low relative humidity

   (c) Higher than standard temperature and high relative humidity

   (d) Lower than standard temperature and high humidity

35. What type of drag are blade tip vortices a form of?

   (a) Profile drag

   (b) Skin drag

   (c) Parasite drag

   (d) Induced drag

36. Why does performance decrease with high humidity?

   (a) Dry air is less dense than moist air

   (b) Water vapour decreases air density

   (c) Moist air is heavier than dry air

   (d) Vapour trails from rotor tips will cause an increase in induced drag

37. Why is negative pitch available on tail rotor blades?

   (a) To counteract the torque of the transmission during autorotation

   (b) To maintain heading with a crosswind from the left (assume North American rotation)

   (c) To make it possible to make a hovering turn to the right

   (d) To make it possible to make a hovering turn to the left

38. What is the main purpose of a tail rotor?

   (a) Assist in making coordinated turns

   (b) Maintain heading in forward flight

   (c) Provide extra thrust and lift

   (d) Counteract the torque force of the main rotor

39. Some helicopters can tilt laterally while hovering and landing in nil wind conditions. What causes the tilt?

   (a) The translating effect of the tail rotor

   (b) Downwash onto the tail boom from the main rotor

   (c) A rolling couple created between the main and tail rotors

   (d) The pilot applying cyclic to counteract the effect of a tilted drive shaft

40. What is the most common type of aerofoil used for rotor blades?

    (a) High lift

    (b) Symmetrical

    (c) Supersonic

    (d) Transonic

41. What surface will need the most power to hover over?

    (a) A concrete ramp

    (b) Smooth water

    (c) Rough uneven ground

    (d) High grass

42. What are the immediate actions required to prevent the development of ground resonance when it appears?

    (a) If RRPM is too low to warrant an immediate takeoff, open throttle fully, raise collective and take off

    (b) Regardless of RRPM, "pin" the helicopter onto the ground with the collective, close the throttle and stop the rotor when safe to do so

    (c) If RRPM is above operating range, lower the collective, close throttle and stop the rotor; if RRPM is below operating range then take off

    (d) If RRPM are in normal operating range, take off; if RRPM is below operating range lower the collective, close the throttle and stop the rotor

43. As a blade flaps up, its centre of mass moves inwards to its axis of rotation, causing a tendency to:

    (a) Slow its rotational velocity, known as Drag Effect

    (b) Stabilize its rotational velocity compensating for dissymmetry of lift

    (c) Slow its rotational velocity, known as Translating Tendency

    (d) Speed up its velocity, known as Coriolis effect

44. What are the forces acting on a helicopter when it is maintaining constant speed, height and direction?

    (a) Lift is equal and opposite to weight, horizontal thrust is equal and opposite to drag

    (b) Lift is equal and opposite to weight, horizontal thrust is greater than and opposite to drag

    (c) Lift is greater than and opposite to weight, thrust is greater than and opposite to drag

    (d) Lift is equal and opposite to weight, horizontal thrust is less than and opposite to drag

45. What is movement of a rotor blade in a plane at right angles to the plane of rotation known as?

    (a) Leading

    (b) Lagging

    (c) Flapping

    (d) Feathering

46. What is the difference between a fully articulated rotor system and a semi-rigid one?

    (a) The fully articulated system can flap and feather, whilst the semi-rigid system can only flap

    (b) The fully articulated system can flap and lead or lag, whilst the semi-rigid system can only flap

    (c) The fully articulated system can flap, feather and drag, whilst the semi-rigid system can only flap and feather

    (d) The fully articulated system can feather, whilst the semi-rigid system can only flap

47. What does washout do?

    (a) It increases the lift coefficient at the tip of the blade

    (b) It decreases the lift coefficient at the tip of the blade

    (c) It sweeps back at the tip of the blade

    (d) It sweeps forward at the tip of the blade

48. How does movement of the collective pitch control change the pitch of the main rotor blades?

    (a) More on the advancing side than the retreating side

    (b) At one point only

    (c) By an equal amount in the same direction

    (d) By an equal amount in opposite directions

49. When hovering in ground effect:

   (a) Less power is needed because the angle of attack is reduced

   (b) Less power is needed because the induced flow is reduced

   (c) More power is needed because the pressure increase under the disc increases drag

   (d) More power is needed because the induced flow is reduced

50. When hovering, the tail rotor has a secondary effect which creates a sideways drift in which direction?

   (a) In the opposite direction to tail rotor thrust

   (b) In the opposite direction to the main rotor

   (c) In the same direction as tail rotor thrust

   (d) It depends on when the power is applied

51. With North American rotation, movement of the cyclic to the left will produce a maximum rotor blade pitch increase in what position?

   (a) At the front

   (b) At the back

   (c) On the advancing side

   (d) On the retreating side

52. How is dissymmetry of lift compensated for?

   (a) The blade flaps to increase the angle of attack on the advancing side

   (b) The blade flaps to decrease the angle of attack on the advancing side

   (c) The flapping hinge allows the blade to feather

   (d) Opposite movement of the cyclic

53. What is phase lag? The delay between:

   (a) A pitch increase from the collective and the blade flapping down

   (b) A pitch increase from the cyclic and the blade flapping down

   (c) A pitch increase from the cyclic and the blade flapping up to maximum

   (d) Movement of the cyclic and the swashplate

54. During a flare, induced flow through the disc will:

   (a) Increase from Coriolis

   (b) Decrease from flow above

   (c) Decrease from flow below

   (d) Stay the same

55. Increased disc loading can move the total reaction closer to the axis of rotation and:

   (a) Increase torque from the rotor

   (b) Decrease torque from the rotor

   (c) Increase the flapping angle

   (d) Increase the gliding angle

56. What is needed to develop vortex ring?

   (a) High rate of descent with power applied, airspeed above translational lift speed

   (b) Low rate of descent with power applied, airspeed above translational lift speed

   (c) Rate of descent over 400 ft per minute with power applied, airspeed low or zero

   (d) Rate of descent below 400 ft per minute with power applied, airspeed low or zero

57. On helicopters that can suffer from mast bumping, how should you react if you inadvertently encounter negative G?

   (a) Forward cyclic, keep straight with the pedals

   (b) Left or right cyclic, and relevant pedal movement

   (c) Raise the collective

   (d) Gentle rearward cyclic to reload the rotor, then roll level

58. If the engine fails in flight:

   (a) The cyclic should be moved to maintain rotor RPM

   (b) Rotor RPM can be maintained by engaging the clutch

   (c) Rotor RPM are restored by flaring

   (d) The freewheel unit allows the engine to disengage from the main gearbox

If this page is a photocopy, it is not authorised!

59. To increase rotor thrust, you could do what?

   (a) Increase the angle of attack of the main rotor blades with the cyclic control

   (b) Increase the angle of attack of the main rotor blades with the collective control

   (c) Reduce the angle of attack of the tail rotor blades with the cyclic control

   (d) Reduce the angle of attack of the tail rotor blades with the collective control

60. What is the (profile) drag force on a rotor blade balanced by?

   (a) Rotor Thrust

   (b) Total Rotor Thrust

   (c) Rotor RPM

   (d) Engine torque

61. Why should the rotor speed not be allowed to fall below the minimum limits?

   (a) The blades might stall

   (b) The clutch might disengage

   (c) The engine might overspeed

   (d) To stop the blades coning too much

62. How do you maintain rotor RPM in an autorotative descent?

   (a) The air coming up creates a lift component

   (b) The reversed airflow counteracts the drag

   (c) The hub and blades have inertia

   (d) Lower the collective

63. What is coning angle? The angle between the longitudinal axis of the rotor blade and the:

   (a) Plane of Rotation

   (b) Rotor Mast

   (c) Tip Path Plane

   (d) Relative airflow

64. What is airflow reversal associated with?

   (a) Upflowing air in autorotation

   (b) Blowback in a carburettor

   (c) Vortex ring

   (d) Flight at high forward speed, starting at the root of the blade

65. How would you correct retreating blade stall in flight?

   (a) Apply forward cyclic

   (b) Apply rear cyclic

   (c) Reduce engine speed

   (d) Reduce collective pitch

66. What does the blue line on the ASI mean?

   (a) V_{NE}

   (b) V_{NE} in autorotation

   (c) V_{NO}

   (d) Minimum single engine speed

67. What is ground resonance?

   (a) A low frequency vibration between the rotor head and the swashplate

   (b) A harmonic between the engine and main rotor gearbox

   (c) A sympathetic vibration from an interaction between the landing gear and the main rotor

   (d) An interaction between the tail rotor and the main rotor gearbox

68. The tail rotor controls the helicopter about which axis?

   (a) Lateral

   (b) Longitudinal

   (c) Normal

   (d) Yaw

69. In the hover, in nil wind conditions, what are the forces acting on a helicopter?

   (a) TRT opposes weight and drag

   (b) TRT is opposite and equal to weight

   (c) TRT opposes drag

   (d) TRT reinforces drag

70. What causes dynamic rollover?

   (a) Too much cyclic movement

   (b) Too much collective movement

   (c) A rolling moment caused by a wheel or skid in contact with the ground

   (d) Negative G conditions

Turbine Engines

1. What are the main engine modules in a light helicopter turbine engine?

   (a) The Air Intake, The Compressor, The Combustion Chamber, The Gas Producer Turbine, The Free Turbine and the Exhaust

   (b) The Oil Tank, The Fuel Control Unit, Power Turbine Governor, Regulator and Gas Outlet

   (c) The Cold Section, The Hot Section The Fuel Regulator, The Exhaust

   (d) The Air Intake, The Centrifugal Compressor, The Rotary Turbine, The Centrifugal Power Turbine, The Gas Discharger

2. What does the compressor bleed valve on a gas turbine engine do?

   (a) It provides P2 air for the cabin heating system

   (b) It bleeds air off the compressor for the combustion chamber

   (c) It stops the engine overheating

   (d) It releases excess air from the compressor and minimises the risk of compressor surge/stall during engine acceleration/deceleration

3. The air fed to the combustion chamber from the compressor of a small gas turbine engine:

   (a) Provides air for combustion and cools the combustion chamber components

   (b) Provides air for combustion and shapes the flame

   (c) Provides air for combustion, shapes the flame and cools the combustion chamber components

   (d) Provides air for combustion only

4. Why do gas turbine engines have maximum Turbine Outlet Temperature starting limits?

   (a) To prevent excess fuel consumption during the start cycle

   (b) To prevent a flame from being ejected from the exhaust during the start cycle

   (c) To maximise the thermal gradient across the engine during starting

   (d) To minimise thermal stresses on engine components during starting

5. What device controls the speed of a free turbine?

   (a) The power turbine governor

   (b) The collective pitch setting

   (c) The anticipator rod on the collective lever

   (d) The fuel control unit (FCU)

6. In a light gas turbine engine, gas producer speed is generally referred to as:

   (a) N_1 or N_G

   (b) T4

   (c) N_2 or N_F

   (d) N_3 or N_R

7. What is the correct immediate action in an active governor failure on a light gas turbine engine?

   (a) Shut down the engine

   (b) Select ground idle

   (c) Enter autorotation

   (d) Control the rotor speed with appropriate collective pitch

COMMUNICATIONS

GENERAL

1. What would be a correct abbreviated reply to "Golf India Tango, radar service terminated"?

   (a)   Radar service terminated, Golf India Tango

   (b)   Golf India Tango

   (c)   India Tango

   (d)   Roger

2. Where would the call *Transmitting Blind Due To Receiver Failure* come from?

   (a)   A ground station

   (b)   An aircraft

   (c)   Tower

   (d)   Approach

3. What does the word *Roger* mean?

   (a)   I have received all your last transmission

   (b)   I understand your last transmission

   (c)   Will comply

   (d)   Received and understood

4. What is the definition of *aeronautical station*?

   (a)   An air station in the aeronautical mobile service

   (b)   A land station in the aeronautical mobile service

   (c)   A relay station

   (d)   A seaborne station

5. What should you do if you make a transmitting error?

   (a)   Repeat the message with the correct words

   (b)   Say *Correction*, followed by the last group or phrase that was correctly transmitted, then the proper version

   (c)   Say *I Say Again*, followed by the last group or phrase that was correctly transmitted, then the proper version

   (d)   Repeat the message twice with the correct words

6. What does the term *Squawk Ident* mean?

   (a)   Identify your callsign

   (b)   Say the transponder code over the microphone

   (c)   Operate the Ident button on your transponder

   (d)   State your position

7. How do you transmit the time of 10:30?

   (a)   Ten Thirty

   (b)   One Zero Thirty

   (c)   Ten Three Zero

   (d)   One Zero Three Zero

8. What frequency do you make the first Mayday call on?

   (a)   121.5 KHz

   (b)   121.5 MHz

   (c)   The one currently in use

   (d)   204.3 MHz

9. How do you transmit the frequency 118.1?

   (a)   One eighteen decimal one

   (b)   One one eight decimal one

   (c)   One one eight decimal one zero

   (d)   One one eight point one

10. What would the abbreviation for the callsign CHEROKEE XY-ABC be?

  (a) Cherokee XY-BC

  (b) Cherokee BC

  (c) XY- BC

  (d) ABC

11. What is the Q code for a True Bearing from a station?

  (a) QDR

  (b) QFE

  (c) QUJ

  (d) QTE

12. What is the Q code on which height is based?

  (a) QNH

  (b) QFF

  (c) QUJ

  (d) QFE

13. On what type of frequency can ATIS be found?

  (a) Discrete VHF only

  (b) VOR frequency only

  (c) Discrete VHF or VOR frequency

  (d) Any ATC frequency

14. What does the word *Urgency* mean?

  (a) A serious situation that does not require immediate assistance.

  (b) A serious situation that requires immediate assistance.

  (c) A condition where safety is compromised.

  (d) A condition concerning the safety of an aircraft.

15. When asking for a message to be repeated, what should you say?

  (a) Words Twice

  (b) Say Again

  (c) Repeat Message

  (d) Speak Slowly

16. When reporting a frequency, when can the use of the word DECIMAL be omitted?

  (a) When there is no likelihood of confusion

  (b) Never

  (c) After the initial call

  (d) By the ground station only

17. What does selecting 7600 on a transponder indicate?

  (a) Distress

  (b) Urgency

  (c) Loss of communications

  (d) Hijacking

18. What is your action in response to the instruction to *Recycle Squawk?*

  (a) Switch to standby and back to ON

  (b) Press the IDENT button

  (c) Reselect the numbers on the control unit

  (d) Set the numbers to 7000

19. What should you do if you are unable to contact a station on a designated frequency?

  (a) Start transmitting blind

  (b) Land at the nearest suitable aerodrome

  (c) Try another appropriate frequency

  (d) Transmit words twice

20. The minimum content of a readback of the message *X-CD Change Frequency To Stephenville Tower 118.7* is:

  (a) Changing Frequency X-CD

  (b) To Stephenville X-CD

  (c) 118.7

  (d) 118.7 X-CD

21. The best signals for VHF communications are obtained when the aircraft is at:

  (a) High altitude at long range

  (b) Low altitude and short range

  (c) High altitude and near the aerodrome

  (d) Low level and long range

22. What is the Q code for the magnetic bearing from a station?

   (a) QDM

   (b) QDR

   (c) QTE

   (d) QNH

23. What does the phrase *Squawk Charlie* mean?

   (a) Press and release the ident button

   (b) Recycle the numbers

   (c) Turn the transponder switch to ALT

   (d) Turn the transponder switch to SBY

24. What would be the callsign of a station controlling surface vehicles in a manoeuvring area?

   (a) Tower

   (b) Ground

   (c) Clearance

   (d) Apron

25. The instruction *Orbit* from ATC means that the aircraft should:

   (a) Carry out one 360 degree turn only

   (b) Carry out a go around

   (c) Reverse the direction of the turn

   (d) Continue with 360 degree turns

26. The time used in aeronautical communications is:

   (a) UTC

   (b) Local mean time

   (c) In minutes only

   (d) Daylight saving time

27. To make your messages more effective you should:

   (a) Use words twice

   (b) Speak slower

   (c) Speak at a constant volume

   (d) Repeat the message

28. When making a blind transmission you should:

   (a) Transmit the message twice

   (b) Transmit each word twice

   (c) Repeat the message on 121.5 MHz

   (d) Wait for visual signals

29. What does the abbreviation AFIS stand for?

   (a) Automatic Flight Information Service

   (b) Aircraft Fire Indication System

   (c) Automatic Flight Instrument System

   (d) Aerodrome Flight Information Service

30. What is the full range of VHF frequencies used for communications?

   (a) 108.0 to 139.95 MHz

   (b) 3 to 30 MHz

   (c) 88 to 108 MHz

   (d) 118.0 to 136.975 MHz

31. What does the message *Readability 3* mean?

   (a) Readable now and then

   (b) Unreadable

   (c) Readable with difficulty

   (d) Readable

32. What phrase below means *Yes*?

   (a) Affirmative

   (b) Roger

   (c) Wilco

   (d) Affirm

33. What is the definition of the phrase *Standby*?

   (a) Wait and I will call you

   (b) Consider the transmission as not sent

   (c) Proceed with your message

   (d) Hold your present position

34. How do you transmit a height of 2500 feet?

   (a) TWO THOUSAND FIVE HUNDRED

   (b) TOO TOUSAND FIFE HUNDRED

   (c) TWO FIFE DUBBEL ZERO

   (d) TWO FIVE HUNDRED

If this page is a photocopy, it is not authorised!

35. What is the correct reply to the instruction *Hold Short At Runway?*

    (a) Wilco

    (b) Roger

    (c) Understood

    (d) Holding

36. If you hear an *All Stations* transmission:

    (a) Do not reply unless asked

    (b) Reply with your callsign

    (c) Acknowledge with *Roger*

    (d) Acknowledge with *Roger And Out*

37. The abbreviation HJ means that an aerodrome is:

    (a) Open between sunrise and sunset

    (b) Open 24 hours

    (c) Open between sunset and sunrise

    (d) Open during unspecified hours

38. What is the definition of *Broadcast?*

    (a) A transmission of information relating to air navigation that is specific to a station or stations

    (b) A transmission of information relating to air navigation that is not specific to a station or stations

    (c) A transmission of information relating to air navigation that is specific to a station or stations using a Flight Information Service

    (d) A weather transmission that is specific to a station or stations

39. What is the definition of *Distress?*

    (a) There is concern for the safety of the aircraft or a person on board or other vehicle but there is no need for immediate assistance

    (b) The aircraft has crashed

    (c) The aircraft is in imminent danger and requires immediate assistance

    (d) The aircraft is being hijacked

40. What condition defines the state of an aircraft in imminent danger?

    (a) Mayday

    (b) Pan

    (c) Distress

    (d) Urgency

41. What do you squawk for radio failure?

    (a) 7600

    (b) 7500

    (c) 7700

    (d) 7000

42. What does a Squawk of 7700 indicate? You:

    (a) Have an emergency

    (b) Are not receiving a radar service

    (c) Are in controlled airspace

    (d) Have a radio failure

43. What is the international emergency frequency?

    (a) 121.500 MHz

    (b) 121.050 MHz

    (c) 121.005 MHz

    (d) 123.500 MHz

44. How do you identify an aerodrome in Newtown with an air/ground frequency?

    (a) Newtown Radar

    (b) Newtown Tower

    (c) Newtown Radio

    (d) Newtown Information

45. What should an urgency message include?

    (a) Callsign, position, route, destination, endurance

    (b) Name of station addressed, aircraft callsign, nature of urgency condition, intention of commander, position, level, heading

    (c) Name of station addressed, callsign, present position, level, ETA destination

    (d) Captains number, rank and name

If this page is a photocopy, it is not authorised!

46. The frequency 121.5 MHz is the:

    (a) International emergency frequency

    (b) International flight safety frequency

    (c) One way air to ground emergency frequency

    (d) Air to air chat frequency

47. What does the ATC message DISTRESS TRAFFIC ENDED mean?

    (a) Normal ATC is resumed after an emergency

    (a) All aircraft are to end their transmissions

    (a) All aircraft on the frequency are to change to another frequency

    (a) ATC is shutting down

48. What is the phrase used by ATC to impose radio silence during an emergency?

    (a) STOP TRANSMITTING MAYDAY

    (b) MAYDAY MAYDAY MAYDAY

    (c) DISTRESS TRAFFIC IN PROGRESS

    (d) RADIO SILENCE

49. What does the word *Out* mean at the end of a radio transmission?

    (a) This exchange of transmissions is ended and no response is expected.

    (b) Waiting for you to respond

    (c) Changing frequency

    (d) The radio is not working

50. On hearing an Urgency message, you should:

    (a) Maintain a listening watch to see if you can assist in any way

    (b) Impose a radio silence on the frequency

    (c) Change frequency because radio silence will be imposed

    (d) Acknowledge the message straight away

51. What automated service provides meteorological and airfield information?

    (a) AFIS

    (b) ATIS

    (c) OFIS

    (d) ATSI

52. How should the callsign *Avia G-BCCB* be abbreviated?

    (a) Avia Golf Charlie Bravo

    (b) Avia Charlie Bravo

    (c) Golf Charlie Bravo

    (d) Bravo Charlie Charlie Bravo

53. When can you use an abbreviated callsign?

    (a) After the ground station uses it

    (b) If it was agreed before flight

    (c) If no confusion arises from its use

    (d) If the pilot requests it

54. What does *Readability 4* mean?

    (a) Your message is readable

    (b) Your message is unreadable

    (c) Your message mostly readable

    (d) Your message has interference

55. What information must you read back?

    (a) Altimeter settings, meteorological information, taxi instructions

    (b) Clearances, frequency changes, SSR codes, level instructions and altimeter settings

    (c) Instructions

    (d) Readability codes

56. When can you use the phrase *Takeoff*?

    (a) Never

    (b) When acknowledging a takeoff clearance

    (c) When requesting an immediate departure

    (d) Any time

57. Ignoring pronunciation, how would you report an altitude of 12,500 feet?

    (a) One Two Thousand Five Hundred

    (b) One Two five Hundred

    (c) One Two Five Double Zero

    (d) Twelve Thousand Five Hundred

58. What is the correct order for the elements of a position report?

    (a) Time at position, Callsign, Position, Level or altitude, Next position, ETA at next position

    (b) Callsign, Position, Level or altitude, Next position, Time at position, ETA at next position

    (c) Callsign, Position, Level or altitude, Time at position, Next position, ETA at next position

    (d) Callsign, Position, Time at position, Level or altitude, Next position, ETA at next position

59. How would you transmit the frequency of 132.875?

    (a) One Three Two Point Eight Seven Five

    (b) One Three Two Decimal Eight Seven Five

    (c) One Three Two Decimal Eight Seven

    (d) One Three Two Point Eight Seven

60. What does the phrase *Vacate Left* mean?

    (a) Clear the runway immediately

    (b) The next exit is on the left

    (c) Turn left to clear the runway at the next convenient exit

    (d) Expedite at the next turn off on the left

61. What does the phrase *Go Around* mean?

    (a) Orbit until the runway is clear

    (b) Make sure you don't hit any aircraft on the manoeuvring area

    (c) Do not descend below 100 feet

    (d) Execute a missed approach

62. With whom do you file an airborne flight plan?

    (a) The nearest radar service

    (b) The FIR Frequency for the area concerned

    (c) The nearest ATS Unit

    (d) Any air/ground radio station

63. What is the correct RTF phraseology for the frequency 121.375?

    (a) One Two One Three Seven Five

    (b) One Two One Decimal Three Seven Five

    (c) One Two One Three Seven

    (d) One Two One Point Three Seven Five

64. What is the correct RTF word for *No*?

    (a) No

    (b) Cancel

    (c) Cannot Comply

    (d) Negative

65. On reading back an ATC instruction, how should the message conclude? With:

    (a) The ground station's callsign

    (a) The aircraft callsign

    (a) Wilco

    (b) Over and Out

66. What does *Verify* mean?

    (a) Say that again

    (b) Check & Confirm

    (c) Can you read back my last message?

    (d) Does my last transmission make sense?

67. What details should you transmit when you want a Special VFR clearance?

    (a) Callsign, type, position, heading, level, ETA at entry point

    (b) Callsign, position, level, ETA at entry point

    (c) Callsign, type, position, ETA at entry point

    (d) Callsign, type, intentions, ETA at entry point

68. How close to a MATZ should you establish two-way communication?

    (a) The greater of 15 nm or 5 mins

    (b) The greater of 10 nm or 10 mins

    (c) The greater of 5 nm or 5 mins

    (d) The greater of 10 nm or 5 mins

69. To cross the base of an airway, what details are required by ATC?

    (a) ID, TAS, Hdg (M), Place and ETA, desired level

    (b) ID, Type, Hdg (M), Place and ETA, desired level

    (c) Callsign, Type, Point of Departure, Position, Heading, Level, Flight Conditions, Place and ETA of crossing

    (d) Callsign, Type, Point of Departure, Flight Conditions, Position, Intended destination

70. When should you report long final and final?

    (a) 2 nm, 1 nm

    (b) 4 nm, 2 nm

    (c) 6 nm, 3 nm

    (d) 8 nm, 4 nm

71. What should you transmit if you cannot carry out an ATC instruction?

    (a) CANNOT COMPLY

    (b) UNABLE

    (c) CANNOT DO

    (d) STAND BY

72. When transmitting for DF purposes, what should the message end with?

    (a) 123456

    (b) DF station callsign

    (c) Aircraft callsign

    (d) True Bearing, True Bearing, True Bearing

73. What is the accuracy of a Class B VDF bearing?

    (a) ±2°

    (b) ±5°

    (c) ±3°

    (d) ±7°

74. Why might ATC may request you to *Confirm Your Level* when your transponder is set to ALT?

    (a) To check where you are

    (b) To check what your altimeter is set to

    (c) To check the accuracy of the altitude figures on the radar screen

    (d) To check that the transponder is working

75. What should you do if you hear a distress message?

    (a) Acknowledge the message and offer to act as a relay station

    (b) Change to another frequency to keep out of the way of rescue crews

    (c) Maintain radio silence but monitor the situation

    (d) Record the position of the craft in distress, inform the appropriate ATC or RCC, at your discretion, whilst awaiting further instructions, proceed to the position given

76. What does the word *Student* mean when used before a callsign?

    (a) Inexperienced pilot

    (b) Practice call

    (c) There is an examiner on board

    (d) Urgent message

77. The emergency frequency of 121.5 MHz:

    (a) May be used to practice urgency and distress procedures

    (b) May be used to practice emergency incidents

    (c) May be used to practice distress procedures

    (d) May not be used to practice emergencies

78. What are the two categories of emergency?

    (a) MAYDAY and PAN

    (b) Emergency and Urgent

    (c) Distress and Emergency

    (d) Distress and Urgency

79. What is an example of a conditional clearance?

    (a) G-PACO, after the landing aircraft, clear to cross

    (b) G-PACO, take off at your discretion

    (c) G-PACO, you are number 2, report final

    (d) G-PACO, exit left after passing the tower

80. What is a Special VFR clearance? One:

    (a) Passed to a flight in difficulty to allow it to enter controlled airspace in IMC conditions

    (b) Passed for flight in controlled airspace in VMC

    (c) Passed to a flight that is unable to comply with IFR, under certain minimum weather conditions

    (d) Passed for flight in controlled airspace to a pilot who does not hold an Instrument Rating

81. What elements are involved in a conditional clearance?

    (a) Identification, condition, subject of the condition, instruction

    (b) Condition, identification, subject of the condition, instruction

    (c) Condition, subject of the condition, identification, instruction

    (d) Instruction, condition, subject of the condition, identification

82. What is the order of priority of messages in the aeronautical mobile service?

(a) Flight regularity, flight safety, meteorological

(b) Flight safety, meteorological, flight regularity

(c) Meteorological, flight regularity, flight safety

(d) Flight regularity, meteorological, flight safety

83. How many times should you transmit the words PAN or MAYDAY?

(a) Once

(b) Twice

(c) Three times

(d) As many times as can be fitted in

84. What altimeter setting is used in a MATZ?

(a) QFE

(b) QNH

(c) QNE

(d) QFF

85. What word means that you have received an ATC message and will comply with it?

(a) Roger

(b) Wilco

(c) Affirmative

(d) Affirm

86. Why would ATC ask you to confirm your level when you have the transponder set to Mode C?

(a) To check you have the right pressure set

(b) To verify the accuracy of Mode C information

(c) To verify your position

(d) To check what mode is selected

87. The service from ATC that provides useful advice and information for the safe and efficient conduct of flights, which may include weather information, the conditions at aerodromes and general traffic information is called what?

(a) Traffic

(b) Flight Information

(c) Basic

(d) Information

88. On a standard overhead join at 2 000 feet, descending to join the circuit pattern, you should make the call "G-PACO _____ Descending". What is the missing word?

(a) Live Side

(b) Dead Side

(c) Crosswind

(d) Downwind

89. What information should you pass if you want to penetrate a MATZ?

(a) Callsign/Type, Departure point and destination, Position, Level and Intentions

(b) Callsign, Position, Altitude, Heading and ETA

(c) Type, Position, Altitude, Heading and ETA

(d) Callsign, Position, Destination and ETA

90. Ignoring pronunciation, how do you transmit the QFE of 995 hPa?

(a) QFE nine nine five hectopascals

(b) QFE nine nine five

(c) nine nine five hectopascals

(d) nine nine five

91. After requesting a radar service, you should include the following information in which order?

(a) Callsign/Type, Departure point and destination, Position, Level and Intentions

(b) Callsign, Position, Altitude, Heading and ETA

(c) Type, Position, Altitude, Heading and ETA

(d) Callsign, Position, Destination and ETA

92. What is a deconfliction service available for?

(a) All flights up to 50 miles

(b) VFR or IFR flights, regardless of flight conditions

(c) VFR flights below 3 000 feet

(d) VFR flights above 3 000 feet

93. If you are told to *Squawk Ident*, what should you do?

(a) Move the transponder switch to Standby

(b) Move the transponder switch to ALT

(c) Operate the transponder SPI (Special Position Identification) switch

(d) Confirm your callsign to ATC

94. What condition defines Distress?

    (a) About the safety of an aircraft or other vehicle, or some person on board or within sight, but immediate assistance is not required

    (b) Being threatened by serious and/or imminent danger, and requiring immediate assistance

    (c) The safety of an person, vessel, vehicle or structure

    (d) A MAYDAY or PAN call is required

95. What prefix should precede a Distress call?

    (a) MAYDAY transmitted once

    (b) MAYDAY transmitted twice

    (c) MAYDAY transmitted three times

    (d) MAYDAY transmitted four times

96. Immediately after the prefix MAYDAY, what should be transmitted?

    (a) Position and altitude

    (b) Callsign

    (c) Type of emergency

    (d) The callsign of the station addressed, if it is known and the circumstances permit

97. In what order should the content of a Distress or Urgency message be transmitted?

    (a) Position, Callsign, Type, Intentions

    (b) Position, Callsign, Intentions

    (c) Callsign, Type, Nature of Emergency, Intentions, Position, FL/Altitude, Heading, Other Useful Information

    (d) Callsign, Nature of Emergency, Intentions

98. If you are given clearance to climb to a height of 3 500 feet, what pressure setting should be included?

    (a) QNE

    (b) QFE

    (c) QNH

    (d) QFF

99. What air traffic services are available outside controlled airspace?

    (a) Flight Information, Basic, Radar, Procedural

    (b) Flight Service, Basic, Approach, Procedural

    (c) Basic, Traffic, Deconfliction, Procedural

    (d) Basic, Radar, Deconfliction, Procedural

100. An unlicensed aerodrome with an Air/Ground communication service should have what callsign?

    (a) (Name of Station) Information

    (b) (Name of Station) Radio

    (c) (Name of Station) Ground

    (d) (Name of Station) traffic

101. What does the code QDM mean?

    (a) Magnetic radial from the station

    (b) Magnetic bearing from the station

    (c) True heading to be steered to reach the station

    (d) Magnetic heading to be steered (assuming no wind) to reach the station

102. LARS is available to help pilots up to FL _____, within _____ nm. The service provided will be _____ or a _____.

    (a) 95, 30, Traffic, Deconfliction

    (b) 65, 30, Traffic, Procedural

    (c) 95, 38, Traffic, Procedurel

    (d) 65, 38, Traffic, Deconfliction

103. What is the correct call when ready for takeoff?

    (a) Ready for takeoff

    (b) Taking Off

    (c) Ready for departure

    (d) Ready for departure clearance

104. When landing at an airfield whose suffix is *Information*, the correct response to the transmission "G-CO, land at your discretion, surface wind 180/5 kts" should be:

    (a) Land at my discretion, G-CO

    (b) Cleared to land, G-CO

    (c) Roger, G-CO

    (d) G-CO

105. Messages relating to climb or descent to a height or altitude should:

    (a) Include the word *To* before *height* or *altitude*

    (b) Not use the word *To* because it could be mistaken for a number

    (c) Include the word *To* before the QFE or QNH

    (d) Include the word *Level* instead of *To*

106. What does a Special VFR clearance allow you to do?

    (a) Fly in bad weather

    (b) Avoid some low flying rules

    (c) Cross airways

    (d) Fly in airspace that normally needs IFR clearance

107. An Air Traffic Service where specific surveillance derived traffic information is provided to assist pilots to avoid other traffic, but the responsibility for avoiding that traffic is down to the pilot is called what?

    (a) Basic

    (b) Traffic

    (c) Procedural

    (d) Deconfliction

108. Under what conditions will a conditional clearance be used for movements on an active runway? When:

    (a) The aerodrome is very busy, but it is safe

    (b) Vehicles without radio need to cross

    (c) The aircraft and vehicles concerned are seen by the controller and pilot, and relate to only one movement

    (d) Aircraft need to cross the runway

109. When asked if you are able to maintain VMC, the correct reply contains what phrase?

    (a) Roger

    (b) Wilco

    (c) Affirm or Negative

    (d) Yes or No

110. What do the initials ATIS stand for?

    (a) Air Traffic Information Service

    (b) Automatic Terminal Information Service

    (c) Aerodrome Traffic Information Service

    (d) Aerodrome Terminal Information Service

111. If you need ATSOCAS, you should pass what details once you have established communication?

    (a) Callsign/Type, Departure point and destination, Position, Level and Intentions

    (b) Callsign, Position, Altitude, Heading and ETA

    (c) Type, Position, Altitude, Heading and ETA

    (a) Callsign, Position, Destination and ETA

112. You may only make SAFETYCOM transmissions below _____ ft above the aerodrome level, or _____ ft above promulgated circuit height, within _____ nm of the aerodrome of intended landing.

    (a) 2 000, 1 000, 10

    (b) 3 000, 1 000, 15

    (c) 2 000, 2 000, 15

    (d) 3 000, 1 500, 10

113. Your position in an emergency message should be given as what?

    (a) GPS

    (b) Present or last known position, FL/Altitude and heading

    (c) Relative to a known position

    (d) Latitude & longitude

114. An Automatic Flight Information Service provides:

    (a) Instructions to aircraft in the ATZ

    (b) Information to aircraft in the ATZ

    (c) Control of aircraft in the ATZ

    (d) Information to aircraft within 25 nm

115. What is a procedural service?

    (a) There is no Basic service, but Deconfliction is provided for unknown traffic

    (b) Basic service plus surveillance

    (c) Basic service, plus deconfliction from participating traffic, provided instructions are complied with

    (d) No Basic service, but traffic information is provided

If this page is a photocopy, it is not authorised!

© Phil Croucher, 2016

116. What type of clearance is this?

"G-PACO, after departure cleared to the zone boundary via Route Bravo. Climb to altitude 2 000 feet QNH 1019. Squawk 3720."

(a) Clearance to the zone boundary

(b) Route clearance

(c) Takeoff clearance

(d) Conditional clearance

117. What does the code QDR mean?

(a) Magnetic radial from the station

(b) Magnetic bearing from the station

(c) True heading to be steered to reach the station

(d) Magnetic heading to be steered (assuming no wind) to reach the station

118. What is the correct pronunciation for the frequency 116.080 MHz?

(a) ONE ONE SICKS POINT ZERO AIT ZERO

(b) WUN WUN SICKS DAYSEEMAL ZERO AIT ZERO

(c) ONE ONE SICKS DECIMAL ZERO AIT ZERO

(d) WUN WUN SICKS POINT ZERO AIT ZERO

119. What does the phrase *Break Break* mean?

(a) The separation between messages transmitted to different aircraft in a very busy environment

(b) The separation between portions of a message transmitted to an aircraft station

(c) The exchange of transmissions has ended and no response is expected

(d) My transmission is ended and I expect a response from you

120. What is the definition of the term *Damp* when it refers to the surface condition of a runway?

(a) There is sufficient water to produce surface film

(b) The surface appears reflective

(c) The surface is soaked but no significant patches of standing water are visible

(d) The surface shows a change of colour due to moisture

121. if you require ATSOCAS, once communications have been established, what details should be passed?

(a) Callsign/Type, present position, time, level, next ETA

(b) Callsign/Type, present position, level, intentions

(c) Callsign/Type, Departure Point and Destination, present position, level, additional details/intentions

(d) Callsign, present position, flight rules, SSR code

122. A pilot who has already established communication with a civil or military ATSU should, in an emergency:

(a) Make a distress call on the frequency in use and maintain the allocated SSR code

(b) Make a MAYDAY call on 121.5 MHz

(c) Select 7700 on the SSR and change to 121.5 MHz to make a distress call

(d) Change to 121.5, make a distress call, and select 7000 on the SSR

123. What maximum number of specific phrases can be included in a message?

(a) 4

(b) 2

(c) 3

(d) 5

124. Which words are not used by the operator of an aeronautical station with the callsign suffix *Information* or *Radio*?

(a) Pass your message

(b) Cleared

(c) Affirm

(d) Correct

125. Why would the callsign prefix *Student* be used?

(a) To alert controllers and other airspace users to the presence of student pilots flying solo

(b) To advise controllers that the purpose of the flight is to conduct a flying lesson

(c) To alert controllers and other airspace users that a flight test with an examiner is in progress

(d) To advise other airspace users (in Class F or G airspace) that manoueuvres are being carried out

126. What are the three main categories of aeronautical communication service?

   (a) Aerodrome Air/Ground Communication Service, Flight Information Service, ATC

   (b) Emergency, Airways, VFR

   (c) ATC, Operations, Meteorological

   (d) Ground, Tower, Approach

127. What is a common and effective way to obtain current meteorological information at the planning stage of a VFR flight?

   (a) By listening to VOLMET or telephoning ATC (where no such VOLMET arrangements exist)

   (b) By obtaining a meteorological briefing from an air traffic controller, a FISO, an air/ground radio operator or a competent meteorological observer as appropriate

   (c) By thoroughly self-briefing before the flight, by consulting all appropriate published meteorological information

   (d) By making a visual assessment of the conditions at the airfield of departure and then obtaining meteorological information through VOLMET once airborne

128. Which phrase communicates that a message should be ignored?

   (a) Cancel my last message

   (b) Disregard

   (c) Forget the last message

   (d) My last transmission is cancelled

129. An Air Traffic Control Service (ATC) can be provided by:

   (a) Licensed Flight Information Service Officers, Affiliated Radio Operators, and Licensed A TC Officers

   (b) Radio Operators holding a CAA issued certificate of competency and Licensed ATC Officers regulated by the CAA

   (c) Licensed ATC Officers regulated by the CAA

   (d) Licensed Flight Information Service Officers and Licensed ATC Officers, both regulated by the CAA

130. What is VOLMET?

   (a) Meteorological reports for certain aerodromes broadcast on specified frequencies

   (b) Meteorological reports and aerodrome information broadcast on a discrete frequency or an appropriate VOR

   (c) Meteorological reports for certain aerodromes including arrival information, broadcast on a discrete frequency

   (d) Meteorological reports broadcast on a discrete frequency or VOR, for one aerodrome

131. What does the term SNOCLO mean?

   (a) The aerodrome is closed due to adverse weather conditions that may affect safe operations and practices, such as heavy snow

   (b) The aerodrome is unusable for takeoff or landing because of heavy snow on the runways or snow clearance

   (c) The aerodrome is closed to sailplanes and non-radio aircraft

   (d) The aerodrome is closed due to adverse meteorological conditions or other operational reason, such as heavy snow or work in progress

132. What is true regarding VHF propagation?

   (a) VHF is practical and usable worldwide, requires no ground based facilities, and reception is of the highest quality over the ocean

   (b) VHF is used for voice communications, reception quality is greatest over land, and its range is approximately limited to line of sight

   (c) VHF occupies the KHz frequency range and has a range of 30 to 300 nautical miles

   (d) VHF ranges from 30 - 300 MHz and its range is approximately limited to line of sight

133. How can you activate a flight plan in flight?

   (a) By asking an ATSU by radio to activate it

   (b) This cannot be done in flight, use the telephone before departure

   (c) By making a request on the FIS frequency, as busy RTF frequencies should not be used

   (d) This can only be done for flights entering controlled airspace, or crossing a Flight Information Region or international boundary

134. What is the correct response to an instruction to *Report Vacated*?

  (a) Runway clear

  (b) Clear of the active

  (c) Vacated the main

  (d) Runway vacated

135. With the QFE set on the altimeter, which word or phrase is used to report vertical distance above an airfield?

  (a) Pressure Altitude

  (b) Altitude

  (c) Height

  (d) Flight Level

136. What meaning is assigned to the word *Roger*?

  (a) Your last message is understood

  (b) I have received all of your last transmission

  (c) I have received all of your last transmission and will comply with it

  (d) Your last message is acknowledged

137. What would the abbreviation for the callsign CHEROKEE G-ABCD be?

  (a) Cherokee G-BC

  (b) Cherokee CD

  (c) G-BC

  (d) CD

138. What is the most correct response to this transmission?

  "G-CO, after the landing A320, via Bravo, cross runway 15m report vacated."

  (a) Via Bravo, cross runway 15, behind landing, and wilco, G-CO

  (b) After the landing A320, via Bravo cross the active, G-CO

  (c) Behind landing, via Bravo, cross, wilco, G-CO

  (d) After the landing A320, via Bravo cross runway 15, wilco, G-CO

139. You suspect that your communications have failed, but the equipment is working and set up correctly. What would be an appropriate subsequent action?

  (a) Land at the nearest suitable aerodrome

  (b) Try to establish communication with other nearby aircraft

  (c) Make a blind transmission

  (d) Squawk 7600 and continue flying

140. What phrase should be used when carrying out radio transmissions for test purposes?

  (a) Radio Check

  (b) Testing (state frequency)

  (c) Testing (state frequency) 1 - 2 - 3

  (d) What is my readability?

141. What is the correct order of priority of these messages in the aeronautical mobile service?

  (a) Flight Regularity messages come before Direction Finding messages

  (b) Flight Safety messages come before Urgency messages

  (c) Direction Finding messages come before Meteorological messages

  (d) Flight Regularity messages come before Urgency messages

142. What should you do having been asked to change frequency and monitor?

  (a) Select the new frequency and use your callsign only

  (b) Select the new frequency and wait for ATC to speak

  (c) Select the new frequency and listen out

  (d) Remain on the current frequency until given another instruction

143. What does the message *Readability 2* mean?

  (a) Readable now and then

  (b) Unreadable

  (c) Readable with difficulty

  (d) Readable

144. What subsequent action is correct if you hear a distress call on the frequency in use but there is no response from ATC?

    (a) retransmit the message exactly as heard and await instructions from the ATSU

    (b) relay the message, making it clear that you are not the aircraft in distress

    (c) squawk 7700 and relay the message, making it clear that you are not the aircraft in distress

    (d) retransmit the message exactly as heard on 121.5 MHz

145. The message *Confirm Squawk* means what?

    (a) Press the transponder's Ident button

    (b) Select Mode C on the transponder

    (c) Confirm what code is set on the transponder

    (d) Confirm your callsign and level

146. What subsequent action is correct if your transmissions remain unanswered by the ATSU with whom you have previously been in contact?

    (a) Make a blind transmission

    (b) Squawk 7600 and check the radios

    (c) Check that you have the correct frequency and that the ATSU are supposed to be open, you are not out of range and the volume is set

    (d) Continue as planned, land as soon as practical

NAVIGATION & RADIO NAVIGATION

GENERAL NAVIGATION

1. A rhumb line:

    (a)   Crosses lines of equal variation at equal angles

    (b)   Passes through the centre of the Earth

    (c)   Crosses meridians at equal angles

    (d)   Crosses great circles at equal angles

2. An agonic line:

    (a)   Joins points having equal variation

    (b)   Joins points having equal gradation

    (c)   Joins points having equal elevation

    (d)   Joins points having no variation

3. A great circle:

    (a)   Crosses meridians at equal angles

    (b)   Is a straight line

    (c)   Is a circle on the surface of a sphere whose plane passes through the centre of the sphere

    (d)   Is a circle on the surface of a sphere whose plane does not pass through the centre of the sphere

4. What type of projection do most aviation charts use?

    (a)   Lambert Conformal Conical

    (b)   Mercator

    (c)   Polar Stereograph

    (d)   Transverse Mercator

5. Which pairs make up the Triangle of Velocities?

    1. Wind direction & speed

    2. TAS & track made good

    3. Heading & TAS

    4. Wind direction required track

    5. Wind direction & ground track

    6. TAS & required track

    7. TAS & crab angle

    8. Track and ground speed

    (a)   1, 2, 3

    (b)   3, 4, 7

    (c)   3, 5, 6

    (d)   1, 3, 8

6. What is a nautical mile equal to?

    (a)   One minute of latitude

    (b)   One minute of longitude at 50° north

    (c)   1.5 statute miles

    (d)   One quarter inch on a 1:500,000 scale map

7. With variation 15°E, deviation 4°W, true track 007° and nil wind, what is the compass heading?

    (a)   356°

    (b)   248°

    (c)   018°

    (d)   026°

8. With variation 22°W, compass heading 358° and nil wind, what is the true heading?

    (a) 022°

    (b) 018°

    (c) 336°

    (d) 334°

9. On a cross country flight from A to B (120 nm) you notice by your drift lines that after 30 miles you now have an opening angle of 9° right of track and a closing angle of 3°. To regain track at your destination you must:

    (a) Steer 9° to the left

    (b) Steer 12° to the left

    (c) Steer 3° to the left

    (d) Steer 6° to the right

10. When tracking 270°, under which of the conditions below will you be able to proceed the furthest distance and return to the point of origin?

    (a) Wind calm

    (b) Wind 270° @ 30 kts

    (c) Wind 090° @ 30 kts

    (d) Wind 360° @ 30 kts

11. With a Pressure Altitude of 6000', a temperature of -20°C, IAS 130 kts, find the density altitude and TAS:

    (a) 3000', 136 kts

    (b) 6200', 118 kts

    (c) 5700', 124 kts

    (d) 8000', 147 kts

12. On a 1:1000000 chart, what earth distance does a line 50 cm long represent?

    (a) 240 nm

    (b) 275 km

    (c) 269 nm

    (d) 176 nm

13. When turning to the South clockwise, on what heading should you stop to end up with 180° on the compass?

    (a) 160°

    (b) 180°

    (c) 200°

    (d) It depends on the latitude

14. On a True heading of 255°, with variation of 5°W and 2°E deviation, what is the compass heading?

    (a) 258°

    (b) 255°

    (c) 266°

    (d) 270°

15. Over 120 nm you use 20 gallons of fuel. If you have 23 gallons left in the tank, how much further could you fly?

    (a) 128

    (b) 118

    (c) 127

    (d) 138

16. A symbol with figures looking like this next to it:

    1200
    (750)

means what? The item is:

    (a) 1200 feet high with obstruction lights at 750 feet

    (b) 1200 feet above sea level with obstruction lights at 750 feet

    (c) 750 feet above sea level and 1200 above ground level

    (d) 750 feet above ground level and 1200 above sea level

17. An aircraft leaves position 01° 20'S 012° 15'W on a track of 360° True for 01:06 mins. If the TAS is 160 kts and the wind is calm, where does it end up?

    (a) 01° 36'N

    (b) 01° 36'S

    (c) 10° 36'N

    (d) 10° 36'S

18. When is the declination (the angular distance above the plane of the Equator) of the sun at its highest?

    (a) Equinox

    (b) Solstice

    (c) Ecliptic

    (d) Meridianal passage

19. As well as the Equator, which of the following are great circles on the Earth's surface?

   (a) Parallels of latitude

   (b) A circle of radius greater than the Earth's

   (c) Any rhumb line

   (d) Meridians of longitude

20. At what point does sunrise or sunset occur?

   (a) when the centre of the Sun's disc is on the observer's horizon

   (b) when the bottom of the Sun's disc is on the observer's horizon

   (c) when the centre of the Sun's disc is 6° below the observer's horizon

   (d) when the top of the Sun's disc (upper limb) is on the observer's horizon

21. The total magnetic force at any point on the Earth's surface (T) resolves into a horizontal component (H) and a vertical component (Z). The angle of dip is:

   (a) the angle between H and Z

   (b) 90° at the magnetic Equator

   (c) the angle between H and T

   (d) the angle between T and Z

22. If the scale of a chart is 1:5000000, which statement is true?

   (a) 1 cm on the chart represents 5000000 nm on the Earth's surface

   (b) 1 cm on the chart represents 5000000 cm on the earth's surface

   (c) The scale of the chart is smaller than the scale of 1: 1000000

   (d) 5000000 cm on the chart represents 1 nm on the Earth's surface

23. Which statement best describes the appearance of meridians on a Direct Mercator chart?

   (a) Straight lines converging towards the poles

   (b) Curved lines converging towards the poles

   (c) Unequally spaced straight lines

   (d) Equally spaced straight lines

24. At what latitude is the ecliptic at the summer solstice?

   (a) 23°27'N

   (b) 66°33'S

   (c) 23°27'S

   (d) 66°33'N

25. What best describes the longitude of a point?

   (a) The shorter angular distance measured East/West from the Greenwich meridian

   (b) The angular distance measured North/South from the Poles

   (c) The longer angular distance measured East/West from the Greenwich meridian

   (d) The angular distance measured North/South from the Equator

26. How far below the observer's horizon is the Centre of the Sun's disc at the beginning or end of civil twilight?

   (a) 18°

   (b) 0°

   (c) 12°

   (d) 6°

27. Where is the compass most accurate?

   (a) At low latitudes

   (b) Over the magnetic poles

   (c) At mid-latitudes

   (d) Over the geographic poles

28. Which statement is correct?

   (a) Meridians of longitude are semi-great circles that are numbered from 0° at the Equator and 90° at the Poles

   (b) Except for the Equator, parallels of latitude are small circles that are numbered from 0° at the Equator and 90° at the Poles

   (c) Meridians of longitude are semi-great circles that are numbered from 0° to 360°

   (d) Parallels of latitude are great circles

29. If you have a track made good of 127° with 5° of right drift, the variation is 10°E and the deviation is 2°W, what compass heading would be required?

(a) 114°

(b) 124°

(c) 134°

(d) 126°

30. If the windspeed is 25 kts, by how many degrees can the wind be off the nose before the crosswind is 18 kts?

(a) 60°

(b) 45°

(c) 50°

(d) 40°

31. What distance will you have travelled if you fly North from 40°S to 24°S?

(a) 960 km

(b) 1778 km

(c) 1567 km

(d) 1200 km

32. Ignoring errors, what is the TAS in the cruise at 85 KIAS at FL 80 with an OAT of ISA -10°?

(a) 94 kts

(b) 98 kts

(c) 93 kts

(d) 89 kts

33. If you set heading at 11:00 UTC to fly to a destination that is 82 nm away on a track of 140°T, with a TAS of 92 kts and a W/V of 020/20, what is the ETA?

(a) 11:30

(b) 11:48

(c) 12:12

(d) 12:15

34. What is the time in terms of UTC if the LMT in Perth, Australia (32°S 116°E) is 15:00?

(a) 15:16

(b) 07:16

(c) 08:45

(d) 23:00

35. You have 50 nm to go to a waypoint and you have been told to arrive in 30 minutes. If the temperature is 5°C and your level is FL 50, in nil wind conditions, what airspeed is required?

(a) 89 kts

(b) 91 kts

(c) 93 kts

(d) 97 kts

36. The Lambert chart is most suited to which areas of the Earth?

(a) The Equator

(b) The Poles

(c) The mid-latitudes

(d) All areas

37. With 30 nm to go, you are 4 nm left of track. By how much must you alter heading to arrive at the destination?

(a) 12° right

(b) 8° right

(c) 6° left

(d) 9° left

38. Which statement is true?

(a) Daylight can end earlier if the horizon is blocked by high ground

(b) Daylight can end earlier if the visibility is poor or there is cloud cover

(c) The duration of twilight changes as you fly North or South

(d) Twilight is always 30 minutes long

39. At FL 60 over terrain that is 1850 feet AMSL, if the QNH is 995 hPa in ISA conditions, how much clearance is available above the terrain? (1 hPa = 30 feet).

(a) 3710 feet

(b) 2915 feet

(c) 3170 feet

(d) 3270 feet

40. What does a straight track drawn on a Lambert chart best represent?

    (a) A rhumb line

    (b) A great circle

    (c) A small circle

    (d) A meridian

41. What navigation aid is shown at number 3?

    (a) NDB

    (b) VOR

    (c) TACAN

    (d) VOR/DME

42. What navigation aid is shown at number 4?

    (a) NDB

    (b) VOR

    (c) TACAN

    (d) VOR/DME

43. What latitude is reached by the ecliptic at the Summer solstice?

    (a) 23° 27'S

    (b) 66° 54'S

    (c) 23° 27'N

    (d) 66° 54'N

44. Travelling East at 60°N, from 20°W to 20°E, what distance will be flown?

    (a) 1200 km

    (b) 2222 km

    (c) 1100 nm

    (d) 1100 km

45. As magnetic latitude increases, the:

    (a) Vertical component of the earth's magnetic field increases and the dip angle decreases

    (b) Horizontal component of the earth's magnetic field decreases and the dip angle increases

    (c) Horizontal component of the earth's magnetic field increases and the dip angle decreases

    (d) Vertical component of the earth's magnetic field decreases and the dip angle increases

The Flight Plan

The next five questions are based on a CAA Southern England 1:500 000 aeronautical chart (see *Appendix*).

A trip is planned from Beaulieu (50° 48' 30N 01° 30'W) to Tangmere (50° 51'N 42'W) with a turning point at Petersfield, just North of Tangmere. The alternate is Chichester (EGHR).

The sample flight plan given in at Figure 6 in the Appendix should be filled out first.

1. What is the magnetic heading from Beaulieu to Petersfield?

    (a) 062°

    (b) 070°

    (c) 075°

    (d) 080°

2. What is the groundspeed from Petersfield to Tangmere?

    (a) 65 kts

    (b) 70 kts

    (c) 75 kts

    (d) 80 kts

3. What is the flight time from Petersfield to Tangmere?

    (a) 8 minutes

    (b) 10 minutes

    (c) 12 minutes

    (d) 13.5 minutes

4. What is the VOR frequency for EGHR?

    (a) 114.25

    (b) 114.75

    (c) 114.95

    (d) There isn't one

5. Given:

> Max All Up Weight: 2500 lbs
> Basic Weight: 1500 lbs
> Pilot weight: 180 lbs
> Fuel: 45 Imperial Gals
> Specific Gravity: 0.79

How much weight is available for passengers and/or baggage?

(a) 424 lbs

(b) 464.5 lbs

(c) 484.5 lbs

(d) 350 lbs

6. Given:

> Start, taxy and runup fuel: 2 US gals
> Planned flight time: 84 minutes
> Diversion Fuel: 20 minutes
> Fuel consumption: 9 US Gals per hour
> Approach, Landing and Missed Approach: 2 US gals
> Overhead reserve at alternate: 5 US gals

What minimum fuel is required?

(a) 23 gals

(b) 24 gals

(c) 24.6 gals

(d) 27.6 gals

7. On the chart, what activity takes place at 50°56'N 01°3.5'W?

(a) Microwaves

(b) Microlights

(c) Gliding

(d) Gliding at low level

8. What kind of traffic might use Fleetlands?

(a) Hovercraft

(b) Seaplanes

(c) Helicopters

(d) Flying boats

9. What does the black dotted line to the South West of Petersfield represent?

(a) A valley

(b) A disused railway

(c) A road under construction

(d) A county boundary

10. What is the total flight time?

(a) 21 minutes

(b) 23 minutes

(c) 25 minutes

(d) 27 minutes

11. You are overhead Glidden Farm (just to the right of track). What magnetic heading will take you to Petersfield?

(a) 048°

(b) 046°

(c) 051°

(d) 056°

12. How high does Danger Area 061 go up to?

(a) 1500 feet

(b) It starts at 1500 feet

(c) 2300 feet

(d) 2500 feet

13. Referring to the extract from the UK AIP at figure 5 in the Appendix, what is the callsign for Chichester?

(a) Chichester Tower

(b) Chichester Information

(c) Goodwood Information

(d) Goodwood tower

14. Referring to the extract from the UK AIP at figure 5 in the Appendix, would you be able to land there at 1800 on Feb 12th?

(a) Yes

(b) No

(c) Ring first

(d) Just turn up

15. Referring to the extract from the UK AIP at figure 5 in the Appendix, what is the ATS frequency?

    (a) 123.45

    (b) 122.45

    (c) 121.45

    (d) 120.45

16. In the extract from the UK AIP at figure 5 in the Appendix, what is the longest runway?

    (a) 14R/32L

    (b) 06/24

    (c) 14L/32R

    (d) 10/28

17. Referring to Figure 1 in the Appendix, if the wind velocity is 180/15, what would be the ETA at Inverness?

    (a) 12:45

    (b) 12:55

    (c) 13:00

    (d) 13:10

RADIO NAVIGATION

1. At 1000' AGL, what is the approximate reception distance of a VOR?

    (a) 30 sm

    (b) 39 sm

    (c) 30 nm

    (d) 39 nm

2. DME gives _____ range distance information, and reception is based on _____ and is _____.

    (a) Horizontal, groundspeed, line of sight

    (b) Slant, altitude, line of sight

    (c) Bearing, groundspeed, not line if sight

    (d) Horizontal, altitude, line of sight

3. With a VOR, one dot's deflection is equal to:

    (a) 4°

    (b) 2°

    (c) 10°

    (d) 5°

4. Full scale deflection of the VOR CDI indicates a course deviation of:

    (a) Less than 10°

    (b) 10°

    (c) 10° or more

    (d) 5°

5. What is one advantage of SSR over ASR?

    (a) Aircraft without transponders may be readily identified

    (b) SSR has a far shorter range

    (c) Increased range and positive identification

    (d) SSR is obsolete

6. When on the ground what is the maximum acceptable error before a VOR is unserviceable for flight?

    (a) 2°

    (b) 4°

    (c) 6°

    (d) 10°

7. Station passage at a VOR is indicated by:

    (a) Slow fluctuations of the CDI

    (b) Rapid movement of the CDI, FROM changes to TO

    (c) CDI remains centered, FROM changes to TO

    (d) Movement of the CDI, TO changes to FROM

8. One disadvantage of the VOR when compared to an ADF is:

    (a) Subject to greater reception errors

    (b) Shorter range

    (c) Affected by storms

    (d) All the above

9. What is the purpose of the aural identification signal for a navigation aid?

    (a) To indicate that it is not undergoing maintenance

    (b) For positive identification

    (c) To indicate the voice signal is available

    (d) Both A and B are correct

10. What does *Line Of Sight* reception mean?

    (a) Prevailing visibility is a limiting factor

    (b) You must be able to see the station

    (c) Curvature of irregularity of the surface of the Earth will prevent VHF reception

    (d) Presence of any obscuring phenomena will prevent VHF reception

11. What is the maximum useful range of a VOR at 1500' AGL? Around:

    (a) 20 nm

    (b) 50 nm

    (c) 100 nm

    (d) 150 nm

12. ADF systems are checked for enroute accuracy of ±10°, but larger errors are possible from propagation disturbances caused by:

    (a) Sunrise or sunset and reflected signals from high terrain

    (b) Refraction of the signals crossing shorelines at less than 30°

    (c) Electrical storms

    (d) All the above

13. DME information is most accurate when the aircraft is _____ with respect to the station:

    (a) High and long

    (b) Low and short

    (c) Low and long

    (d) High and short

14. The ADF should be used with caution during:

    (a) IFR conditions

    (b) Thunderstorms

    (c) Summer time

    (d) Early fall

15. When you tune an ADF and there is no ident:

    (a) There is no voice

    (b) It is not being monitored

    (c) It is not to be used for navigation

    (d) It is serviceable and you should use it

16. How might VDF accuracy be decreased?

    (a) Night effect

    (b) Coastal effect

    (c) Mountain effect

    (d) Site and propagation errors

17. Tracking away from an NDB on a track of 030° with 2° starboard drift (i.e. to the right), what should the relative bearing indication be?

    (a) 002° relative

    (b) 182° relative

    (c) 180° relative

    (d) 000° relative

18. In what frequency band does the VOR operate in?

    (a) UHF

    (b) SHF

    (c) VHF

    (d) VLF

19. Tracking towards a VOR on radial 245°, to get correct indications, what should be set on the OBS?

    (a) 245° with TO indicated

    (b) 245° with FROM indicated

    (c) 065° with TO indicated

    (d) 065° with FROM indicated

20. SSR data is:

    (a) Shown on the same screen as primary data

    (b) Shown on a screen next to the primary PPI

    (c) Subject to interference

    (d) Displayed in red

21. What Q code do you use to request a true bearing from a VDF station?

    (a) QFE

    (b) QTE

    (c) QDM

    (d) QDR

22. How does the VOR work?

    (a) The airborne receiver measures the difference between the relative bearing and the QDM

    (b) The airborne receiver measures the phase difference between two signals transmitted by the station for a QDR

    (c) The airborne receiver measures the phase difference between the QDR and QDM

    (d) The airborne receiver measures the phase difference between two signals received at the station

23. What type of distance is shown by a DME?

    (a) Actual range

    (b) Slant range

    (c) Corrected slant range

    (d) Level range

24. What equipment is essential for SSR to work?

    (a) Transcender

    (b) Transducer

    (c) Transponder

    (d) Transmitter

25. How can you increase the range of primary radar?

    (a) Place the antenna above surrounding obstacles

    (b) Make the antenna rotate faster

    (c) Use a narrow antenna

    (d) Make the antenna rotate slower

26. In which frequency band does DME operate?

    (a) VHF

    (b) MF

    (c) LF

    (d) UHF

27. SSR information is:

    (a) mandatory for aircraft in controlled airspace

    (b) not displayed on a screen

    (c) displayed on a screen next to the primary radar screen

    (d) displayed on the same screen as primary radar information

28. How many satellites do you need in view to obtain a 3 dimensional position fix?

    (a) 3

    (b) 4

    (c) 2

    (d) 5

29. What information is obtainable from the VOR?

    (a) Relative bearing

    (b) Magnetic bearing

    (c) Range and bearing

    (d) Range

30. If your heading is 130°(M) and an NDB has a relative bearing of 055°, what is the QDM to the NDB?

    (a) 175°

    (b) 185°

    (c) 195°

    (d) 165°

31. The VOR display shown indicates what radial?

    (a) 174°

    (b) 172°

    (c) 168°

    (d) 006°

32. Using the picture in Q 31, which way must you turn to intercept the inbound course selected?

    (a) Right

    (b) Left

    (c) Maintain heading

    (d) You must go the in the other direction

33. What is the accuracy of a Class B VDF bearing?

    (a) ±2°

    (b) ±10°

    (c) ±5°

    (d) less than

FLIGHT COMPUTER PRACTICE

1. At 90 kts TAS heading 045° on the compass, what is the expected track if the forecast wind is 075°/12 kts? Deviation is -2 and variation is 7°E.

(a) 053°

(b) 047°

(c) 044°

(d) 058°

2. If the wind is 320° at 18 kts, what is the track and groundspeed for a heading of 205°T and TAS of 145 kts?

(a) 212°T 151 kts

(b) 207°T 141 kts

(c) 197°T 149 kts

(d) 199°T 153 kts

3. At FL 120 the wind is 290°/20 kts and an aircraft is heading 005°M with a CAS of 170 kts. If the OAT is 12°C and variation is 3°W what is its track and groundspeed?

(a) 58°T 189 kts

(b) 007°T 207 kts

(c) 009°T 168 kts

(d) 001°T 199 kts

4. At FL 350, the temperature is -48°C, at 280 kts CAS. The heading is 005°M, variation is 0° and the wind is 160° at 90 kts. What is the track and groundspeed?

(a) 352°M 530 kts

(b) 011°M 545 kts

(c) 000°M 560 kts

(d) 358°M 570 kts

5. A heading of 180°T at 230 kts TAS results in a track of 172°T and a groundspeed of 258 kts. What is the wind?

(a) 305°/45 kts

(b) 300°/35 kts

(c) 320°/50 kts

(d) 295°/40 kts

6. Tracking the 035° radial from a VOR (magnetic) with a variation of 10°W requires a heading of 041°M at a TAS of 180 kts. If the DME reads a groundspeed of 192 kts what is the wind?

(a) 140°/25 kts

(b) 150°/20 kts

(c) 180°/15 kts

(d) 165°/10 kts

7. A helicopter is follows a straight power line which follows a true bearing of 334° for 4 nm. The temperature is 28°C, the pressure altitude zero and it takes 3 minutes to follow the straight section at a CAS of 90 kts. If the heading is 324°M and variation is 4°E what is the wind?

(a) 280°/12 kts

(b) 285°/22 kts

(c) 295°/15 kts

(d) 280°/17 kts

8. Desired track: 110°T

Variation: 5°E

TAS: 125 kts

Forecast wind: 040°/12 kts

What is the required magnetic heading and the expected groundspeed?

(a) 105° and 125 kts

(b) 110° and 120 kts

(c) 100° and 120 kts

(d) 095° and 125 kts

9. Track followed: 342°T

TAS: 65 kts

Wind experienced: 210° at 12 kts

What is the heading to fly, and how long will the 18 nm leg take?

(a) 339° and 17 minutes

(b) 335° and 15 minutes

(c) 347° and 14 minutes

(d) 349° and 16 minutes

10. The track from A to B is 165°T. The aircraft flies at 140 kts CAS at FL170 with a temperature of -10°C. What is the heading (M) to fly from A to B and the expected groundspeed in a wind of 200°/45 kts? Variation is 20°E.

    (a) 168° and 155 kts

    (b) 178° and 160 kts

    (c) 175° and 150 kts

    (d) 153° and 145 kts

11. Wind: 230°/70 kts

    320 kts CAS

    Required track 270°T

    Temperature -25°

    FL 220

    Variation 7°W

What is the required magnetic heading and the expected groundspeed?

    (a) 267° and 270 kts

    (b) 264° and 405 kts

    (c) 271° and 395 kts

    (d) 278° and 380 kts

12. Given the following:

    OAT ISA+10

    FL 230

    CAS

    170 kts

What is the TAS?

    (a) 247 kts

    (b) 241 kts

    (c) 255 kts

    (d) 230 kts

13. Flying a TAS of 450 kts at FL310 in ISA what is the Mach number?

    (a) 0.77

    (b) 0.75

    (c) 0.81

    (d) 0.72

14. For the following:

    TAS 212 kts

    FL 330

    ISA -10°

What is the Mach number?

    (a) 0.38

    (b) 0.61

    (c) 0.58

    (d) 0.71

15. Given a fuel quantity of 35 US gallons with a specific gravity of 0.81 what is the weight of the fuel?

    (a) 232 kg

    (b) 151 kg

    (c) 122 kg

    (d) 107 kg

16. Given the following:

    Altitude with QNH 1010 hPa set: 13,000 feet

    OAT: 12°C

What is the true altitude?

    (a) 14 200 feet

    (b) 13 200 feet

    (c) 11 900 feet

    (d) 12 400 feet

17. To fly a TAS of 120 kts what CAS must be flown at FL 70 if the OAT is +7°C?

    (a) 120 kts

    (b) 134 kts

    (c) 107 kts

    (d) 102 kts

18. At an indicated altitude of 23,000 feet at -15°C, what is the approximate true altitude?

    (a) 21 700 feet

    (b) 22 500 feet

    (c) 24 500 feet

    (d) 23 800 feet

19. If the temperature is -20°C and the PA 2 000 feet, what is the TAS of an aircraft flying at a CAS of 105 kts?

 (a) 113 kts

 (b) 105 kts

 (c) 108 kts

 (d) 102 kts

20. At FL90 what is the TAS of an aircraft flying at 85 kts if the OAT is 20° above ISA?

 (a) 95 kts

 (b) 90 kts

 (c) 80 kts

 (d) 100 kts

21. Given:

 Pressure Altitude: 40 000 feet

 OAT: -75°C

 CAS: 280 kts

What is the true airspeed?

 (a) 450 kts

 (b) 540 kts

 (c) 490 kts

 (d) 590 kts

22. Given:

 Pressure Altitude: 12 340 feet

 True Air Temperature: -4°C

What CAS should you fly at to maintain a TAS of 140 kts?

 (a) 105 kts

 (b) 115 kts

 (c) 125 kts

 (d) 107 kts

23. What is the Density Altitude when the air temperature is 86°F and the Pressure Altitude is 6344 feet?

 (a) 9726 feet

 (b) 9926 feet

 (c) 8000 feet

 (d) 7260 feet

24. How long will it take to climb to 12 500 feet from an airport whose elevation is 6344 feet and the rate of climb is 650 feet per minute?

 (a) 6 minutes

 (b) 7 mins 40 secs

 (c) 9 mins 28 secs

 (d) 12 mins

25. How much distance will you cover climbing to 5 000 feet at 375 feet per minute and 180 kts?

 (a) 25 nm

 (b) 30 nm

 (c) 40 nm

 (d) 50 nm

26. How fast must you climb to cross a fix 6.7 nm from takeoff (elevation 6344 feet) at 8 800 feet AMSL? Groundspeed is 97 kts.

 (a) 573 fpm

 (b) 593 fpm

 (c) 613 fpm

 (d) 623 fpm

27. If the fuel flow is 15.8 gallons per hour, and fuel available is 48 gallons, how much endurance do you have?

 (a) 2 hrs 55 mins

 (b) 3 hrs 30 mins

 (c) 3 hrs 2 mins

 (d) 4 hrs 2 mins

28. How much range do you have at 123 kts over 3 hours?

 (a) 350 nm

 (b) 375 nm

 (c) 400 nm

 (d) 425 nm

29. How far have you travelled at 108 kts for 70 minutes?

 (a) 100 nm

 (b) 125 nm

 (c) 150 nm

 (d) 175 nm

30. What is your groundspeed if you take 9 mins 26 seconds to cover 17 nm?

    (a) 102 kts

    (b) 104 kts

    (c) 106 kts

    (d) 108 kts

31. How long will it take to cover 231 nm at a groundspeed of 123 kts?

    (a) 1 hr 45 mins

    (b) 1 hr 53 mins

    (c) 1 hr 57 mins

    (d) 1 hr 59 mins

32. How much fuel will you need over 1 hour 52 mins at 16 gals per hour?

    (a) 25 gals

    (b) 28 gals

    (c) 30 gals

    (d) 32 gals

Fill in the missing boxes:

No	G/S	Time	Distance
33	120 kts	1:15	
34	105 kts	0:52	
35	145 kts	1:33	
36	168 kts	1:40	
37	152 kts	0:35	
38	110 mph	1:22	
39	133 mph	2:15	
40	108 mph	2:02	
41	210 mph	0:48	
42	183 mph	1:25	
43	184 kts		62 nm
44	108 kts		268 nm
45	165 kts		100 nm
46	198 kts		202 nm
47	87 kts		127 nm
48	208 mph		104 sm
49	122 mph		583 sm
50	346 mph		213 sm
51	56 mph		298 sm

No	G/S	Time	Distance
52	100 mph		250 sm
53		0:48	68 sm
54		1:48	204 sm
55		2:02	400 sm
56		1:35	108 sm
57		0:28	96 sm
58		0:13	26 nm
59		1:47	356 nm
60		2:03	457 nm
61		1:04	203 nm
62		0:58	108 nm
63	116 mph	1:04	
64	156 mph	0:53	
65	209 mph	1:56	
66	98 mph	2:54	
67	358 mph	4:59	
68	122 kts	0:47	
69	330 kts	1:13	
70	98 kts	2:56	
71	106 kts	3:26	
72	208 kts	1:37	
73	129 mph		28 sm
74	116 mph		13.5 sm
75	220 mph		66 sm
76	192 mph		16 sm
77	157 mph		21 sm
78	175 kts		500 nm
79	149 kts		144 nm
80	118 kts		124 nm
81	137 kts		183 nm
82	102 kts		7.64 nm
83		2:34	930 sm
84		0:5.6	20 sm
85		1:40	248 sm
86		0:48	80 sm
87		1:17	140 sm
88		10:00	1000 nm
89		1:23	385 nm
90		0:40	125.5 nm

No	G/S	Time	Distance	No	G/S	Time	Distance
91		6:40	660 nm	130	57.6		
92		0:1.1	1.56 nm	131	2100		
93	15			132	0.138		
94	210			133		306	
95	14.5			134		23.7	
96	178			135		164	
97	57			136		678	
98	820			137		13 340	
99	95			138		16.5	
100	127			139		115	
101	265			140		239	
102	38			141		3 670	
103		44.5		142		95	
104		650		143			53
105		3.9		144			678
106		800		145			115
107		0.126		146			45.6
108		156		147			61
109		20		148			5280
110		26.5		149			13.4
111		1.67		150			1.67
112		409		151			897
113			57.6	152			136
114			135				
115			15.5				
116			120.5				
117			184.5				
118			16				
119			20 840				
120			1521				
121			9.6				
122			111				
123	62						
124	137						
125	356						
126	20.3						
127	122						
128	115						
129	1.36						

No	PA Ft	Temp C	IAS mph	TAS mph
153	10 000	0	178	
154	15 000	-20	160	
155	12 000	-25	180	
156	8 000	10	164	
157	30 000	10	192	
158	28 000	-40	190	
159	1 000	5	85	
160	4 000	-20	190	
161	5 500	15	135	
162	7 200	22	158	
163	4 000	40	89	
164	3 000	10	77	

No	PA Ft	Temp C	IAS mph	TAS mph
165	12 500	-10	103	
166	9 000	-3	120	
167	18 000	-15	134	
168	23 500	-35	174	
169	8 000	5	85	
170	9 500	0	117	
171	3 000	-22	174	
172	30 000	-45	350	
173	1 500	38	122	
174	3 750	22	116	
175	22 500	-34	248	
176	17 000	-24	186	
177	13 500	-3.5	154	
178	11 000	0	122	
179	8 000	1	117	
180	16 400	-11	157	
181	10 000	10	142	
182	6 300	11	178	
183	15 500	-32		346
184	13 000	-20		136
185	10 500	-10		134
186	11 450	-2		178
187	8 000	-9		124
188	4 500	22		145
189	5 000	30		110
190	2 500	40		120
191	3 000	35		154
192	5 500	20		124
193	22 000	-33		256
194	30 000	-45		422
195	19 000	-23		222
196	11 500	-12		203
197	10 000	0		164
198	12 000	-9		120
199	7 500	16		167
200	4 000	15		145
201	2 000	20		200
202	1 670	16		135
203	28 000	-38		278

No	PA Ft	Temp C	IAS mph	TAS mph
204	16 000	-27		210
205	12 500	-14		184
206	16 000	-16		160
207	1 000	40		138
208	2 750	38		110
209	30 000	-40		456
210	13 500	-28		190
211	4 500	0		157
212	2 000	20		200

No	TH	TAS mph	TC	GS mph	W/V
213	162	132			320/16
214	36	168			135/23
215	347	128			110/34
216	122	100			35/35
217	236	137			345/26
218	122	139			119/21
219	189	214			16/11
220	122	316			256/34
221	56	114			116/46
222	108	108			180/18
223	189	146			360/21
224	356	213			101/13
225	89	103			267/26
226	112	235			116/13
227	167	126			346/24
228			153	113	222/22
229			189	214	124/17
230			239	187	46/34
231			162	102	111/11
232			347	168	137/17
233			002	118	352/23
234			046	137	119/33
235			305	129	54/26
236			107	43	187/25
237			167	102	349/33
238			216	202	121/30

If this page is a photocopy, it is not authorised!

No	TH	TAS mph	TC	GS mph	W/V
239			111	97	183/22
240			271	174	192/19
241			001	203	122/29
242			083	143	138/27
243		136	163		165/24
244		199	222		104/29
245		208	161		218/36
246		309	298		132/46
247		122	009		090/15
248		239	036		267/27
249		162	162		162/16
250		119	137		351/19
251		139	317		221/30
252		183	213		114/26
253		171	227		213/29
254		196	305		098/28
255		209	300		123/22
256		163	122		347/27
257		356	267		119/21
258	100	122	104	116	

Find the groundspeeds:

No	Dist	Time	G/S
1	90	:50	
2	75	2:00	
3	60	:40	
4	35	:16	
5	110	:120	
6	65	:30	
7	12	:10	
8	120	1:55	
9	115	:50.5	
10	90	1:40	

Find the times:

No	Dist	Time	G/S
1	80		67
2	120		60

No	Dist	Time	G/S
3	150		70
4	90		130
5	95		190
6	110		220
7	170		80
8	115		90
9	300		115
10	45		83

Find the distances:

No	Dist	Time	G/S
1		:80	40
2		:30	90
3		2:00	85
4		:120	120
5		:37	146
6		2:10	123
7		1:50	175
8		:25	88
9		1:30	62
10		:07	78

Fill in the missing boxes:

No	Dist	Time	G/S
1	120	2:00	
2	156	:120	
3	104	:42	
4	75		125
5	36		120
6	42		143
7		3:00	60
8		1:10	76
9		1:37	112
10	166	1:32	
11	82		115
12		:46	111
13	81		107
14	113	:80	
15	8		117

No	Dist	Time	G/S
16		:07	110
17	120		72
18	80	:43	
19	125		104
20	150		137

Find the fuel consumption:

No	Fuel	Time	Gals/Hr
1	42	3:00	
2	36	3:30	
3	33	2:45	
4	6	:26	
5	30	3:15	

Find the flying time:

No	Fuel	Time	Gals/Hr
1	40		8
2	38		11
3	37		6.5
4	26		12
5	40		15

Find the fuel used:

No	Fuel	Time	Gals/Hr
1		2:00	6
2		2:20	11
3		3:45	12.5
4		1:50	7.5
5		1:18	7

Fill in the missing boxes:

No	Fuel	Time	Gals/Hr
1	39	4:00	
2	27	3:30	
3	16.5		8
4	25.3		8
5		3:00	7
6		4:10	9
7	42		14

No	Fuel	Time	Gals/Hr
8	37	2:18	
9	22.7		9.1
10		3:14	10
11		3:00	6.0
12	25		8.3
13	80	6:10	
14	11	:35	
15	58		15.5
16	70	5:15	
17		3:30	6
18		2:15	8.4
19	23.5	3:12	
20	6.2	:41	

Find the true altitude:

No	Ind Alt	Temp	True
1	20,000	-15	
2	13,000	-10	
3	30,000	-30	
4	10,000	10	
5	6,000	20	
6	14,000	5	
7	8,000	-20	
8	18,000	-5	
9	8,000	10	
10	15,000	0	

Find the temperatures:

No	Ind Alt	Temp	True
1	20,000		22,000
2	25,000		26,000
3	18,000		18,500
4	10,000		9,200
5	11,500		12,000
6	10,000		9,500

Find the indicated altitudes:

No	True	Temp	PA	Ind
1	20,000	-25	21,000	

No	True	Temp	PA	Ind
2	10,000	-10	9,800	
3	19,000	-30	18,000	
4	25,500	10	26,000	
5	4,900	25	5,000	
6	5,500	25	6,000	

Find the TAS:

No	IAS	Ind Alt	Temp	TAS
1	190	10,000	-15	
2	200	20,000	-30	
3	150	5,000	-20	
4	180	12,000	-10	
5	140	3,000	5	
6	140	4,000	-5	
7	120	4,000	-30	
8	210	7,000	-15	
9	165	15,000	-20	
10	190	12,000	15	

Find the IAS:

No	IAS	Ind Alt	Temp	TAS
1		12,000	-10	150
2		20,000	5	200
3		18,000	10	165
4		6,000	-20	125
5		5,000	20	135
6		7,000	-5	107

Find the Indicated Altitude:

No	IAS	Ind Alt	Temp	TAS
1	175		-15	200
2	230		-35	225
3	180		-10	185
4	145		15	150
5	118		15	125
6	110		10	130

Fill in the empty spaces:

No	IAS	Ind Alt	Temp	TAS
1	140	5,000		156
2	178	12,000	-20	
3	235		-35	270
4		16,000	-25	260
5	116		-5	125
6	115	17,000		160
7	158	12,000	-20	
8		18,300	-18	165
9	165	18,500		210
10	190		-45	180

WIND TRIANGLES
Find the course, groundspeed and drift:

No	W/V	Hdg	A/S	Cs	G/S	Dft
1	090/30	350	120			
2	050/20	260	140			
3	270/25	180	125			
4	300/22	360	110			
5	225/25	045	170			
6	360/30	100	135			
7	315/26	041	117			
8	180/27	090	128			
9	360/12	299	130			
10	360/11	080	90			

Find the wind speed, direction and drift:

No	W/V	Dft	Hdg	A/S	Cs	G/S
1			090	120	090	120
2			355	135	360	130
3			045	118	038	128
4			192	140	183	120
5			090	165	103	178
6			271	65	263	72
7			158	68	158	78
8			085	78	085	60
9			285	85	270	94
10			183	155	180	161

Find the heading and groundspeed:

No	W/V	Hdg	A/S	Cs	G/S
1	320/30		140	260	
2	050/20		120	230	
3	045/20		130	270	
4	090/32		110	170	
5	180/28		125	090	
6	260/15		160	180	
7	050/30		174	315	
8	050/11		110	360	
9	180/32		092	045	
10	270/32		140	180	

Fill in the missing spaces:

No	W/V	Hdg	A/S	Cs	G/S	Dft
1	270/32		115	120		
2	240/20		140	080		
3	090/22	183	135			
4	184/18	350	105			
5		270	160	270	140	
6		180	90	188	75	
7	120/20		130	170		
8	175/20	180	125			
9		255	100	265	88	
10	186/25		140	152		
11	180/25		192	270		
12	350/?	090	125			8R
13	270/?	180	150			11L
14	250/20			350	110	
15	045/20			080	157	

AIR LAW & OPERATIONS

GENERAL

1. An aircraft overtaking another in flight should pass:

   (a) To the right

   (b) To the left

   (c) Over

   (d) Under

2. A vertical position based on 1013.2 hPa is reported as..

   (a) Altitude

   (b) Flight Levels

   (c) Height

   (d) Quadrantals

3. The Transition Altitude is that at or below which vertical position is controlled by reference to what?

   (a) Altitude

   (b) Flight Levels

   (c) Height

   (d) Quadrantals

4. What minimum radio equipment is needed for Class D airspace in UK, below FL 100, under VFR/Special VFR?

   (a) VOR, ADF, ILS

   (b) VHF Comms

   (c) VHF Comms, VOR, ADF, ILS

   (d) VHF Comms, ADF

5. Who is responsible for safe conduct of a VFR flight?

   (a) ATC

   (b) The PIC + ATC

   (c) The PIC

   (d) The operator

6. What does FIR mean?

   (a) Forward Looking Infra Red

   (b) Flight Information Region

   (c) Flight In Rain

   (d) Flight Incident Recording system

7. What is a Control Zone?

   (a) Notified airspace starting at ground level in which ATC service is given to IFR flights

   (b) Notified airspace starting at 3000 feet in which ATC service is given to IFR and VFR flights

   (c) Notified airspace starting at 3000 feet in which ATC service is given to IFR flights

   (d) Notified airspace starting at ground level in which ATC service is given to IFR and VFR flights

8. What is an airway?

   (a) A Control Zone

   (b) A Control Area

   (c) A Restricted Area

   (d) None of the above

9. What is a visual contact approach?

   (a) One that is conducted wholly under Visual Meteorological Conditions

   (b) An instrument approach with all or part of it completed by visual reference to terrain

   (c) One with all or part of it completed underneath the cloud base

   (d) An approach during which the copilot looks out of the window whilst the Captain flies the approach

10. On what occasions would you consider diversion?

    (a) Weather below minima

    (b) Runway obstructed

    (c) Failure of ground services and unacceptable delays

    (d) All of the above

11. When a runway is described as flooded:

    (a) It should not be used

    (b) Significant patches of standing water are visible

    (c) Extensive standing water is visible

    (d) The surface is completely covered with water - you need a flying boat

12. What altimeter setting should be used for terrain clearance en route?

    (a) QNH

    (b) Regional QNH

    (c) QFF

    (d) QNE

13. What is the normal circuit direction?

    (a) To the left

    (b) To the right

    (c) As directed by ATC

    (d) As directed by the signals area

14. At night you see the white navigation lights of an aircraft about 3 nm ahead whose range is decreasing. What should you do?

    (a) Keep the same distance

    (b) Slow down

    (c) A risk of collision with the aircraft ahead exists and you should turn right to overtake

    (d) A risk of collision with the aircraft ahead exists and you should fly over it well clear

15. To what side of a line feature should you fly when following it?

    (a) The left

    (b) The right

    (c) Overhead

    (d) Within sight

16. A flying machine overtaking another while taxying must do so on which side?

    (a) The right

    (b) The left

    (c) It may not

    (d) It must keep well clear

17. A helicopter and an aeroplane are converging at a 90° angle in flight, with the helicopter to the right of the aeroplane. Which has the right of way, and why?

    (a) The helicopter, because the aeroplane has the helicopter on its right

    (b) The aeroplane, because aeroplanes have right-of-way over helicopters

    (c) The helicopter, because helicopters have the right-of-way over aeroplanes

    (d) The aeroplane, because it is less able to move aside quickly

18. On a VFR flight approaching an aerodrome, you observe a steady red signal. What does this indicate?

    (a) You are approaching a danger area. Remove yourself from the vicinity

    (b) Keep away from the circuit

    (c) Give way to other aircraft and continue circling

    (d) Airport Unsafe, do not land

19. When two aircraft are approaching head on, or approximately so, and there is a danger of collision, each aircraft shall:

    (a) alter heading to the right

    (b) alter heading to the right or left enough to avoid a collision

    (c) initiate a climb or descent

    (d) alter heading to the left

20. Approaching an aerodrome, you observe a series of white flashes directed towards you. What does this indicate?

    (a) You are cleared to land

    (b) Land at this aerodrome and proceed to the apron after clearances have been given

    (c) Return to the aerodrome

    (d) Continue circling

21. In an aerodrome circuit, a red flashing light from the Tower means what?

    (a) You are approaching a danger area. Remove yourself from the vicinity

    (b) Keep away from the circuit

    (c) Give way to other aircraft and continue circling

    (d) Airport unsafe or unavailable, do not land

22. Two aircraft of the same category are approaching an airport to land. The right-of-way belongs to the aircraft:

    (a) at the higher altitude

    (b) that is more maneuverable, and that aircraft may, with caution, move in front of or overtake the other aircraft

    (c) at the lower altitude, but the pilot shall not take advantage of this rule to cut in front of or to overtake the other

    (d) with the higher speed

23. What frequency should you use to try and contact an intercepting aircraft?

    (a) 121.5 MHz

    (b) The one in use

    (c) Flight Information

    (d) 123.45 MHz

24. What does a series of green flashes to an aircraft in flight mean?

    (a) Join the circuit, but do not land

    (b) Return for landing - clearance will be sent in time

    (c) Join downwind

    (d) You are joining the circuit the wrong way

25. What is the signal to an unauthorised aircraft in or about to enter a R-, D- or P-area?

    (a) Flashing Red Light

    (b) Steady Red Light

    (c) Red and white Flares

    (d) A series of projectiles discharged from the ground at intervals of 10 seconds showing red and green lights or stars

26. What does a red pyrotechnic from a control tower to a flying aircraft mean?

    (a) You are joining the circuit the wrong way

    (b) Despite previous instructions, don't land for now

    (c) Animals on the runway

    (d) Keep circling

27. At night, you can see the green light of another aircraft. If both are converging, who has the right of way?

    (a) You, because you are to the right of the other aircraft

    (b) The other, because is to your right

    (c) You, because you are to the left of the other aircraft

    (d) The other, because is to your left

28. Helicopter A is overtaking helicopter B. Which one has the right of way?

    (a) Helicopter B - the pilot should expect to be passed on the left

    (b) Helicopter B - the pilot should expect to be passed on the right

    (c) Helicopter A - the pilot should alter course to the right to pass

    (d) Helicopter A - the pilot should maintain heading

29. An aeroplane is overtaking a helicopter. Which one has the right of way?

    (a) The aeroplane - its pilot should alter course to the left to pass

    (b) The helicopter - the pilot should expect to be passed on the left

    (c) The helicopter - the pilot should expect to be passed on the right

    (d) The aeroplane - its pilot should maintain heading

30. During a night flight, an aircraft is flying from right to left in front of you. What light(s) would you see?

    (a) Steady red

    (b) Steady green

    (c) Flashing red

    (d) Steady white

31. In the signals area of an aerodrome, a white dumb-bell means:

    (a) Landing direction is parallel with the shaft towards the cross-arm

    (b) Land on hard surfaces only

    (c) Land and taxi on hard surfaces only

    (d) Do not land

32. In the absence of ATC, what should your transponder code be?

    (a) Mode A 2000

    (b) Mode C 2000

    (c) Mode A 2100

    (d) Mode C 2100

33. In the UK, to whom must an accident be reported by the quickest means available?

    (a) The Chief Inspector of Air Accidents and the local police

    (b) The CAA

    (c) The nearest ATS unit

    (d) The operator of the aircraft and the police

34. A manual, acceptable to the state of the operator of an aircraft, that contains normal, abnormal and emergency operating procedures, checklists, limitations, performance information, details of aircraft systems and other relevant material, is called what?

    (a) An aircraft operating manual

    (b) An operations manual

    (c) Standard Operating Procedures (SOPs)

    (d) A training manual

35. What is defined as "A control area or portion thereof established in the form of a corridor equipped with radio navigation aids"?

    (a) An ATS Preferred Route

    (b) An ATS Route

    (c) An Airway

    (d) A Controlled Airway

36. Which of the following is *aerodrome traffic*?

    (a) All traffic on the movement area of an aerodrome

    (b) All traffic on the movement area of an aerodrome and flying in its vicinity

    (c) Local flying machines in or near the visual circuit

    (d) Any traffic flying through the aerodrome traffic zone

37. What is "an airspace of defined dimensions within which activities dangerous to the flight of aircraft may exist at specified times"?

    (a) A Restricted Area

    (b) A Restricted Zone

    (c) A Danger Area

    (d) A Danger Zone

38. What is an area around an aerodrome, from ground level to a specified altitude within which an Air Traffic Control service is provided?

    (a) A Control Zone

    (b) An Aerodrome Traffic Zone

    (c) A Traffic Zone

    (d) A Control Area

39. What is the third item in a position report?

    (a) Position

    (b) Altitude

    (c) Estimate

    (d) Time

40. When does night exist?

    (a) From the end of evening civil twilight until the start of morning civil twilight

    (b) From 30 minutes before sunset until 30 minutes after sunrise

    (c) When the centre of the sun's disc is 6° below the horizon

    (d) When the centre of the sun's disc is 6° above the horizon

41. A control unit tells you that they have radar contact. What does this mean?

(a) They know which blip you are on the screen

(b) Radar identity is established

(c) Radar identity is established, and radar instructions will be given until it is terminated

(d) Radar identity is established, and you may follow your own navigation

42. Which statement is true about noise abatement?

1. It only applies to commercial aircraft that can reduce power after takeoff

2. Suitable routings for aerodromes can be found in the AIP

3. It must be observed by all aircraft

(a) 2

(b) 3

(c) 1, 2, 3

(d) 1 and 3

43. A red parachute flare is:

(a) An urgency signal

(b) A distress signal

(c) A warning signal

(d) Of no significance

44. On the ground the letters LLL are formed in the snow. This is a "Ground-air signal" meaning:

(a) Operation completed

(b) Require medical assistance

(c) We have found only some personnel

(d) We have found all personnel

45. What is the reply from a surface craft meaning that it is able to comply with a request for assistance from another one in distress?

(a) Hoisting the Red Ensign

(b) Hoisting two black balls on the main mast

(c) Hoisting the *Code Pennant*

(d) Hoisting the *Blue Peter*

46. If an aircraft is missing, it is an:

(a) Incident

(b) Serious incident

(c) Accident

(d) Lost aircraft

47. What does a white dumb-bell with a black bar across each circular part of it, perpendicular to the shaft mean?

(a) Land and taxi on runways and taxiways only

(b) You must still only take off and land on runways, but other manoeuvres need not be confined to runways and taxiways

(c) You must still only take off and land on runways, but other manoeuvres are confined to runways and taxiways

(d) You may land on taxiways if they are clear

48. What does the sign XX lying on the ground mean?

(a) We are not able to continue

(b) Operation completed

(c) Require medical assistance

(d) We found only some personnel

49. How would a ground party signal that they have found only some personnel?

(a) ++

(b) LLL

(c) Y

(d) NN

50. Who is responsible for initiating an accident investigation?

(a) The Captain

(b) The Operator

(c) The Police

(d) The Authority of the state where the accident happened

51. If an aircraft wishes to divert a surface craft towards another in distress, the first action is what?

    (a) Flash the landing lights

    (b) Flash the navigation lights

    (c) Rock the wings

    (d) Circle the surface craft at least once

52. For how long every day must SAR facilities be provided?

    (a) 12 hours

    (b) 24 hours

    (c) Between sunset and sunrise

    (d) Between sunrise and sunset

53. Having intercepted a distress call and passed the information to ATC, what is your next action when asked to standby?

    (a) Stay where you are

    (b) Proceed to the position in the distress message

    (c) Carry on, but maintain a listening watch

    (d) Get ready to copy a message

54. High intensity obstacle lights should be:

    (a) Flashing blue

    (b) Flashing white

    (c) Fixed red

    (d) Fixed white

55. When it becomes apparent that an aircraft is in difficulty, the decision to initiate the alert phases is the responsibility of the:

    (a) Air traffic control and flight information centres

    (b) Flight information or control organisations

    (c) Air traffic co-ordination services

    (d) Search and rescue co-ordination centres

56. The ground-air visual code for *Require Assistance* is:

    (a) V

    (b) X

    (c) N

    (d) Y

57. The ground-air visual signal code LL indicates what?

    (a) Operation completed

    (b) All well

    (c) Require medical assistance

    (d) Nothing found. Will continue to search

58. What is Air Traffic?

    (a) Aircraft in flight or in the process of taking off or landing

    (b) Aircraft within the FIR

    (c) Aircraft in flight or operating on the manoeuvring area and apron

    (d) Aircraft in flight or operating on the manoeuvring area

59. The notification to a Rescue Co-ordination Centre shall contain which emergency phase as appropriate?

    (a) INCERFA - when no communication has been received from an aircraft within a period of 30 minutes

    (b) ALERFA- when an aircraft has been cleared to land and fails to land within 30 minutes

    (c) DETRESFA- when an aircraft has been cleared to land and fails to land within 5 minutes

    (d) ALERFA- when an aircraft fails to arrive within 30 minutes

60. What does a black ball suspended from a mast in the signals square mean?

    (a) Parachute dropping

    (b) Low flying aircraft

    (c) No circuits

    (d) Takeoffs and landings not necessarily in the same direction

61. A marshaller moving both arms up and down to and from a horizontal position to a helicopter pilot means what?

    (a) Move back

    (b) Move downwards

    (c) Land

    (d) Take off

62. What colour is a mandatory fixed aerodrome signal?

   (a)   Red on white

   (b)   White on red

   (c)   Black on white

   (d)   White on black

63. What colour are aerodrome information signs?

   (a)   Red on white

   (b)   White on red

   (c)   Black on yellow or yellow on black

   (d)   Yellow on blue

64. Of what do civil aerodrome identification beacons comprise?

   (a)   A red beacon flashing a 2 letter Morse group

   (b)   A white beacon flashing a 2 letter Morse group

   (c)   A yellow beacon flashing a 2 letter Morse group

   (d)   A green beacon flashing a 2 letter Morse group

65. How are taxiway markings coloured?

   (a)   Orange

   (b)   Green

   (c)   Yellow

   (d)   Red

66. What does a pair of yellow parallel lines with another set of parallel broken yellow lines across a taxiway mean?

   (a)   A runway intersection

   (b)   A holding point on an instrument runway beyond which no part of an aircraft may project without permission from ATC

   (c)   The start of a runup area

   (d)   The end of the apron

67. What colour are runway surface markings?

   (a)   Orange

   (b)   Green

   (c)   Yellow

   (d)   White

68. The transition level shall be:

   (a)   the highest available flight level below the transition altitude

   (b)   the lowest available flight level for use above the transition altitude

   (c)   published in the RAC section of the AIP

   (d)   determined by the PIC

69. Runway end lights shall be:

   (a)   Fixed unidirectional lights showing white in the direction of the runway

   (b)   Fixed unidirectional lights showing red in the direction of the runway

   (c)   Fixed lights showing variable white

   (d)   Fixed lights showing variable red

70. Which is correct regarding runway end lights?

   (a)   Omnidirectional lights showing red

   (b)   Showing red in the direction of the runway

   (c)   Omnidirectional lights showing green

   (d)   Showing green in the direction of the runway

71. Runway threshold identification lights are:

   (a)   Showing fixed green

   (b)   Showing flashing green

   (c)   Showing fixed white

   (d)   Showing flashing white

72. What is the colour of runway edge lights?

   (a)   Fixed lights showing blue

   (b)   Fixed lights showing green

   (c)   Fixed lights showing white

   (d)   Fixed lights showing red

73. ICAO was formed as a result of which convention?

   (a)   The Chicago Convention

(b) The Tokyo Convention

(c) The Rome Convention

(d) The French Convention

74. For what purpose was ICAO established?

(a) Making aeronautical standards adopted by all states

(b) Making proposals for aeronautical regulations in the form of 18 annexes

(c) Making standards and recommended practices for contracting states

(d) Making standards and recommended practices applied without exceptions by all states signatory of the Chicago Convention

75. Under the Chicago Convention, the (A) of a State shall be deemed to be the land areas and territorial waters adjacent thereto under the (B), suzerainty, protection or mandate of such State.

(a) A Territory, B Jurisdiction

(b) A Jurisdiction, B Sovereignty

(c) A Territory, B Sovereignty

(d) A Jurisdiction, B Territory

76. What documents should be carried on a flight abroad?

(a) Certificate of Registration, Certificate of Airworthiness, Aircraft Radio Station Licence, Passenger List (names, places of embarkation and destination), Cargo Manifest and detailed declarations of the cargo

(b) Certificate of Registration, Certificate of Airworthiness, Flight Crew Licences, Journey Log Book, Aircraft Radio Station Licence, Passenger List (names, places of embarkation and destination), Cargo Manifest and detailed declarations of the cargo

(c) Certificate of Registration, Certificate of Airworthiness, Flight Crew Licences, Journey Log Book, Aircraft Radio Station Licence

(d) Certificate of Registration, Certificate of Airworthiness, Journey Log Book, Aircraft Radio Station Licence, Passenger List (names, places of embarkation and destination), Cargo Manifest and detailed declarations of the cargo

77. What does the term *State Of Registry* mean?

(a) The State or country in which an aircraft was made

(b) The State or country in which an aircraft is currently registered and in whose register details of the aircraft and its ownership are registered

(c) The State or country in which an aircraft's crew is licensed

(d) The State or country in which an aircraft is maintained

78. What items are temporarily exempt customs duty between Contracting States?

(a) Spares and small quantities of alcohol for personal use

(b) Fluid consumables (fuel, oil, etc.)

(c) Essential equipment remaining on board

(d) Fuel, lubricating oils, spare parts and regular equipment remaining on board

79. In which section of AIP are contained information elements relating to areas and/or routes for which meteorological service is provided?

(a) RAC

(b) COM

(c) MET

(d) GEN

80. Whenever AIS information is operationally significant, temporary and of short duration it will be issued as what?

(a) A PIREP

(b) A navigation warning

(c) A NOTAM

(d) A SNOTAM

81. Which part of the AIP concerns Location Indicators?

(a) GEN

(b) FAL

(c) COM

(d) RAC

82. What are the aims and objectives of ICAO Annex 17 (Security)?

    (a)   To safeguard civil aviation against acts of unlawful interference

    (b)   To safeguard civil aviation against hijackers

    (c)   To safeguard civil aviation against acts of piracy

    (d)   To safeguard the Contracting State against acts of unlawful interference

83. Who establishes the national security program?

    (a)   Each Contracting State

    (b)   Each State Of Registry

    (c)   Each Contracting State's police organisation'

    (d)   The Authority

84. What is the correct phrase if an intercepting aircraft wants you to follow it?

    (a)   Follow me

    (b)   Follow

    (c)   Behind

    (d)   Intercepted

85. To report unexpected very bad weather, what would you send?

    (a)   Air report

    (b)   METAR

    (c)   PIREP

    (d)   SIGMET

86. If a runway is closed for one year for maintenance, where should it be noted?

    (a)   AIP

    (b)   NOTAM

    (c)   AFTN

    (d)   AIP + NOTAM, including supplements.

87. How are flight safety, air navigation and technically related changes to the AIP distributed?

    (a)   PIREP

    (b)   NOTAM

    (c)   AIRAC

    (d)   AIP

88. Temporary, long-term modification (3 months or more) and short-term extensive or graphical information is published as follows:

    (a)   NOTAM

    (b)   Trigger NOTAM

    (c)   AIP Supplements

    (d)   AIP Amendments

89. If radio communication is established during an interception but communication in a common language is not possible, which phrase should be pronounced by the intercepting aircraft to request the intercepted aircraft to descend for landing?

    (a)   Let down

    (b)   Descend

    (c)   Descend for landing

    (d)   You land

90. The information concerning charges for aerodromes/heliports and Air Navigation Services are on the following part of the AIP?

    (a)   GEN

    (b)   FAL

    (c)   RAC

    (d)   AD

91. If an intercepting aircraft performs an abrupt breakaway manoeuvre, such as a climbing turn of 90° or more without interfering with your line of flight:

    (a)   You must land at the aerodrome below you

    (b)   You must follow

    (c)   You have been released

    (d)   The interceptor has to go - another will be taking over shortly

92. A notice containing information concerning flight safety, air navigation, technical, administration or legislative matters and originated at the AIS of a state is called:

    (a)   Aeronautical Information Publication (AIP)

    (b)   Aeronautical Information Circular (AIC)

    (c)   AIRAC

    (d)   NOTAM

93. Which part of the AIP contains a list with "Location Indicators"?

   (a) ENR

   (b) GEN

   (c) LOC

   (d) AD

94. What is most correct about the Aeronautical Information Publication (AIP)?

   (a) A notice containing information that does not qualify for the origination of a NOTAM or for inclusion in an AIC

   (b) A publication containing aeronautical information of a lasting character essential to air navigation

   (c) A publication issued by the appropriate authority containing aeronautical information of a short basis essential to air navigation

   (d) AIPs are navigational information issued in two volumes by each contracting State

95. What doe this symbol mean when displayed on the ground by survivors? > or V

   (a) What direction should I proceed?

   (b) Proceeding in this direction

   (c) Assistance required

   (d) Need medical help

96. A contracting State shall take measures for the safety of passengers subjected to unlawful interference until:

   (a) their journey can be continued

   (b) during the investigation

   (c) returned to the point of origin

   (d) as requested by the passengers

97. With regard to the Aeronautical Information Service, whenever the information to be distributed is operationally significant and of a temporary nature and of short duration it will be issued as what?

   (a) An AIC

   (b) A NOTAM

   (c) An AIRAC

   (d) An ATC

98. A checklist of valid NOTAMS shall be distributed at regular intervals of:

   (a) 15 days

   (b) 28 days

   (c) Not more than 1 month

   (d) 42 days

99. For how long is a JAR-FCL licence issued?

   (a) Life

   (b) 24 months

   (c) 5 years (60 months)

   (d) 10 years

100. In the UK, which aircraft (unless specifically exempted) require noise certificates?

   (a) Multi-engined aeroplanes, and aeroplanes with constant speed propellers

   (b) Aeroplanes and helicopters over 5 700 kg MAUW

   (c) All helicopters

   (d) All of the above

101. How long is a Part med Class 2 medical certificate valid for?

   (a) 6 months over 40, 24 months over 40

   (b) 12 months over 40, 48 months under 40

   (c) 18 months over 40, 36 months under 40

   (d) 24 months over 40, 60 months under 40

102. What is an "entry in a licence stating special conditions, privileges or limitations pertaining to that licence"?

   (a) A rating

   (b) A type rating

   (c) An endorsement

   (d) A signature

103. A licence holder shall, without undue delay, seek the advice of the appropriate authority when becoming aware of a decrease in medical fitness, such as any illness involving incapacity to function as a member of a flight crew throughout a period of …?

   (a) 21 days

   (b) 21 days or more

   (c) 28 days

   (d) 28 days or more

104. Which Annex contains information about aircrew licensing?

   (a) Annex 1

   (b) Annex 2

   (c) Annex 6

   (d) Annex 14

105. What is the sole objective of accident or incident investigation?

   (a) Their prevention and to allocate responsibility

   (b) Their prevention from recurring

   (c) Their prevention and to provide evidence

   (d) Their prevention and to advise on improvements

106. Must a licence holder seek the advice of the Authority when subject to an illness involving their incapacity to function as a member of a flight crew over 18 days?

   (a) Yes

   (b) No

   (c) Depends on the illness

   (d) If the doctor says so

107. What is the State Of Registry?

   (a) The State that issued the PIC's licence

   (b) The State that issued the aircraft's C of A

   (c) The State in whose Registry the aircraft is entered

   (d) The State where the aircraft is maintained

108. What is a skill test?

   (a) A demonstration of skill for licences, including oral examinations

   (b) A demonstration of skill for ratings, including oral examinations

   (c) A demonstration of skill for licences or ratings, including oral examinations

   (d) A demonstration of skill for licences or ratings

109. What is currency for a PIC carrying passengers?

   (a) 3 circuits within the previous 90 days in an approved simulator or on type

   (b) 3 takeoffs, approaches and landings in any aircraft within the previous 90 days

   (c) 3 takeoffs and landings within the previous 90 days in an approved simulator or on type

   (d) 3 takeoffs and landings in 90 days on type

110. How do you revalidate a helicopter type rating?

   (a) Perform a 2-hour recurrency check with an instructor in the last 3 months of validity

   (b) Do 12 hours in the last 3 months of validity

   (c) Pass a proficiency check with an instructor in the last three months of validity

   (d) Pass a proficiency check with an authorised examiner in the last three months of validity

111. The privileges of an unrestricted FI are to conduct flight instruction for the issue of a CPL:

   (a) If the FI has completed at least 15 hours on the relevant type in the preceding 12 months

   (b) If the FI has completed at least 500 hours of flight time as a pilot of aeroplanes including at least 200 hours of flight instruction

   (c) Without restriction

   (d) If the FI has completed 200 hours of flight instruction

112. *Normal Residency*, with regard to licensing, means the place where you usually live for at least:

   (a) 5 months a year

   (b) 6 months a year

   (c) 185 days a year

   (d) 215 days a year

113. What is the minimum age for an applicant for a Flight Instructor Rating?

   (a) 18 years

   (b) 20 years

   (c) 21 years

   (d) 23 years

114. If there is a 90 minute delay to a filed flight plan for a flight in uncontrolled airspace, what should you do?

   (a) Use the current flight plan as it is still valid

   (b) Use the current flight plan, but inform ATC

   (c) Cancel the first flight plan and submit a new one

   (d) Submit a new plan which cancels the first one

115. What medical certificate classes exist?

   (a) 1, 2, 3 and 4

   (b) 1, 2 and 3

   (c) 1 only

   (d) 1 and 2

116. What does a red square panel with a diagonal yellow stripe in the signals area indicate?

   (a) Use landing areas with caution

   (b) The runway (and hence the aerodrome) is closed

   (c) The manoeuvring area is in a poor state and special care must be exercised when landing

   (d) Taxi with caution

117. What must you do to make your licence valid on receipt?

   (a) Send the enclosed receipt back to the Authority

   (b) Sign it with ink

   (c) Keep it in a wallet with the medical certificate

   (d) Staple it to your radio licence

118. Before flying into the airspace of a foreign state in which you are going to land, you must:

   (a) ensure that the aircraft is registered, airworthy and has all the relevant documents on board

   (b) ensure that a current C of A is on board

   (c) inform the Search & rescue organisation

   (d) ensure that crew licences are current

119. Which of the following is correct regarding noise certificates?

   (a) Subsonic aircraft able to take off within 500 m are exempt

   (b) Microlight aircraft are exempt

   (c) All aeroplanes except certain STOL types require a noise certificate

   (d) Aeroplanes with variable pitch propellers and turbine engines require noise certificates

120. For an international flight, a pilot must hold a licence issued or rendered valid by:

   (a) The authority of the country in which the aircraft is registered

   (b) The authority of any contracting ICAO state

   (c) The authority of any EASA state

   (d) The authority of the country in which the aircraft is operated

121. If your pilot licence does not fully comply with international standards, it:

   (a) Cannot be used

   (b) May only be used in the issuing State

   (c) Must be endorsed with the names of States that allow its use

   (d) Must be endorsed with information on how the licence does not comply

122. Which rules of the air regarding entry and departure of international air traffic have precedence?

   (a) International ones as agreed by all States

   (b) Those laid down by JAA, and now EASA

   (c) Those of the foreign State concerned

   (d) Those between the State of Registry and the foreign State concerned

123. For customs purposes, any Contracting State:

   (a) must direct any aircraft intending to land in its territory to land at a Customs aerodrome

   (b) has the right to direct any aircraft intending to land in its territory to land at a Customs aerodrome

   (c) may require multiple copies of the General Declaration

   (d) does not require use of the General Declaration

124. What is the maximum distance between points of reference for visual navigation?

    (a) 25 nm

    (b) 25 km

    (c) 60 nm

    (d) 60 km

125. A C of A issued by one Contracting State is recognised by others if:

    (a) It was issued under agreed (ICAO) standards

    (b) It was issued under JAA/EASA standards

    (c) It is current

    (d) There are no deferred defects

126. An aircraft must comply with the rules of the airspace it is in. Who ensures compliance with this rule?

    (a) The State of Operation

    (b) The State of Registry

    (c) The Pilot

    (d) The State of Operation and The State of Registry

127. If its C of A is not compliant, an aircraft may:

    (a) not participate in international navigation

    (b) participate in international navigation with prior permission of the States concerned

    (c) not fly until the C of A is compliant

    (d) Operate with a Permit to Fly

128. Who is responsible for ensuring that an aircraft and conditions are fit for the intended flight?

    (a) The organisation hiring out the aircraft

    (b) The aircraft owners

    (c) The PIC

    (d) The organisation operating the aircraft

129. Who has the final authority with regard to operating a flight?

    (a) The aircraft owner

    (b) The aircraft commander

    (c) The pilot manipulating the controls at the time

    (d) ATC

130. What should an aircraft registration mark be inscribed on?

    (a) A rust proof metal plate

    (b) A stainless steel plate

    (c) A fireproof metal plate

    (d) A waterproof metal plate

131. For how long must a newly prepared weight schedule be preserved? Up to:

    (a) When the next one is ready

    (b) 6 months after the next weight schedule is prepared

    (c) 12 months after the next weight schedule is prepared

    (d) 18 months after the next weight schedule is prepared

132. Where are all UK registered aircraft subject to the Air Navigation Order and Rules Of The Air regulations?

    (a) In the airspace of any ICAO contracting state

    (b) Within UK airspace

    (c) Anywhere

    (d) Where they conflict with the Rules of the State in which they are operating

133. Of the following, what minor repairs and replacements may be carried out by an aircraft's owner/operator?

    (a) Replacement of unserviceable spark plugs or landing gear tyres

    (b) Adding ballast weight

    (c) Changing radios, as long as they are switchable

    (d) Changing batteries

134. What is the minimum safety equipment to be carried on any flight?

    (a) First aid kit, spare fuses, portable fire extinguisher

    (b) First aid kit, life jackets, portable fire extinguisher

    (c) First aid kit, oxygen, portable fire extinguisher

    (d) First aid kit, passenger briefing cards, portable fire extinguisher

135. Of the following, under ICAO, what documents must be carried on international flights?

    (a) C of A, C of R, Radio Licence

    (b) C of A, C of S, Crew Licence

    (c) Passports

    (d) Insurance certificate, crew licences

136. When does a C of A become invalid?

    (a) If the aircraft is overhauled, repaired or modified otherwise than in an approved manner

    (b) If the Check A has not been done

    (c) If the aircraft flies too many hours

    (d) Outside the provisions of the preflight inspection

137. What may a flying machine be classified as?

    (a) A power driven heavier than air aircraft

    (b) A helicopter or an aeroplane

    (c) A helicopter because it does not use a propeller

    (d) A power driven aircraft

138. When an aircraft registered in one ICAO Contracting State lands in another one, the authorities there:

    (a) May only search the aircraft with advance notice

    (b) May only search the aircraft for contraband control purposes

    (c) Have the absolute right to search the aircraft without unreasonably delaying it

    (d) May search the aircraft only with the permission of its commander

139. ICAO Contracting States agree that:

    (a) Aircraft of other Contracting States may make flights across their territory if at least one landing is made within those territories

    (b) Aircraft of other Contracting States may make flights across their territory without prior permission

    (c) Aircraft of other Contracting States on scheduled services may make flights across their territory without prior permission

    (d) Other than those engaged on Scheduled Services, aircraft of other Contracting States may make flights into or across their territories without prior permission

140. What are Visual Meteorological Conditions (VMC) determined in terms of?

    (a) Equal to or better than specified minima for RVR and cloud ceiling

    (b) Equal to or better than specified minima for visibility, distance from cloud and cloud ceiling

    (c) Equal to or better than specified minima for visibility and cloud ceiling

    (d) Equal to or better than specified minima for visibility

141. The Certificate of Registration:

    (a) Need not be carried on flights within 25 nm of the departure point

    (b) Must be carried on all flights

    (c) Must be carried on international flights, but not necessarily on domestic flights

    (d) May be a photocopy

142. What document contains the approved limitations within which an aircraft is considered to be airworthy?

    (a) The Weight & Balance Schedule

    (b) The Flight Manual, including any placards

    (c) The Maintenance Schedule

    (d) The Minimum Equipment List

143. What should a PPL holder without an Instrument Rating do if ATC issues an instruction to climb to a level that would not enable the PPL holder to maintain VMC?

    (a) Climb to that level and revert to the instrument appreciation training previously given

    (b) Ignore the instructions

    (c) Turn back to the departure point

    (d) Carry on at the present height or heading and request new instructions that will maintain VMC

144. How close may you fly to any person, vessel, vehicle or structure without permission from the CAA, except for taking off or landing under normal aviation practice?

    (a) 1 000 feet

    (b) 500 feet

    (c) 1 000 metres

    (d) 500 metres

145. In a level cruise at night, you see a red navigation light at a similar height on a steady relative bearing of 020°. Is there a risk of collision?

    (a)   Yes, turn right

    (b)   Yes, but you have right of way

    (c)   Yes, change your level

    (d)   No

146. You see a red light at night. What could it be on?

    (a)   An airship

    (b)   A glider or free balloon

    (c)   A glider

    (d)   A free balloon

147. You are taxying on the manoeuvring area and converging with a vehicle that is towing another aircraft. Unless ATC says otherwise, which one must give way?

    (a)   The towing vehicle

    (b)   That with the other on its left

    (c)   You

    (d)   That with the other on its right

148. What does a white T in the signals area with a white disc next to its cross arm in line with the stem mean?

    (a)   Takeoffs and landings are in the same direction

    (b)   Takeoff and landing directions do not necessarily coincide

    (c)   The aerodrome is unmanned - land with caution

    (d)   Watch out for parachutists

149. What is an altimeter reading based on QNH reported as?

    (a)   Height

    (b)   Altitude

    (c)   A Flight Level

    (d)   Elevation

150. In Class D airspace, what may VFR traffic expect to receive?

    (a)   Separation from IFR and VFR flights

    (b)   Separation from IFR flights

    (c)   Separation from VFR flights

    (d)   Traffic information on all other flights

151. What is an Approach Control Service? An ATC Service for:

    (a)   Arriving and departing IFR flights

    (b)   Arriving and departing VFR flights

    (c)   Arriving and departing controlled flights

    (d)   IFR and VFR flights within a control zone

152. For whom is an Alerting Service provided?

    (a)   Aircraft with a current flight plan

    (b)   Aircraft subject to unlawful interference

    (c)   Aircraft known by ATC to be operating in the relevant Flight Information regions

    (d)   Aircraft with a current flight plan filed within the last 24 hours

153. From where does a Control Zone extend from?

    (a)   A specified altitude

    (b)   A specified height

    (c)   A specified Flight Level

    (d)   The surface

154. What is a defined area on an aerodrome used for parking aircraft on called (it may also be used for loading or unloading, fuelling and maintenance)?

    (a)   A parking slot

    (b)   A manoeuvring area

    (c)   A parking bay

    (d)   An apron

155. What does a double white cross displayed horizontally in the signals area mean?

    (a)   The aerodrome is not open

    (b)   Take off or land on grass areas only

    (c)   Use right hand circuits

    (d)   Gliders are flying at the aerodrome

156. When may an aerodrome with a public licence be closed?

    (a)   When the landing surface is unfit

    (b)   When the visibility is too low

    (c)   In snow

    (d)   When the weather is below minima

157. Given:

> Minimum Safe Altitude: 3 000 feet
> Track: 086° (T)
> Variation: 4°W
> Estimated Drift: 10°L
> Regional QNH: 3500 feet

What is the lowest appropriate level to fly at?

   (a) 3 500 feet on the QNH

   (b) FL 30

   (c) FL 35

   (d) FL 50

158. Where would you find details of the privileges pertaining to a UK pilot's licence?

   (a) The AIP

   (b) The Rules Of The Air (ICAO Annex 2)

   (c) In the Air Navigation Order (ANO) as amended

   (d) In the licence

159. If your fuel state is becoming critical, how would you alert ATC to the problem?

   (a) Declaring an emergency (MAYDAY/PAN)

   (b) Use the phrase *minimum fuel*

   (c) Use the phrase *low fuel*

   (d) Use the phrase *final reserve fuel*

160. Near aerodromes, what is the vertical position of aircraft at or below the transition altitude expressed in?

   (a) Height

   (b) Altitude

   (c) A Flight Level

   (d) Elevation

161. What should you do having flown clear of severe weather conditions that were not forecast?

   (a) Warn others with a blind transmission

   (b) Submit a special air-report to ATC

   (c) Report it after you land

   (d) Report it when you close the flight plan

162. If a PIC receives an ATC clearance that is considered to be unsuitable:

   (a) An amended clearance should be requested

   (b) It should be ignored

   (c) It should be followed

   (d) The flight should not take place

163. The privileges of a PPL licence holder are to act as PIC or co-pilot of any aircraft:

   (a) for remuneration

   (b) being used for domestic, business or pleasure purposes

   (c) engaged in non-revenue flights for which they are appropriately certified

   (d) engaged in revenue earning flights for which they are appropriately certified

164. If you, holding a pilot licence, become aware of the need for a surgical operation, what should you do?

   (a) Without undue delay, seek the advice of the Authority or an authorised medical examiner

   (b) Without undue delay, seek the advice of the consultant, who is obliged to report the circumstances to the Authority

   (c) Without undue delay, seek the advice of the authorised medical examiner, who must report the circumstances to the Authority

   (d) Without undue delay, seek the advice of any doctor, who must report the circumstances to the Authority

165. In order to be credited for a licence or rating, what must flight time have been flown in?

   (a) Any aircraft with a valid C of A

   (b) Any aircraft with at least a permit to fly

   (c) Any category of aircraft for which the rating is sought

   (d) The same category of aircraft for which the rating is sought

166. What is the transponder code for a general emergency situation?

    (a) 7000

    (b) 7500

    (c) 7600

    (d) 7700

167. Once a Search & Rescue operation has been started, who is responsible for alerting individual SAR units?

    (a) Local ATC

    (b) The aircraft operator

    (c) The Rescue Coordination Centre (RCC)

    (d) The commander

168. If a person on the ground is seriously injured by something that falls off an aircraft, although that aircraft's flight is not impaired, this is:

    (a) An incident

    (b) An occurrence

    (c) An accident

    (d) None of the above

169. When may you transfer your licence from one JAA/EASA state to another?

    (a) Once you have been issued with a work permit

    (b) Once you have been resident for more than 75 days

    (c) Once you have been resident for more than 105 days

    (d) Once employment or normal residency is established in that state

170. An aircraft being overtaken has:

    (a) to slow down

    (b) the right of way

    (c) to increase speed

    (d) to turn right to get out of the way

171. For recency purposes, you must have made 3 takeoff and landings (including circuits) within how long?

    (a) The past year

    (b) The past 120 days

    (c) The past 90 days

    (d) The past 30 days

172. You may not act as PIC unless your licence has a:

    (a) Valid class rating

    (b) Valid type rating, if required

    (c) Valid IMC rating

    (d) Valid class and type rating

173. How long is a helicopter type rating valid for?

    (a) 13 months

    (b) 12 months

    (c) 24 months

    (d) Indefinitely, as long as currency is maintained

174. An applicant for a licence or rating is credited _____ all solo, dual instruction or PIC time towards the total flight time needed for the licence or rating:

    (a) in full with

    (b) with half of

    (c) with a quarter of

    (d) with three quarters of

175. Under the Chicago Convention, the regulations relating to entry and departure from a State are those of:

    (a) The State of registry

    (b) The State in question

    (c) JAA/EASA

    (d) All States involved in the flight

176. Under the Chicago Convention, the duty to ensure compliance with rules and regulations pertaining to aircraft in flight rests with whom?

    (a) The State of registry

    (b) The State of registry and the State over whose territory the flight takes place

    (c) The State over whose territory the flight takes place

    (d) ICAO

177. Who is responsible for ensuring that, taking into account the best weather information available, a flight can safely be made?

    (a)   The Chief Flying Instructor, if the aircraft is hired from a club

    (b)   The commander of the aircraft

    (c)   The owner of the aircraft

    (d)   The operator of the aircraft

178. For how long must weight schedules be preserved?

    (a)   Until the next weighing

    (b)   6 months after the next weighing

    (c)   12 months after the next weighing

    (d)   24 months

179. For converging aircraft:

    (a)   Aeroplanes must give way to helicopters and airships

    (b)   Aeroplanes must give way to helicopters and other aeroplanes towing gliders

    (c)   Aeroplanes and helicopters must give way to aeroplanes towing gliders

    (d)   Aeroplanes must give way to helicopters

180. The identity of Prohibited, retsricted and Danger areas is composed of what?

    (a)   Nationality letters for Location Indicators assigned to the state or territory, followed by the letter P, R or D and figures

    (b)   The letter P, R or D and figures

    (c)   Nationality letters for Location Indicators assigned to the state or territory, followed by the letter P, R or D

    (d)   The letter P, R or D

181. When aircraft are converging, the one with right of way should maintain its:

    (a)   Speed and heading

    (b)   Height and speed

    (c)   Height and heading

    (d)   Heading, height and speed

182. On an aerodrome, how is an area that is to be used only for takeoff and landing by helicopters indicated?

    (a)   A square white box

    (b)   A large white letter H

    (c)   A white circle with a number inside

    (d)   A red letter H

183. When does the duration of an initial medical examination begin:

    (a)   On the date of certificate issue

    (b)   On the date of licence renewal

    (c)   On the date of the assessment

    (d)   On the date of licence delivery

184. When are you considered to be overtaking? When the faster aircraft is converging within:

    (a)   90° of the extended centreline of the slower aircraft

    (b)   70° of the extended centreline of the slower aircraft

    (c)   60° of the extended centreline of the slower aircraft

    (d)   45° of the extended centreline of the slower aircraft

185. How is an altimeter reading based on QFE reported?

    (a)   Altitude

    (b)   Flight Level

    (c)   Height

    (d)   Quadrantal

186. What type of airspace satisfies these conditions?

    • IFR and VFR flights are permitted, and all flights are subject to ATC

    • IFR flights are separated from other IFR flights and receive traffic information about VFR flights

    • VFR flights receive traffic information about all other flights

    (a)   Class C

    (b)   Class D

    (c)   Class F

    (d)   Class G

187. What are the objectives of ATC?

    1. Prevent collisions between aircraft in the air and on the manoeuvring area

    2. Expedite and maintain an orderly flow of traffic

    3. Provide advice and information useful for the safe and efficient conduct of flights

    4. Notify appropriate organisations about aircraft in need of Search & rescue, and to assist those organisations

    (a) 1, 3, and 4

    (b) 1, 2, and 3

    (c) 1, 2, 3, and 4

    (d) 1 and 4

188. What is a Terminal Control Area (TMA)?

    (a) A control zone with at least 1 major aerodrome

    (b) A control area with at least 1 major aerodrome

    (c) A control area at the confluence of ATS routes near one or more major aerodromes

    (d) A control area designed to handle transiting traffic at higher levels

189. What do large white diagonal crosses up to 300 m apart along a section of a runway indicate?

    (a) The section between them is unfit for takeoff but OK for landing

    (b) The section between them is unfit for landing but OK for takeoff

    (c) The section between them is unfit for landing but OK for taxying

    (d) The section between them is unfit for aircraft movement

190. How is the direction of takeoff indicated in the signals square?

    (a) A red and white striped arrow pointing in the relevant direction

    (b) A red and yellow striped arrow pointing in the relevant direction

    (c) A white T, with direction towards the cross arm

    (d) A white T, with direction from the cross arm

191. What does the word *territory* mean?

    (a) Land areas only

    (b) Nearby lands and waters under a State's sovereignty, suzerainty, protection or mandate

    (c) Land areas and waters up to 3 nm

    (d) Land areas and waters up to 5 nm

192. How would you file a flight plan if you cannot do it at the departure aerodrome?

    (a) Use the telephone to call the destination

    (b) Fax it to the destination

    (c) Submit it in flight to the first ATS unit you contact

    (d) Submit the flight plan, by telephone or radio, to the ATS unit serving the departure aerodrome

193. In which UK Wake Vortex category are large helicopters included?

    (a) Small

    (b) Light

    (c) Medium

    (d) Heavy

194. What transponder code means *communication failure*?

    (a) 7000

    (b) 7500

    (c) 7600

    (d) 7700

195. If you are unfit to be flight crew for medical reasons (injury, etc), what happens to the medical certificate?

    (a) It remains current until you get better

    (b) It remains current for 21 days

    (c) It remains current for 42 days

    (d) It is deemed to be suspended

196. When may a PPL holder fly for aerial work, aside from flight instruction?

    (a) Photography

    (b) Dropping Parachutists

    (c) Towing gliders

    (d) Dropping Parachutists and towing gliders

197. What type of airspace satisfies these conditions?

    • IFR and VFR flights are permitted, and all flights are subject to ATC

    • All flights are separated from each other

    • VFR flights receive traffic information about other VFR flights

    (a) Class C

    (b) Class D

    (c) Class F

    (d) Class G

198. What must passengers be briefed on as a minimum (by the PIC) before flight?

    (a) Emergency exits

    (b) Emergency exits and use of safety belts

    (c) Emergency exits and use of safety belts or harnesses, oxygen equipment and lifejackets

    (d) Action in the event of ditching

199. What does the term *night* usually mean?

    (a) The time between sunset and sunrise

    (b) The time between sunrise and sunset

    (c) When it is dark

    (d) The time between the end of evening civil twilight and the beginning of morning civil twilight on the following day

200. What is an alternate aerodrome?

    (a) The intended destination after the first landing

    (b) A place where an aircraft may proceed when it becomes impossible or undesirable to proceed to, or land at, the aerodrome of intended landing

    (c) One which can be used to operate from on a temporary basis

    (d) One with better weather than the original destination

201. Under what conditions may a helicopter operate in less than 500 metres visibility in Class G airspace?

    (a) The pilot must have an IMC rating

    (b) Clear of cloud with the surface in sight if the speed is reasonable regarding visibility

    (c) Clear of cloud

    (d) At least 500 feet from any cloud

202. When should Performance Class 3 helicopters carry lifejackets or flotation devices? Over water beyond:

    (a) 5 nm from land

    (b) 500 metres from land

    (c) Autorotational distance from land

    (d) 1 nm from land

203. What minimum visibility (1) and distance from cloud (2) must a VFR aircraft in Class C airspace observe?

    (a) (1) 5 km at or above 3050 m (10 000 ft AMSL (2) 1500 m horizontally and 300 m (1 000 ft) vertically

    (b) (1) 8 nm at or above 3050 m (10 000 ft AMSL (2) 1500 m horizontally and 300 m (1 000 ft) vertically

    (c) (1) 8 km at or above 3050 m (10 000 ft AMSL (2) clear of cloud, in sight of the surface

    (d) (1) 8 km at or above 3050 m (10 000 ft AMSL (2) 1500 m horizontally and 300 m (1 000 ft) vertically

204. Under the Chicago Convention:

    (a) all aircraft of other contracting states, including those engaged on scheduled services may make flights into or across its territory without prior permission

    (b) only those aircraft engaged on scheduled services may make flights into or across its territory without prior permission

    (c) all aircraft of other contracting states may make flights across its territory provided only that at least one landing is made within the territory

    (d) other than those engaged on scheduled services, all aircraft of other contracting states may make flights into or across its territory without prior permission

205. If you suffer a significant personal injury and are considered unfit to act as flight crew, your medical certificate:

(a) remains current, if your ratings are current

(b) requires a currency check within 21 days

(c) is suspended

(d) requires a full initial medical

206. At aerodromes where takeoffs and landings are not confined to a runway, the pilot of an aeroplane about to take off shall position and manoeuvre so as to leave clear any aircraft which is taking off:

(a) on the right

(b) on the right if the circuit is right hand and on the left if it is left hand

(c) on the left

(d) on the left if the circuit is right hand and on the right if it is left hand

207. When does a Certificate of Airworthiness cease to be valid?

(a) if the aircraft, or any of its equipment, is overhauled, repaired or modified otherwise than in an approved manner

(b) in a State other than the State of issue

(c) until the Check A servicing has been signed for in the Technical Log

(d) during a refuelling stop until the refuelling is completed

208. Low intensity obstacle lights on vehicles other than those used for emergency or security shall be:

(a) fixed red

(b) fixed blue

(c) flashing blue

(d) flashing yellow

209. Low intensity lights on fixed objects shall be:

(a) flashing red

(b) fixed red

(c) flashing yellow

(d) fixed orange

210. Under Annex 2, the pilot of an aircraft:

(a) must comply with all instructions received from ATC

(b) may deviate from rules and regulations for safety reasons only

(c) is only responsible for adherence to rules and regulations when acting as the

(d) pilot flying

(e) may deviate from the rules and regulations provided that he is willing to accept full responsibility

211. What additional information is transmitted over SSR Mode C?

(a) Altitude based on regional QNH

(b) Aircraft height based on sub-scale setting

(c) Pressure altitude based on 1013.25 hPa

(d) Height based on QFE

212. To operate radio transmitting apparatus over the territory of a contracting state:

(a) the radio station and the operator must be suitably licensed by the state of registry

(b) the operator, but not the radio station, must be suitably licensed by the state of registry

(c) either the radio station or the operator may be suitably licensed by the state of registry

(d) the radio station, but not the operator, must be suitably licensed by the state of registry

213. Aircraft on VFR flights should normally have at least the following equipment:

(a) attitude indicator, magnetic compass, sensitive pressure altimeter and airspeed indicator

(b) turn coordinator or indicator, sensitive pressure altimeter, airspeed indicator, engine RPM gauge

(c) magnetic compass, sensitive pressure altimeter and airspeed indicator

(d) magnetic compass, accurate timepiece, sensitive pressure altimeter and airspeed indicator

214. On approach, you encounter windshear with a decreasing headwind. If you do nothing, what will the aircraft do?

    1. Its rate of descent will decrease

    2. Its rate of descent will increase

    3. It will have an increasing airspeed

    4. It will have a decreasing airspeed

Which combination is correct?

    (a) 2 and 4

    (b) 1 and 4

    (c) 2 and 3

    (d) 1 and 3

215. Windshear is commonly associated with:

    1 - Thunderstorms

    2 - Frontal passage

    3 - Virga

    4 - Roll cloud

    5 - Inversions

    (a) 1, 3 & 4

    (b) 1 & 3

    (c) 1, 2, 3, 4 and 5

    (d) 1 only

216. You notice a fast and high increase in IAS without any changes in engine power and attitude. Other pilots have already reported windshear. What must you do?

    (a) Reduce the selected thrust rapidly to reach a speed just above the stall, then try a precision landing

    (b) Take a level flight attitude to reduce speed, then come back to glide path from above

    (c) Maintain the glide path, accept a positive speed deviation, monitor the speed evolution

    (d) Reduce the selected thrust rapidly, maintain the glide path

217. Wake turbulence is generated when:

    (a) Generating lift (including hovering helicopters)

    (b) Flying at high speed

    (c) Using high engine RPM

    (d) Flying with its gear and flaps extended

218. Observations and studies about the behaviour of birds on the ground, ahead of an aircraft taking off and having reached an average speed of 135 kt, show that birds fly away:

    (a) About two seconds beforehand

    (b) About ten seconds beforehand

    (c) As soon as they hear the engine noise

    (d) From the beginning of the takeoff run

219. The effect of wake turbulence is strongest behind a:

    (a) heavy aeroplane with large wingspan, flying slowly

    (b) heavy aeroplane, flying slowly, in light wind conditions and zero flap

    (c) light aeroplane, flying fast, in strong wind conditions

    (d) light aeroplane, flying slowly, with flaps in the landing position

220. When could an aircraft encounter wake turbulence?

    (a) Departing from a crossing runway after another aircraft rotated before the intersection

    (b) Departing from a crossing runway after another aircraft landed before the intersection

    (c) When climbing in light wind conditions, upwind of another departing aeroplane

    (d) When holding downwind of a runway before a departing aircraft's rotation point

221. When should lifejackets be inflated?

    (a) in the aircraft before ditching to provide added crash protection

    (b) after leaving the aircraft, but before entering a dinghy or the water

    (c) once in the water unless a passenger cannot swim or is infirm or disabled

    (d) once the passenger has climbed into the dinghy, or on entering the water if one is not available

222. Which statements are true?

1. The position of a holding point ensures safe clearance between the holding aircraft and any passing in front of it

2. You can only cross the red stop bars after receiving the proper clearance

3. You can only cross the yellow line after receiving the proper clearance

4. You may only cross two solid and two broken yellow lines after checking left and right and receiving clearance

(a) 2 and 4

(b) 1 and 3

(c) 1 and 4

(d) 3 and 4

223. A runway is contaminated if:

(a) It is wet

(b) It has more than 3mm of wet snow over 25% of the surface

(c) It is flooded

(d) It is damp

224. After an emergency landing that involves an evacuation, you should:

1. Move the passengers upwind, with a fire extinguisher and first aid kit

2. Clear the runway vis the first available taxiway

3. Stop the engine, keep the battery on for the radio

4. Turn off all systems

(a) 1 and 3

(b) 1 and 2

(c) 1 and 4

(d) 1, 3 and 4

225. "The length of the takeoff run available plus the length of the clearway if provided" defines what?

(a) Takeoff Run Available (TORA)

(b) Takeoff Distance Available (TODA)

(c) Accelerate/Stop Distance Available (ASDA)

(d) The runway length

226. What is the definition of flight time for an aeroplane?

(a) The time from the release of the brakes until the aircraft comes to rest at the end of the runway after landing

(b) The time from when the engine is started until it is shut down at the end of the flight

(c) The time from takeoff until the engine stops

(d) The time from when an aircraft first moves under its own power with the intent of taking off until it comes to rest after the flight

227. If you become doubtful as to your position on the manoeuvring area, you must:

(a) Stop the aircraft, except if you are on a runway, notify ATC and ask for clarification

(b) Notify ATC and continue taxying without stopping. If on a runway, get off as quickly as possible unless otherwise instructed

(c) Notify ATC and stay where you are until otherwise instructed

(d) If on a runway, vacate as quickly as possible and stop. Otherwise, continue taxying slowly

228. What is a safe forced landing?

(a) An unavoidable landing or ditching with a reasonable expectancy of no injuries to persons in the aircraft or on the surface.

(b) A planned landing or ditching with a reasonable expectancy of no injuries to persons in the aircraft or on the surface.

(c) A planned landing or ditching with a reasonable expectancy of limited injuries to persons in the aircraft or on the surface.

(d) An unavoidable landing or ditching with a reasonable expectancy of limited injuries to persons in the aircraft or on the surface.

229. What is the best course of action if you see smoke and flames coming from the engine cowling during start?

    (a) Open the door and discharge the fire extinguisher into the smoke. Master switch and electrics off, notify ATC and evacuate aircraft

    (b) Close the window and discharge the extinguisher into the smoke

    (c) Inform ATC. Master switch and electrics off, evacuate aircraft and await the fire service

    (d) Continue turning the engine, mixture lean, fuel off, throttle open. If the fire remains, turn the Master switch off and evacuate the aircraft

230. What is the most common cause of carburettor fires when the engine is started?

    (a) Overpriming beforehand

    (b) Excess fuel in the float chamber

    (c) Accelerator pump failure

    (d) Butterfly valve stuck

231. During a climb after takeoff, you encounter windshear with an increasing tailwind. If you don't do anything, the aircraft:

    1. rate of climb will decrease

    2. rate of climb will increase

    3. will have an increasing indicated airspeed

    4. will have a decreasing indicated airspeed

Which combination is correct?

    (a) 2 and 4

    (b) 1 and 4

    (c) 2 and 3

    (d) 1 and 3

232. A runway is contaminated if:

    (a) It is wet

    (b) It has more than 3mm of wet snow over 25% of the surface

    (c) It has water patches

    (d) It is damp

233. Which statements are true?

    1. The position of a holding point ensures safe clearance between the holding aircraft and any passing in front of or behind it

    2. You may not cross red stop bars

    3. You can only cross the yellow line after receiving the proper clearance

    4. You may only cross two solid and two broken yellow lines after checking left and right and receiving clearance

    (a) 2 and 4

    (b) 1 and 3

    (c) 1 and 4

    (d) 3 and 4

234. How may warnings of approaching microbursts be provided?

    1. From ATC

    2. From other pilots

    3. From transmissometers

    4. An increase in airspeed and reduced rate of descent at a constant pitch and power setting

    5. A decrease in airspeed and increased rate of descent at a constant pitch and power setting

    (a) 1, 2, 3

    (b) 1, 3, 4

    (c) 1, 2, 4

    (d) 1, 3, 5

235. When could an aircraft encounter wake turbulence?

    (a) Landing on a crossing runway after another aircraft rotated before the intersection

    (b) Departing from a crossing runway after another aircraft landed before the intersection

    (c) When climbing in light wind conditions, upwind of another departing aeroplane

    (d) When holding downwind of a runway before a departing aircraft's rotation point

236. Wake turbulence:

(a) Can be a hazard to light aircraft within 3 rotor diameters of a hovering helicopter

(b) decreases with speed

(c) stops when the landing gear touches the runway

(d) is less of a problem from helicopters

237. "The length of the takeoff run available plus the length of the stopway if provided" defines what?

(a) Takeoff Run Available (TORA)

(b) Takeoff Distance Available (TODA)

(c) Accelerate/Stop Distance Available (ASDA)

(d) The runway length

238. What is the name of a manual that contains procedures, instructions and guidance for use by operational personnel within an organisation?

(a) A training manual

(b) Standard Operating Procedures (SOPs)

(c) An operations manual

(d) A flight manual

239. Who is the Pilot In Command (PIC)?

(a) The sole manipulator of the controls

(b) The person responsible for the safe conduct of the flight

(c) The pilot designated by the owner or operator of an aircraft as such and charged with the safe conduct of the flight

(d) The pilot in the captain's seat

240. Which statement is correct about light signals given to an aircraft on the ground?

(a) Steady red means stop

(b) Flashing green is clearance to take off at pilot's discretion

(c) Steady red means move clear of the landing area

(d) Steady green means you can cross the runway

241. Which statement is correct about operating from contaminated runways?

(a) Use maximum takeoff power

(b) It should be avoided

(c) Apart from a little extra wheel drag, such operations are routine

(d) Use the lowest approved flap and power settings

242. Which statement is correct about the selection of runway landing direction?

(a) It is selected by ATC. Use it or divert

(b) ATC should make sure that the runway in use is the best one aligned with the wind

(c) You can only request an alternative if the wind is beyond crosswind limitations

(d) You can request an alternative if the crosswind and/or tailwind, or any other condition, exceeds your limits

243. What is the best course of action after an engine failure over water in a single-engined aeroplane?

(a) Set the speed for maximum range, and plan to land parallel to the swell as close to the wind direction as possible. Make a distress call, squawk 7500 and prepare for ditching.

(b) Make a distress call, squawk 7600, head for land while trying to restart the engine

(c) Make a distress call, squawk 7700, head towards any shipping if there is no land within reach, try to restart the engine and plan to land parallel to the swell rather than directly into wind

(d) Set the speed for maximum endurance, and plan to land parallel to the swell as close to the wind direction as possible. Make a distress call, squawk 7500 and prepare for ditching.

244. Which statement is correct about light signals given to an aircraft on the ground?

(a) Flashing red means stop

(b) Flashing green is clearance tooperate on the manoeuvring area

(c) Steady red means move clear of the landing area

(d) Steady green means you can cross the runway

245. What are the best initial actions if the engine of a single-engined aeroplane fails in the cruise?

   (a)   Close throttle, mixture ICO, fuel off, ignition off, make distress call, select field, descend as rapidly as possible

   (b)   Check the fuel, carb heat off, check ignition on and try to restart the engine

   (c)   Master switch off, electrics off, cabin heat off, make distress call, select field, attempt to land

   (d)   Check fuel, carb heat on, ignition on, try to restart the engine

246. Which statement is true?

   (a)   A microburst contains up- and downdraughts

   (b)   A thunderstorm 5 nm downwind of an airfield is more dangerous than one 5 nm upwind

   (c)   A microburst can be associated with the passage of a warm front

   (d)   Downdraughts can be found beneath thunderstorms and virga

247. On approach, you encounter windshear with an increasing headwind. If you do nothing, what will the aircraft do?

   1. Its rate of descent will decrease

   2. Its rate of descent will increase

   3. It will have an increasing airspeed

   4. It will have a decreasing airspeed

Which combination is correct?

   (a)   2 and 4

   (b)   1 and 4

   (c)   2 and 3

   (d)   1 and 3

248. When ditching, you should:

   (a)   Use best range speed, squawk 7600 and make a distress call

   (b)   Use best endurance speed

   (c)   Land as slowly as possible into a rising swell

   (d)   Make a distress call and squawk 7700

249. When is an aircraft unlikely to encounter wake turbulence?

   (a)   Landing on a crossing runway after another aircraft rotated beyond the intersection

   (b)   Departing from a parallel runway after another aircraft has executed a missed approach

   (c)   Departing from a crossing runway after another aircraft has rotated before the intersection

   (d)   When crossing behind and below a departing aeroplane in light winds

250. What is General Aviation?

   (a)   Aircraft operations other than commercial air transport or aerial work operations

   (b)   Operations that include photography or survey

   (c)   Operations that include search and rescue

   (d)   Aircraft operations other than commercial air transport or aerial work operations

251. What is *A defined rectangular area on the ground, selected or prepared as a suitable area over which an aircraft may make a portion of its initial climb to a specified heigh*t called?

   (a)   Stopway

   (b)   Take Off Run Available

   (c)   Clearway

   (d)   Take Off Distance Available

252. What is the best course of action if you see smoke that has an acrid smell in the cockpit?

   (a)   Open the door and discharge the fire extinguisher into the smoke. Master switch and electrics off, notify ATC and land at the nearest aerodrome

   (b)   Close the window and discharge the extinguisher into the smoke

   (c)   Inform ATC. Master switch and electrics off, cabin heat off, land at the nearest aerodrome

   (d)   Mixture lean, fuel off, throttle open. If the fire remains, turn the Master switch off and land at the nearest aerodrome

FLIGHT PERFORMANCE & PLANNING

6

GENERAL

1. What is the total weight of an aircraft, together with its total contents at any time, called?

   (a)   Tare weight

   (b)   Gross weight

   (c)   All Up Weight

   (d)   Factored Weight

2. Given:

   Takeoff weight: 2400 lbs

   C of G: 91 inches aft of datum

   Planned fuel burn: 180 lbs, at 90 inches aft of datum

What is the landing C of G?

   (a)   90 ins aft of datum

   (b)   89 ins aft of datum

   (c)   91 ins aft of datum

   (d)   93 ins aft of datum

3. If air density reduces, what happens to take off distance? It:

   (a)   Increases

   (b)   Reduces

   (c)   Stays the same

   (d)   It depends on the QNH

4. In the choices below, which combination of weight and C of G position results in a safe configuration?

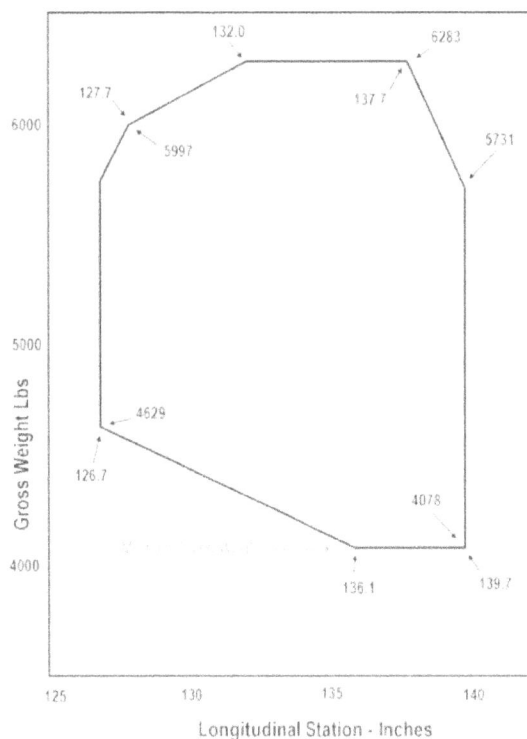

   (a)   5000 lbs 135 ins

   (b)   6000 lbs 142 ins

   (c)   3000 lbs 125 ins

   (d)   5000 lbs 125 ins

5. Why does the engine speed drop when you apply carburettor heat?

(a) Ice temporarily forms on the butterfly

(b) The accelerator pump is disconnected

(c) The air is less dense and less charge gets into the engine

(d) The ICO is linked to the carb heat lever

6. How much is 300 lbs of fuel in litres if the specific gravity is 0.72?

(a) 41.5

(b) 275

(c) 85

(d) 189

7. Given an aircraft weighing 1750 lbs with a total moment of 160 000, what is the new total moment if 100 lbs of fuel is added at station 80?

(a) 175 000

(b) 157 000

(c) 218 000

(d) 168 000

8. To carry full passengers with maximum baggage:

(a) You can carry full fuel

(b) You don't need to worry about the fuel load

(c) You can only carry 75% fuel

(d) the fuel must be adjusted to keep within limits

9. An oil tank with 2 gallons in it with a specific gravity of .85 is 10 inches aft of the datum. What is its moment?

(a) 150 lb/ins

(b) 170 lb/ins

(c) 180 lb/ins

(d) 175 lb/ins

10. If the barometric pressure falls, what happens to the altimeter reading?

(a) It decreases

(b) It increases

(c) It stays the same

(d) It starts to rise, then falls

11. What is the Landing Mass for this aircraft, given:

Standard Empty Mass: 1764 lbs

Optional Equipment: 35 lbs

Pilot + Front seat passenger: 300 lbs

Cargo Mass: 350 lbs

Ramp Fuel = Block Fuel: 60 gals

Trip Fuel: 35 gals

Fuel density: 6 lbs/gal

(a) 2659 lbs

(b) 2449 lbs

(c) 2599 lbs

(d) 2799 lbs

12. The datum is a reference from which all moment (balance) arms are measured. Its precise position is given in the control and loading manual and it is located:

(a) At or near the focal point of the axis system

(b) At or near the natural balance point of the empty aircraft

(c) At a convenient point which may not physically be on the aircraft

(d) At the rear

13. A specific measured distance from the datum or some other point identified by the manufacturer, to a point in or on the aircraft is called a:

(a) Zone number

(b) Station number

(c) Specification number

(d) Range number

14. When using the weight information in a typical flight manual, you need to know that if items have been installed in addition to the original equipment, the:

(a) Maximum allowable gross weight is increased

(b) Allowable useful load is decreased

(c) Allowable useful load remains unchanged

(d) Allowable useful load is increased

If this page is a photocopy, it is not authorised!

15. What does density altitude increase with?

(a) Increases in temperature and moisture content of the air, and a decrease in pressure

(b) An increase in temperature only

(c) Increases in pressure, temperature, and moisture content of the air

(d) A decrease in temperature only

16. If the reference datum line is placed at the nose of an aircraft rather than some other location aft:

(a) Measurement arms will be in positive numbers

(b) Measurement arms will be in negative numbers

(c) Measurement arms will be in positive and negative numbers

(d) Numbers will not be used at all

17. Zero fuel weight is the:

(a) Basic operating weight without crew, fuel, and cargo

(b) The maximum weight of an aircraft, beyond which any additional weight must consist entirely of fuel

(c) Dry weight plus the weight of full crew, passengers, and cargo

(d) The weight of the aircraft plus crew

18. An aircraft is considered to be in balance when:

(a) The average moment arm falls within its C of G range

(b) All moment arms fall within the C of G range

(c) The movement of the passengers will not cause the moment arms to fall outside the C of G range

(d) The movement of the cargo will not cause the moment arms to fall outside the C of G range

19. What determines whether the value of a moment is preceded by a + or a - sign?

(a) The location of the datum with reference to the C of G

(b) The location of the weight with reference to the datum

(c) The result of a weight being added or removed, and its location relative to the datum

(d) The result of a weight being added or removed

20. The Centre of Gravity of an aircraft is normally computed along the:

(a) Lateral axis

(b) Longitudinal axis

(c) Vertical axis

(d) Horizontal axis

21. The Centre of Gravity of an aircraft is determined by:

(a) Dividing total moments by total weight

(b) Multiplying total arms by total weight

(c) Dividing total arms by total moments

(d) Dividing total weight by total moments

22. If all index units are positive when computing weight and balance, the datum would be at the:

(a) Nose, or out in front

(a) Centreline of the skids or wheels

(a) Centreline of the nose or tailwheel, depending on the type of aircraft

(a) By the main rotor mast

23. The centre of gravity:

(a) May only be moved if permitted by the regulating authority and endorsed in the certificate of airworthiness

(b) Is in a fixed position and is unaffected by loading

(c) Must be maintained in a fixed position by careful distribution of the load

(d) Can be allowed to move between defined limits

24. Moment (balance) arms are measured from a specific point to the body station at which the mass is located. That point is known as:

(a) The datum

(b) The focal point

(c) The axis

(d) The Centre of Gravity

25. Two identical aircraft, one with a light load and one with a heavy load are in an idle power descent, from the same height. Both experience the same atmospheric conditions. How will the heavy aircraft perform?

   (a) It will descend shallower, at faster speed, with a greater rate of descent

   (b) It will descend steeper, at faster speed, with a greater rate of descent

   (c) It will descend steeper, at slower speed, with a greater rate of descent.

   (d) No difference

26. If a static vent gets blocked in the cruise, how are the barometric instruments affected in a climb?

   (a) The altimeter reads the same, the ASI over-reads

   (b) The altimeter reads the same, the ASI under-reads

   (c) The altimeter under-reads, the ASI over-reads

   (d) The altimeter under-reads, the ASI under-reads

27. Increasing all up weight does what to rate of climb?

   (a) Increase it

   (b) Decrease it

   (c) Decrease it at higher altitudes

   (d) Have no effect

28. Using the following table, at 10°C and 2000 feet, how far will it take to climb to 50 ft at 2600 lbs?

Gross Wt (lbs)	PA (ft)	-25°C	-5°C	15°C	35°C
2150	SL	373	401	430	458
	2000	400	434	461	491
	4000	428	462	494	527
	6000	461	510	585	677
	8000	567	674	779	896
2500	SL	531	569	613	652
	2000	568	614	660	701
	4000	611	660	709	759
	6000	654	727	848	986
	8000	811	975	1144	1355
2850	SL	743	806	864	929
	2000	770	876	929	1011
	4000	861	940	1017	1102
	6000	939	1064	1255	1538
	8000	1201	1527	-	-

   (a) 689 feet

   (b) 698 feet

   (c) 896 feet

   (d) 869 feet

29. A steep turn at constant altitude and speed requires:

   (a) An increase in power and angle of attack to maintain height

   (b) An increase in angle of attack to maintain height

   (c) An increase in power to maintain height

   (d) No adjustments to maintain height

30. The load factor in a turn in level flight with constant TAS depends on:

   (a) The radius of the turn and the bank angle

   (b) The TAS and the bank angle

   (c) The radius of the turn and the weight of the aeroplane

   (d) The bank angle only

31. A higher OAT:

   (a) Does not have any noticeable effect on climb performance

   (b) Reduces the angle of climb but increases the rate of climb

   (c) Reduces the angle and the rate of climb

   (d) Increases the angle of climb but decreases the rate of climb

32. Which of the following combinations has an effect on the angle of descent in a glide?

   (a) Configuration and mass

   (b) Configuration and angle of attack

   (c) Mass and altitude

   (d) Altitude and configuration

33. The absolute ceiling:

   (a) Is the altitude at which the best climb gradient attainable is 5%

   (b) Is the altitude at which the aeroplane reaches a maximum rate of climb of 100 ft/min

   (c) Is the altitude at which the rate of climb is theoretically zero

   (d) Can be reached only with minimum steady flight speed

If this page is a photocopy, it is not authorised!

34. The optimum cruise altitude increases:

    (a) If mass is decreased

    (b) If OAT is increased

    (c) If the tailwind component is decreased

    (d) If mass is increased

35. What will be the effect on performance if aerodrome pressure altitude is decreased?

    (a) It will increase the takeoff distance required

    (b) It will increase the takeoff ground run

    (c) It will increase the accelerate stop distance

    (d) It will decrease the takeoff distance required

36. True airspeed is determined by correcting:

    (a) Calibrated airspeed for nonstandard temperature and altitude

    (b) Indicated airspeed for density altitude

    (c) Calibrated airspeed for pressure altitude

    (d) Equivalent airspeed for the air density variation from the standard value at sea level

37. What effect has a tailwind on max endurance speed?

    (a) No effect

    (b) Tailwind only effects holding speed

    (c) The IAS will be increased

    (d) The IAS will be decreased

38. How does the best angle and best rate of climb vary with increasing altitude?

    (a) Both decrease

    (b) Both increase

    (c) Best angle of climb increases while best rate of climb decreases

    (d) Best angle of climb decreases while best rate of climb increases

39. During climb to the cruising level, a headwind component:

    (a) Decreases the climb time

    (b) Decreases the ground distance flown during that climb

    (c) Increases the amount of fuel for the climb

    (d) Increases the climb time

40. Carrying an extra passenger will cause climb performance to be:

    (a) Degraded

    (b) Improved

    (c) Unchanged

    (d) Unchanged, if a short field takeoff is adopted

41. A constant headwind

    (a) Increases the descent distance over ground

    (b) Increases the angle of the descent flight path

    (c) Increases the angle of descent

    (d) Increases the rate of descent

42. Density Altitude:

    (a) Is used to calculate the FL above the Transition Altitude

    (b) Is used to determine performance

    (c) Is equal to the pressure altitude

    (d) Is used to establish minimum clearance of 2.000 feet over mountains

43. If the pressure altitude is 4,500 feet, and the temperature is 20°C, the density altitude will be nearest to:

    (a) 7,300 feet

    (b) 6,100 feet

    (c) 5,400 feet

    (d) 4,500 feet

44. If the aerodrome elevation is 6,000 feet ASL, and the altimeter setting is 995 hPa, what is the pressure altitude?

    (a) 6,500 feet

    (b) 4,640 feet

    (c) 4,600 feet

    (d) 4,200 feet

45. To determine pressure altitude before takeoff, the altimeter should be set to:

    (a) The current altimeter setting

    (b) The field elevation and the pressure reading in the altimeter setting window noted

    (c) 29.92" Hg or 1013 hPa and the altimeter indication noted

    (d) The regional pressure setting

46. Why will an engine produce more power on a dry day than on a humid day?

   (a) Because a molecule of water weighs more than a molecule of nitrogen or oxygen

   (b) Increased air density

   (c) Humidity increases the density

   (d) Decreased air density

47. What atmospheric condition change will cause an increase in air density?

   (a) Increased temperature

   (b) Increased pressure

   (c) Increased humidity

   (d) Decreased pressure

48. How does temperature decrease affect performance?

   (a) It will cause an increase in takeoff distance and decrease rate of climb

   (b) It will cause a decrease in takeoff distance and increase rate of climb

   (c) No change

   (d) Depends on the wind

49. If the OAT is 10°C and the dewpoint is 7°C, can you expect carburettor ice?

   (a) Yes

   (b) No

   (c) It depends on relative humidity

   (d) It depends on temperature

50. Which of the following combinations adversely affects takeoff and initial climb performance?

   (a) High temperature and high relative humidity

   (b) Low temperature and high relative humidity

   (c) High temperature and low relative humidity

   (d) Low temperature and low relative humidity

51. With pressure altitude 12,000 ft, true air temperature +50 °F, the approximate density altitude is:

   (a) 14,130 feet

   (b) 11,900 feet

   (c) 13,500 feet

   (d) 18,150 feet

52. The speed for best rate of climb is:

   (a) V_O

   (b) V_Y

   (c) V_X

   (d) V_2

53. An increase in atmospheric pressure has, among other things, what consequences on takeoff performance?

   (a) A reduced takeoff distance and degraded initial climb performance

   (b) A reduced takeoff distance and improved initial climb performance

   (c) An increased takeoff distance and degraded initial climb performance

   (d) An increased takeoff distance and improved initial climb performance

54. With pressure altitude 7,000 ft, true air temperature +15 °C, what is the approximate density altitude?

   (a) 5,000 feet

   (b) 9,500 feet

   (c) 8,500 feet

   (d) 7214 feet

55. What should the standard temperature be at 10,000 feet?

   (a) -5 °C

   (b) +5 °C

   (c) -15 °C

   (d) +15 °C

56. What conditions are favourable for a surface-based temperature inversion?

   (a) Broad areas of cumulus with smooth, level bases at the same altitude

   (b) Area of unstable air rapidly transferring heat from the surface

   (c) Area of stable air rapidly transferring heat from the surface

   (d) Clear, cool nights with calm or light wind

57. An increase in aircraft weight has, among other things, what consequences on takeoff performance?

(a) A reduced rate of climb and greater maximum operating altitude

(b) Reduced acceleration and landing speed

(c) An increase in takeoff speed and takeoff run

(d) Reduced range and increased endurance

58. An aircraft weighs 2400 lbs and its total moments are 216 000 aft of datum. If fuel weighing 600 lbs is loaded 12 feet aft of datum, what will the aircraft's C of G be?

(a) 74.4 ins aft of datum

(b) 100.8 ins aft of datum

(c) 94 ins aft of datum

(d) 110 ins aft of datum

59. What is included in the Basic Empty Mass (BEM) of an aircraft?

(a) Usable fuel

(b) Unusable fuel and engine oil

(c) Unusable fuel and disposable load

(d) Pilot and engine oil

60. What does 350 lbs of fuel at a specific gravity of 0.74 equate to in litres?

(a) 211 litres

(b) 184 litres

(c) 404 litres

(d) 292 litres

61. How heavy is 300 litres of fuel with a specific gravity of 0.76?

(a) 327 kg

(b) 476 lbs

(c) 389 lbs

(d) 502 lbs

62. What time should be entered into the flight plan form (Box 13) for the departure aerodrome and time details?

(a) Wheels off time in UTC

(b) Off-block time in UTC

(c) The time of obtaining clearance

(d) The time of the first radio call

63. How is the flight time to the Scottish FIR boundary (EGPX) entered in the ICAO flight plan form if it takes 1 hour twenty minutes to get there after takeoff?

(a) ETA EGPX0120

(b) EET/EGPX0120

(c) RMK/EET/EGPX0120

(d) EST/EET/EGPX0120

FIXED WING

1. What is the part of a runway called that can support the weight of an aeroplane during takeoff?

(a) Takeoff Distance Available (TODA)

(b) Takeoff Run Available (TORA)

(c) Clearway

(d) Stopway

2. Compared to the still air TAS, what is the TAS for best range in a strong tailwind?

(a) The same

(b) A bit higher

(c) A bit lower

(d) A lot lower, in proportion to the tailwind

3. Increasing an aeroplane's gross weight will (A) the speed at which it rotates and (B) the V_2 speed. What combination correctly completes the above sentence?

(a) A decrease, B decrease

(b) A increase, B decrease

(c) A increase, B increase

(d) A decrease, B increase

4. For runway surfaces:

(a) An upsloping runway will increase the takeoff run required but decrease the landing distance

(b) A downsloping runway will increase the takeoff run required but decrease the landing distance

(c) An upsloping runway will decrease the takeoff run required but decrease the landing distance

(d) A downsloping runway will increase the takeoff run required but decrease the landing distance

5. How is maximum range in a glide achieved?

(a) Maintaining a relatively low angle of attack

(b) Maintaining a negative angle of attack

(c) Maintaining a relatively high angle of attack

(d) Maintaining a neutral angle of attack

6. How does greater weight affect gliding for max range?

(a) Angle of attack is greater and airspeed is slower

(b) The glidepath is shallower and airspeed is slower

(c) The glidepath is steeper and airspeed is slower

(d) The glidepath is steeper and airspeed is faster

7. When gliding, the rate of descent will be (A) and the distance flown will be (B) in a tailwind:

(a) A unchanged, B increased

(b) A increased, B decreased

(c) A decreased, B unchanged

(d) A decreased, B decreased

8. Increasing gross weight will (A) the stall speed, (B) the takeoff run required, and (C) landing distance required:

(a) A decrease, B decrease, C increase

(b) A decrease, B decrease, C decrease

(c) A increase, B increase, C decrease

(d) A increase, B increase, C increase

9. Why are full flaps selected for approach and landing?

(a) It increases the safe flying speed and provides a flatter approach path, which improves vision

(b) It reduces the approach speed to reduce the landing distance required and provides a steeper approach path, which improves vision

(c) Engine power is reduced and a flatter approach path is provided, which improves vision

(d) It reduces the approach speed and provides a flatter approach path, which improves vision

10. If you increase approach and landing speeds above those recommended:

(a) Landing distance is unaffected

(b) Landing distance is reduced

(c) Landing distance is increased

(d) The tyres will wear faster

11. How do you achieve maximum range? By flying:

(a) At just below minimum drag speed

(b) At the lowest safe density altitude

(c) At the speed that provides the minimum power/airspeed ratio

(d) At maximum endurance speed + 10%

12. A downsloping runway requires (A) takeoff distance and (B) landing distance:

(a) A less, B more

(b) A more, B less

(c) A more, B more

(d) A less, B less

13. The landing speed, in terms of TAS, for a particular weight and configuration of the aircraft will:

(a) Remain constant regardless of altitude

(b) Decrease as atmospheric pressure is decreased

(c) Increase as altitude is increased

(d) Decrease as altitude is increased

14. Why do we normally take off into wind? To:

(a) Reduce the Take Off Run Available (TORA)

(b) Reduce the Take Off Distance Required (TODR)

(c) Reduce the groundspeed

(d) B and C

15. How is an aeroplane affected if it is loaded too far aft at maximum all up weight?

(a) It will need ballast in the baggage compartment

(b) It will be harder to flare on landing

(c) Its range will be reduced

(d) It will be easier to flare on landing

16. What is the usual indicated operating range of an aircraft vacuum system?

(a) 1.5-2.5 ins

(b) 6.5-7.5 ins

(c) 5.5-7.5 ins

(d) 3.5-5.5 ins

17. What effect would having the flaps partially extended in cruise flight have?

   (a) Reduced rate of climb capability

   (b) Decreased Lift coefficient

   (c) Decreased Drag coefficient

   (d) Increased rate of climb capability

18. What will happen to the lift produced by the wing of an aeroplane maintaining a constant TAS? It will:

   (a) Decrease as altitude increases

   (b) Increase as altitude increases

   (c) Remain constant with altitude

   (d) Decrease as altitude decreases

19. If thrust available exceeds that required for level flight:

   (a) The aircraft accelerates if altitude is maintained

   (b) The aircraft descends if airspeed is maintained

   (c) The aircraft decelerates if it is in the region of reversed command

   (d) The aircraft decelerates if the altitude is maintained

20. What happens to a wing that is evenly contaminated with a small amount of ice?

   (a) Weight is increased, drag is reduced

   (b) Weight is increased, drag is increased, lift is significantly reduced

   (c) Drag and Lift coefficients are increased due to the extra weight

   (d) Weight is increased and rate of descent is reduced

21. Climbing at constant power and airspeed, the lift that opposes the weight of the aircraft will be:

   (a) Slightly greater than the weight

   (b) A lot greater than the weight

   (c) Less than the weight

   (d) The same as the weight

22. The TORA plus the clearway is called what?

   (a) TODA

   (b) ASDA

   (c) EMD

   (d) Stopway

23. What is the gradient of a runway with one end at 420 feet and the other at 465 ft above sea level?

   (a) 2.25%

   (b) 1.95%

   (c) 1.65%

   (d) 1.35%

24. In the graph, what airspeed gives maximum range?

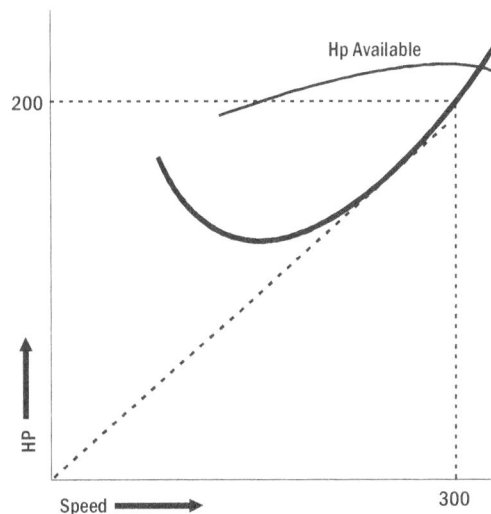

   (a) The bottom of the power required curve

   (b) Where the HP curve crosses power required

   (c) Where the tangent from the origin touches the power required curve

   (d) The start of the power required curve

25. Using wing flaps in the takeoff position during takeoff:

   (a) Is done for safety reasons

   (b) provides a large increase in lift and drag and a reduction in takeoff safety speed (V_2)

   (c) Increases lift with a small drag penalty, and reduces stall, unstick and takeoff safety speeds, the ground run and angle of climb

   (d) Provides a small increase in lift with a large drag penalty

26. Increasing an aircraft's all up weight by 15% increases the landing distance by how much?

(a) 10%

(a) 12%

(a) 15%

(b) 20%

27. The IAS at which an aeroplane stalls in straight and level flight is not affected by a change in:

(a) altitude

(b) wing loading

(c) TAS

(d) speed

28. A wing will enter a stalled condition when:

(a) The airspeed is too slow

(b) The angle of attack is too large

(c) The angle of incidence equals the angle of attack

(d) The angle of attack is within 5% of the angle of incidence

29. The target speed at 50 ft on the approach that will allow a full stop landing within the landing distance should be at least:

(a) 1.43 x the stalling speed in the landing configuration

(b) 1.3 x the stalling speed in the landing configuration

(c) 1.25 x the stalling speed in the landing configuration

(d) 1.5 x the stalling speed in the landing configuration

30. Your aeroplane is in a steep dive with a fixed pitch propeller. Excessive engine RPM would:

(a) be prevented by reducing the throttle setting

(b) not occur because the propeller acts as a flywheel

(c) not be a problem because the clutch in the propeller hub would disengage

(d) not occur because of the increased drag from the propeller

31. For what purpose is the best rate of climb used? To gain the greatest amount of height:

(a) with the longest travel over the surface

(b) with the shortest travel over the surface

(c) in the shortest period of time

(d) as gently as possible

32. What happens to the TAS for the best rate of climb when climbing to altitude?

(a) It increases

(b) It decreases

(c) It remains more or less the same

(d) It increases at a greater rate

33. You are in cloud and notice ice forming on the wing. What is the best action?

(a) Climb above the cloud

(b) Find a warmer part of the cloud

(c) Make a 180° turn or descend into warmer air (terrain permitting), or both

(d) Carry on and hope that it will go away

34. Which of the following would result in degraded performance and handling qualities?

(a) A Normal Category aeroplane that is constantly doing extreme manoeuvres at maximum weight

(b) Any aeroplane operated above its normal landing weight

(c) An aeroplane constantly operated at V_{NE}

(d) Any aeroplane that is overweight

35. What restrictions apply to aeroplanes in the Normal category?

(a) Max weight below 5700 kg, no spinning or aerobatics, max bank angle of 60°

(b) Max weight below 2400 kg, some aerobatics, max bank angle of 45°

(c) Max weight below 5700 kg, some aerobatics, max bank angle of 30°

(d) Max weight below 5700 kg, no spinning or aerobatics, max bank angle of 90°

36. If an aeroplane with a lift/drag ratio of 6:1 was at 6000 feet, how far would it glide in still air conditions? Around:

(a) 3 nm

(b) 2 nm

(c) 6 nm

(d) 12 nm

37. Published performance data is based on aircraft operating on:

(a) Long grass

(b) Short grass

(c) A hard runway with a maximum slope of 5°

(d) A level, hard, dry runway

38. Why does altering the power setting of an aeroplane change the pitch attitude?

(a) The propeller has a gyroscopic effect

(b) The thrust line is not aligned with the drag line

(c) The difference between parasite and induced drag

(d) The lift line is not in line with the drag line

39. In straight and level cruise, how is any instability caused by increased lift compensated for?

(a) By the pilot, with a change in power

(b) An up force from the tailplane

(c) A down force from the tailplane

(d) A downwards force from the ailerons

40. You notice that your TAS is a lot less than your groundspeed when landing. What is happening?

(a) There is an inversion

(b) The runway is moving

(c) You have a tailwind

(d) You have a headwind

41. You want the aircraft to maintain a constant attitude after changing the power. The elevator trim:

(a) Should be adjusted once the speed has stabilised after the power change

(b) Does not need adjustment

(c) Should be adjusted just before the power change

(d) Should be adjusted at the same time as the power change

42. By how much should the landing distance on wet short grass be factored?

(a) 1.2

(b) 1.4

(c) 1.35

(d) 1.8

43. by how much should the landing distance on dry grass less than 8 inches long be factored?

(a) 1.1

(b) 1.2

(c) 1.15

(d) 1.4

44. Why should the airspeed be kept relatively high during a prolonged climb?

(a) You will get the required height as quickly as possible.

(b) It gives a smoother airflow over the tailplane

(c) The airflow over the engine compensates for the lower speed for cooling purposes

(d) It brings you nearer to the best angle of climb

45. How much extra landing distance do you need if the runway slopes down by 2%?

(a) 5%

(b) 10%

(c) 12.5%

(d) 13%

46. A runway 2500 feet long has an elevation at each end of 400 feet and 375 feet. Taking off from the lower end, what is the average slope?

(a) 1.1% upslope

(b) 0.1% downslope

(c) 11% upslope

(d) 0.1% upslope

47. In the graph, what airspeed gives maximum endurance?

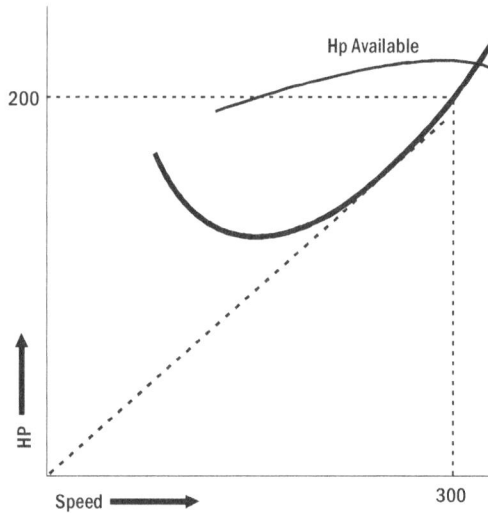

(a) The bottom of the power required curve

(b) Where the HP curve crosses power required

(c) Where the tangent from the origin touches the power required curve

(d) The start of the power required curve

48. Using the graph at Figure 8 in the Appendix, with flaps at the approach setting, in ISA conditions at 4 000 feet and a 10 knot headwind, what would be the approximate takeoff distance to reach a screen height of 50 feet for an aircraft weighing 3 400 lbs?

(a) 2 800 feet

(b) 3 000 feet

(c) 2 000 feet

(d) 1 900 feet

49. An aircraft weighing 2450 lbs without speed fairings is cruising at 4 000 feet PA in ISA +20 conditions with the engine set at 1900 RPM. Using the table at Figure 13 in the Appendix, determine the %BHP, TAS and fuel flow.

(a) 48, 87, 5.6

(b) 50, 89, 5.8

(c) 49, 85, 5.6

(d) 53, 92, 6.0

50. Using this extract from a flight plan and fuel log, what fuel should be left in the tanks on arrival at C?

WP		ETA	Fuel Rem	ATA	Fuel Act
A		10:25	33.3	10:25	33.3
B		11:05	27.3	11:05	27.6
C		11:55	22.9		

(a) 23.9 gallons

(b) 26.2 gallons

(c) 27.5 gallons

(d) 21.9 gallons

51. What effects on performance arise from overloading?

(a) Faster acceleration and shorter takeoff runs

(b) Increased range, decreased endurance

(c) Increased takeoff speed and decreased stalling speed

(d) Increased takeoff distance and stalling speed

52. Which runway surface will use the greatest takeoff distance?

(a) A hard, dry surface

(b) Short, dry grass

(c) Long, dry grass

(d) Long, wet grass

53. How will a 2% downslope affect the landing distance?

(a) It will increase by 10%

(b) It will decrease by 10%

(c) It will increase by 20%

(d) It will increase by 15%

54. How will a 10% increase in mass affect the landing distance?

(a) It will decrease by 20%

(b) It will decrease by 10%

(c) It will increase by 20%

(d) It will increase by 15%

55. An overweight aeroplane:

(a) will have a higher stalling speed and better climb performance

(b) will have a lower takeoff speed and a longer takeoff run

(c) will perform unpredictably, handle badly and may suffer structural damage

(d) will have a higher stalling speed and reduced climb performance

56. Using the table below, what will be the maximum rate of climb for an aircraft at 5 000 PA with an OAT of 10°C?

PA (ft)	KIAS	Rate Of Climb (FPM)			
		-20C	0C	20C	40C
SL	79	830	770	705	640
2000	77	720	655	595	535
4000	76	645	585	525	465
6000	74	530	475	415	360
8000	72	420	365	310	250
10000	71	310	255	200	145
12000	69	200	145	-	-

(a) 535 fpm

(b) 575 fpm

(c) 500 fpm

(d) 475 fpm

57. If the stalling speed in the landing configuration is 45 kts, what is the approximate minimum approach speed?

(a) 52 kts

(b) 46 kts

(c) 55 kts

(d) 59 kts

58. Which profile represents a takeoff with zero flaps?

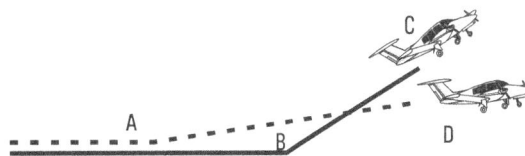

(a) A to C

(b) A to D

(c) B to C

(d) B to D

59. An aeroplane takes off at sea level on a standard day and climbs to 3 500 ft PA. using the table, how long does it take, over what distance, and how much fuel does it use?

PA	°C	KIAS	ROC	From Sea Level		
				Mins	Fuel	Dist
SL	15	79	720	0	0.0	0
1 000	13	78	670	1	0.4	2
2 000	11	77	625	3	0.7	4
3 000	9	76	575	5	1.2	6
4 000	7	76	560	6	1.5	8
5 000	5	75	515	8	1.8	11
6 000	3	74	465	10	2.1	14
7 000	1	73	415	13	2.5	17
8 000	-1	72	365	15	3.0	21
9 000	-3	72	315	18	3.4	25
10 000	-5	71	270	22	4.0	29
11 000	-7	70	220	26	4.6	35
12 000	-9	69	170	31	5.4	43

Flaps up, Full throttle, ISA conditions. Add 1.1 gallons for start, taxi and takeoff. Increase time, fuel and distance by 10% for each 10°C above standard temperature.

(a) 5.5 minutes, 2.5 gallons, 7 nm

(b) 7.5 minutes, 4.5 gallons, 9nm

(c) 6.5 minutes, 5.5 gallons, 8nm

(d) 8.5 minutes, 3.5 gallons, 9nm

HELICOPTERS

1. In the HIGE chart at Figure 7 in the Appendix, what is the maximum weight for the helicopter to hover IGE on a 16°C day at a Pressure Altitude of 8000 feet?

(a) 1695 lbs

(b) 1725 lbs

(c) 1785 lbs

(d) 1795 lbs

2. Which statement is true regarding helicopter weight and balance?

(a) The moment of tail-mounted components is subject to constant change

(b) Regardless of internal or external loading, lateral axis C of G control is ordinarily not a factor in maintaining helicopter weight and balance

(c) Weight and balance procedures for aeroplanes generally also apply to helicopters

(d) The Zero Fuel Weight is not important

3. As altitude increases, the V_{NE} of most helicopters:

(a) Increases

(b) Remains the same

(c) Decreases

(d) Depends on the density altitude

4. The most power is needed to hover over which type of surface?

(a) Rough/uneven ground

(b) Concrete ramp

(c) High grass

(d) Water

5. What is one significant aspect of taking off from a helipad 120 feet above the ground? As you rotate:

(a) You don't need power in hand

(b) You could be in the height/velocity curve

(c) Drift down is not required

(d) Floats should be set manually if an engine fails

6. Is the centre of London a hostile environment?

(a) No

(b) Yes

(c) Not for Category B aircraft

(d) Not for Category A aircraft

7. How does high density altitude affect rotorcraft performance?

(a) It increases rotor drag, which requires more power for normal flight

(b) It decreases rotor drag, which requires more power for normal flight

(c) Engine and rotor efficiency is reduced

(d) Engine and rotor efficiency is increased

8. During downwind landings, pilots should expect a faster:

(a) Groundspeed at touchdown, longer ground roll, likelihood of overshooting

(b) Groundspeed at touchdown, shorter ground roll, likelihood of undershooting.

(c) Airspeed at touchdown, longer ground roll, and better control

(d) Airspeed at touchdown, shorter ground roll, no change in control

9. A helicopter is loaded so that the C of G is aft of the allowable limits. Which statement is true about this situation?

(a) This condition would become more hazardous as fuel is consumed, if the main fuel tank is aft of the rotor mast

(b) If the helicopter should pitch up during high-speed flight, there may not be enough forward cyclic control to lower the nose

(c) In an autorotation, enough aft cyclic control may not be available to flare

(d) There is no effect

10. A helicopter is loaded so that the C of G is forward of the allowable C of G limits. What is true about this situation?

(a) It would become less hazardous as fuel is consumed if the fuel tank is aft of the rotor mast

(b) Should the machine pitch up during cruise flight, there may not be enough forward cyclic control to lower the nose

(c) In an autorotation, enough cyclic control may not be available to flare properly to land

(d) There is no effect

11. Improper loading of a helicopter which exceeds fore or aft C of G limits is hazardous because:

(a) Coriolis effect might be translated to the fuselage

(b) Reduction or loss of effective collective pitch control

(c) Reduction or loss of effective cyclic pitch control

(d) The main rotor mast might be subject to lateral stress

12. The C of G range in single-rotor helicopters is:

(a) Much greater than that for aeroplanes

(b) More restricted than that for aeroplanes

(c) Approximately the same as that for aeroplanes

(d) Exactly the same as that for aeroplanes

13. Aft centre of gravity in a helicopter limits the:

(a) Ability to stop, flare, or recover from a steep descent

(b) Center of pressure travel along the blades

(c) Upper allowable airspeed range

(d) Lower allowable airspeed range

14. Too much forward cyclic during flight may be due to:

(a) A tendency of the nose to pitch up due to transverse flow effect

(b) Critical aft C of G

(c) Excessive forward speed at maximum gross weight

(d) Sloppy control linkage

15. While hovering, too much forward cyclic is needed to maintain position over the ground. If flight is continued, this situation will be:

(a) Aggravated if the fuel tanks are forward of the C of G

(b) Unimproved regardless of the where the fuel tanks are

(c) Aggravated if the fuel tanks are aft of the CG

(d) Normal

16. In the cruise, an extreme aft longitudinal centre of gravity in a helicopter:

(a) Moves the cyclic away from its forward stop and increases the stress in the rotor head

(b) Brings the cyclic stick closer to its forward stop and decreases the stress in the rotor head

(c) Moves the cyclic stick away from its forward stop and decreases the stresses in the rotor head

(d) Brings the cyclic stick closer to its forward stop and increases the stress in the rotor head

17. What is the longitudinal C of G for this aircraft?

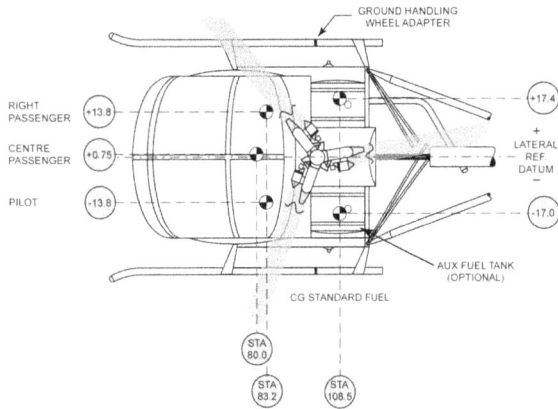

Item	Wt	Arm	Mom
Aircraft	1400	85	
Pilot	210		
Pax C	150		
Pax R			
Zero Fuel			
Fuel	200		
Total			

(a) 89.67

(b) 89.68

(c) 89.69

(d) 89.70

18. Using the following data, what is the C of G of a helicopter, if the pilot weight is 190 lbs and the front passenger weight is 210 lbs, and there is 50 lbs of baggage, with 35 US Gals on board? (SG is 6.6)

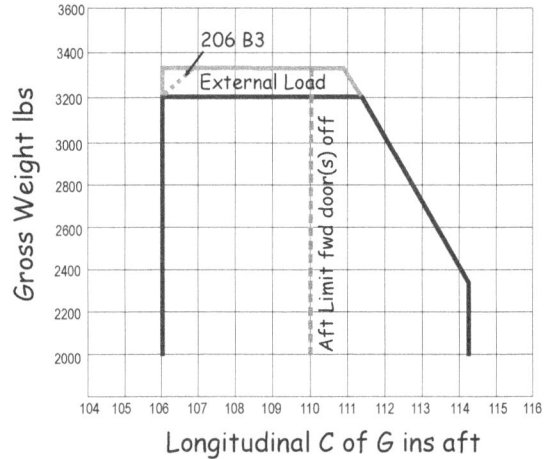

Is the C of G within limits for the flight?

Item	Wt	Arm	Moment
Aircraft	1881	116.5	
Front pax		65	
Rear Pax		104	
Baggage		147.50	
Zero Fuel CG			
Fuel	310		
Total			

Fuel (US Gals)/Moment

5	109.40
10	110.00
15	110.30
20	110.40
25	110.50
30	110.50
35	110.70
40	111.10
45	112.10
50	113.10

(a) 108.55, Yes

(b) 108.55, No

(c) 108.33, Yes

(d) 108.33, No

© *Phil Croucher, 2016*

If this page is a photocopy, it is not authorised!

19. What is the most favourable combination of conditions for rotorcraft performance?

    (a) Low density altitude, low gross weight, and moderate to strong wind

    (b) Low density altitude, high gross weight, and calm to light wind

    (c) High density altitude, low gross weight, and moderate to strong wind

    (d) High density altitude, high gross weight, and calm to light wind

20. Performance of a helicopter can be determined by:

    (a) The highest altitude that can be maintained in a hover after liftoff

    (b) The formula pi times the rotor diameter divided by the blade area

    (c) Knowing the density altitude, gross weight, and surface wind

    (d) The load factor

21. With 28 US gallons already on board, how many litres must be added to make the total 96 US gallons?

    (a) 199

    (b) 254

    (c) 157

    (d) 372

22. Referring to Figure 4 in the Appendix, what is the fuel flow at 2000 ft with 20.3 inches Hg MAP?

    (a) 9.6 gal/hour

    (b) 55 lbs/hour

    (c) 10.1 gal/hour

    (d) 60.5lbs/hour

23. The V_{NE} of a helicopter is effectively determined by:

    (a) engine power available, it occurs at the upper intersection of the power available and power required curves

    (b) the ability of the tail rotor to balance the torque produced at high speeds

    (c) retreating blade stall and/or the advancing blade approaching the speed of sound

    (d) maximum collective pitch available to counteract retreating blade stall

24. If the helicopter in the picture experiences a total engine failure at 20kts, it will:

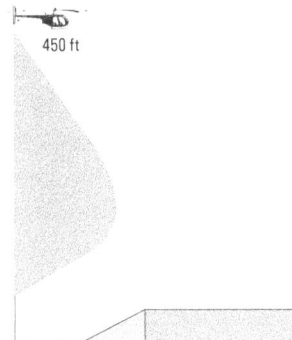

450 ft

    (a) be guaranteed a safe autorotational landing

    (b) not be able to make a safe autorotational landing as it must descend into the low speed section

    (c) be in a position where, depending on the skill and reactions of the pilot, a safe autorotational landing may be made

    (d) not be able to make a safe autorotational landing as its airspeed must be above 35 kts

25. Referring to Figure 3 in the Appendix, what is the rate of climb at 9000 ft at 1,800 lbs?

    (a) 460 fpm

    (b) 740 fpm

    (c) 720 fpm

    (d) 600 fpm

METEOROLOGY

GENERAL

1. Isobars connect points of equal:

   (a) Temperature

   (b) Pressure

   (c) Windspeed

   (d) Humidity

2. What does the term *inversion* mean?

   (a) Pressure decreases with height

   (b) Pressure increases with height

   (c) Temperature decreases with height

   (d) Temperature increases with height

3. An air mass is an extensive body of air within which:

   (a) Temperature and humidity are almost uniform horizontally

   (a) Temperature & humidity do not change with height

   (a) Temperature and pressure are almost uniform vertically

   (a) Pressure and humidity are almost uniform in any direction

4. How is advection heating characterised?

   (a) Air being heated from below

   (b) Air being heated by moving over a warm surface

   (c) Air being heated by subsidence

   (d) Air being heated by the sun

5. Which of the following indicates that the wind has backed?

   (a) 050° changing to 070°

   (b) 130° changing to 310°

   (c) 050° changing to 040°

   (d) 190° changing to 195°

6. Which of the following terms indicate vertical motion?

   (a) Trough

   (b) Advection

   (c) Conduction

   (d) Convergence

7. What process changes water vapour directly to ice crystals?

   (a) Condensation

   (b) Freezing

   (c) Evaporation

   (d) Deposition (Sublimation)

8. What process changes frost directly to water vapour?

   (a) Condensation

   (b) Melting

   (c) Sublimation

   (d) Evaporation

9. What does the term *gradient* describe?

   (a) The wind strength

   (b) The horizontal change in pressure with distance

   (c) The steepness of the pressure drop

   (d) The steepness of the lapse rate

10. What is the essential difference between a gust and a squall?

    (a) Speed

    (b) Direction

    (c) Duration

    (d) Change

11. The lapse rate generally means a rate of change in:

    (a) Pressure

    (b) Wind

    (c) Temperature

    (d) Any of the above

12. How can orographic lift be caused?

    (a) Rising ground

    (b) Rough ground

    (c) Wind

    (d) Any of the above

13. What might radiant cooling cause?

    (a) Fog

    (b) A shallow lapse rate

    (c) Stability

    (d) Any of the above

14. Through an isothermal layer, what is the lapse rate?

    (a) Negative

    (b) Zero

    (c) Positive

    (d) Atmospheric

15. What is the Troposphere?

    (a) The boundary between the Tropopause and the Stratosphere

    (b) Part of the atmosphere above the Stratopause

    (c) Part of the atmosphere below the Tropopause

    (d) The boundary between the Mesosphere and the Thermosphere

16. As air rises, why does it cool?

    (a) The surrounding air is cooler at higher levels

    (b) Air becomes more moist

    (c) It contracts

    (d) It expands

17. Where is the Tropopause lower?

    (a) In the summer than in the winter

    (b) Over the Equator than over the North Pole

    (c) Over the North Pole than over the Equator

    (d) In the Southern Hemisphere

18. Why are areas of sinking air generally cloudless? Because as the air sinks it:

    (a) Is heated by compression

    (b) Reached warmer layers

    (c) Loses water vapour

    (d) Is heated by expansion

19. What does the term *moisture in the air* refer to?

    (a) Clouds

    (b) Precipitation

    (c) Fog

    (d) Water vapour

20. If the surface temperature is 22°C, what would the temperature at 10 000 feet be?

    (a) 2°C

    (b) 9°C

    (c) 6°C

    (d) 7°C

21. What is True Altitude?

    (a) Actual height above sea level after correcting for all errors

    (b) Altitude above the surface

    (c) Altitude reference to the standard datum plane

    (d) Altitude shown on a radar altimeter

22. ISA specifies a sea level temperature of ___°C, a sea level pressure of ___ hPa, moisture in the air as ___, and lapse rate of ___°C per thousand feet.

(a) 60, 1013, Nil, 2.0

(b) 15, 29.92, 10%, 1.98

(c) 15, 1013.25, Nil, 1.98

(d) 15, 1013, 10%, 2.0

23. What degree of turbulence would you expect beneath cumulonimbus clouds?

(a) Nil

(b) Moderate

(c) Moderate to severe

(d) Light

24. What is a low pressure system also known as?

(a) A col or depression

(b) A cyclone or col

(c) A cyclone or depression

(d) An Anticyclone

25. What is a high pressure system also known as?

(a) Trowal

(b) Anticyclone

(c) Trough

(d) Col

26. If sea level pressure remains constant, the altitude of a given pressure level would be _____ in warm air:

(a) Higher

(b) Lower

(c) Same

(d) It depends on the water vapour content

27. Density altitude is the:

(a) Altitude reference to the standard datum plane

(b) Altitude read directly from the altimeter

(c) Pressure altitude corrected for non-standard temperature

(d) Altitude above the surface

28. What causes wind?

(a) Changes in humidity

(b) Changes in lapse rates

(c) Vertical pressure differences

(d) Horizontal pressure differences

29. If the wind is from the North, where does the low pressure lie?

(a) To the North

(b) To the South

(c) To the East

(d) To the West

30. From where do land breezes flow?

(a) Sea to land during the day

(b) Land to sea during the day

(c) Land to sea at night

(d) Sea to land at night

31. Descending from 4000 feet AGL, what would you expect the wind to do?

(a) Veer and then back

(b) Back and decrease speed

(c) Veer and decrease speed

(d) Veer and increase speed

32. How would you find pressure altitude?

(a) Set 1013 in the altimeter setting window and read the indicated altitude

(b) Set the altimeter to zero feet and read the value in the altimeter window

(c) Set the altimeter to the field elevation and read the value in the altimeter setting window

(d) Set the field elevation in the altimeter setting window and read the indicated altitude

33. At a cold front:

(a) Warm air is compressed as colder air rises over it

(b) Fog forms from the interaction of warm and cold air

(c) Warmer air is lifted as colder air pushes under it

(d) Temperature rising owing to an increase in pressure

34. A warm air mass moving slowly over very cold ground would most likely result in:

(a) Moderate clear air turbulence in the lower levels

(b) Smooth flight conditions in the lower levels

(c) Thunderstorm activity

(d) An overcast of Stratocumulus

35. What are the effects of cold weather in mountains at night?

(a) The altimeter reads lower than the actual altitude

(b) The altimeter reads higher than actual altitude

(c) You must set the altimeter to standard pressure

(d) The static ports might freeze over

36. How are the lower levels of the atmosphere heated?

(a) By conduction, from the Earth's surface

(b) By radiation from the Sun

(c) By advection

(d) By convection

37. The dry adiabatic lapse rate is 3°C/1000 feet, which is the rate at which dry air cools when it:

(a) Descends

(b) Rises

(c) Accepts moisture

(d) Releases moisture

38. If the wind backs gradually from SE to NE when a low pressure system moves past a station, where has the centre of the low passed? To the _____ of the station.

(a) South

(b) West

(c) Northeast

(d) North

39. What does term *convergence* mean?

(a) The advance of a cold air mass upon a warm air mass

(b) The transfer of heat by warm air rising up through cooler layers

(c) A neutral area of mid pressure

(d) The accumulation of air caused by air flowing towards the centre of a high pressure area

40. What is radiation fog caused by?

(a) Warm, moist air moving over a cold surface

(b) Loss of heat to the atmosphere over land on clear nights with light winds

(c) Adiabatic expansion and cooling of the air mass as it moves up a slope

(d) Saturation of cold air by precipitation falling form overlying warm air

41. Which of the following is true concerning the passage of a cold front?

(a) The wind direction will veer, temperature will decrease and dew point will increase

(b) The wind will back, temperature and dewpoint will increase

(c) The wind will veer, temperature and dewpoint will decrease

(d) The wind will back, temperature will decrease but the dew point will remain constant

42. From the warm air side, how would you recognise passage through a warm front?

(a) Port drift

(b) Starboard drift

(c) An increase in temp

(d) A sudden improvement in the weather

43. Flying in a constant direction you notice the following cloud sequence: cirrus, cirrostratus, altostratus, nimbostratus. What are you approaching?

(a) A cold front from the cold air side

(b) A warm front from the cold air side

(c) An occluded warm front from the warm air side

(d) A warm front from the warm air side

44. What is advection fog caused by?

(a) Warm dry air passing over a cold moist surface

(b) Cold moist air passing over a warm surface

(c) Warm moist air passing over a cold surface

(d) Diurnal effect

45. When might carburettor icing be greatest?

    (a)   +10°C, high humidity, high cruise RPM

    (b)   -10°C, high humidity, low cruise RPM

    (c)   +10°C, low humidity, idle RPM

    (d)   +10°C, high humidity, idle RPM

46. In temperatures well below standard, how might the altimeter read?

    (a)   Lower than the actual height

    (b)   Correctly, providing the local altimeter setting is used

    (c)   Higher than the actual height

    (d)   Correctly, if the standard altimeter setting is used

47. Flying along a shoreline in warm weather, what is an extensive fog bank offshore most likely to be?

    (a)   Advection fog

    (b)   Radiation fog

    (c)   Sublimation

    (d)   Arctic sea smoke

48. You park overnight where the altimeter reads 600 feet. During the night a low pressure system moves into the area, so in the morning the altimeter might read:

    (a)   Lower

    (b)   Higher

    (c)   Same as before

    (d)   The subscale would read higher

49. With a pressure altitude of 6000', OAT of -20°C and an IAS of 130 kts, what is your density altitude and TAS?

    (a)   3000', 136 kts

    (b)   6200, 118 kts

    (c)   5700', 124 kts

    (d)   8000', 147 kts

50. What cloud type is usually associated with steady rain?

    (a)   Altostratus

    (b)   Altocumulus

    (c)   Stratocumulus

    (d)   Nimbostratus

51. Clouds form when moist warm air overruns cold air because the warm air:

    (a)   Is cooled by the cold air underneath

    (b)   Is cooled by the surrounding cold air aloft

    (c)   Becomes unstable due to cooling from below

    (d)   Cools because of expansion as it is forced to rise

52. The following cloud progression is observed: cirrus, altostratus, nimbostratus. What can you expect?

    (a)   The passage of a cold front

    (b)   Anticyclonic weather

    (c)   The passage of a warm front

    (d)   Clearing skies and a decrease in temperature

53. What are fallstreaks or virga?

    (a)   Strong katabatic winds in mountainous areas and accompanied by heavy precipitation

    (b)   Water or ice particles falling out of a cloud that evaporate before reaching the ground

    (c)   Strong downdraughts in the polar jet stream, associated with jet streaks

    (d)   Gusts associated with a well developed Bora

54. Freezing rain encountered during a climb is normally evidence that:

    (a)   A layer of warmer air exists above

    (b)   A climb can be made to a higher altitude without encountering more than light icing

    (c)   A descent can be made to a lower altitude without encountering more than light icing

    (d)   Ice pellets at higher altitudes have changed to rain in the warmer air below

55. Which of the following are medium level clouds?

    (a)   Cumulonimbus

    (b)   All convective clouds

    (c)   Altostratus and altocumulus

    (d)   Cirrocumulus and cirrostratus

56. The amount of water vapour which air can hold depends on what?

   (a) Dewpoint

   (b) Air temperature

   (c) Stability of the air

   (d) Humidity

57. What cloud types would indicate convective turbulence?

   (a) Cirrus

   (b) Nimbostratus

   (c) Towering cumulus

   (d) Lenticular

58. Which of the following cloud types is least likely to produce precipitation?

   (a) NS

   (b) CI

   (c) AS

   (d) CB

59. What type of cloud can produce hail showers?

   (a) CB

   (b) NS

   (c) CS

   (d) AC

60. In which of the following regions does polar maritime air originate?

   (a) Round the British Isles

   (b) Baltic Sea

   (c) Black Sea

   (d) East of Greenland

61. In which of the following situations can freezing rain be encountered?

   (a) Ahead of a cold front in the winter

   (b) Ahead of a warm front in the winter

   (c) Behind a warm front in the summer

   (d) Ahead of a cold front in the summer

62. How does freezing rain develop?

   (a) Snow falls through a layer where temperatures are above 0°C

   (b) Rain falls through a layer where temperatures are below 0°C

   (c) Through melting of snow grains

   (d) Through melting of ice crystals

63. Clouds, fog or dew will always be formed when:

   (a) Water vapour is present

   (b) Water vapour condenses

   (c) Relative humidity reaches 98%

   (d) Temperature and dew point are nearly equal

64. *Ceiling* is defined as the height above the Earth's surface of the:

   (a) Lowest reported obscuration and the highest layer of clouds reported as overcast

   (b) Lowest layer of clouds or obscuring phenomena reported as broken, overcast, and not classified as thin or partial

   (c) Lowest layer of clouds reported as scattered, broken, or thin

   (d) Lowest visible moisture

65. Which degree of aircraft turbulence is determined by the following ICAO description?

There may be moderate changes in aircraft attitude and/or altitude but the aircraft remains in positive control at all times. Usually, small variations in air speed. Changes in accelerometer readings of 0.5 to 1.0 g at the aircraft's centre of gravity. Occupants feel strain against seat belts. Loose objects move about. Food service and walking are difficult

   (a) Light

   (b) Moderate

   (c) Severe

   (d) Violent

66. The density of air is:

    (a) Inversely proportional to pressure and temperature

    (b) Directly proportional to pressure and temperature

    (c) Directly proportional to pressure and inversely proportional to temperature

    (d) Inversely proportional to pressure and directly proportional to temperature

67. Which of the following is a cause of stratus forming over flat land?

    (a) Radiation during the night from the earth's surface in moderate wind

    (b) Unstable air

    (c) Convection during the day

    (d) The release of latent heat

68. Which of the following processes within a layer of air may lead to the building of CU and CB clouds?

    (a) Convection

    (b) Radiation

    (c) Subsidence

    (d) Frontal lifting within stable layers

69. What are the characteristics of cumuliform clouds?

    (a) Small water droplets, stability, no turbulence and extensive areas of rain

    (b) Large water droplets, stability, no turbulence, showers and mainly rime ice

    (c) Large water droplets, instability, turbulence, showers and mainly clear ice

    (d) Small water droplets, instability, turbulence, extensive areas of rain and rime ice

70. Which of the following types of clouds are evidence of unstable air conditions?

    (a) ST, CS

    (b) SC, NS

    (c) CI, SC

    (d) CU, CB

71. Which of the following clouds are classified as medium level clouds in temperate regions?

    (a) SC, NS

    (b) CI, CC

    (c) AS, AC

    (d) CS, ST

72. How does moderate turbulence affect an aircraft?

    (a) Changes in altitude or attitude occur but the aircraft remains in positive control

    (b) Rapid and somewhat rhythmic bumpiness is experienced without appreciable changes in altitude or attitude

    (c) Large, abrupt changes in altitude or attitude occur but the aircraft may only be out of control momentarily

    (d) Continued flight in this environment will result in structural damage

73. What is the main composition of high level clouds?

    (a) Supercooled water droplets

    (b) Water droplets

    (c) Water vapour

    (d) Ice crystals

74. Which of the following cloud is classified as low level?

    (a) ST

    (b) CS

    (c) AS

    (d) CC

75. Which of the following clouds may extend into more than one layer?

    (a) Nimbostratus

    (b) Stratus

    (c) Altocumulus

    (d) Cirrus

76. Which of the following types of cloud is most likely to produce heavy precipitation?

   (a) NS

   (b) CS

   (c) SC

   (d) ST

77. What process in an air mass leads to the creation of wide spread NS and AS coverage?

   (a) Sinking

   (b) Lifting

   (c) Convection process

   (d) Radiation

78. In this TAF:

```
FCNL31 281500

EGAM 281601 14010KT 6000 -RA SCT025
BECMG 1618 12015G25KT SCT008 BKN013
TEMPO 1823 3000 RA BKN005 OVC010
BECMG 2301 25020KT 8000 NSW BKN020
=
```

What lowest cloud base is forecast for arrival at 2100 UTC?

   (a) 250 ft

   (b) 500 ft

   (c) 500 m

   (d) 800 ft

79. In the TAF extract in Q 78, what visibility is forecast for 2400 UTC?

   (a) 2000 m

   (b) 500 m

   (c) Between 500 m and 2000 m

   (d) Between 0 m and 1000 m

80. In the TAF extract in Q78, what does the abbreviation VV001 mean?

   (a) RVR less than 100 m

   (b) RVR greater than 100 m

   (c) Vertical visibility 100 m

   (d) Vertical visibility 100 ft

81. What does the term METAR signify?

   (a) A METAR is a warning of dangerous meteorological conditions within a FIR

   (b) A METAR is a flight forecast, issued by the meteorological station several times daily

   (c) A METAR is a landing forecast added to the actual weather report as a brief prognostic report

   (d) A METAR is the actual weather report at an aerodrome and is generally issued in half-hourly intervals

82. What does the abbreviation PROB30 mean?

   (a) Conditions will probably last for at least 30 minutes

   (b) Probability of 30%

   (c) The cloud ceiling should lift to 3000 ft

   (d) Change expected in less than 30 minutes

83. A METAR describes the weather:

   (a) Expected at a station at a given time

   (b) Expected at a station over a twelve hour period

   (c) Observed at a station at the time of the report

   (d) Observed at a station during the previous day

84. Would you expect to carry out a visual approach at this airfield?

```
EGLL 0550 21008 0600 R0560 45FG
9///// 18/17 1020 GRADU 3000 7ST006
```

   (a) No

   (b) Maybe

   (c) Yes, no problem

   (d) Yes, after about another 5 mins

85. Vertical visibility is shown on METAR/TAF reports when the sky is:

   (a) Overcast

   (b) Partially obscured

   (c) Obscured

   (d) Clear

86. The station originating this METAR observation has a field elevation of 3,500 feet MSL. If the sky cover is one continuous layer, what is the thickness of the cloud layer? (Top of overcast reported at 7,500 feet MSL).

```
151250Z 17006KT 4SM OVC005 13/11
A2998
```

(a) 2,500 feet

(b) 3,500 feet

(c) 1,500 feet

(d) 3,000 feet

87. In a TAF during the summer, for the time of your landing you note: TEMPO TS. What is the maximum time this deterioration in weather can last?

(a) 120 minutes

(b) 10 minutes

(c) 20 minutes

(d) 60 minutes

88. In the following TAF:

```
BECMG 1821 2000 BKN004 PROB30 BECMG
2124 0500 FG VV001
```

What does BECMG indicate?

(a) The new conditions are achieved between 1800 and 2100 UTC

(b) A quick change to new conditions between 1800 and 1900 UTC

(c) Many short term changes in the original weather

(d) Many long term changes in the original weather

89. In the above TAF extract (see q 88), what does BKN004 mean?

(a) 5 - 7 oktas, ceiling 400 ft

(b) 1 - 4 oktas, ceiling 400 ft

(c) 4 - 8 oktas, ceiling 400 m

(d) 1 - 4 oktas, ceiling 400 m

90. How long from the time of observation is a TREND in a METAR valid?

(a) 2 hours

(b) 9 hours

(c) 1 hour

(d) 30 minutes

91. In the TAF in q 88, what surface wind is forecast for the same ETA?

(a) 120°/15 kt gusts 25 kt

(b) 140°/10 kt

(c) 300°/15 kt maximum wind 25 kt

(d) 250°/20 kt

92. In the TAF in q 88, what minimum visibility is forecast for the same ETA?

(a) 5 km

(b) 5 nm

(c) 6 km

(d) 3 km

93. If a wind of 08010KT is reported on a METAR, what would be the wind velocity at 2000 feet above the ground?

(a) 11020KT

(b) 08015KT

(c) 05020KT

(d) 08005KT

94. What does the abbreviation NOSIG mean?

(a) No report received

(b) No weather related problems

(c) Not signed by the meteorologist

(d) No significant changes expected over the next 2 hours

95. In which of the following 1850 UTC METAR reports, is the probability of fog formation, in the coming night, the highest?

(a) VRB01KT 8000 SCT250 11/10 Q1028 BECMG 3000 =

(b) 22004KT 6000 -RA SCT012 OVC030 17/14 Q1009 NOSIG =

(c) VRB02KT 2500 SCT120 14/M08 Q1035 NOSIG =

(d) 00000KT 9999 SCT300 21/01 Q1032 NOSIG =

96. What does a TAF time group of 0220 mean?

    (a) It is a long range TAF that is valid between 0200 - 2000 local time

    (b) It is a long range TAF that is valid between 0200 - 2000 UTC

    (c) The observation was made at 0220 UTC

    (d) The observation was issued at 0220 UTC

97. What is an AIRMET service?

    (a) A telephone service for aircrew without access to forecast charts, in text form, in plain language issued via the AFTN

    (b) A telephone, telex or fax service for aircrew without access to forecast charts, in plain language

    (c) A telephone, telex or fax service for private pilots at smaller airfields

    (d) A telephone, telex or fax service for aircrew unable to understand normal reports

98. The following VOLMET report was issued at 0450 UTC at some time in the Autumn in UK:

```
Surface Wind:    150/5 kts
Visibility:      2000 m
Weather:         Nil
Temperature:     9C
Dewpoint:        8C
QNH:             1029 hPa
Trend:           NOSIG
```

If sunrise is at 0600 UTC, in the two hours following the report, what is the most probable meteorological phenomenon that might develop?

    (a) CAVOK

    (b) Advection fog

    (c) Radiation fog

    (d) A low cloud base

99. You are flying into wind and see lenticular clouds ahead of you on top of a range of hills. What is ahead?

    (a) Strong anabatic currents above the hills

    (b) Strong katabatic currents above the hills

    (c) Strong katabatic currents in the lee of the hills

    (d) Strong downdraughts just before you get to the ridge, with the possibility of severe turbulence in or below roll cloud, with turbulence and strong updraughts after passing the ridge

100. With mountain waves, where might you expect the severest turbulence?

    (a) Midway between the rotor and lenticular clouds

    (b) Just above any roll clouds

    (c) Just below the ridge

    (d) In or below roll clouds, downwind of the ridge

101. Which of the following is true of windshear in the lowest levels?

    (a) It is unlikely if there is an inversion close to the surface

    (b) It is found under thunderstorms

    (c) It is common in mountain waves

    (d) You can get it 15-20 minutes ahead of a moving thunderstorm

102. How far ahead of the surface position of a typical warm front in the UK might you expect to see rain?

    (a) 50 miles

    (b) 100 miles

    (c) 200 miles

    (d) 300 miles

103. Which frontal system is most likely to produce thunderstorms?

    (a) A cold front

    (b) A warm front

    (c) A warm occlusion

    (d) A trough of low pressure

104. Mist is restricting your visibility at 2000 feet. How would you improve your view of the ground ahead?

    (a) Fly close to the top of the mist layer

    (b) Fly higher

    (c) Fly lower

    (d) Fly close to the ground

105. Where might you see frontal fog?

    (a) Behind a cold front

    (b) Ahead of a cold front

    (c) Ahead of a warm or occluded front

    (d) Where a cold front meets the surface

106. Which list below describes clouds in the order of Low, Medium and High?

    (a) Stratus, Cumulonimbus, Cirrocumulus

    (b) Cumulonimbus, Stratocumulus

    (c) Nimbostratus, Altocumulus, Cirrus

    (d) Altocumulus, Cumulus

107. What levels of cloud do one or more coloured rings around the Sun or Moon indicate?

    (a) High

    (b) Low

    (c) High or Medium

    (d) Medium

108. How can you recognise unstable air?

    (a) Cumulus cloud with poor visibility and drizzle

    (b) Layered cloud with light rain and good visibility

    (c) Cumulus cloud with showers and generally good visibility

    (d) Layered cloud with continuous moderate rain and poor visibility

109. From which cloud are you most likely to get hail?

    (a) AC

    (b) NS

    (c) SC

    (d) CB

110. What does the use of the word *Nimbus* or *Nimbo* in a cloud's name indicate?

    (a) Wispy, with ice crystals

    (b) Rain bearing

    (c) Medium cloud

    (d) Extensive vertical development

111. Which of the following clouds are normally associated with drizzle?

    (a) Cumulonimbus and nimbostratus

    (b) Cirrostratus and stratocumulus

    (c) Nimbostratus

    (d) Stratus

112. If the wind at 2000 feet is 335/15 kts, what runway might you expect to land on?

    (a) 18

    (b) 31

    (c) 27

    (d) 36

113. What is water vapour?

    (a) A gas that takes up a large proportion of the Earth's atmosphere

    (b) A liquid suspended as clouds in the Earth's atmosphere

    (c) A liquid that falls as rain

    (d) A gas that condenses to form clouds in the Earth's atmosphere

114. When is the earth likely to be coldest when there is no cloud cover?

    (a) An hour before dawn

    (b) Around midnight

    (c) Around sunrise

    (d) Just after midnight and dawn

115. If the temperature at 1 000 feet is 24°C and the temperature at 2 000 feet is 20°C, in what condition would the air between the two altitudes be?

    (a) Stable

    (b) Conditionally Unstable

    (c) Unstable

    (d) Dry

116. What might happen to an air mass that starts off over North America in Winter and heads towards UK over the Atlantic?

    (a) It will cool down

    (b) It will become unsaturated

    (c) It will become saturated

    (d) Its humidity will increase from the warmer ocean

117. Flying towards low pressure at 4000 feet in the Northern hemisphere, what will happen to your aircraft?

    (a) It would slow down from the headwind

    (b) It would drift to the right

    (c) It would drift to the left

    (d) It would go faster from the tailwind

118. A moderate Westerly wind crosses a range of hills that lie N-S. Where is the most hazardous position?

    (a) Going towards the hills from the East

    (b) Going away from the hills to the East

    (c) Parallel to the hills, on the West side

    (d) Parallel to the hills, on the East side

119. Where is the likeliest place to get severe icing in a Cb?

    (a) Near the centre

    (b) Above the freezing level

    (c) 1 000 feet either side of the freezing level

    (d) Where the temperature is between 0 to -20°C

120. Where is the likeliest place to get rain ice?

    (a) Below the freezing level before a warm front

    (b) Below the freezing level behind a warm front

    (c) Above the freezing level before a warm front

    (d) Above the freezing level behind a warm front

121. Which condition will not produce carburettor icing?

    (a) Cruising 200 feet below cloud, with OAT 2°C

    (b) Descending with idle RPM in clear air with OAT of 17°C

    (c) Climbing in cloud with an OAT of -2°C

    (d) All the above will produce icing

122. The visibility forward of an aircraft if flight is:

    (a) RVR

    (b) Met visibility

    (c) Flight visibility

    (d) In-flight visibility

123. If the full Moon is in the West, where will the best visibility be? Looking:

    (a) North

    (b) South

    (c) East

    (d) West

124. Where is the surface wind from in this METAR?

```
071650Z 18006KT 9000 20/18 Q1020
```

    (a) From the South at 6 kts

    (b) From the South at 60 kts

    (c) From the North at 6 kts

    (d) From the West at 6 kts

125. What is the layer of the atmosphere closest to the Earth where light aircraft operate?

    (a) Stratosphere

    (b) Ionosphere

    (c) Troposphere

    (d) Mesosphere

126. What type of air mass produces cold, moist and unstable air over the UK?

    (a) Polar Continental

    (b) Arctic Continental

    (c) Polar Maritime

    (d) Returning Polar Maritime

127. How does the Pressure Gradient Force move air?

    (a) From low pressure to nearby low pressure areas

    (b) From high pressure to nearby high pressure areas

    (c) From low pressure to high pressure

    (d) From high pressure to low pressure

128. What is the phenomenon that replaces cold air with warm air at the surface?

   (a) Warm front

   (a) Warm occluded front

   (a) Cold front

   (a) Cold occluded front

129. What kind of weather is associated with a winter anticyclone in the UK?

   (a) Subsiding air keeps the clouds in one place, which increases humidity and reduces visibility

   (b) Subsiding air is cooled adiabatically, and may create an inversion, trapping smoke, haze and dust beneath it, leading to anticyclonic gloom and poor visibility

   (c) Subsiding air is warmed adiabatically, and may create an inversion, trapping smoke, haze and dust beneath it, leading to anticyclonic gloom and poor visibility

   (d) Subsiding air warms the surface which creates a low pressure and rain

130. If you have starboard drift in the Northern hemisphere, what might be happening to your altimeter?

   (a) It would be over-reading

   (b) It would be under-reading

   (c) Nothing

   (d) It would over-read at first, then settle down

131. What weather is most likely when an unstable air mass is lifted orographically?

   (a) Cumulus with extensive vertical development

   (b) Stratus

   (c) Cumulus cloud with icing

   (d) Lenticular cloud

132. What weather would you expect in a cold sector?

   (a) Scattered cloud with moderate visibility

   (b) Scattered cumulus with good visibility

   (c) Scattered stratus with good visibility

   (d) Broken stratus with poor visibility

133. What is the definition of VOLMET?

   (a) A report of weather conditions made by a pilot during routine matters

   (b) A report made by a pilot during the approach

   (c) A continuous radio broadcast of forecast weather conditions at selected aerodromes

   (d) A continuous radio broadcast of actual weather conditions at selected aerodromes

134. How far ahead should you request a Special Forecast for a flight less than 500 nm?

   (a) 2 hours

   (b) 3 hours

   (c) 4 hours

   (d) 6 hours

135. What does this symbol mean?

   (a) Severe icing

   (b) Moderate turbulence

   (c) Moderate aircraft icing

   (d) Rain coming from cloud

136. What does this symbol mean?

   (a) Sharp lapse rate

   (b) Lightning

   (c) Thunderstorms

   (d) Downdraughts

137. What is this?

   (a) A warm front

   (b) A cold front

   (c) An occlusion

   (d) None of the above

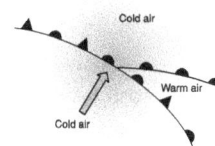

138. What type of heat energy causes weather?

   (a) Reradiation from clouds

   (b) Direct radiation from the Sun

   (c) Condensation of water vapour

   (d) Reradiation from the surface of the Earth

139. What happens to humidity if the temperature of an unsaturated parcel of air is reduced?

    (a) It will stay the same

    (b) It will stay the same at first, then decrease

    (c) It will increase

    (d) It will decrease

140. What is the balanced flow of wind around curved isobars called?

    (a) Cyclostrophic wind

    (b) Geostrophic wind

    (c) Gradient wind

    (d) Pressure Gradient Force

141. What cloud is formed by orographic uplift in stable air over mountain ranges?

    (a) Cumulus

    (b) Stratus

    (c) Cumulonimbus

    (d) Lenticularis

142. What sort of weather is usually associated with Polar Maritime air moving across the UK?

    (a) Stratus, advection fog and drizzle

    (b) Cool temperature, clear skies, good visibility

    (c) Convective cloud, showers and thunderstorms

    (d) Warm temperatures, stratus and fog

143. What is the greatest danger from an occluded front?

    (a) There could be thunderstorms embedded in stratiform cloud

    (b) You could get advection fog near the surface position

    (c) You could get severe rime ice

    (d) Strong downdraughts

144. What kind of icing hazards are associated with cloudless conditions?

    (a) Rime and clear ice

    (b) Carburettor icing and hoar frost

    (c) Clear ice only

    (d) Mixed ice

145. What is the most dangerous stage in the development of a thunderstorm to aircraft at low levels?

    (a) Developing stage

    (b) Mature stage

    (c) Dissipating stage

    (d) All the above

146. At a remote landing spot that is 240 feet above mean sea level, if the QNH is 1023, what would be the QFE if 1 hPa is equal to 30 feet?

    (a) 1010 hPa

    (b) 1012 hPa

    (c) 1015 hPa

    (d) 1016 hPa

147. How often is a spot wind chart (Form 214) issued in the UK, and how long is it valid for?

    (a) 8 hours, 8 hours

    (b) 8 hours, 18 hours

    (c) 6 hours, 6 hours

    (d) 2 hours, 2 hours

148. What does this symbol mean? ≡

    (a) Freezing fog

    (b) Mist

    (c) Widespread fog

    (d) Sky obscured

149. What does NOSIG mean in a METAR?

    (a) Nothing significant happening

    (b) No significant change in the two hours after the observation

    (c) No significant change until the next observation

    (d) No significant weather

150. If the surface temperature is 19°C and the dewpoint is 9°C, where might the base of any cumulus cloud be?

    (a) 4 000 feet

    (b) 5 600 feet

    (c) 3 700 feet

    (d) 6 400 feet

151. What type of cloud is this?

(a) Stratus

(b) Cumulonimbus

(c) Alto stratus

(d) Cumulus

152. A microburst:

(a) Has a life time of more than 30 minutes

(b) Is always associated with thunderstorms

(c) Occurs only in tropical areas

(d) Has a diameter up to 4 km

153. In a single thunderstorm cell when do up- and downdrafts occur simultaneously?

(a) Cumulus stage

(b) Dissipating stage

(c) In all stages

(d) Mature stage

154. Clear ice is dangerous because it:

(a) Is translucent and only forms at leading edges

(b) Is not translucent and forms at the leading edges

(c) Spreads out and contains many air particles

(d) Is heavy and is difficult to remove from the aircraft surfaces

155. In which air mass might extremely low temperatures encountered?

(a) Polar maritime air

(b) Tropical continental air

(c) Arctic maritime air

(d) Polar continental air

156. In the spot wind reading below (from Form 214), what is the temperature at 4,000 ft?

```
57N 0230E

24 320 60 -35
18 310 45 -21
10 310 25 -08
05 310 20 +01
02 310 20 +07
01 300 20 +09
```

(a) +2°C

(b) +3°C

(c) +4°C

(d) +5°C

157. In the forecast weather form (215) at Figure 9 in the Appendix, in what direction and at what speed is the trough at the top of the chart moving?

(a) NW, 20 kts

(b) SE, 20 kts

(c) It isn't moving - the windspeed is 20 kts

(d) S, with the wind from the NW at 20 kts

158. In the forecast weather form (215) at Figure 9 in the Appendix, in Area A, what does the following mean?

```
ISOL 1200 M +TSGS
```

(a) Surface visibility isolated 1500 metres, with heavy hailstorms

(b) Surface visibility isolated 1500 metres, with light hail and heavy snow

(c) Surface visibility isolated 1500 metres, with heavy thunderstorms containing small hail or snow pellets and snow on mountains

(d) Surface visibility isolated 1500 metres, with light snow and heavy hail

159. In the forecast weather form (215) at Figure 9 in the Appendix, at what altitude is the 0°C isotherm in Area C?

(a) 400 feet

(b) 40 feet

(c) 4000 feet

(d) There isn't one

160. Using the forecast weather form (215) at Figure 9 in the Appendix to plan the route given in the Flight Plan section of the Navigation chapter, and assuming no interference from danger areas, licence restrictions, icing, etc., what is the most reasonable course of action?

  (a) Wait until later in the day when the weather will improve

  (b) Cloud base and visibility are within limits - go when ready

  (c) Thunderstorms are forecast - don't go

  (d) Go, but follow the coast instead

161. What are standard ISA conditions?

  (a) 1013 hPa, 15°C

  (b) 1013.25 hPa, 59°F

  (c) 1013 hPa, 10°C

  (d) 1012 hPa, 15°C

162. How is the atmosphere mainly heated?

  (a) Radiation from the Sun

  (b) Radiation from the Earth

  (c) Insolation from the Sun

  (d) Advection

163. What is radiant energy arriving from the Sun called?

  (a) Insolation

  (b) Insulation

  (c) Radiation

  (d) Convection

164, Where is the diurnal range of temperature normally greatest?

  (a) Inland

  (b) Over the sea

  (c) By the coast

  (d) Where there is no cloud

165. In which part of the atmosphere does most weather occur?

  (a) Troposphere

  (b) Tropopause

  (c) Stratosphere

  (d) Stratopause

166. In ISA conditions, what would you expect the temperature at 4 000 feet above MSL to be?

  (a) 15°C

  (b) 23°C

  (c) 7°C

  (d) 12°C

167. What is the reduction of temperature with increase in altitude called?

  (a) The lapse rate

  (b) An inversion

  (c) Convection

  (d) Refraction

168. What is the primary cause of weather?

  (a) The Earth's tilt

  (b) The presence of water vapour

  (c) Temperature differentials around the Earth

  (d) Winds blowing the rain around

169. What is the pressure gradient?

  (a) The rate of change of pressure with height, around 30 ft per hPa

  (b) The generating force of the gradient wind, which then blows along the pressure gradient

  (c) The change of pressure with distance, measured horizontally at right angle to the isobars

  (d) The rate of change of pressure over time

170. How may pressure be defined?

  (a) Mass per unit area

  (b) Weight per unit area

  (c) Mass per unit volume

  (d) Force per unit area

171. At an indicated altitude of 4 500 ft, with a Regional QNH of 998 hPa in ISA conditions, you fly into an airmass that is colder than ISA. What will be your true altitude?

  (a) There is not enough information

  (b) Higher than 4 500 ft

  (c) 4 500 ft

  (d) Lower than 4 500 ft

172. If the surface wind at midnight in Summer is 180/10 kts, what would the wind velocity be at 2000 feet?

    (a) 210°/20 kts

    (b) 170°/30 kts

    (c) 210°/5 kts

    (d) 130°/15 kts

173. What would the ISA temperature be at 3 500 ft over UK in Winter, inside a polar continental air mass?

    (a) +8°C

    (b) -18°C

    (c) -7°C

    (d) +7°C

174. Which conditions are most likely to lead to radiation fog?

    (a) Cloudy day, high relative humidity, wind 5-7 knots

    (b) Cloudless night, high relative humidity, wind 5-7 knots

    (c) Cloudless night, high relative humidity, no wind

    (d) Cloudless day, low relative humidity, no wind

175. Airport A is 250 ft AMSL (QNH 1013 hPa) and Airport B is 1000 ft AMSL (998 hPa). If an aircraft is overhead A at 6 000 ft and sets heading for B, what will its height be at B if 1 hPa = 30 ft?

    (a) 4,550 ft

    (b) 4,950 ft

    (c) 4,550 ft

    (d) 5,050 ft

176. Cold, moist, unstable air arriving over the UK is most likely to be from a:

    (a) polar continental air mass

    (b) returning polar continental air mass

    (c) tropical maritime air mass

    (d) polar maritime air mass

177. When warmer air slides over colder air, there is a:

    (a) cold front with a typical slope of around 1:150

    (b) cold front with a typical slope of around 1:50

    (c) warm front with a typical slope of around 1:50

    (d) warm front with a typical slope of around 1:150

178. If the temperature of an unsaturated parcel of air decreases (under constant pressure), relative humidity will:

    (a) stay the same

    (b) increase

    (c) decrease

    (d) stay the same to start with and then increase

179. Which cloud type is formed by orographic uplift in stable air over mountain tops?

    (a) Fractus

    (b) Castellanus

    (c) Cumulus

    (d) Lenticularis

180. What is lenticular cloud associated with?

    (a) Warm fronts

    (b) Cold fronts

    (c) Mountain waves

    (d) Occlusions

181. Which conditions are most likely to cause induction system icing in a piston engine?

    (a) Cold weather, low humidity, high power settings

    (b) Warm weather, high humidity, high power settings

    (c) Warm weather, high humidity, low power settings

    (d) Cold weather, high humidity, low power settings

182. What does this symbol mean?

    (a) Severe turbulence

    (b) Moderate turbulence

    (c) Icing

    (d) Thunderstorm

183. What does the weather code MIFG mean?

    (a) Mist and Fog

    (b) Shallow Fog

    (c) Advection Fog

    (d) Upslope fog

184. What does the code NSC mean in a TAF?

    (a) Not Sure about Cloud amounts

    (b) No Significant Cloud

    (c) Nil Strato Cumulus

    (d) No Significant Chance of making an approach

IMC Rating

Note: Many IMC Rating questions, particularly for instruments, meteorology and flight plans, are covered in previous sections. Put another way, they won't be found here!

1. How long is an IMC rating valid for?

   (a)   13 months

   (b)   12 months

   (c)   36 months

   (d)   25 months

2. What can you do with an IMC Rating?

   (a)   Operate out of sight of the surface when outside controlled airspace

   (b)   Operate under IFR in controlled airspace

   (c)   Operate under Special VFR in controlled airspace out of sight of the surface with a flight visibility of at least 5km

   (d)   Take off or land below cloud when visibility is below 1 km

3. Which of the following is (are) true?

   1. Flight visibility must be at least 1800 m for you to take off or land below cloud.

   2. Under Special VFR, flight visibility must be 3 km or more, clear of clouds and with the surface in sight.

   3. You can operate out of sight of the surface when outside controlled airspace.

   4. There must be instrument approach procedures from which you can land when flight visibility is 600 m or more.

   5. You may operate as commander in IMC outside controlled airspace.

   (a)   1, 2, 3, 4 & 5

   (b)   1, 2, 3 & 5

   (c)   2, 3, 4 & 5

   (d)   1 only

4. Flying an ILS approach, what would the instrument show if the OBS knob were turned without changing your aircraft's heading?

   (a)   The glideslope needle will stay where it is, while the localiser needle will move left and right

   (b)   The localiser needle will stay where it is, while the glideslope needle will move up and down

   (c)   Nothing

   (d)   Both needles will move

5. Where may you exercise IMC rating privileges?

   (a)   All UK airspace including the Channel Islands and the Isle of Man, in Class D or E airspace when IFR is required

   (b)   All UK airspace including the Channel Islands and the Isle of Man and the Republic of Ireland in Class D or E airspace when IFR is required

   (c)   All EASA countries, in Class D or E airspace when IFR is required

   (d)   All ICAO countries, in Class D or E airspace when IFR is required

6. Which statement about Deconfliction Service is true?

   (a)   A controller may offer a vector that leads into the centre of a thunderstorm

   (b)   You need a Mode S transponder

   (c)   ATC instructions allow you into airspace you normally would not have permission to enter

   (d)   You must comply with all instructions and clearances

7. What minimum flight visibility is required for an approach and landing?

    (a)   1 nm

    (b)   1 500 m

    (c)   1 800 m

    (d)   3 km

8. What instrument flight rules must be complied with outside controlled airspace?

    (a)   Minimum height, the requirement to file a flight plan and obtain a clearance

    (b)   Minimum height and position reporting

    (c)   Position reporting

    (d)   Minimum height and the quadrantal rules

9. What colour are the Outer and Middle marker lights for the ILS?

    (a)   Blue, white

    (b)   Blue, amber

    (c)   White, Amber

    (d)   Amber, white

10. The ILS display shown indicates what deflection?

    (a)   1.5°

    (b)   6°

    (c)   3°

    (d)   2°

11. If you took your IMC rating test on 12th March 2014, but the paperwork was not completed until 15th May 2014, when would it need to be renewed?

    (a)   30th April 2016

    (b)   31st March 2016

    (c)   15th May 2016

    (d)   31st May 2016

12. To comply with IFR, you must fly at least (1) above the highest obstacle within (2) of the aircraft.

    (a)   (1) 1 500 ft (2) 2 nm

    (b)   (1) 1 500 m (2) 2 nm

    (c)   (1) 1 000 ft (2) 5 nm

    (d)   (1) 2 000 ft (2) 5 nm

13. What is the maximum safe deviation below a glideslope?

    (a)   Full scale deflection

    (b)   Half scale deflection

    (c)   None is allowed

    (d)   3 dots

14. In which airspace may you fly?

APPENDIX (CHARTS, ETC)

FIGURE 1

Flight Plan Glasgow-Inverness

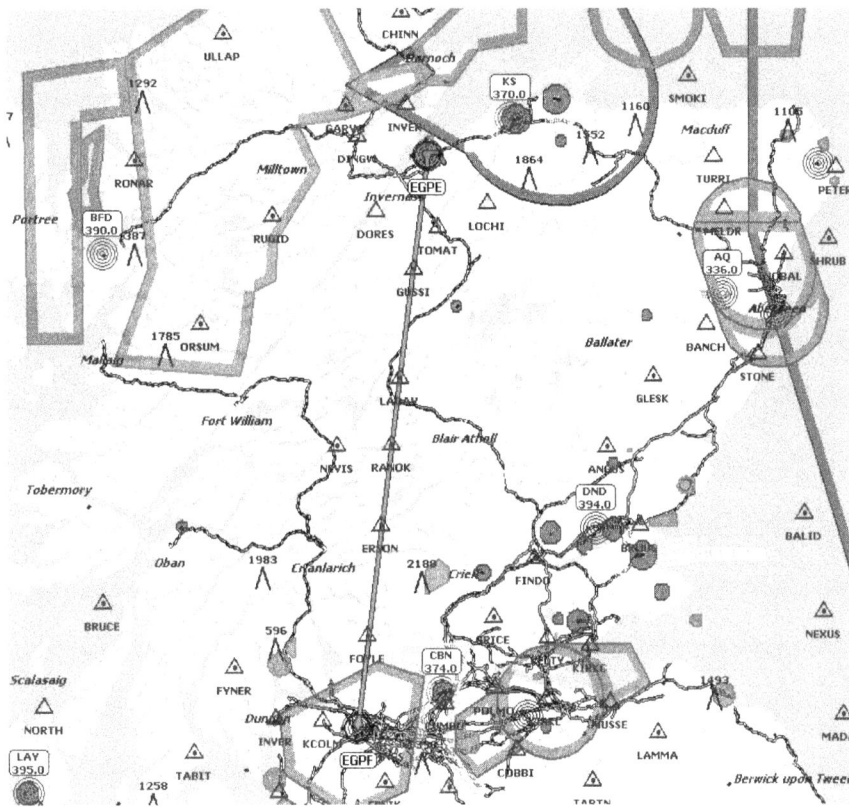

Time	From	To	FL/ Alt	Safety Alt	TAS	W/V	Track T	Drift	Hdg T	Var	Hdg M	G/S	Dist	Time	ETA
1200	EGPF	EGPE	4500	4300	90	180/15	007			+ 5.5			104		
Alternate										Totals →					

This is higher ↓   ↓ Than this

FIGURE 2

Pressure Altitude/Density Altitude

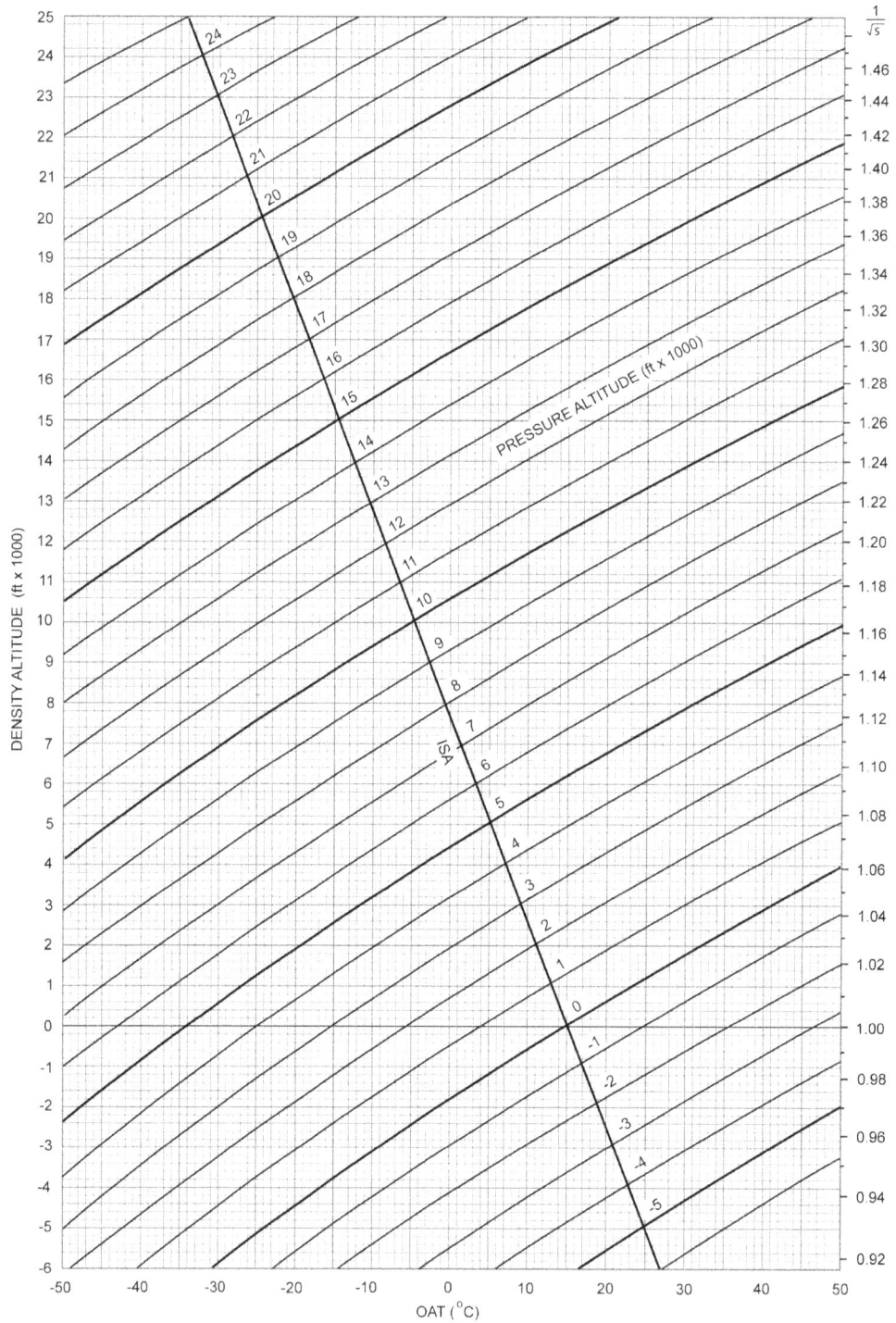

FIGURE 3

ROC Graph

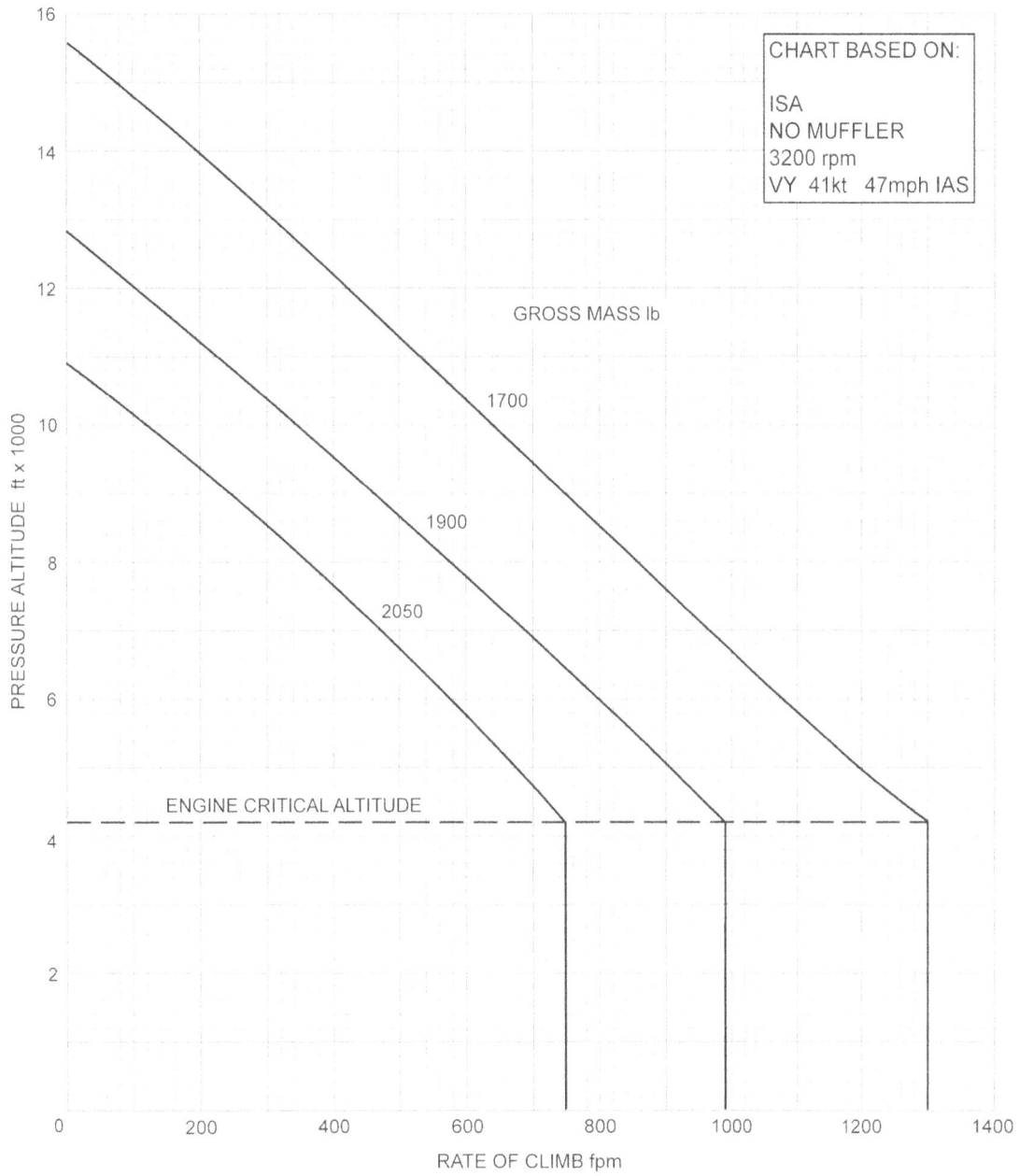

FIGURE 4

Fuel Flow

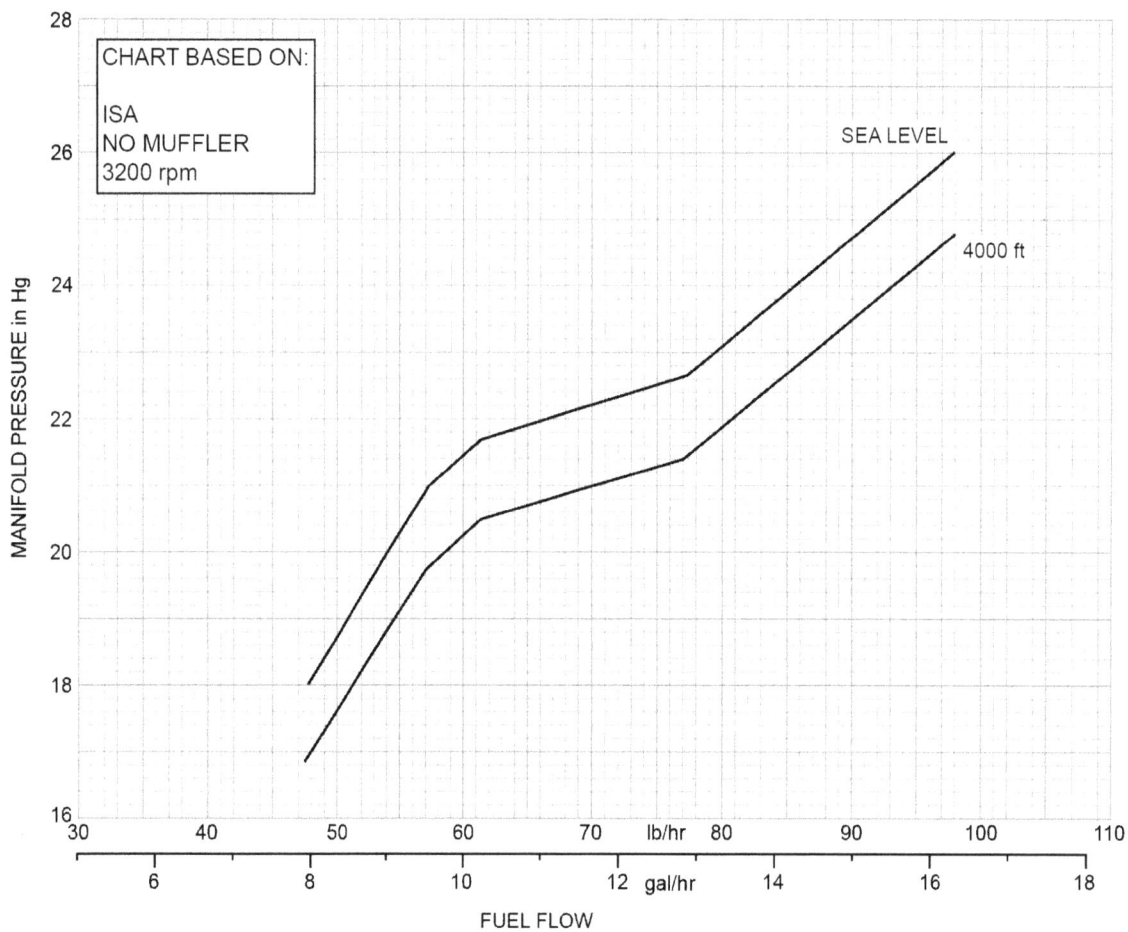

FIGURE 5

Extracts from the AIP

EGHR AD 2.2 - GEOGRAPHICAL & ADMINISTRATIVE DATA

1. ARP Coordinates and Site at Aerodrome:	**Lat:** 505134N **Long:** 0004533W Mid-point of Runway 10/28
2. Direction & Distance From The City:	1.5 nm NNE of Chichester
3. Elevation/Reference Temperature:	110 ft °C
4. Geoid undulation at AD ELEV PSN:	149 feet
5. MAG VAR/Annual change:	W1.9° (2009) - 0.14° decreasing
6 AD Administration:	Goodwood Road Racing Company Ltd
Address:	Goodwood, Chichester, West Sussex, PO18 0PH
Telephone:	01243 755061 (ATS) 01243 755060 (GRRC Admin) 01243 755066 (Goodwood Flying School) 01243 755064 (Engineering)
Fax:	01243 755062 (ATS) 01243 755065 (GRRC Admin) 01243 755085 (Goodwood Flying School) 01243 780312 (Engineering)
7. Types of traffic permitted (IFR/VFR):	VFR
8. Remarks:	

EGHR AD 2.3 - OPERATIONAL HOURS

1. AD Administration:	**Winter:** Nov, Feb and Mar 0900-1700; Dec-Jan 0900-1600 **Summer:** 0800-1700; other time by arrangement.
2. Customs & Immigration	By arrangement.
3. Health & Sanitation	
4. AIS Briefing Office:	
5. ATS reporting Office (ARO):	
6. MET Briefing Office:	
7. ATS:	As AD hours. See also AD 2.18.
8. Fuelling:	As AD except for the last 15 minutes.
9. Handling:	
10. Security:	
11. De-icing:	
12. Remarks:	This aerodrome is PPR. PPR by telephone recommended. PPR in writing outside published hours.

EGHR AD 2.4 - HANDLING SERVICES & FACILITIES

1. Cargo handling facilities:	
2. Fuel/Oil types:	AVTUR JET A-1, AVGAS 100LL. Oil: W80, W100, S80, S100, Multi.
3. Fuelling facilities/capacity:	
4. De-icing facilities:	
5. Hangar space for visiting aircraft:	
6. Repairs facilities for visiting aircraft:	
7. Remarks:	

EGHR AD 2.13 - DECLARED DISTANCES

RWY	TORA (m)	TODA (m)	ASDA (m)	LDA (m)	Remarks:
06	799	799	799	710	
24	799	799	799	799	
14R	1104	1199	1199	1073	
32L	1115	1199	1199	1051	
10	613	613	613	613	
28	613	613	613	613	
14L	726	726	726	726	
32R	726	726	726	726	

EGHR AD 2.17 - ATS AIRSPACE

Designation and lateral limits	Vertical	Class
Chichester/Goodwood Aerodrome Traffic Zone (ATZ) Circle radius 2 nm centred on longest notified runway (14R/32L) 505134N 0004533W	2000 ft aal/ SFC	G
4. ATS unit call sign: Language(s): 5. Transition Altitude: 6. Remarks:	Goodwood Information English Hours: See AD 2.18	

EGHR AD 2.18 - ATS COMMUNICATION FACILITIES

Service	Callsign	Channel MHz	Hours Of Operation		Remarks
AFIS	Goodwood Information	122.450	**Winter** Nov, Feb, Mar 0900-1700 Dec, Jan 0900-1600 Other times by arrangement	**Summer** 0800-1700 and by arrangement	ATZ hours coincident with AFIS hours but not by arrangement

FIGURE 6

Time	From	To	FL/ Alt	Safety Alt	TAS	W/V	Track T	Drift	Hdg T	Var	Hdg M	G/S	Dist	Time	ETA
11:00	BEAULIEU	PTSFLD		1200	90	180/15				5W					
	PTSFLD	TANGMERE		1200	90	180/15				5W					

Totals ⟶

Alternate

Time	From	To	FL/ Alt	Safety Alt	TAS	W/V	Track T	Drift	Hdg T	Var	Hdg M	G/S	Dist	Time	ETA
	TANGMERE	EGHR		1200	90	180/15				5W					

FIGURE 7

Hover Ceiling IGE

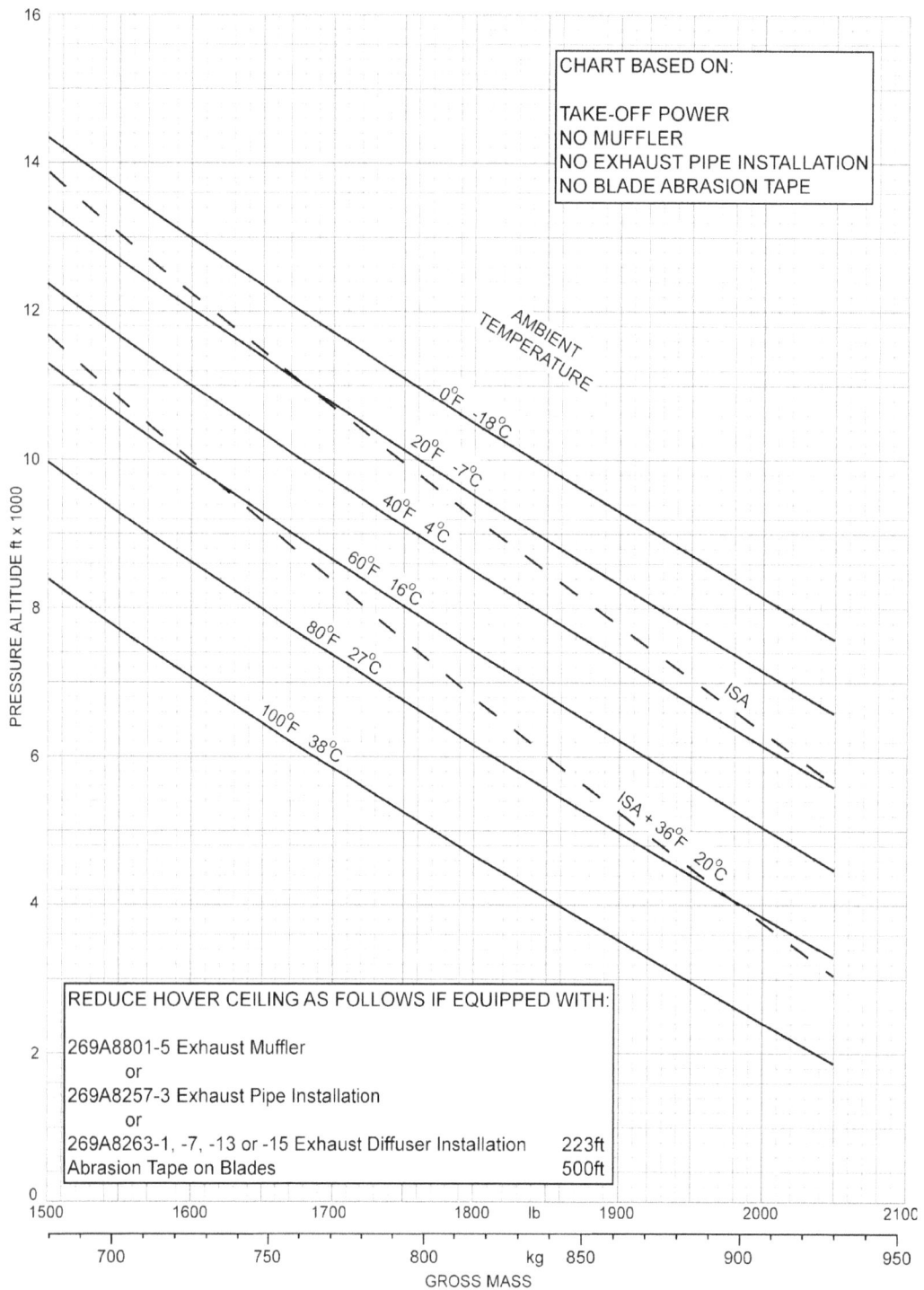

CHART BASED ON:

TAKE-OFF POWER
NO MUFFLER
NO EXHAUST PIPE INSTALLATION
NO BLADE ABRASION TAPE

AMBIENT TEMPERATURE

0°F   -18°C
20°F   -7°C
40°F   4°C
60°F   16°C
80°F   27°C
100°F   38°C

ISA
ISA + 36°F   20°C

REDUCE HOVER CEILING AS FOLLOWS IF EQUIPPED WITH:

269A8801-5 Exhaust Muffler	
or	
269A8257-3 Exhaust Pipe Installation	
or	
269A8263-1, -7, -13 or -15 Exhaust Diffuser Installation	223ft
Abrasion Tape on Blades	500ft

PRESSURE ALTITUDE ft x 1000

GROSS MASS

FIGURE 8

Takeoff Distance Graph

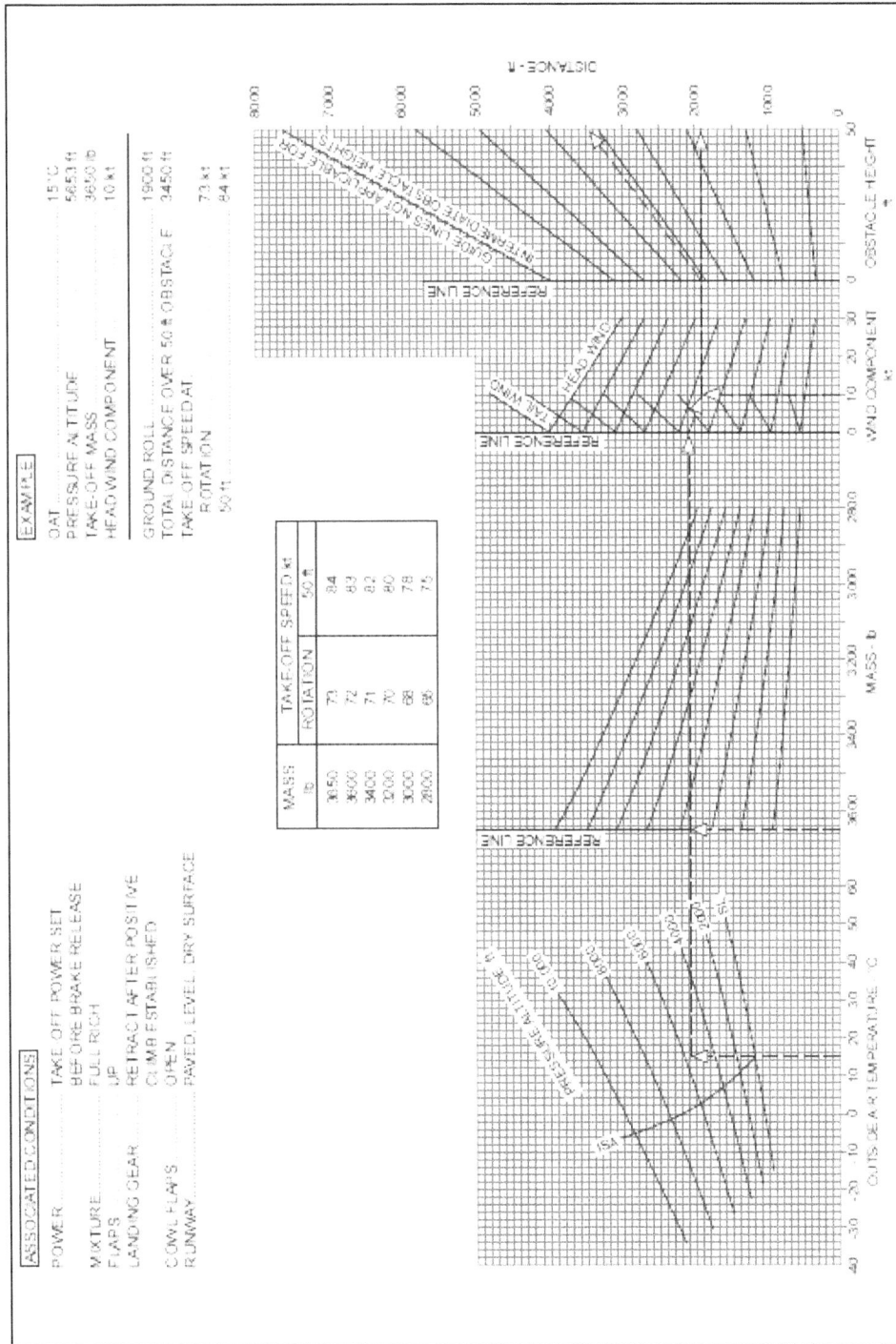

FIGURE 9

Form 215 Weather Chart

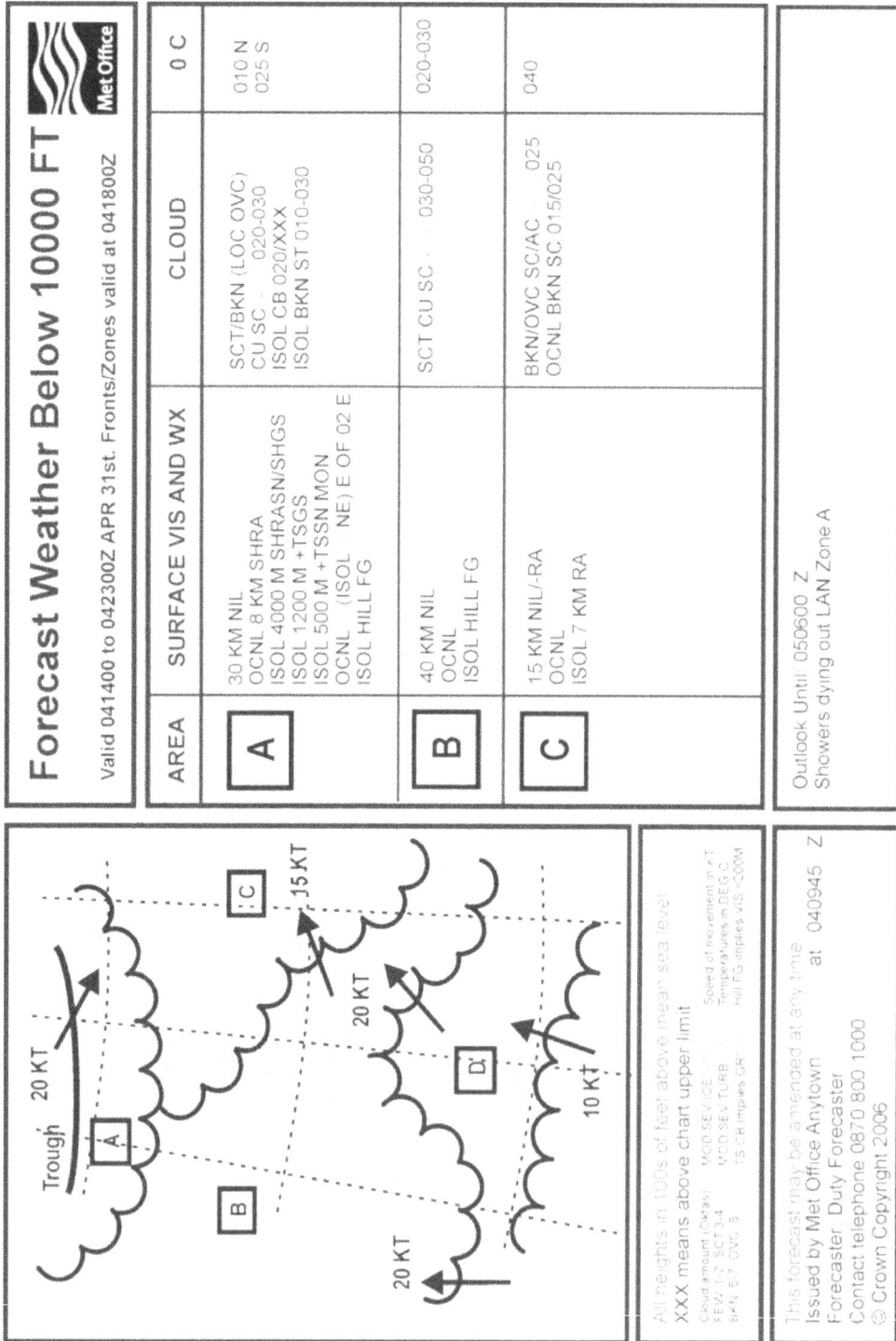

Forecast Weather Below 10000 FT

Valid 041400 to 042300Z APR 31st. Fronts/Zones valid at 041800Z

AREA	SURFACE VIS AND WX	CLOUD	0 C
A	30 KM NIL OCNL 8 KM SHRA ISOL 4000 M SHRASN/SHGS ISOL 1200 M +TSGS ISOL 500 M +TSSN MON OCNL (ISOL NE) E OF 02 E ISOL HILL FG	SCT/BKN (LOC OVC) CU SC 020-030 ISOL CB 020/XXX ISOL BKN ST 010-030	010 N 025 S
B	40 KM NIL OCNL ISOL HILL FG	SCT CU SC 030-050	020-030
C	15 KM NIL/-RA OCNL ISOL 7 KM RA	BKN/OVC SC/AC 025 OCNL BKN SC 015/025	040

Outlook Until: 050600 Z
Showers dying out LAN Zone A

All heights in 100s of feet above mean sea level
XXX means above chart upper limit

Cloud amount (Oktas)
FEW 1-2 SCT 3-4
BKN 5-7 OVC 8

MOD SEVICE
MOD SEV TURB
TS CB implies GR

Speed of movement in KT
Temperatures in DEG C
Hill FG implies VIS <200M

This forecast may be amended at any time at 040945 Z
Issued by Met Office Anytown
Forecaster Duty Forecaster
Contact telephone 0870 800 1000
© Crown Copyright 2006

FIGURE 10

Inches/Millibars Conversion

hPa (Mb)	Inches (of Mercury)									
	0	*1*	*2*	*3*	*4*	*5*	*6*	*7*	*8*	*9*
970	28.64	28.67	28.70	28.73	28.76	28.79	28.82	28.85	28.88	28.91
980	28.94	28.97	29.00	29.03	29.05	29.08	29.11	29.14	29.17	29.20
990	29.23	29.26	29.29	29.32	29.35	29.38	29.41	29.44	29.47	29.50
1000	29.53	29.56	29.59	29.62	29.65	29.68	29.71	29.74	29.77	29.80
1010	29.83	29.86	29.89	29.92	29.95	29.97	30.00	30.03	30.06	30.09
1020	30.12	30.15	30.18	30.21	30.24	30.27	30.30	30.33	30.36	30.39
1030	30.42	30.45	30.47	30.50	30.53	30.56	30.59	30.62	30.65	30.68
1040	30.71	30.74	30.77	30.80	30.83	30.86	30.89	30.92	30.95	30.98

Temperature Compensation

°C	ISA Dev	Height above touchdown or above aerodrome in feet								
		200	*300*	*400*	*500*	*600*	*700*	*800*	*900*	*1000*
-0	-15	20	20	30	30	40	40	50	50	60
-10	-25	20	30	40	50	60	70	80	90	100
-20	-35	30	50	60	70	90	100	120	130	140
-30	-45	40	60	80	100	120	130	150	170	190
-40	-55	50	80	100	120	150	170	190	220	240
-50	-65	60	90	120	150	180	210	240	270	300

FIGURE 11

Speed Conversion

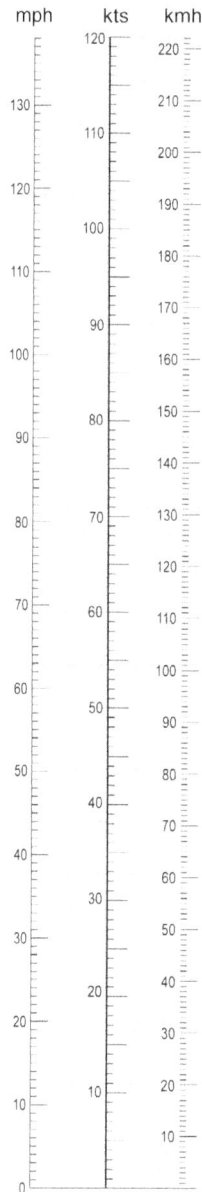

KT	MPH (approx)	KmH (approx)
1	1	2
2	2	4
3	3	6
4	5	7
5	6	9
6	7	11
7	8	13
8	9	15
9	10	17
10	12	19
20	23	37
30	35	56
40	46	74
50	58	93
60	69	111
70	81	130
80	92	148
90	104	167
100	115	185
110	127	204

1 KT = 1.151 MPH or 1.852 KmH

FIGURE 12

Temperature Conversion

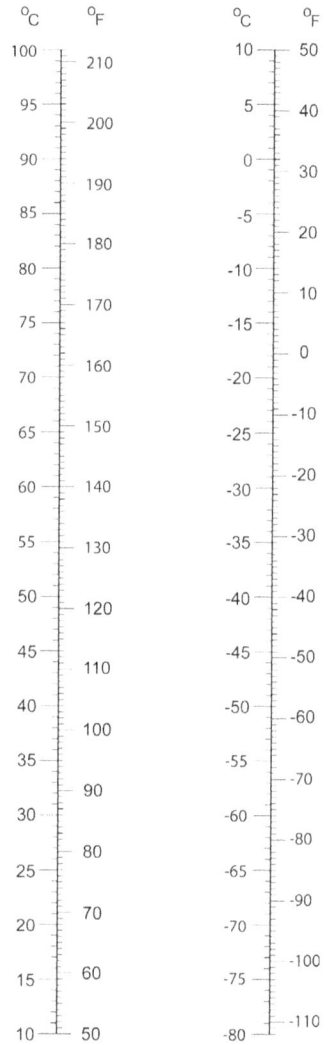

TEMPERATURE
CONVERSION

$^{\circ}F = (^{\circ}C \times 9/5) + 32$

$^{\circ}C = (^{\circ}F - 32) \times 5/9$

FIGURE 13

Cruise Performance Table
2450 lbs

PA (Feet)	RPM	ISA -20			ISA			ISA +20		
		%BHP	KTAS	GPH	%BHP	KTAS	GPH	%BHP	KTAS	GPH
2000	2250	-	-	-	79	115	9.0	74	114	8.5
	2200	79	112	9.1	74	112	8.5	70	111	8.0
	2100	69	107	7.9	65	106	7.5	62	105	7.1
	2000	61	101	7.0	58	99	6.6	55	97	6.4
	1900	54	94	6.2	51	91	5.9	50	89	5.8
4000	2300	-	-	-	79	117	9.1	75	117	8.6
	2250	80	115	9.2	75	114	8.6	70	114	8.1
	2200	75	112	8.6	70	111	8.1	66	110	7.6
	2100	66	106	7.6	62	105	7.1	59	103	6.8
	2000	58	100	6.7	55	98	6.4	53	95	6.2
	1900	52	92	6.0	50	90	5.8	49	87	5.6
6000	2350	-	-	-	80	120	9.2	75	119	8.6
	2300	80	117	9.2	75	117	8.6	71	116	8.1
	2250	76	115	8.7	71	114	8.1	67	113	7.7
	2200	71	112	8.1	67	111	7.7	64	109	7.3
	2100	63	105	7.2	60	104	6.9	57	101	6.6
	2000	56	98	6.4	53	96	6.2	52	93	6.0

Without speed fairings, decrease speeds by 2 kts

FIGURE 14

Exam Practice Form

Use the pencil provided

To answer the question carefully fill in the appropriate box containing the correct letter thus:

If you need to answer, erase the mark completely and re-mark the correct answer as above

Make no other marks apart from the answer below this line

NAME

VENUE

SUBJECT

TIME ALLOWED   Hours   Minutes

CANDIDATE SIGNATURE

DATE

1	21	41	61	81
2	22	42	62	82
3	23	43	63	83
4	24	44	64	84
5	25	45	65	85
6	26	46	66	86
7	27	47	67	87
8	28	48	68	88
9	29	49	69	89
10	30	50	70	90
11	31	51	71	91
12	32	52	72	92
13	33	53	73	93
14	34	54	74	94
15	35	55	75	95
16	36	56	76	96
17	37	57	77	97
18	38	58	78	98
19	39	59	79	99
20	40	60	80	100

ANSWERS

HUMAN FACTORS

1 (D). Carbon monoxide (CO) is toxic gas that is created through the effects of incomplete combustion, when not enough oxygen has been available to create the proper waste product, which is carbon dioxide (CO_2). It typically gets into the cockpit from faulty engine exhausts, but other sources relevant to aviation can include cigarette smoke and cabin heaters. You can buy carbon monoxide detectors from most pilot shops that will act as an early warning, because it is colourless, tasteless, odourless and non-irritating, so is otherwise extremely hard to detect.

The precise way that the effects of carbon monoxide work on the body are complex and not yet fully understood, but when it is not ventilated it binds to haemoglobin* better than oxygen does, and makes it retain any oxygen it carries, so the blood oxygen content increases while the body does not get the supplies that it needs.

*The principal oxygen-carrying compound in blood. It allows more oxygen to be taken up than in plain solution.

The symptoms of CO poisoning can resemble those of food poisoning and the flu, but without the associated high temperatures. A headache is the most common symptom. Others include:

- feeling sick (nausea) and dizziness
- feeling tired and confused
- vomiting with abdominal pain
- shortness of breath, difficulty breathing (dyspnoea)

The longer you breathe in CO gas, the worse the symptoms will get. You may lose your balance, vision and memory and, eventually, consciousness. This can happen within two hours if there is a lot of CO in the air, but the symptoms can occur over a number of days or months.

Later symptoms include:

- confusion
- memory loss
- co-ordination problems

To recover, turn off the cabin heat and open the air vents. Use 100% oxygen if you have it.

2 (C). See Q 1.

3 (D). See Q 1.

4 (A). See Q 1.

5 (D). See Q 68.

6 (A). On the ground we maintain our balance with impressions from the eyes, the vestibular apparatus in the inner ear and various sensations from the muscles, joints, skin, etc. as coordinated by the nervous system, more or less in that order of importance. In essence, we grow used to being parallel to the trees and at right angles to the ground, and things feel strange when we are not.

Flying is subject to illusions, especially when carrying out extreme manoeuvres and/or at night. The input from your senses is interpreted (rightly or wrongly) by your conscious and subconscious minds. The former handles the visual aspects, and the latter all the rest, through the peripheral nervous system, part of which, if you remember, runs your body automatically. When the subconscious becomes confused about your position in space (it assumes you are on the ground), the only link between you and reality is the visual system linked to the conscious mind, which is a lot slower and less capable in its processing ability. The eyes are not affected by acceleration, centrifugal force or gravity, which is why you must rely on your instruments when you get disorientated.

Disorientation is the state of confusion that you get when the brain receives conflicting messages, such as a feeling of turning detected by the inner ear, but not confirmed by the eyes, which frequently produces nausea. It refers to a loss of your bearings in relation to position or movement, and it is more likely to happen when you are subject to colds, in IMC, and frequently changing between inside and outside visual references. The "leans" (or *somatogyral illusion*) is the classic case, which occur because your semicircular canals get used to a particular sustained motion in a very short time. If you start a turn and keep it going, your canals will think this is normal, because they lag, or are slow to respond (they only respond to change). When you straighten up, they will try to tell you you're turning in the opposite direction, where you're actually flying straight and level. Your natural inclination is to obey your senses, but your instruments are there as a cross-reference. In fact, the whole point of instrument training is to overcome this dependence on your senses. More dangerous is recovering from a spin of 2-3 turns, where, without visual reference, you think you are actually turning the opposite way and enter another spin in the original direction when you try to correct it. Eventually an extreme nose-up condition results, which turns into an extreme nose-down attitude and a tight graveyard spiral before entering Terrain Impact Mode. To combat the leans, close your eyes and shake your head vigorously from side to side for a couple of seconds, which will topple the semi-circular canals.

The three *semicircular canals* in the ear monitor **angular accelerations**. Two are vertical and one is horizontal (the vertical ones are at right angles to each other, so they can detect rotary motion in any plane). They use the fluid in the inner ear, which acts against sensory hairs (cupula) to send electrical signals to the brain so you can tell which way is up. The hairs enter the walls of the canals at a point called the *ampulla*. If your head is turned to the left, the fluid's inertia makes it stay where it is, but the canal's movement bends the hairs to the left. The signal is then sent to the brain for interpretation.

The danger lies when such movement is too slow to detect in the first place, and is gradually increased. This is especially true when you are affected by gravity and centrifugal force at the same time, as when in a steep turn.

The types of acceleration include:

- **Linear** During linear acceleration, you can get the impression of pitching up or climbing (*somatogravic illusion*), making you want to push the nose down. This is because the fluid in the inner ear flows backwards. The eyes help to overcome this, but at night, with no visual clues, say on takeoff, this can be mistaken for a steep climb in which you put the nose down and could hit the ground. The effect is more pronounced at night going into a black hole from a well-lit area, unfortunately confirmed by the artificial horizon, which suffers from the same effect. You get a pitch-down illusion from deceleration. The danger here is that lowering the gear or flaps causes the machine to slow down, which makes you think you are pitching down and want to bring the nose up, which could cause a stall at the wrong moment on approach.

- **Radial** (centripetal) - about an external axis, as found when spinning.

- **Angular** - about an axis through the body

While the semicircular canals sense *angular* acceleration, the **otolith organs** on the top of the cochlea in the inner ear pick up changes in *linear* movement. The otolith organs consist of the *utricle*, for horizontal movement, and the *saccule*, for vertical. They both have sensory hairs at the bottom with calcium carbonate crystals at their ends. The crystals provide the inertia needed to bend the hairs, which send signals down sensory nerve fibres which are interpreted by the brain as motion.

Note: Alcohol in the fleshy stalk of the otoliths may persist for days after all traces of alcohol have vanished from the blood. It is not unusual for even small movements of the head to cause disorientation or motion sickness up to three days after alcohol was last consumed.

Additional sources of positional information include *somatosensory receptors* inside the skin, joints and muscles. As they respond to pressure and stretching signals, they can be an important source of information about your equilibrium. They are called the "seat of the pants" sense because it was thought that you could tell which way was up by the seat of your pants sensing the most pressure. **The seat of the pants sense is completely unreliable as an attitude indicator when your body is moving in the aerial environment.**

7 (D).

8 (A). Pilots generally are discouraged from giving blood (or plasma) when actively flying, because a donation may lead to a reduced tolerance of altitude. If you give blood, try to leave a gap of 24 hours afterwards, including for bone marrow donations. Although your arm will fill back up in a very short time, and for most donors there are no noticeable after-effects, there is still a slight risk of faintness or loss of consciousness as your blood takes about 3 months to regain the same level of platelets and haemoglobin. Having donated blood, you should rest supine for about 15-20 minutes, drink plenty of fluid and not fly for 24 hours.

9 (D). One drink at 6000 feet is the same as two at sea level.

10 (B). See Q1.

11 (C). Diving before flight should be avoided, as extra nitrogen is absorbed while breathing pressurised gas, which will dissolve out as you surface again. When you go flying too soon, this is accentuated, and the symptoms can appear as low as 8,000 feet. A diver 30 feet under water is under twice the normal sea level pressure. Don't fly for 12 hours if the depth involved is less than 30 feet, or 24 hours if the dive exceeds 30 feet.

12 (D).

13 (A). Carbon monoxide, hypoxia, or smoking cigarettes can affect night vision, as can fatigue, drugs or alcohol. Bright sunlight can blind you. Vision is affected least by wearing sunglasses during the day.

14 (C). See Q 74.

15 (D).

16 (C). Hypoxia is a condition where the oxygen concentration in the blood is below normal, or where oxygen cannot be used by the body, but anaemia can produce the same effect, as can alcohol. You may also have donated blood, or have an ulcer, or be a smoker, with your haemoglobin affected by carbon monoxide. A blockage of 5-8%, typical for a heavy smoker, gives an equivalent altitude of 5-7000 feet before you get airborne! Short-term memory impairment starts at 12 000 feet. In short, hypoxia is a *reduced partial pressure* in the lungs.

The effects of hypoxia are similar to those of alcohol, but classic signs are:

* *Personality changes.* You get jolly, aggressive and less inhibited

* *Judgment changes.* Your abilities are impaired; you think you can do anything with less self-criticism

* *Muscle movement.* Becomes sluggish, not in tune with your mind

* *Short-term memory loss,* leading to reliance on training, or long-term memory

* *Sensory loss.* Blindness occurs (colour first), then touch, orientation and hearing

* *Loss of consciousness.* You get confused first, then semi-conscious, then unconscious

* *Blueness*

17 (D).

18 (D).

19 (A). Hyperventilation is simply overbreathing, caused by exhaling more than you inhale. The excess oxygen causes CO_2 to be washed out of the bloodstream, so that the plasma gets too alkaline, and the arteries reduce in size, meaning that less blood gets to the brain.

The usual cause is worry, fright or sudden shock, but hypoxia can be a factor - in fact, the symptoms are similar to hypoxia and include:

* Dizziness
* Motion sickness
* Heat
* Vibration
* Pins and needles, tingling
* Blurred sight
* Hot/Cold feelings
* Anxiety
* Impaired performance
* Loss of consciousness

The last one is actually one of the best cures, since the body's automatic systems take over to restore normality. Whenever you are unsure of whether you are suffering from hyperventilation or hypoxia, treat for hypoxia, since this will almost always be the root cause. You can treat hyperventilation by talking aloud through the procedure to calm the emotions and reduce the rate of breathing.

20 (C). See questions 11, 16 & 19.

21 (D). The DERP gives you the best visibility outside and inside while making as few head movements as possible. The pilot compartment should be designed for a clear, undistorted, and adequate external field of vision, so seats need to be adjustable to position your eyes as close to the

DERP as possible for the best views while manipulating the controls (including the instruments).

If you sit lower than the ideal position, you can lose a lot of vision downwards, so you might see fewer runway lights, and approach and flare judgment may suffer.

On changing to an aircraft with a higher eye position, you may not be able to see the overshoot area, and initially taxi faster than you should.

22 (C). Boyle, an Irish physicist, discovered that, for a perfect gas, if *temperature* remains constant, the volume of a gas varies inversely with its pressure, so if you double the pressure of a gas, you halve its volume so, as you climb, and pressure reduces, the volume of the gases within various body cavities, such as the middle ear, sinuses, the gut, lungs and teeth, increases and may cause pain and/or discomfort.

23 (C). Gas in the ears normally vents via the Eustachian tubes. If these are blocked (say with a cold), the pressure on either side of the eardrum is not balanced, which could lead (at the very least) to considerable pain, and (at worst) a ruptured eardrum. It is called aerotitis.

Sinus cavities* are also vulnerable to imbalances of pressure, and are affected in the same way as eardrums are. Aerosinusitis is caused by differences in pressure between the sinus cavity and the ambient air.

*Although associated with the nose, the *sinuses* are hollow spaces or cavities inside the head surrounding the base of the nose and the eye sockets. Amongst other things, they act as sound boxes for the voice. Being hollow, they provide structural strength whilst keeping the head light; there are normally between 15-20 of them. Blockages arise from fluid that can't escape through the narrow passages - pain results from fluid pressure. Blocked sinuses can give you severe headaches, and you will get them from a bad cold. Changes are similar to those of the middle ear, but they are affected equally by ascents or descents.

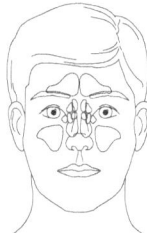

24 (D). There are over 200 harmful chemicals in cigarette smoke, which are more concentrated in sidestream smoke, which has not been filtered through the cigarette, so passive smokers face the worst risks (cigarettes release ten times more air pollution than a diesel engine - it is a Group A carcinogen). Here are some of the chemicals involved and common places they may also be found:

- Carbon monoxide (car exhausts)
- Arsenic (rat poison)
- Ammonia (window cleaner)
- Acetone (nail polish remover)
- Hydrogen cyanide (gas chambers)
- Naphthalene (mothballs)
- Sulphur compounds (matches)
- Formaldehyde (embalming fluid)

Otherwise, the addictive substance in tobacco is **nicotine**, and the substance that stops the alveoli doing their work is tar. There is also carbon monoxide (CO).

Nicotine reduces the diameter of the arteries, which stimulates the release of adrenalin, to increase heart rate and blood pressure. The risk of heart attack or strokes is increased in the order of 100%, and gangrene by 500%.

25 (C).

26 (D).

27 (C).

28 (A).

29 (A). The bends, chokes and creeps are all to do with decompression sickness. The **leans** are to do with disorientation.

30 (A). See Q 19.

31 (D). If you bend over in your seat, for example, to pick up a pencil wile the aircraft is in a turn, you could get disorientated. See Q 6.

32 (A). See Q 1.

33 (B). The partial pressure of oxygen is reduced at that level and you may be subject to hypoxia.

34 (D). Evaporation occurs through the skin and lungs, and water leaves through the kidneys as urine.

35 (B). Oxygen is required after 10,000 feet.

36 (C). The partial pressure of a gas is its pressure in proportion to its presence in a mix of gases. Although the air gets thinner as you climb, the ratio of gases remains the same, so there is still 21% oxygen at 35 000 feet. However, there is an altitude (around 33 700 feet) where the pressure is so low that the partial pressure is less than that at sea level, so you must breathe oxygen under pressure.

37 (D). It is the carbon dioxide (and acidity) level in the blood that regulates respiration, not the body's need for oxygen. If you breathed in helium instead of oxygen, your

rate of breathing would hardly change. The levels are monitored by several chemical receptors in the medulla that are very sensitive to CO_2. When the level is higher than normal, as it might be if you exercise hard, the rate of breathing is speeded up.

38 (C).

39 (C). Hypoxia is a condition where the oxygen concentration in the blood is below normal, or where oxygen cannot be used by the body.

40 (C). Also called *Effective Performance Time*, the times of useful consciousness (from interruption of the oxygen supply to when you are exposed to hypoxia) are short:

Height (feet)	Seated	Moderate Activity
20 000'	30 mins	5 mins
30 000'	1-2 mins	
35 000'	30-90 secs	
40 000'	15-20 secs	

Note: The figures depend on cabin pressure altitude, vary individually, and are affected by physical activity, strength and time of decompression

Another definition states that TUC is the amount of time an individual can perform flying duties efficiently with inadequate oxygen supply, or the time from the interruption of the oxygen supply or exposure to an oxygen-poor environment, to the time when useful function is lost (it is *not* the time to total unconsciousness). Officially, it is: *The time during which you can act with physical and mental efficiency and alertness from when you are exposed to hypoxia,* or *when you lose the available oxygen supply.*

41 (B). See Q 16.

42 (A).

43 (D). Refer to 1.

44 (D).

45 (D). See Qs 19 and 37.

46 (A).

47 (B). Whatever your body gets up to, the processes involved must be coordinated and integrated. This is done by the central nervous system, with a little help from the endocrine system. The Peripheral Nervous System connects the Central Nervous System with the sense organs, muscles and glands, and therefore with the outside world. The PNS is divided into:

- the **somatic** nervous system, which contains the peripheral pathways for communicating with the environment and control of skeletal muscles, and

- the **autonomic** nervous system, which regulates vital functions over which you have no conscious control, like heartbeat and breathing (unless you're a high grade Tibetan monk, of course), or anything that is not to do with skeletal muscle. The ANS in turn consists of the:

  - **sympathetic**
  - **parasympathetic**

  nervous systems. The former prepares you for fight-or-flight (see *Stress,* below) and tends to act on *several organs at once*, while the latter calms you down again, *acting on one organ at a time*. Being under the influence of fight-or-flight is like being in a powerful car in permanent high gear, which you can't do all the time - you need rest & relaxation to allow time for the parasympathetic system to kick in, such as meditation, or a snooze in the back of the aircraft (when landed). Being in such a high state of readiness all the time produces steroids, and can lead to depression.

48 (A).

49 (A). It takes the liver about 1 hour to eliminate 1 unit of alcohol from the blood. Officially, alcohol leaves the body at 15 milligrams per 100 ml of blood per hour, but one figure is 0.01-0.015 mg% per hour. A blood alcohol level of 60 mg/100 ml will therefore take 4 hours to return to normal. 1 unit is, or used to be, the same as 1 measure of spirit, a glass of wine or half a pint of beer. The number of units per week beyond which physical damage is likely is 21 for men and 14 for women.

50 (D). See Q 8.

51 (A).

52 (B).

53 (C). See Q 6.

54 (D). To avoid erroneous assumptions, we need to maintain a continuous mental model of what is going on around us. Officially, situational awareness is "the ability to accurately perceive what is happening in- and outside the aircraft, plus the ability to understand the meaning of different elements in the environment and the projection of their status in the near future." To do this successfully, you have to know how things should be to recognise what's wrong!

Situational awareness refers to your knowledge of **all relevant information**. The information that contributes to situational awareness comes in through the senses, and is transformed by the brain into a mental model of the situation, through the process of perception.

For a good example of situational awareness, imagine yourself overtaking two trucks, one behind the other, in your car. The one behind is going faster than the one in front, and you know that there is a lot of momentum involved in driving a truck, so you figure it isn't going to slow down, but is more likely to want to overtake instead. You therefore expect the rear truck to want to occupy the lane you are in, so you either slow down, speed up or move over to the next lane to give it room (advanced drivers call this reading the road). In aviation terms, it can be likened to keeping a mental picture of what aircraft are around you, and what they are doing, by listening to ATC transmissions. SA involves knowledge of the past, present and future, and requires **anticipation**, so you need vigilance and continual alertness, with regard to what *may* happen on top of what *is* happening. Being a pilot, most of the information you will base a decision on comes from your instruments and navigation equipment, but this can be affected by your physical state.

55 (A). The body can only cope with certain amounts of G-force, which comes from the effects of acceleration, that increase your weight artificially. When there is no acceleration, you are subject to 1G. We are often subject to acceleration forces beyond our design limits, hence some illusions when the mind misinterprets the proper clues. Linear or Transverse acceleration (Gx) concerns forward and backward movement, with speed only. Under forward linear acceleration, you might think you are climbing.

56 (B). Disorientation is a feeling of turning detected by the inner ear, **but not confirmed by the eyes**, frequently producing nausea. See Q 6.

57 (C). A wider runway tends to make you think the ground is nearer than it actually is, so you might fly low and overshoot:

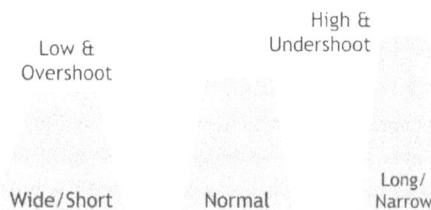

A narrow runway looks as if it is further away and delays your reactions, possibly leading to an undershoot. In the diagram above, all three landing strips are the same distance and angle away from the aircraft, but the one on the left is wider and shorter (looks nearer, and low on the glideslope, so you might carry out a higher approach) and the one on the right is longer and thinner (looks further away and high on the glideslope, so you might go lower and land short while trying to keep the same sight picture).

58 (A). The relatively bright lighting makes the runway appear to be nearer. An object brighter than its surroundings (such as a well-lit runway), will appear closer, so on an approach, you might start early and be lower than you should.

59 (A). The illusions you might get with sloping ground include:

Problem	Illusion	Risk
Downslope	Too low	High approach
Upslope	Too high	Low approach
Rain	Closer	Low approach
Narrow	Too high	Low approach
Wide	Too low	High approach & flare
Bright lts	Too low	High approach

In short, if your approach angle is meant to be 3°, and the runway is already sloping up by 1°, you will think you are approaching too steeply, and *vice versa*. An approach to a downsloping runway should therefore be started higher, with a steeper angle, because the perceived glide path angle is smaller than that of the actual glide path. However, the slope away from the aircraft presents a smaller image to your eyes, and you see less of the runway, so you try to see more by flying too high to correct the apparent undershooting. An approach to an upsloping runway should be started lower, at a shallower angle - good reasons why you should use VASIS when provided.

60 (C). See Q 59.

61 (C). In haze, objects appear to be further away due to their lack of brightness.

62 (A). The fact that somebody has more qualifications than you (and this includes Prime Ministers) does not mean that they know what they are doing! You should first of all express any doubts and be prepared to escalate the situation by being assertive and prepared to take control.

63 (B).

64 (A). The sloping cloud layer may be mistaken for the correct horizon, and you may try to compensate in the opposite direction.

65 (A). A high speed aircraft approaching head-on will grow the most in size very rapidly in the last moments, so it's possible for it to be hidden by a bug on the windscreen for a high proportion of its approach time. Lack of relative movement makes an object harder to detect.

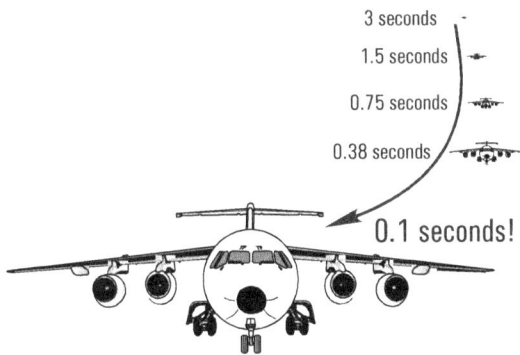

3 seconds
1.5 seconds
0.75 seconds
0.38 seconds

0.1 seconds!

You should be able to see another aircraft directly at 7 miles, or 2.5 miles if it was 45° off - at 60° it's down to half a mile!

66 (B). 600 kts is 10 nm per minute. 5 km is 2.7 nm.

67 (B). Use your flight computer to calculate the time from the 500 kt rate of closure. 500 kts is 8 and a bit miles per minute.

68 (B). The eye is a dual sensor, in terms of central and peripheral vision. The latter is imprecise, but it covers a large area. Central vision is more exact, and narrowly focussed. You can only read instruments with central vision. The eye is nearly round, and its rotation in its socket (and focussing) is controlled by external muscles. It has three coatings, or layers of membrane:

- the **sclerotic**, which has a transparent area at the front called the cornea. Behind the cornea is the *lens*, whose purpose is to finish the job of bending light rays inwards and focus them on the retina. Its shape is changed by the ciliary muscles surrounding it. This change of shape is *accommodation*, which can be affected by age or fatigue. When you are tired, accommodation is diminished, resulting in blurred images.

- the **choroid**, which lines the sclerotic and contains tiny blood vessels

- the **retina**, at the back of the eye, which is the light sensitive part that detects electromagnetic waves at light frequencies, and converts them to electrical

signals that are interpreted by the cerebral cortex in the brain. It is sensitive to hypoxia

The fluid in the eye retains its shape and keeps the sensory ligaments tight. The ciliary muscles have to work to overcome this tension, which is why your eyes get tired after a lot of focussing on near objects.

The lens may be dislodged by careless rubbing of the eyes (for example when the humidity is low), an accidental knock or increased G forces.

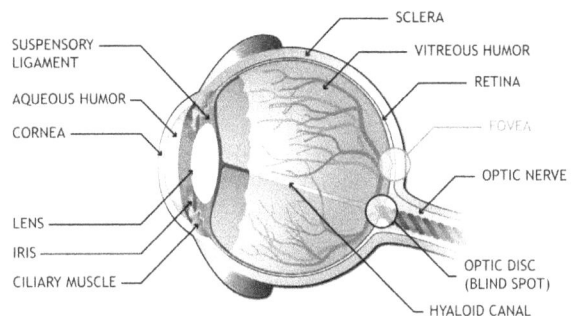

As the cornea does not have its own blood supply, it gets its oxygen from the ambient air. Mild hypoxia and dehydration, from low humidity on the flight deck, may increase the potential for cornea damage when using contact lenses. Decompression may result in bubble forming under a contact lens.

Note: If you are cleared to use contact lenses, a pair of ordinary spectacles must be carried while you are exercising the privileges of your licence. Aircrew who wear spectacles must carry a spare pair during flight in any case.

The lens, iris and cornea control the amount of light entering the eye through the *pupil*, which is the black bit inside the coloured iris. Most of the refraction needed for focussing takes place over the curved surface of the cornea, which has a fixed focus, and the final adjustments are done by the lens through accommodation (the lens performs about 25% of the whole process).

Generally, vision is better with more light, but too much will produce glare (older people need twice as much light to see well than younger people do). The iris appears black because any light that does not get absorbed by the retina is usually absorbed by a layer behind it called the *retinal pigment epithelium*. If it wasn't, your vision would be blurred by randomly scattered light. Redeye occurs when not all the light can be absorbed and some is reflected back.

70% of light is refracted by the cornea, and 30% by the lens. The more your iris is open, the less *depth of field** you have, so in darkness it is hard to see beyond or before the point of focus, and you may need glasses to help.

*The depth of field is an area either side of the focus point in which everything is sharp. The wider the iris, the shorter this distance is, and *vice versa*.

The retina is composed of ten very thin layers, with nerve endings that act as light sensors (actually, *neurons*) which are called *rods* and *cones*, in the ninth. Their names arise from the way they are shaped. Each is more efficient than the other in different kinds of light. Cones are sensitive to day or high-intensity light and rods are used at night or in low-intensity light. As the periphery of the retina consists mainly of rods, peripheral vision is less precise because they only see shades of grey and vague shapes (you see colours because the vibrations they give out are strong enough to wake the cones up, and the brain mixes the colours received by them). The cones need at least the light of a half moon to function at all.

The rods contain *visual purple*, also known as *rhodopsin*, which builds up over 30-45 minutes as light decreases until the approximate level of moonlight, which is when the rods take over from the cones. As rods are sensitive to shorter wavelengths of light, in very low light, blue objects are more likely to be seen than red (neither will be in colour), which is why cockpit lighting is sometimes red because it affects the rods (used for night vision) less than white light does.

Light waves from objects in the *right* visual field fall on the *left* half of each retina, for transmission to the *left* cerebral hemisphere, and *vice versa*. This is so that each side of the brain has input from both eyes at once, and that both of them work in concert.

The *optic nerve* carries signals from the eye to the brain. The point where it joins the retina is mostly populated with cones, so you can get a blind spot in the direct field of vision at night. You don't normally notice it because the brain superimposes the images from each eye.

Once light falls on the retina, the visual pigment is bleached, which creates an electrical current. However, once bleached, the pigment must be reactivated by a further chemical reaction, which is called *nystagmus*, caused by the eye jerking to a new position, there to remain steady. The movement period is edited out by the brain, and the multiple images are merged, so continuous vision is actually an illusion, as an *after image* is produced when light falls on the retina - that is, the image of what you are looking at remains there for a short period, as light has a momentum. As the eye does not need to be seeing

constantly (and can therefore be regarded as a detector of *movement*), it can spend the spare time in repair and replacement of tissue. 30-40 images per second are taken in the average person, and an image takes about 1/50th of a second to register. It has also been discovered that, when we blink, the visual cortex in the brain (the bit that interprets what the eye sees) closes down for that period. As it happens, if 90% of a rat's visual cortex is removed, it can still perform quite complex tasks that require visual skills. Similarly, a cat can have up to 98% of its optic nerves severed without much effect.

69 (D). See Q 5.

70 (A). The short eye movements encourage you to focus on particular spots.

71 (C). The eardrum is the boundary between the outer ear and the middle ear.

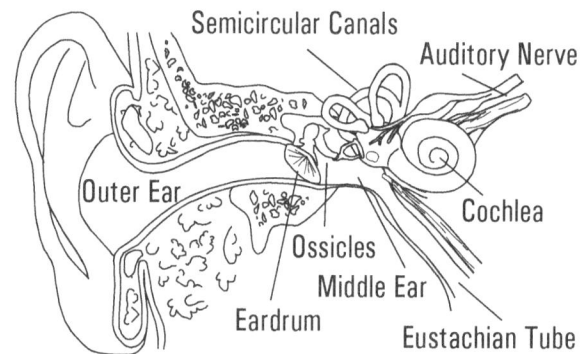

Sound waves make it vibrate, and the vibrations are transmitted by a chain of linked bones in the middle ear (the smallest ones in the body) known as the *hammer*, *anvil* and *stirrup* (collectively, the *ossicles*) to the *cochlea* in the inner ear (via the *oval window*), which is full of fluid.

The cochlea is a tube which narrows progressively. It contains thousands of fibres (*cupula*) of different lengths that vibrate in sympathy with various frequencies. The fibres are linked to the brain and, as with sight, it is now, when the signal reaches the brain, that we "hear". The audible range of the human ear is 16-20 Hz to 20 KHz, with the most sensitive range between 500-4000 Hz.

As you climb and the outside air pressure reduces, the eardrum will bulge outwards, and *vice versa*. This difference in pressure is equalised by air leaking out through the *Eustachian Tube*, which is a canal that connects the middle ear to the back of the throat. The tube is normally collapsed as it can just about cope with walking uphill, but air expanding in the middle ear is enough to open it up (thus, pressures equalise more easily in the climb). When you descend, however, the pressure goes the other way and tends to keep the tube closed. Swallowing opens it up, allowing air to enter, which is why it helps to clear the ears when changing altitude. Blocked Eustachian tubes can be responsible for split eardrums, due to the inability to equalise pressure. As the eardrum takes around 6 weeks to heal, the best solution is not to go flying with a cold.

72 (C). At night, look slightly to one side, as the rods that are sensitive to lower levels of light are outside the fovea, at the peripheral of the retina (scan slowly as well).

73 (D). It is harder to detect because it is not moving relative to your aircraft.

74 (A). The eye needs to latch on to something, which is difficult with a clear blue sky, or on a hazy day. With an empty field of vision, your eyes will focus at relatively short distances, between 1-2 metres ahead, and miss objects further away (*empty field myopia*). In other words, you effectively become short-sighted (myopic). The ratio of looking in- and outside should be 5:15 seconds.

75 (D). The Design Eye Reference Point allows pilots to obtain the best visibility outside and inside. The pilot compartment should be designed for a clear, undistorted, and adequate external field of vision, but not necessarily for what sizes of pilot it can hold, so seats need to be adjusted to position your eyes as close to the DERP as possible for the best views while manipulating the controls. You should be aware of the hazards and compromises associated with seating positions away from the DERP. If you sit lower than the ideal position, you can lose vision downwards, so you might see fewer runway lights, and approach and flare judgement may suffer.

76 (D).

77 (B). As part of the fight or flight mechanism, the release of adrenalin increases the heart rate and blood pressure.

78 (C). Incapacitation is mostly caused by acute gastro-intestinal disorders from suspect food and drink.

79 (A). The 3-needle altimeter was a classic example of poor design that led to accidents, where people confused the hundred- and thousand-foot needles.

80 (D). See Q 57.

81 (C).Although the symptoms of colds and sore throats, etc. are bad enough on the ground, they may actually become dangerous in flight by either distracting or harming you by getting more serious with height (such as bursting your eardrums, or worse). If you're under treatment for anything, including surgery, not only should you not fly, but you should also check that there will be no adverse effects on your physical or mental ability, as many preparations combine chemicals, and the mixture could make quite a cocktail. No drugs or alcohol should be taken within a few hours of each other, as even fairly widely accepted stuff such as aspirin can have unpredictable effects, especially in relation to hypoxia (it's as well to keep away from the office, too - nobody else will want what you've got). Particular ones to avoid are antibiotics (penicillin, tetracyclines), tranquilisers, antidepressants, sedatives, stimulants (caffeine, amphetamines), anti-histamines and anything for relieving high blood pressure, and, of course, anything not actually prescribed. Naturally, you've got to be certifiable if you fly having used marijuana, or worse.

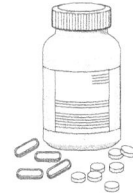

82 (C). Disorientation is a feeling of turning detected by the inner ear, but not confirmed by the eyes, frequently producing nausea. Using the instruments will provide the required confirmation. See Q 6.

83 (B).

84 (A). Very often, controls are selected by feel if a pilot is keeping up a good scan outside the cockpit. If the controls feel similar they may be confused.

85 (C).The circulatory (or cardiovascular) system is actually a double system which is joined at the heart.

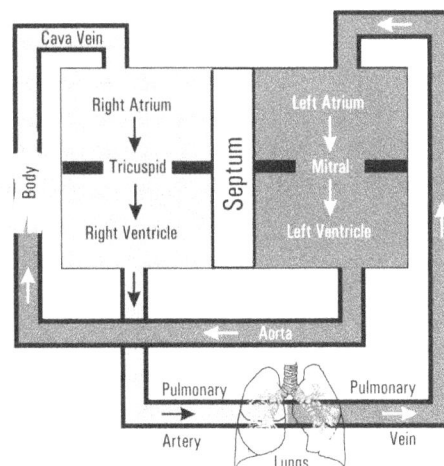

There is one circulation to the lungs (pulmonary) and one to the rest of the body (systemic). It consists of the heart, arteries, arterioles, capillaries, veins (over many miles!) and blood, and provides a transport system that links the external environment to the tissues and distributes essential substances, such as hormones, oxygen and nutrients around the body. It also removes carbon dioxide and other waste products from the tissues and delivers them to the lungs, kidneys and liver.

86 (C).

87 (B).

88 (C).

89 (A).

90 (A).

91 (C). The fact that somebody isn't talking does not mean they are not communicating (some female silences can be quite eloquent!) It is said that 7% of communication is accomplished verbally, 38% by unconscious signals, such as the tone of voice, and the remainder (55%) by non-verbal means, such as body language. In fact, before language was invented it was the only way to get your point across. It's certainly the most believed means of communication, since it will most likely reflect the true feelings of the person concerned.

Non-verbal communication can accompany the verbal kind, such as a smile during a face-to-face chat. It may be acknowledgement or feedback (a nod of the head). It can also be used when the verbal type is impossible, such as a thumbs-up when it's noisy. Body language can be very subtle, but powerful. For example, the word *No* with a smile will be interpreted quite differently from one accompanied by a smack in the mouth.

Non-verbal communication may also include written information or notes between pilots, but technology makes this even more important - it is the main way that systems speak to you - newer displays present data graphically. Unfortunately, the side-by side seating arrangements in the cockpit tend to lessen the effects of body language, so the choice of words (and their packaging) assumes a greater importance.

Note: Elements of body language should not be taken in isolation - folded arms may not mean hostility, but that the other person is merely cold. Always interpret body language based on three or four indications.

92 (C).

93 (D). Divided attention is the alternative management of several matters of interest at (almost) the same time, as when monitoring the progress of a flight whilst making a radio call (time sharing).

94 (A). See Q 1.

95. (B). The most common problems (in the normal pilot's lifestyle, anyway) are low blood sugar (*functional hypoglycaemia*), or eating too much (*reactive hypoglycaemia*), caused by missed meals and the like. Although you may think it's better to have the wrong food than no food, be careful when it comes to eating chocolate bars in lieu of lunch, which will cause your blood sugar levels to rise so rapidly that too much insulin is released to compensate, which drives your blood sugar levels to a *lower* state than they were before - known as *rebound hypoglycaemia*. Here, the sugar is pushed into all cells of the body and not specifically reserved for the Central Nervous System. Apart from eating "real food", you will minimise the risks of this if you eat small snacks frequently instead of heavy meals after long periods with nothing. Complex (slow release) carbohydrates are best, like pasta, etc.

Hypoglycaemia is bad enough in the short term, but long-term can be regarded as a *disease*, aside from being responsible for alcohol cravings. Although not life threatening, it is a forerunner of many worse things and should be looked at. The important thing to watch appears to be the suddenness of any fall in blood sugar, and a big one can often trigger a heart attack. A high protein diet will tend to even things out, as protein helps the absorption of fat, which is inhibited if too much insulin is about. Warning signs include shakiness, sweatiness, irritability or anxiety, difficulty in speaking, headache, weakness, numbness or tingling around the lips, inability to think straight (or lack of concentration), palpitations and hunger. At its worst, hypoglycaemia could result in a coma, but you could also get seizure and fainting. Eat more if you exercise more.

96 (C). See Q 6.

97 (B). See Q 53.

98 (B). See Q 54.

99 (D). See Q 91.

100 (A).

101 (A).

102 (D).

103 (C). See Q 19.

104 (A). See Q 68.

105 (A). See Q 16.

106 (A).

107 (B). See Q 53.

108 (A). See 71.

109 (B). See Q 49.

110 (B). See Q 68.

111 (C).

112 (B).

113 (C).

114 (A).

115 (C).

116 (C).

117 (A).

118 (D).

119 (D).

120 (D).

POF & AGK

General

1 (C). The actual answer should be **density**, which is affected by temperature, pressure and humidity - for example, water (vapour) has $^5/_8$ of the density of dry air. Aircraft performance is affected in two ways - the reaction over the lift producing surfaces and the power output from the engine both reduce when air becomes less dense. Only two answers have the word density in them, and one of them includes oxygen as a choice, which has nothing to do with it.

2 (B). At 10,000 feet, the temperature should be -5°C, and it is 5°C colder than that.

3 (B). In the standard atmosphere, the temperature lapse rate is 1.98°C per thousand feet.

4 (D).

5 (A). Monocoque is a development of *stressed skin*, where the outside covering is rigid and takes the stresses of flight, and supporting devices inside, like *formers* held together by *stringers*, or *longerons*, help keep it in shape (see above).

Formers (or *frames*) are assembled one after the other, changing in size as required. They will absorb torsion and

bending loads. Longerons (or stringers, which are shorter and tend to run just between formers) run fore and aft, keeping the formers together, spreading the load between them and stiffening the structure in general. *Bulkheads* are similar to formers, but tend to be found at either end of a fuselage, or a compartment, or when more strength is required. A *firewall* can be a bulkhead, being a fireproof partition that separates an engine compartment from the cabin. It is normally made of stainless steel, and on an aeroplane the engine is bolted to it.

An egg is a good example of a monocoque structure, which is handy, as *cocque* is French for *eggshell*. Monocoque therefore means *single shell*. Aside from saving weight, the big advantage of monocoque is that it leaves more space inside the aircraft. Older flying boats, made of wood, were among the earliest examples, but large-diameter aircraft cannot use monococque because the skin would be too thick. Semi-monocoque is a compromise which uses longerons to take some of the strain.

6 (C). The answer given is the only one that would create any more heat.

7 (C).

8 (C). Without water vapour we wouldn't have weather!

9 (D).

10 (C).

11 (D). The venturi speeds up the airflow coming into the carburettor, which reduces the pressure enough to allow atmospheric pressure to push the fuel into the main jets.

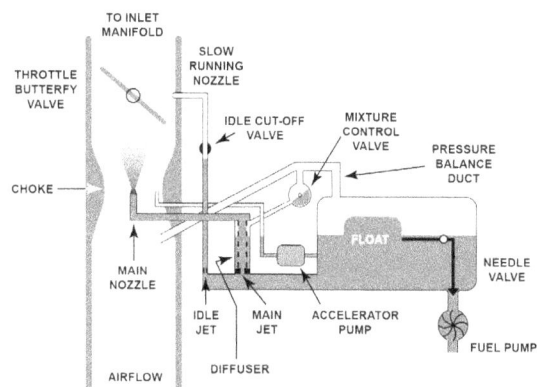

12 (A). With the application of heat, the air becomes less dense and the ratio of the fuel/air mixture becomes upset. The pressure in the manifold will reduce and the mixture will get richer.

13 (B).

14 (B).

15 (C). Water vapour has 5/8 of the density of dry air. This will affect the lift producing surfaces and the power output from the engine.

16 (C).

17 (B).

18 (C).

19 (D).

20 (A). Some say 15:1.

21 (B).

22 (A).

23 (A).

24 (B).

25 (A). As pressure falls, the air molecules are allowed to expand away from each other. This decreases air density.

26 (D).

27 (C).

28 (B). The stability of an aircraft expresses its ability to return to its original state through the results of the original disturbance.

29 (B). The VSI uses two sources of airflow to produce its readings, but these are created within the case of the instrument. Air from only one source goes into it, from the static ports.

30 (C).

31 (B). When the aircraft initiates a right turn from the North, its dip makes it initially indicate a turn in the opposite direction (that is, the compass will turn left). The amount of this initial error is about equal to the latitude. For example, at 30°N, if a right turn from North is initiated, the compass will initially turn to 330°. If the turn is to the left, the compass will turn right to 030°. Therefore, the compass **lags** when turning from North. If turning to the North, you will have to roll straight and level 30° before reaching the heading that you want.

When turning from the South, the compass **leads** by the amount of degrees of latitude. If you are turning to the South, you must roll back to straight and level about 30° past South.

32 (C).

33 (C).

34 (C). BCF is efficient but deadly because it creates a heavy gas that excludes oxygen from the fire - and the pilot! The cabin should be vented.

35 (D).

36 (B).

37 (D).

38 (B).

39 (B). The magneto is always live, except when the primary circuit is broken. This is accomplished normally with a switch that opens the primary circuit so that no magnetic flux is created.

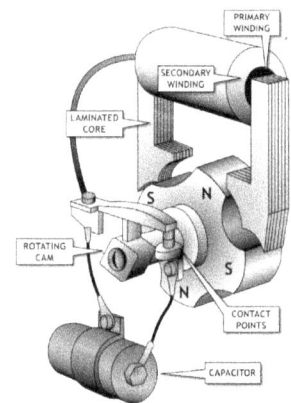

40 (D).

41 (B). A trick question! 59°F is 15°C.

42 (D).

43 (C). As the altimeter relies solely on static input, if the static source becomes blocked, it cannot react at all.

44 (B). Carbon monoxide is a poisonous gas that may come from the heater or the exhaust.

45 (C).

46 (B). The ASI has two inputs, from the pitot head and the static source. If the latter becomes blocked, the instrument now behaves like an altimeter and will increase its readings as you climb, because the pitot source is now mistaken for a static source.

47 (A). If you climb at constant IAS, you will be climbing at a constant dynamic pressure, but air density decreases, so you need more velocity to produce the same dynamic pressure.

48 (D). Dynamic pressure is measured through the pitot head and static pressure through the static source. If you subtract static from dynamic pressure, the remaining pressure can be used to represent airspeed.

49 (B).

50 (B). From HIGH to LOW, the altimeter will be HIGH.

51 (B). The only time any instrument gives you true information is in standard ISA conditions.

52 (C). When the surface temperature is well below ISA (starting at -16°C), add about 10% between -16°C - -30°C. For example, at -20°C at 500 feet, your altimeter should be reading 570 ft.

53 (A).

54 (B).

55 (B). The VSI uses static pressure as a source which is split up to go inside the case and through a capillary tube, to slow the flow down. The time lag between the two flows moves the needle and indicates whether you are climbing or descending. If the static source becomes blocked, there will be no reaction at all.

56 (C).

57 (C).

58 (D).

59 (B).

60 (B).

61 (B).

62 (B). The reading on the oil pressure gauge is the pressure of the oil on the *outlet* side of the pressure pump. In other words, the oil pressure in a piston engine is measured immediately downstream of the oil pump.

63 (A). A dry sump system keeps the oil in a tank *outside* the engine (sometimes above it for gravity feed), and the oil is force fed under pressure to where it is needed - the sump in this case is used merely as a collector for stray oil dripping off the components inside. Because the engine parts aren't having to make their way through oil in the sump, it has less work to do and more power is therefore available. Less oil is also needed.

The "oil pump" is actually two pumps running on the same shaft - the scavenge pump and the engine oil pump.

The scavenge pump (which pulls oil *from* the engine) has the greater capacity in order to keep the sump dry, or to stop oil accumulating in the engine, especially after an unusual attitude, where oil might not necessarily be in the collection area until the machine is righted again, and the pump must cope with the surge (also, overnight, the crankcase drains into the sump and there will be oil remaining when the machine is started if the pumps were the same size). In addition, because air gets mixed with oil

as it does its work, it becomes frothy, gaining a greater volume, which the scavenge pump has to handle.

64 (B).

65 (B). A wet sump system is very simple, because the engine oil is kept in a sump which is under (and part of) the engine, where the crankshaft and other moving parts rotate, splashing it all around (*splash and mist lubrication*). When you start the engine, the oil is sucked from the sump through a filter to the galleries around the engine casing. It is generally thought that wet sump systems do not use a pump, but they can, as with the Piper Cherokee. Wet sump systems tend not to be used on modern aero engines, as the bearings are starved of oil when the aircraft is inverted. They are also nor used on helicopters because the engine is typically placed in a vertical position.

66 (B). Pressure is regulated by the *oil pressure relief valve*, which compensates for oil pump speed and viscosity variations with engine speed changes through the tension on its spring - in fact, engine oil pressure is adjusted by changing the spring pressure*. If oil pressure gets too high here, the pressure relief valve dumps it back to the reservoir. One symptom of problems with the relief valve is *lower than normal oil pressure*, with *steady oil temperature*.

67 (D).

68 (A).

69 (B). A bit of a trick question this. The *cycles* involved are Induction, Compression, Power and Exhaust, but the *sequence of events* is as stated.

One complete stroke of the piston is used for each of the operations involved. If you have only one cylinder, the power stroke is the only one that does any useful work - the other three simply wear the engine out. It makes sense, therefore to have more than one cylinder, at least four, so that you get a power stroke somewhere in the engine for each cycle. With six cylinders, some power strokes will overlap, but the power stroke is not used for the full run of the piston anyway. The overlap also helps remove the need for a flywheel, to save weight.

It all starts with the piston at *Top Dead Centre* (TDC), ready to start moving down to decrease the pressure in the cylinder, and suck in a fuel/air mixture from the carburettor, through the inlet valve, which has just opened (left, below). Atmospheric pressure also helps to force the fuel and air in.

Left: Induction Right: Compression

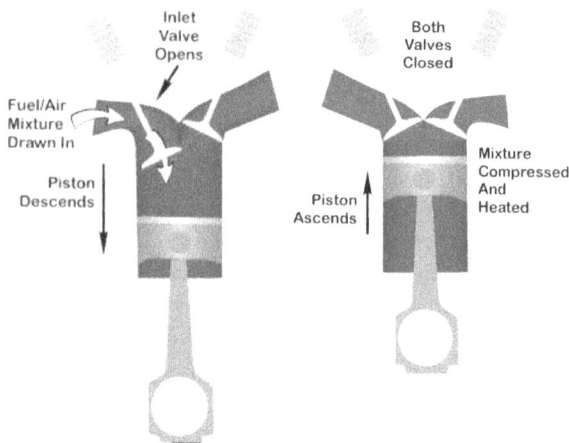

The valve closes as the piston reaches Bottom Dead Centre (BDC), so the chamber is filled to maximum. With both valves closed, the piston starts moving up again (right, above), compressing and therefore heating the mix, as well as increasing its density, which helps the flame ignite quicker because the particles are closer together (the heating helps to increase the pressure).

For a very short period the volume remains relatively constant while the spark plug fires and causes the pressure and temperature to increase rapidly as the fuel ignites.

The spark plug actually fires just before TDC, with a spark from a high-voltage electric current provided by the magneto, which is rotating in sympathy with the engine. It is timed this way to give the fuel time to catch fire, and produce the optimum expansion at 10° *after* TDC, which is when it is actually required. Under power (i.e. at high speeds) the spark can occur as much as 30° beforehand (when idling, it is more like 10°).

The ignited gases expand adiabatically, and the temperature drops because the volume increases as the piston is forced downwards, in a smooth movement, making the crankshaft rotate, plus whatever is attached to

it (left, above). Then the crankshaft's rotation, assisted by a flywheel, if there is one, forces the piston up again with the exhaust valve open to let the burnt gases escape.

Left: Power Right: Exhaust

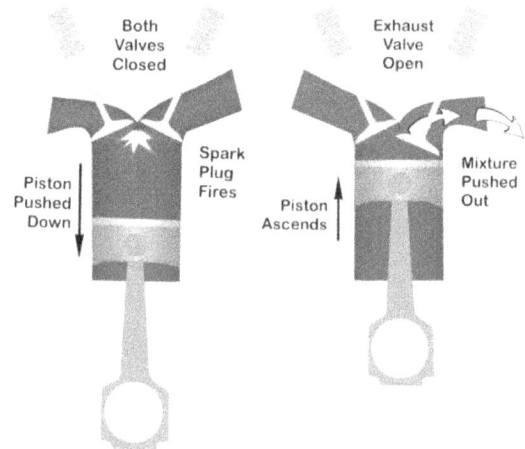

Note: Although there were four cycles, the crankshaft only went round twice (and the camshaft once). Valves open and close once each for every two revolutions of the crankshaft. At 2400 RPM, that's 20 times a second.

70 (C). If you join batteries in *series*, that is, one after the other, with the positive of one connected to the negative of the next (left, below), you will get a voltage which is the *sum* of them both, but with the same *current capacity as one*.

If you join them in *parallel*, with the positive and negative connected to each other (right, below) you would get the *voltage* of *one* battery, but the *current capacity* of *all* of them, so you can use them for longer.

This is because anything connected in series keeps the same current, and anything in parallel keeps the voltage. As a typical aircraft runs on a 24-volt system, you would therefore connect two (12v) car batteries in series (better yet, two sets in parallel).

71 (A).

72 (D). An ammeter's needle should always be showing in the + side of the gauge (not too much!), to show a positive charge going into the battery. It is connected to the battery positive lead. With the battery on and the engine off, the needle will show a negative reading in the minus range, or a discharge. If a discharge is shown with the engine running, the generator is not up to the job and the difference has to be made up by the battery. Switch things off until you get a positive reading.

73 (B).

74 (D).

75 (B).

76 (B).

77 (D).

78 (B).

79 (B).

80 (A).

81 (B).

82 (B).

83 (B). The stagnation point is at the point of impact just under the leading edge:

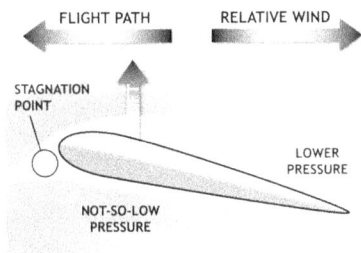

That's where the air molecules are brought to rest for an instant before being given the choice of going over or under an aerofoil, so between the top and bottom edges, there is only a difference of one molecule. The essential point to note is that the flow does not divide precisely at the tip of the aerofoil, but at some point under the leading edge, which effectively increases the upper surface of the aerofoil, and will carry on doing so as the angle of attack is increased, up to the stall point.

That is, as the angle of attack increases, the stagnation point moves downwards on the profile, to increase the size of the upper area.

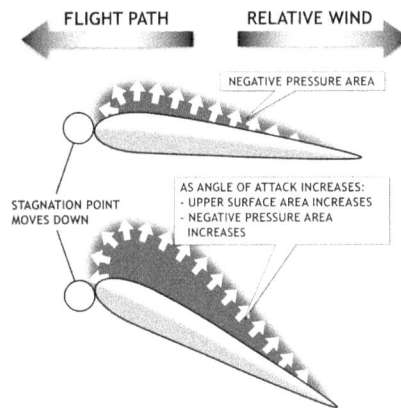

This explains why an aerofoil will still produce lift when it is upside down, although it will require a much higher angle of attack. The stagnation point can also be used as a trigger for stall warning devices.

84 (D).

85 (C).

86 (C).

87 (C).

88 (D).

89 (A).

90 (B).

91 (D).

92 (A).

93 (B).

94 (B).

95 (C).

96 (A).

97 (D).

98 (D).

99 (A).

100 (C).

101 (D).

102 (A).

103 (A).

104 (B). Static pressure is inversely proportional to altitude, so if you know the static pressure, you can figure out how high you are (in the standard atmosphere).

The altimeter is a barometer with the scale marked in feet rather than millibars. It does not measure the true height, but the weight of the air above the aircraft, which compresses the capsule inside.

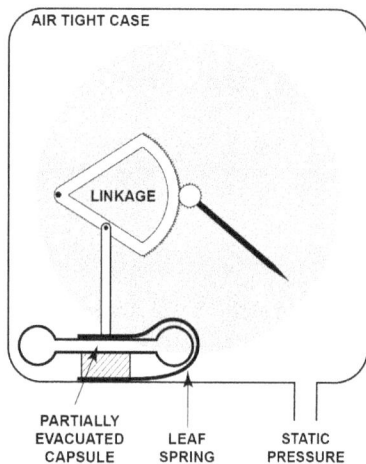

Inside a *sensitive* altimeter are *two* aneroid capsules (vacuums), which are corrugated for strength and kept open with a large leaf spring (a *simple* altimeter is a little more basic, with only one capsule - they are commonly used as cabin altimeters on pressurised aeroplanes since, at high altitudes, the capsule's movements are difficult to detect). The capsules' movements as you go up and down are magnified through the spring by a "suitable linkage" that connects directly to the pointer, using jewelled bearings. If the capsules expand, as they would when you go up, the pointer increases the reading. There is also a temperature compensation system to correct any spring and linkage tensions. Outside, there is a small knob, linked to a subscale which is visible through a small window. Rotating the knob causes the subscale to move and adjust the instrument to an *altimeter setting*.

Only in standard ISA conditions will the true altitude be indicated directly. When it is extremely cold (below about -16°C), it will be a lot lower than shown, so corrections must be applied (altitudes given with radar vectors from ATC are corrected already). If this is something you need to take note of, you could perhaps mark the corrections directly on to the approach chart, next to the heights they refer to (you must recalculate *every* significant height).

105 (A).

106 (C).

107 (B).

108 (A). See Q 69.

109 (D).

110 (C).

111 (B).

112 (D).

113 (B).

114 (C).

115 (A).

116 (B).

117 (A).

Aeroplanes

1 (D). The centre of pressure of an aerofoil moves steadily forward as the angle of attack is increased, until the stall when it moves rapidly backwards. As it moves behind the centre of gravity, it makes the nose pitch down.

2 (B).

3 (B).

4 (B). Washout involves the twisting of an aerofoil in an attempt to even out the distribution of lift along its span. The effect is that the tip has a lesser angle of attack than the root does. The root will therefore stall quicker than the tip will.

5 (A). On any dial, green shading means that you can operate continuously in that range. Amber/Yellow shading tends to be for minutes, while red is for seconds.

6 (C).

7 (C). Any time an aircraft is overstressed, it should be reported to the engineers.

8 (C). The heavier an aircraft is, the faster it has to go to lift the same weight. The stalling speed increases with aircraft weight.

9 (B).

10 (C). Slots are openings between an extended slat and the leading edge of a wing that create a venturi effect as air flows from the lower to the upper surface at high angles of attack. Because this air has lots of energy, it re-energises

the boundary layer and extends the laminar flow by reducing eddies. This reduces loss of lift and drag, and increases the stalling angle of attack. Slots may go across the length of the wing, or just where the ailerons are. Slots can be manually operated, which means they are unpopular with pilots, or automatic, so they are unpopular with designers.

11 (D).

12 (B).

13 (D).

14 (C).

15 (C). Making the control load increase reduces the chances of the control being moved from its trimmed position.

16 (B). Depending on the net result of power and control positions, it may take more physical force to keep the aircraft in a particular attitude. That is to say, for any combination of power and control position, they will move freely with a certain range, but take a lot of force to go outside of it - an increase of speed from the trimmed position at low speed has more effect on stick force than it does at high speed. These extra forces can be trimmed out with a wheel or similar device in the cockpit which operates a very small control surface in the elevator (for example), so you have a control surface within a control surface. Such a trim tab is hinged at the rear of the starboard elevator and is usually controlled by two handwheels through a chain, cable, rod and gear system in the opposite direction to the elevator (when the autopilot is engaged, pitch adjustments are made by a servo motor connected to the tab). The wheel moves the surface up or down in the airflow, which moves the elevator the opposite way and does the work you would otherwise have to do to keep it there. If the trim wheel is moved forward, it forces the trim surface upwards, which creates more lift between it and the elevator, which therefore is forced down, creating more lift underneath the tail which lifts and forces the nose down. The thing to remember is that the control column, when moved forward, moves the elevator down, whereas the trim wheel moves its attached surface up. If the elevator gets jammed, the controls reverse. **As they are independently controlled, trim tabs remain fixed for all positions of the controls they serve**. Power affects trim tabs, as more airflow varies the sensitivity of the controls. Reducing power makes the nose pitch down because the trim tab has become less effective and cannot hold the nose in position.<p>

Trim surfaces may also be found on rudders, depending on the complexity of the machine, which helps when you have to fly with one engine out.

17 (B).

18 (A).

19 (B).

20 (B).

21 (C). See Q 55.

22 (A).

23 (A).

24 (C). At high speeds, control surfaces may flutter because of buffeting, especially if the wings are flexible with a high aspect ratio. To prevent this, a streamlined balancing weight (usually lead) is fitted forward of the control surface's hinge. It may be inside the control surface itself, or fitted externally (Mass Balance). Sometimes, part of the control surface is placed forward of the hinge line, so that airflow hitting it will help the pilot move the controls (known as aerodynamic balance).

25 (B).

26 (B).

27 (C).

28 (D).

29 (C). Propellers are just aerofoils with a twist in them (washout) to spread the lift evenly over the whole length, as the tips run faster than the centre and need less angle of attack (the word pitch is sometimes used loosely to describe this). In fact, the blade is twisted to keep the local angle of attack constant along the blade, although the real purpose is to balance the amount of lift. The basic propeller is averaged to cope with many flight conditions, so is not perfect for them all, particularly taking off. The real problem is that you have to make the engine run faster to get more performance from a fixed pitch propeller, and engines work best within a certain speed range. Not only that, once the airflow becomes more than the propeller can cope with, thrust decreases.

30 (C). See Q29.

31 (C). A rotating propeller creates various forces which may be allowed for in the design stages, including gyroscopic precession, where lifting the tail tends to make the nose yaw to the left. **Torque results from the airframe going the opposite way to the direction of**

rotation. The effect is to produce a roll, which is countered by washout on the upgoing wing.

32 (C). Takeoff flap increases the angle of attack, which produces more lift, hence the shorter run required on takeoff.

33 (C).

34 (A). A retractable landing gear unit will normally have an oleo-pneumatic shock-absorber strut, supported in a trunnion bearing which is fixed to a strengthened box section in the fuselage. It is braced longitudinally by drag struts and laterally by sidestays.

The shock strut takes the loads during taxi, takeoff and landing. The basic design is two telescoping cylinders (cylinder and piston) filled with hydraulic fluid and compressed air or nitrogen under pressure. The piston is the lower one, with the hydraulic fluid, and the cylinder has the gas. There is a hole between them that allows the fluid through during compression and out during extension. There is a tapered metering pin that controls the size of the hole and the amount of fluid transferred.

A **torsion link assembl**y avoids rotation of the piston rod relative to the gear oleo strut.

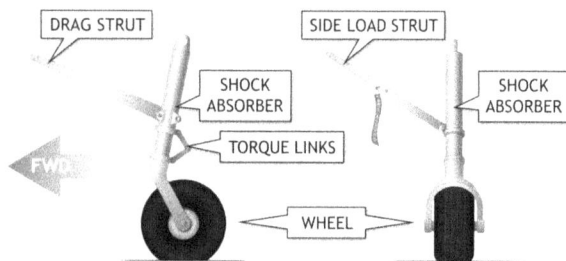

35 (D). An aeroplane's rated strength is a measure of the load the wings can carry without being damaged. Light aircraft can take total loads in three categories:

- *Normal*, 3.8 x gross weight

- *Utility*, 4.4 x gross weight

- *Acrobatic*, 6 x gross weight

Naturally, there is a safety factor involved, but the above should not be exceeded. Normal or utility categories do not allow manoeuvres with high positive and negative load factors. Bank angles would normally be inside 60°.

36 (B).

37 (C).

38 (B). Aircraft tyres have a lot to cope with, including high speeds, heat, abrasion and high braking loads.

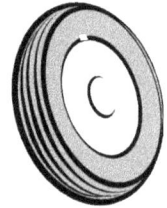

When they touch the runway, and have to spin rapidly in a short time, they can creep round the wheel rim. However, the most likely time for creep is when the tyre is newly fitted.

Creep is the circumferential movement of a tyre in relation to the wheel flange. Aside from the stress, creep can force the valve assembly to one side, so it is usual to monitor it by checking the alignment marks that are placed on the tyre when it is fitted (the white mark near the rim in the picture). If the movement reaches half the width of the paint marks, it's time to consult an engineer. A red spot is used to match up the tyre with the rim when balancing (a red band is a balance mark), and a grey/green one is an awl hole (vent position) that allows trapped gas between plies to escape.

The greatest tyre wear happens during braking, and the greatest tyre stress occurs during taxying. Under-inflated tyres wear most on their shoulders.

39 (C).

40 (C).

41 (A).

42 (A).

43 (B).

44 (C).

45 (A).

46 (A).

47 (C).

48. (D). See Q 35.

49 (A). You can calculate the glide range in still air by multiplying the L/D ratio by your altitude. The answer will be in feet, so divide it by 6080 to get nautical miles. So, from 6000 feet with a L/D ratio of 6:1, you will glide for 36 000 feet, or around 6 nm. The glide range is not affected by weight, and neither is the glide angle - only the glide speed.

50 (C).

51 (C).

52 (D).

53 (A).

54 (A).

55 (C). An aircraft needs to be controlled around three axes:

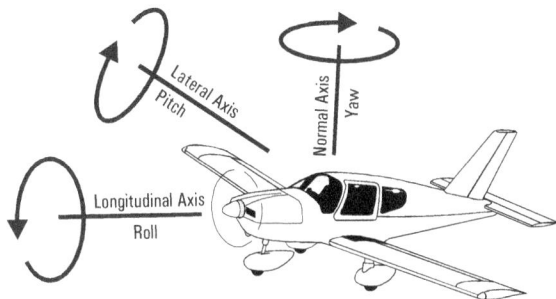

- The **longitudinal axis** extends fore and aft, through the fuselage. Movement about it is **roll**, controlled by the ailerons on small aircraft. On bigger aircraft, spoilers supplement the ailerons. On large and high speed aircraft, two sets of ailerons can be used, one set for high speed only.

- The **lateral axis** runs from wing tip to wing tip (i.e. it parallels the span). Movement around this axis is **pitch** and is controlled by the elevators.

- The **vertical** or **normal** axis is perpendicular to the longitudinal and lateral axes. Movement around it is **yaw,** primarily controlled by the rudder.

56 (A).

57 (B).

58 (C).

59 (A).

60 (B).

61 (D).

62 (A).

63 (A).

64 (B).

65 (B).

66 (B).

67 (D).

68 (A).

69 (B).

70 (D).

71 (D).

72 (C).

73 (A). Wings (plus tailplanes and elevators) are designed and manufactured in a similar way to the fuselage, but *ribs* are the equivalent of formers, which are held in place with *spars*, that perform like longerons.

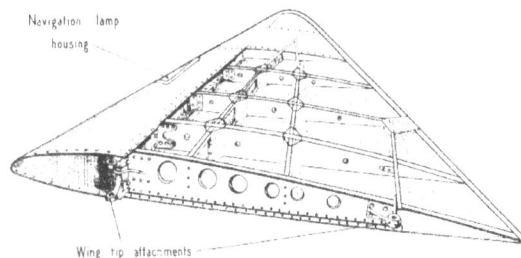

The ribs produce the basic framework and are in line with the airflow. To keep them light but strong, holes may be cut out in them but strength is maintained by curling the edges of the holes through 90° (stiffeners may be fitted vertically to a rib to increase the strength in this direction). The ribs are attached to the skin and the main spars to produce a rigid structure.

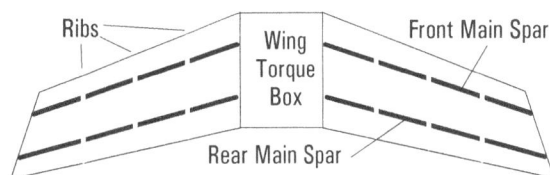

Spars are the main structural members running for the length of the wing, which support all distributed loads as well as concentrated weights such as those from the fuselage, landing gear and engines. The front spar may have engine mounts attached to it and landing gear can be fitted between them (the rear spar normally has the ailerons attached and may be the support for high lift devices such as flaps).

74 (D).

75 (C).

76 (B).

77 (C).

78 (D).

79 (B).

80 (C). Various colour codes are specified for ASIs.

The *green arc* covers the range of speeds for normal operations, and the red line (in a light aircraft, anyway) is the speed not to be exceeded, V_{NE}, which varies inversely with altitude. The blue line is the single engine safety speed. A white arc represents the flap operating range. The limits are:

- Yellow scale: V_{NO}–V_{NE}

- Green scale: V_{S1}-V_{NO}

- White scale: V_{S0}-V_{FE}

At low levels, limiting speeds will be expressed as IAS.

Helicopters

1 (C). The downwash should be of the same velocity along the length of a rotor blade. Unfortunately, the tip rotates at a much faster speed than the root does, often approaching the speed of sound.

This causes a large difference between the lift force at each end. When a blade's speed doubles, as it might (and more) at the tip, the lift created is quadrupled because lift varies as the square of the speed. To stop it bending upwards, a blade's tip must be made stronger, which is expensive, so the lift (and drag) is evened out along the blade instead, by twisting it from root to tip.

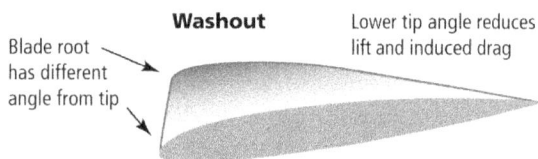

Washout
Blade root has different angle from tip
Lower tip angle reduces lift and induced drag

This process is called *washout*, which affects the C_L part of the lift formula, or by tapering it towards the end, affecting the S component.

Unfortunately, the high twisting required for best hover performance produces vibration and oscillations at high speeds, so a compromise is made - between 6-12° of washout produces most of the advantages for hovering and avoids most of the disadvantages of speed. The Bell 206, for example, has a washout of -10° from root to tip.

2 (C).

3 (A).

4 (A).

5 (A). High winds and gusts can cause the main rotor blades to flap up and down during starting and stopping and be a danger to both people near them and the helicopter itself, as the droop stops could be damaged, or a particularly flexible blade could hit the tail boom (two-bladed helicopters are especially vulnerable), or people walking about. At certain critical speeds (50-100 RPM), blades will pass in and out of the stall. Holding the cyclic in the direction of the wind (and applying the rotor brake) will keep the pitch of the advancing blade to a minimum and stop it lifting in the first place.

However, the cyclic is less effective at low RPM, so other ways of minimising the effect include parking away from the downwind side of obstructions or the downwash or slipstream of other machines, keeping the collective down, or accelerating and decelerating the blades as quickly as possible. In addition, *point the nose out of wind*, so the lowest deflection is away from the tail boom.

With clockwise-rotating blades, have the wind coming from the port side, and *vice versa* - the wind will lift the blades over the tail boom when slowing down or starting up (but they will be down at the front, so warn your passengers). Having the wind from the rear helps you keep an eye on the low blade at the front, but it means landing downwind.

6 (D). See Q5.

7 (D). See Q5.

8 (C).

9 (C).

10 (D). The pressure created by an aerofoil at any point may be represented by a vector at right angles to its surface, whose length is proportional to the difference between absolute pressure at the point and the free stream static pressure. All of them can be represented by a single vector acting at a particular point, the Centre of Pressure.

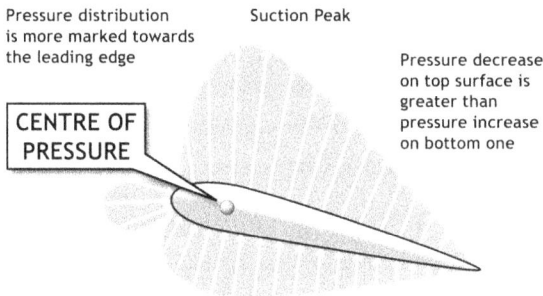

Pressure distribution is more marked towards the leading edge

Suction Peak

Pressure decrease on top surface is greater than pressure increase on bottom one

CENTRE OF PRESSURE

The C of P is a theoretical point on the chord line through which the resultant of all forces (i.e. the total reaction) is said to act. Its position is usually around 25% of the way from the leading edge, simply because more lift is generated there, but it moves steadily forward as the angle of attack is increased, until just before the stalling angle, when it moves rapidly backwards (the C of P's most forward point is just before the stalling angle). This is why an aeroplane's nose drops when the wings stall and the C of P moves behind the C of G.

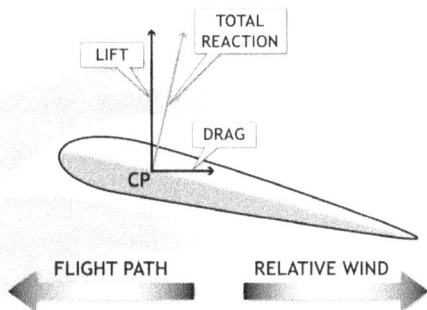

TOTAL REACTION

LIFT

DRAG

CP

FLIGHT PATH   RELATIVE WIND

In a helicopter, the C of P of each blade moves backwards and forwards with each revolution as its angle of attack changes. This means twisting moments and extra loads on the control links. The Centre of Pressure should therefore be as close to the feathering axis as possible to reduce control system loads. The position of the C of P is independent of the angle of attack for its usual values (i.e. below the stall).

Forward movement of the C of P is classed as unstable, because it ends up forward of the aerofoil's C of G and makes things worse.

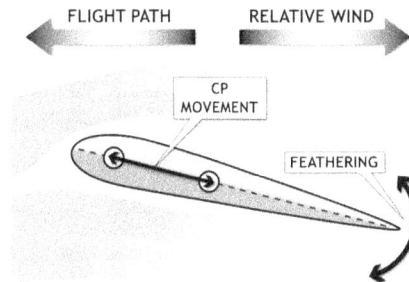

FLIGHT PATH   RELATIVE WIND

CP MOVEMENT

FEATHERING

With an unsymmetrical aerofoil, upper surface lift can act through a different point than lower surface lift, which produces a couple, since there will be a Centre of Pressure for the upper and lower surfaces (the lower one tends to be forward of the upper one). In a symmetrical aerofoil, of course, the two tend to be opposite each other, which is preferred for helicopters, because the CP will then not move so much, if at all. Too much movement imposes a strain on the pitch control arms.

11 (C). As a blade flaps up, its centre of gravity will move inboard, so it will tend to accelerate. When it flaps down, it will decelerate, so the blades can speed up or slow down according to whether the blades are flapping up and down, or according to the radius of the disc.

12 (C).

13 (A). See Q 10.

14 (D). You get the same amount of lift from applying a large acceleration to a small mass of air (as you would in the hover), or a small acceleration to a larger mass. In the case of the hover, the air entering the disc from above will already have gained some speed. In forward flight, on the other hand, it only gets a relatively small acceleration, as it has not had much of a chance to get out of the way, which makes the rotors operate more efficiently (up to a point, where it is offset by an increase in drag).

So, as a helicopter starts to move from the hover into forward flight, a loss of lift will make it settle slightly and seem to lose power, without you moving any controls, as you lose the ground cushion. However, the airflow also becomes more horizontal, effectively **reducing the induced flow** when the air doesn't get to go directly through the blades (it is diverted before it gets to them).

Now, without increasing power, the helicopter will climb and continue its acceleration, so, on takeoff, to maintain a smooth flight path, you can expect to increase collective pitch slightly, then decrease it.

The extra lift (or reduction in the power required) is called translational lift. It occurs because **the reduction in induced flow allows the angle of attack to become larger**, within the blade pitch angle. The relative airflow now moves towards the plane of rotation, as it does when you are in the ground cushion, so the Total Reaction moves closer to the axis of rotation, making the drag vector smaller. This produces an increase in rotor RPM on top of the climb from the increased rotor thrust, assuming collective pitch and power stay the same.

15 (C). In the hover, the tail rotor provides more of a force in the relevant direction than is actually needed to counteract the main rotor torque, and a single-rotor helicopter with North American rotation (anticlockwise viewed from the top) will drift laterally to the right if not corrected.

The tail rotor is doing more work because it is impractical to place any part of the force at the front. In the picture on the left, above, the blades rotate around the centre, and points A are counterbalanced with a double force BB, as with a typical tail rotor. If you cancel out one each of A and B at the bottom, you are left with a side loading that causes movement **in the direction of the anti-torque force**. Also, the tail rotor is out on the end of the tailboom, and has a moment arm, and leverage, to increase the effect as it produces thrust of its own.

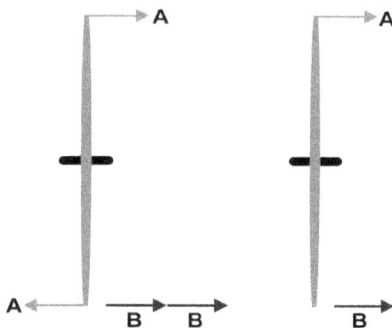

The correction for this residual movement can be done simply by holding the cyclic control slightly off-centre. Other ways include offsetting the mast in the first place, rigging the controls (a mixing unit moves the cyclic proportionally to the collective), or causing the disc to tilt when the collective is raised. None, however, eliminate it completely, and it will not work for semirigid heads because the trunnion bearings are centred at the mast.

The amount of anti-torque from the tail rotor depends on the power setting - more will be required in the hover, for example, so the "power pedal" will be more forward than normal. The power pedal is the left one for a helicopter whose blades go round anti-clockwise when viewed from above (*North American rotation*). It is called that because, not only does it apply more anti-torque in the required direction, but its use also uses power from the engine and may cause the RRPM to droop, which is why a little throttle application is needed when you use it, otherwise the helicopter would descend.

Note: Tail rotor drift is why the helicopter will go one way or the other (depending on which way the blades go round) when the engine fails in the hover. It is also why, when slinging, you need a clear space on that side so you can go there safely, and the ground crew need to be taught to go the opposite way.

This is also known as *translating tendency*.

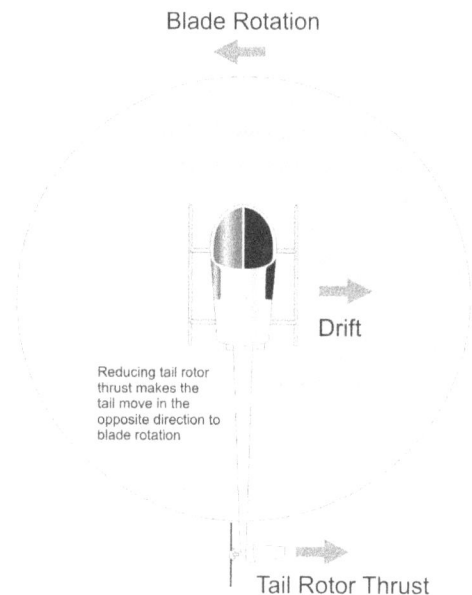

16 (B). In the descent, the vertical upflow alters the direction of the relative airflow, which is in the plane of rotation at the root, and causes an increased angle of attack because there is no induced flow. When the root stalls, the already small downwash is effectively cancelled out by the upwash.

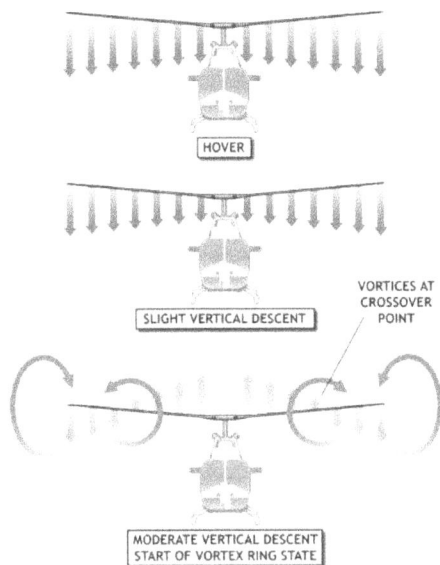

At the tip, the vortices are strengthened, to increase the induced flow and *reduce* the angle of attack. Eventually, the only thrust that balances aircraft weight comes from the middle sections, which is very erratic. Thus, once into the Vortex Ring state you would be very lucky to get out of it, since the controls become significantly less responsive*. However, you can get out of the incipient stage by removing one of the three ingredients that cause you to catch up with your own downwash, namely:

- Low speed (typically less than translation, 10 kts)
- Over 30% power applied
- 300-500 fpm ROD

17 (D). Ground effect is a condition of improved performance in the hover, within about one rotor diameter of the surface. It can also be achieved in forward flight, when very low over the ground, but the maximum effect is at zero airspeed (the reason why ground effect does not show very well at 100 knots is that induced power is very low there).

The slowing down and stagnation of the downwash as it hits the ground underneath the helicopter increases the pressure underneath the disc that opposes and reduces the induced flow, and reduces the effect of the tip vortices.

As the angle of attack increases, the TR vector becomes more vertical, and longer, resulting in less induced drag and a subsequent reduction in the power needed to hover (a Bell 206 will typically need 15% less in the ground cushion). Because you have more lift, you have to lower the collective to maintain your position, so the blade pitch angle is lower.

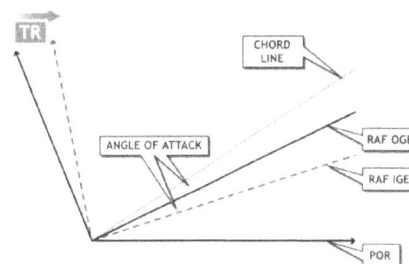

Ground effect is also due to the reduction in tip vortices that are present when any aerofoil is producing lift, because of its downward and outward flow. The vortices normally reduce the efficiency of the rotor disc so that some of the lift "leaks away" at the edges of the disc - here, the leaking away is reduced. Don't forget the upward flow through the centre of the disk which helps to reduce the aerodynamic download from the downwash hitting the fuselage, which in turn reduces the effective weight of the helicopter.

As ground effect depends on a streamline flow, it can be reduced by:

- the *surface you are hovering over* (the harder and smoother the better, and the more level)
- the *wind*, which will vary the direction of the downwash from under the blades. Any wind above about 10 kts will produce translational lift

The effect of ground cushion on a hovering helicopter is greatest on level ground with a hard surface and no wind, and is most effective at a skid height below 4 ft. Over long grass, the power required to hover will be greater than that required over a smooth surface because of greater recirculation of air through the rotor disc.

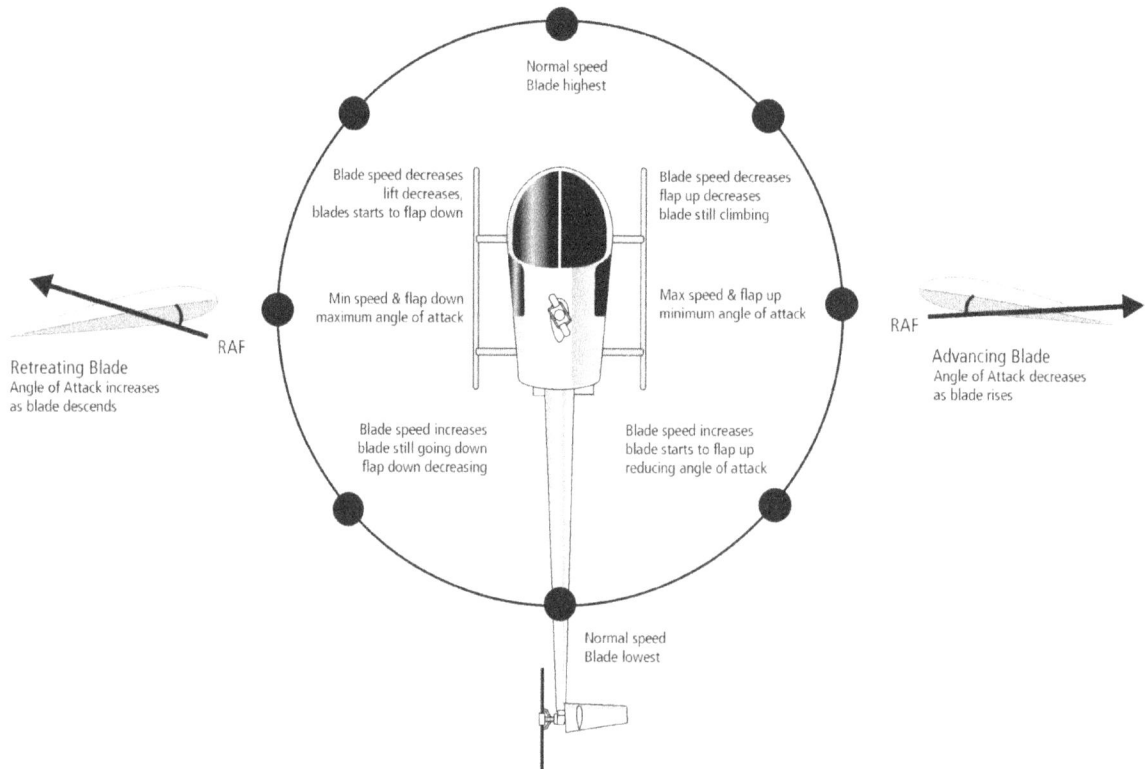

Normal speed
Blade highest

Blade speed decreases
lift decreases,
blades starts to flap down

Blade speed decreases
flap up decreases
blade still climbing

Min speed & flap down
maximum angle of attack

Max speed & flap up
minimum angle of attack

RAF

RAF

Retreating Blade
Angle of Attack increases
as blade descends

Advancing Blade
Angle of Attack decreases
as blade rises

Blade speed increases
blade still going down
flap down decreasing

Blade speed increases
blade starts to flap up
reducing angle of attack

Normal speed
Blade lowest

18 (C). Flapback (see above picture) is an uncommanded change in disc attitude away from the wind, or direction of flight. Dissymmetry of lift and phase lag cause a pitch-up tendency as the helicopter increases speed, and *vice versa*.

This is a side effect of trying to cure the problems due to dissymmetry of lift with flapping, and is the real reason for phase lag, as opposed to "precession". It is a change of disc attitude (away from the wind) that occurs without any control movement, as might be found when hovering, where a small gust will lift the disc up from that direction without altering the TRT. If you use the cyclic to move the disc back, only the control orbit (the plane in which the pitch links move) is affected, meaning that the only thing that will change is the cyclic position - the fuselage attitude will stay the same, so you lose a little cyclic range (the loss of cyclic range is another limitation on forward speed).

If you initiate a control input, the disc responds, then flaps back more *the other way*, so you have to continually apply the original control input to keep going until everything equalises. Luckily, forward speed should be limited by other factors (discussed under V_{NE}) before you reach the end of your cyclic travel.

As the advancing blade passes over the tailboom, it gets faster and produces more lift, which means that it climbs.

Because of the V^2 part of the lift formula, the lift produced is way more than that of the retreating blade, and its maximum relative airspeed (and therefore lift) is gained at the front of the disc, because the climb starts 90° after it starts to increase its relative speed, and its maximum lift point is 90° after that, which is a shift of 180° overall. There is a 90° difference between maximum flapping *velocity* (abeam) and *displacement* (at the front).

As well, there is more induced flow at the rear of the disc which increases the difference between the front and rear angles of attack.

19 (B). In forward flight, the advancing blade develops more lift because the forward speed of the helicopter is added to its rotational speed.

On the other side of the disc, however, the blade going backwards (the retreating blade) generates *less lift* because of its relatively *reduced* speed (rotational speed *minus* forward speed). This makes it fly down because it is trying to increase its angle of attack to maintain the lift.

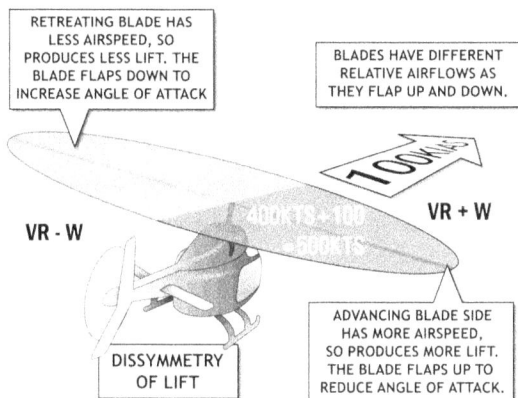

RETREATING BLADE HAS LESS AIRSPEED, SO PRODUCES LESS LIFT. THE BLADE FLAPS DOWN TO INCREASE ANGLE OF ATTACK

BLADES HAVE DIFFERENT RELATIVE AIRFLOWS AS THEY FLAP UP AND DOWN.

VR - W

VR + W

DISSYMMETRY OF LIFT

ADVANCING BLADE SIDE HAS MORE AIRSPEED, SO PRODUCES MORE LIFT. THE BLADE FLAPS UP TO REDUCE ANGLE OF ATTACK.

The end result is that one side of the disc will produce more thrust than the other. In the picture above, there is a 200 kt difference in airflows, which is reflected in the amount of lift produced on either side.

At low speeds, this imbalance tends to cancel out but, at higher speeds, it becomes more significant because lift varies as the *square* of the speed. If you increase collective pitch in forward flight, the advancing and retreating blades get the same increase in angle of attack, but the advancing blade develops more lift than the retreating blade and nose-up flapping results.

Note: The advancing blade is the one with an increased relative wind from its airspeed, and it goes in the same direction as the helicopter, so if you are hover-taxiing sideways to the left in a machine with N American rotation, the advancing blade is in front of you. Similarly, if you are hovering with a wind from the left. Going backwards with a clockwise rotor, it will be on the right. In a stationary hover (relative to the ground), the position of the advancing or retreating blades relative to the pilot depends on the direction of rotation of the main rotor and the wind. In flight, it just depends on the direction of rotation of the main rotor.

20 (A). As a blade flaps up, its centre of gravity will move inboard, so it will tend to accelerate. When it flaps down, it will decelerate, so the blades can speed up or slow down

according to whether the blades are flapping up and down, or according to the radius of the disc. This makes the blade move backwards and forwards in its mounting. The drag hinge allows it to do so.

21 (D).

22 (D).

23 (C). The total reaction is split into two vectors, one vertical and one horizontal. The horizontal vector provides the forward movement.

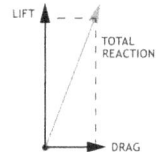

24 (D). Centrifugal force keeps rotor blades stiff in the horizontal position when they are rotating, but when lift is generated, they will rise and form a *coning angle* between the blade and the Tip Path Plane, the size of which is determined by the lift produced and the centrifugal force applied, plus the weight of the blade itself.

25 (A).

26 (A).

27 (B).

28 (B).

29 (B).

30 (B).

31 (C).

32 (B).

33 (C).

34 (C).

35 (D).

36 (B).

37 (A).

38 (D).

39 (C).

40 (B).

41 (D).

42 (D).

43 (D).

44 (A).

45 (C).

46 (C).

47 (B).

48 (C).

49 (B). See Q 17.

50 (C). See Q 15.

51 (B).

52 (B).

53 (C).

54 (C).

55 (B).

56 (C).

57 (D).

58 (D).

59 (B).

60 (D).

61 (D).

62 (A).

63 (C). See Q 24.

64 (D).

65 (D).

66 (B).

67(C).

68(C).

69 (B).

70 (C).

Turbines

1 (A).

2 (D).

3 (C).

4 (D).

5 (D).

6 (A).

7 (A).

COMMUNICATIONS

1 (B). After satisfactory communication has been established, and if no confusion is likely to arise, the ground station may abbreviate callsigns. A pilot may only abbreviate a callsign if it has first been abbreviated by the aeronautical station. The shortened version would typically be the national identifier followed by the last two letters. For example, G-BFRM becomes G-RM.

Other information may be given, such as: "Basic service available from Wrayton on 125.750". The reply would then be: "Changing to Wrayton 125.750, G-RM."

2 (B). A blind transmission is one from a station where 2-way communications cannot be established, but it is believed that the called station can receive it (ICAO). If you cannot establish communication on any designated aeronautical station frequency, or with any other aircraft, transmit your message twice on that frequency, including the addressee for whom the message is intended, preceded by the phrase *Transmitting Blind* in case the transmitter is still functioning.

If the receiver fails, transmit reports twice at the scheduled times or positions on the designated frequency preceded by the phrase 'TRANSMITTING BLIND DUE TO RECEIVER FAILURE'.

3 (A). **Note**: Under no circumstances is this to be used in reply to a question requiring a direct answer in the affirmative (AFFIRM) or negative (NEGATIVE).

4 (B). A *land* station in the aeronautical mobile service, that is, a transmitting or receiving node, on land, a ship or a platform at sea, or a satellite (one would logically include *in the air*, but it would appear not). Normally, control is exercised by the ground station (meaning that you must do what they tell you), except for distress calls, which are controlled by the station initiating the call. Between aircraft, the one *called* has control.

5 (B). CAP 413 Chapter 2 1.11.1 refers. When an error is made in a transmission the word 'CORRECTION' shall be spoken, the last correct group or phrase repeated and then the correct version transmitted. If a correction can best be made by repeating the entire message, use the phrase 'CORRECTION I SAY AGAIN' before transmitting the message a second time.

6 (C). CAP 413 Table 7. Operate the special position indication (i.e the ident button) on your transponder.

7 (D). CAP 413 Chapter 2 para 1.4.2 All numbers, except those contained in paragraph 1.4.2 b) shall be transmitted by pronouncing each digit separately as follows:

(a) When transmitting messages containing aircraft callsigns, altimeter settings, flight levels (except FL100, 200, 300 etc. which are expressed as 'Flight Level (number) HUNDRED'), headings, wind speeds/directions, pressure settings, airspeed, transponder codes and frequencies, each digit shall be transmitted separately

(b) All numbers used in the transmission of altitude, height, cloud height, visibility and runway visual range information which contain whole hundreds and whole thousands shall be transmitted by pronouncing each digit in the number of hundreds or thousands followed by the word HUNDRED or TOUSAND as appropriate. Combinations of thousands and whole hundreds shall be transmitted by pronouncing each digit in the number of thousands followed by the word TOUSAND and the number of hundreds followed by the word HUNDRED

Thus, numbers (as used for altitude, cloud height, visibility and RVR information) should generally be spoken individually, except for whole thousands (or hundreds) where they occur as round figures. 65 is therefore *six-five*, while 2000 is *two thousand*. Eleven thousand is *One One Thousand*. In other words, combinations of thousands and whole hundreds must be transmitted by pronouncing each digit in the number of thousands, followed by the word *Thousand*, followed by the number of hundreds, followed by the word *Hundred*.

For example:

- Altitude 800 (Eight Hundred)
- 1,500 (One Thousand Five Hundred)*
- 6,715 (Six Seven One Five)
- 12,000 (One Two Thousand)
- 200 (Two Hundred)

Altitude above sea level is expressed in thousands of feet, plus hundreds, but flight levels use separate digits, thus 2500 is said as two thousand five hundred, but FL 100 is *flight level one zero zero.** You would express a heading separately, e.g. *two five zero* for 250°.

CAP 413 Chapter 2 para 1.5.1. **When transmitting time**, only the minutes of the hour are normally required, but the hour should be included if there is any possibility of confusion. Time checks shall be given to the nearest minute and preceded by the word 'TIME'. Coordinated Universal Time (UTC) is to be used at all times, unless specified. 2400 hours designates midnight, the end of the day, and 0000 hours the beginning of the day.

8 (C). The one currently in use.

9 (B). One one eight decimal one.

10 (B). Cherokee BC.

11 (D). CAP 413 Chapter 6 para 1.7.1. A pilot may request a bearing or heading using the appropriate phrase or Q code to specify the service required. Each aircraft transmission shall be ended by the aircraft call sign. A VDF station will provide the following as requested:

- **QDR** – Magnetic bearing from the station (i.e. Approach G-ABCD request QDR G-ABCD).
- **QDM** – Magnetic heading to be steered (assuming no wind) to reach the VDF station (i.e. Approach G-ABCD request QDM G-ABCD).
- **QTE** – True bearing from the station (i.e. True bearing, True bearing, Approach G-ABCD request True bearing (or QTE) G-ABCD).

12 (D). QFE is the altimeter subscale setting that indicates **height** above either aerodrome elevation, threshold elevation, or helideck elevation.

13 (C). CAP 413 Chapter 10 para 7.5.1. To alleviate RTF loading at some busy airports, *Automatic Terminal Information Service* (ATIS) messages are broadcast to pass routine arrival/departure information on a **discrete RTF frequency or on an appropriate VOR**. Pilots inbound to these airports are normally required, on first contact with the aerodrome ATSU, to acknowledge receipt of current information by quoting the code letter of the broadcast. Pilots of outbound aircraft are not normally required to acknowledge receipt of departure ATIS except when requested on the actual ATIS broadcast. If, however, pilots report receipt of a departure ATIS broadcast the QNH should be included, thereby allowing ATC to check that the quoted QNH is up-to-the-minute.

14 (A). CAP 413 Chapter 8 para 1.2.1. *Urgency* - A condition concerning the safety of an aircraft or other vehicle, or of some person on board or within sight, but does not require immediate assistance. It has priority over all other messages except Distress.

15 (B). CAP 413 Table 7 - Repeat all, or the following part of your last transmission.

16 (B). CAP 413 1.4.3. Numbers containing a decimal point shall be transmitted with the decimal point in appropriate sequence being indicated by the word decimal.

17 (C). Loss of communications.

18 (C). Reselect the numbers on the control unit.

19 (C). CAP 413 1.18 Communication Failure, Air–Ground. Check the following:

- You are using the correct frequency
- The station you are calling is open for watch
- You are not out of radio range
- The Receiver volume is correctly set

If the above are OK, the aircraft equipment may not be working correctly.

When an aircraft station is unable to establish contact with the aeronautical station on the designated frequency it shall attempt to establish contact on another frequency appropriate to the route being flown. If this attempt fails, the aircraft station shall attempt to establish communication with other aircraft or other aeronautical stations on frequencies appropriate to the route.

If you still cannot establish communication on any designated frequency, or with any other aircraft, you must transmit your message twice on the designated frequency, including the addressee for whom the message is intended, preceded by the phrase 'TRANSMITTING BLIND' in case the transmitter is still working.

If you think the transmitter has failed, check or change the microphone. Listen out on the designated frequency for instructions. It should be possible to answer questions by using the carrier wave if the microphone is not working.

If the receiver fails, transmit reports twice at the scheduled times or positions on the designated frequency preceded by the phrase 'TRANSMITTING BLIND DUE TO RECEIVER FAILURE'.

An aircraft being provided with air traffic control service, advisory service or aerodrome flight information service is to transmit information regarding the intention of the PIC with respect to the continuation of the flight.

20 (D). 118.7 X-CD.

21 (C). VHF reception is line-of-sight and as such will not curve to follow the Earth surface, so you have to be high enough to receive your selected station at a particular distance. As an example, when crossing the Irish Sea, you must be above 3000 feet to hear either Shannon or London Information. However, If using the VOR at high altitudes, you might get station overlap and erroneous readings, so don't use VOR bearing information beyond the published protection range (see the AIP).

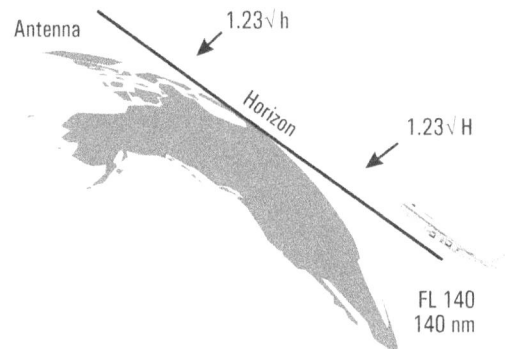

22 (B). See Q 11.

23 (C). A Mode C transponder is directly attached to an encoding altimeter (or, more precisely, an altitude digitiser, which selects a different code to that selected in the window), but only Pressure Altitude (or FL) information based on 1013.25 (or 29.92) information is sent from the aircraft (in 100-foot increments) - the conversion to local pressure, if required, is done inside the ATC computer. ATC will not be able to see changes when you move the altimeter subscale. Mode C is selected by switching to ALT, after switching on for Mode A. The pulses are 21 microseconds apart. You should always use Mode C unless directed otherwise.

24 (B). Ground.

25 (D). CAP 413 1.5.7. Occasionally an aircraft may be instructed to make a complete turn (known as an orbit or a 360 degree turn), for delaying purposes or to achieve a required spacing behind preceding traffic. **Note:** A 360 turn is spoken of a "TREE SIXTY TURN".

26 (A). UTC. See Q 7.

27 (C). Speak at a constant volume.

28 (A). See Q 2.

29 (D). Aerodrome Flight Information Service.

30 (D). 118.0 to 136.975 MHz.

31 (C). CAP 413 Table 11. To check a radio, call up another station (if they're not busy) and ask how they read you (don't take more than about ten seconds). They should reply with a grading on the following scale:

© *Phil Croucher, 2016*

If this page is a photocopy, it is not authorised!

- 1 - unreadable

- 2 - readable now and then

- 3 - readable with difficulty

- 4 - readable

- 5 - perfectly readable

"Reading you Strength Three", for example.

32 (D). Affirm.

33 (A). CAP 413 Table 7. Wait and I will call you. **Note:** No onward clearance to be assumed. The caller would normally re-establish contact if the delay is lengthy. STANDBY is not an approval or denial.

34 (B). See Q 7.

35 (D). *Hold* means stop before reaching the specified location. Note: It is only used in limited circumstances where no defined point exists (e.g. where there is no suitably located holding point), or to reinforce a clearance limit. See CAP 413 1.7.12 & 13.

36 (A). CAP 413 1.10.3. When a ground station wishes to broadcast information to all aircraft likely to receive it, the message should be prefaced by the call 'All stations'. No reply is expected to such calls unless individual stations are subsequently called upon to acknowledge receipt.

37 (A). Open between sunrise and sunset.

38 (B). ICAO definition.

39 (C). CAP 413 Chapter 8 para 1.2.1.

40 (C). Distress.

41 (A). 7600.

42 (A). Have an emergency.

43 (A). 121.500 MHz.

44 (C). Newtown Radio.

45 (B). CAP 413 Chapter 8 para 1.5. The emergency message shall contain the following information (time and circumstance permitting) and, whenever possible, should be passed in the order given:

(a) 'MAYDAY/MAYDAY/MAYDAY' (or 'PAN PAN/PAN PAN/PAN PAN')

(b) Name of the station addressed (when appropriate and time and circumstances permitting)

(c) Callsign

(d) Type of aircraft

(e) Nature of the emergency

(f) Intention of the PIC

(g) Present or last known position, flight level/altitude and heading

(h) Pilot qualifications*

(i) Any other useful information e.g. endurance remaining, number of people on board (POB), aircraft colour/markings, any survival aids.

*There is no ICAO requirement to include pilot qualifications in a distress message, but this information should be included whenever possible in UK emergency messages as it may help the controller to plan a course of action best suited to your ability. It could include:

- *Student* - Solo student pilots can prefix the aircraft callsign with STUDENT to indicate their lack of experience. Although intended primarily for *ab initio* students, the prefix shall also be used in other circumstances where, for example, the holder of a valid licence is returning to flying practice after a significant absence and is undergoing renewal training involving solo flight conducted as a student under supervision of a flight instructor.

- *No Instrument Qualification*

- *IMC Rating*

- *Full Instrument Rating*

46 (A). CAP 413 Table 7.

47 (A). CAP 413 Chapter 8 para 1.13.2. When an distress incident has been resolved, the station which has been controlling the emergency traffic will transmit a message indicating that normal working may be resumed.

48 (A). STOP TRANSMITTING MAYDAY.

49 (A).

50 (A). Maintain a listening watch to see if you can assist in any way.

51 (B). **ATIS** (*Automatic Terminal Information Service*) is a repetitive broadcast on available VHF frequencies, VOR and NDB (not the ILS) at major aerodromes, to reduce congestion on VHF frequencies. You should listen and take down the details before you contact ATC, inbound or outbound. ATIS broadcasts should be updated whenever a significant change occurs, and should not last over 30 seconds. The information given need not be repeated, except for the altimeter setting.'

The items are transmitted in this order:

- ATIS ID
- Time (24 hour clock)
- Wind Velocity (Degrees/Knots)
- Visibility (Metres)
- Low Cloud (oktas/feet)
- Medium Cloud (oktas/feet)
- High Cloud (oktas/feet)
- Temp/Dew Point (Degrees)
- Altimeter (hPA/Inches)
- Runway in use
- Anything else useful, such as runway missing, lights out, etc.

Visibility less than 5 km is reported in metres, and in km above that.

52 (B). See Q 1.

53 (A). See Q 1.

54 (A). See Q 35.

55 (B). Clearances are valid only in controlled airspace, and there will be some form of the word "clear" in the text to identify them. **Clearances must always be read back** (although you don't need to read back the wind velocity). In general, anything that affects communication, identification or position information.

56 (B). CAP 413 Chapter 2 para 1.14.3. The words *Take Off* are used only when an aircraft is cleared for takeoff. At all other times the word *Departure* is used.

57 (A). For heights, whole thousands should be pronounced digit by digit, followed by the word *Thousand*.

58 (D). CAP 413 Chapter 3 para 1.7. 1. This is the order of items in a position report:

- Callsign
- Position
- Time at position
- Level or altitude
- Next position
- ETA at next position

59 (B). CAP 413 Chapter 2 para 1.4.4. All six figures shall be used when identifying frequencies irrespective of whether they are 25 kHz or 8.33 kHz spaced.

Exceptionally, when the final two digits of the frequency are both zero, only the first four digits need be given. Technically, an 8.33 kHz frequency is a "channel", but the word "channel" is not used in RTF.

60 (C).

61 (D).

62 (B).

63 (B). See Q 59.

64 (D).

65 (B).

66 (B).

67 (D). CAP 413 Chapter 6 para 1.5.2. A full flight plan is not required for Special VFR flight but the pilot must give brief details of the callsign, aircraft type and pilot's intentions, including ETA at entry point. A full flight plan is required if the pilot wishes his destination to be notified.

68 (A). CAP 413 Chapter 10 para 3.32.3. Pilots requiring a MATZ, and where appropriate, ATZ penetration service must establish two way RTF communication on the appropriate frequency with the aerodrome controlling the zone when 15 nm or 5 minutes' flying time from the boundary whichever is the sooner, and request approval to penetrate the MATZ, and if appropriate ATZ. When requested by the controller to 'pass your message' the pilot should pass the following information:

- Aircraft Callsign/Type
- Departure Point and Destination
- Present Position
- Level
- Additional details/Intention (e.g. Flight Rules, Next Route Point)

69 (C). CAP 413 Chapter 7 para 1.5.

70 (D). CAP 413 Chapter 4 para 1.8.1. Aircraft reports Long Final (between 8 and 4 miles) when aircraft is on a straight in approach.

71 (D). CAP 413 Table 7. I cannot comply with your request, instruction or clearance. Unable is normally followed by a reason.

72 (C). CAP 413 Chapter 6 para 1.7.1. A pilot may request a bearing or heading using the appropriate phrase or Q code to specify the service required. Each aircraft transmission shall be ended by the aircraft call sign.

73 (B).

Class	Bearing	Position
A	±2°	5 nm
B	±5°	20 nm
C	±10°	50 nm
D	<C	<C

74 (C). An encoding altimeter is used with a transponder in Mode C so that your altitude can be shown on a radar display.

The encoding assembly is mechanically activated by the aneroid capsule. Older versions consist of a light source, various lenses and an encoder disc with a special pattern on it (in eleven concentric circles) that works like a bar code when the light is reflected from it to produce binary inputs that correspond to 100-ft increments in altitude. One turn of the disc covers the complete range of the altimeter. Naturally, there are now digital versions of the same thing that can also be fitted externally.

Note: The adjustment knob on the altimeter does not affect what ATC see on their radar screens! All encoding systems transmit your altitude corrected to 29.92 inches, or 1013.25 hPa. The ground equipment makes any regional corrections directly. You won't get into trouble for small deviations, say, of 200 feet or so, but you may be treated as an amateur and directed around their airspace, rather than being allowed a more direct routing.

75 (D). Under ICAO Annex 12, para 5.7, if you hear a distress transmission, you must:

• Acknowledge the transmission (if somebody else does that before you, then it may be a good idea to maintain radio silence)

• Record the position of the craft in distress, if given

• Take a bearing on the transmission

• Inform the appropriate ATS unit or RCC

• At your discretion, whilst awaiting further instructions, proceed to the position given. Once there, if a rescue is in progress, do not interfere without checking with whoever is in charge

76 (A). See Q 45.

77 (B). CAP 413 Chapter 8 para 1.8.1. Pilots may simulate emergency incidents (BUT NOT THE STATE OF DISTRESS) on 121.5 MHz or 243.0 MHz to enable them to gain experience of the ATC service provided. Before calling, pilots should listen out on the emergency

frequency to ensure that no actual or practice incident is already in progress.

78 (D). CAP 413 Chapter 8 para 1.2.1. The states of emergency are classified as follows:

• **Distress**. A condition of being threatened by serious and/or imminent danger and of requiring immediate assistance.

• **Urgency**. A condition concerning the safety of an aircraft or other vehicle, or of some person on board or within sight, but does not require immediate assistance.

79 (A). CAP 413 Chapter 4 para 1.5.3. A conditional clearance depends on the actions of another aircraft, such as when being given clearance to cross a runway after a taxying aircraft has passed. Correct identification of the aircraft involved is essential. Conditional clearances must be given in this order:

• Identification

• The condition (specify)

• The subject of the condition

• The instruction

For example: "G-PACO - Behind* the A 340, Line up". Your reply: "Behind the A 340, Line Up, G-PACO".

Note: This implies the need for you to identify the aircraft or vehicle causing the conditional clearance.

Readback must be in full and in the same sequence as given, with the condition first.

*In the UK, the word *After* is used because the ICAO one, *Behind*, has been misinterpreted.

80 (D). According to the UK AIP, clearance for Special VFR flight in the UK is an authorization by ATC for **a pilot** (not a flight) to fly within a **Control Zone** while unable to comply with IFR (under ICAO, the aircraft should be IFR equipped - see Annex 6). Special VFR clearance is only granted when traffic conditions permit it to take place without hindrance to normal IFR flights, but certain notified lanes, routes and local flying areas may be used. It should be requested by the pilot.

81 (A). See Q 79.

82 (B). Messages must be dealt with in this order:

- Distress
- Urgency
- Direction Finding
- Flight Safety (ATC messages, avoiding weather)
- Meteorological
- Flight Regularity (parts and materials)
- UN Charter
- Government messages
- Service communications
- All others

83 (C).

84 (A). Vertical position is reported as height.

85 (B).

86 (B).

87 (B). CAP 413 Glossary: A Basic Service is an ATS provided for the purpose of giving advice and information useful for the safe and efficient conduct of flights. This may include weather information, changes of serviceability of facilities, conditions at aerodromes, general airspace activity information, and any other information likely to affect safety.

The avoidance of other traffic is solely the pilot's responsibility.

88 (B). CAP 413 Chapter 4 para 1.8.3. A standard overhead join comprises the following:

- Overfly at 2000 ft above Aerodrome Elevation.
- If not already known, determine the circuit direction from the signals square, other
- traffic or windsock.
- Descend on the 'dead side' to circuit height.
- Join the circuit by crossing the upwind end of the runway at circuit height.
- Position downwind.

89 (A). See Q 68.

90 (A).

91 (A). CAP 413 Chapter 6 para 1.17.3. Once communication has been established the pilot should pass the following information:

- Aircraft Callsign/Type
- Departure Point and Destination
- Present Position
- Level
- Additional details / Intention (e.g. Flight Rules, Next Route Point)

92 (B). CAP 413 Glossary. A Deconfliction Service is a surveillance based ATS where, in addition to the provisions of a Basic Service, the controller provides specific surveillance derived traffic information and issues headings and/or levels aimed at achieving planned deconfliction minima against all observed aircraft in Class F/G airspace, or for positioning and/or sequencing. However, the avoidance of other traffic is ultimately the pilot's responsibility.

93 (C).

94 (B).

95 (C).

96 (D).

97 (C).

98 (B).

99 (C).

100 (B).

101 (D). See Q 11.

102 (A). CAP 413 Chapter 6 para 1.16.1. LARS is an ATS surveillance service available to assist pilots flying outside controlled airspace up to and including FL95. LARS is normally provided within 30 nm of the nominated unit and is a secondary service provided at the discretion of the controller. Therefore, when primary task loadings are high, LARS may not be available. The service provided will be a Traffic Service or a Deconfliction Service.

103 (C). See Q 56.

104 (C).

105 (A). CAP 413 Chapter 3 para 1.2.3. Care must be taken to ensure that misunderstandings are not generated as a consequence of the phraseology employed during these phases of flight. For example, levels may be reported as altitude, height or flight levels according to the phase of

flight and the altimeter setting. Therefore, when passing level messages, the following conventions apply:

- The word 'to' is to be omitted from messages relating to FLIGHT LEVELS.

- All messages relating to an aircraft's climb or descent to a HEIGHT or ALTITUDE employ the word 'to' followed immediately by the word HEIGHT or ALTITUDE.

Furthermore, the initial message in any such RTF exchange will also include the appropriate QFE or QNH.

106 (D). See Q 80.

107 (B).

108 (C).

109 (C).

110 (B).

111 (A). See Q 91.

112 (A). CAP 413 Chapter 4 para 6.2.3. SAFETYCOM transmissions shall only be made when aircraft are not more than 2000 ft above aerodrome level, or not more than 1000 ft above promulgated circuit height (if applicable) and within 10 nm of the aerodrome of intended landing.

113 (B).

114 (B).

115 (C).

116 (B).

117 (B). In other words, a radial.

118 (B).

119 (A).

120 (D).

121 (C).

122 (A).

123 (C).

124 (B).

125 (A).

126 (A).

127 (C).

128 (B).

129 (C).

130 (A).

131 (B).

132 (D).

133 (A).

134 (D).

135 (C).

136 (B).

137 (B).

138 (D).

139 (B).

140 (A).

141 (C).

142 (C).

143 (A).

144 (B).

145 (C).

146 (C).

NAVIGATION

General Navigation

1 (C). Rhumb Lines are regularly curved lines on the surface of the Earth that cut each meridian at the same angle, and maintain a constant direction with respect to True North.

2 (D).

3 (C). Great Circles have planes that go through the centre of the Earth, or, in other words, are circles whose centre and radius are that of the Earth, so they will always divide it into two equal parts. The name comes from the fact that it is the largest circle you can obtain, so only one Great Circle can be drawn through two points on the surface of the Earth that are not diametrically opposed. The shortest distance between any two points on the surface of a sphere is the smaller arc of the Great Circle joining them. Radio waves follow Great Circle routes. Arcs are measured in degrees.

The definition includes lines of longitude and the Equator. Since meridians are half lines of longitude, they are semi-great circles, so a meridian and its antimeridian together make a Great Circle.

4 (A). These velocities go together:

- Heading & Airspeed
- Track & Groundspeed
- Wind Direction & Speed

You have to find mixed pairs, such as heading and groundspeed, rather than the combinations mentioned above, because you start with a mix in the first place (you usually know the airspeed and track already). Given any four, you can figure out the others by measurement, but you can do this mechanically with the flight computer.

5 (D). The Lambert Conformal is what most of today's aeronautical charts are based on, as the meridians are straight, even if they converge towards the North, beyond the limits of the map. This means that Great Circles are nearly straight lines*, so they are good for radio bearings, and rhumb lines will be curves concave to the nearer pole. Great Circles that are not meridians are curves concave to the Parallel of Origin.

*Even for the 2750 miles distance between San Francisco and New York, the distance between the two at mid-longitude would be no more than ten miles.

6 (A). 1 nautical mile (nm) is 6080 feet, or 1852 m. The JAR syllabus is limited to where 1 degree of arc = 60 nm (1 degree has 60 minutes)

7 (A).

8 (C).

9 (B).

10 (A).

11 (A).

12 (C). First multiply the scale by the chart distance to get an earth distance of 50 000 000 cm. Convert to kilometres by dividing by 100 to get metres, then 1000 - 500 km. Convert that to nm (divide by 1.852) to get 269 nm.

13 (C).

14 (A).

15 (D). 6 nm per gallon!

16 (D).

17 (A).1.1 hours at 160 kts is 176 nm, or 2° 56 minutes. Subtract the distance South of the Equator to get the distance North of the Equator.

18 (B).

19 (D).

20 (D). It is refraction that accounts for twilight. *Civil twilight* exists when the centre of the Sun's disk is within 6° of the horizon, during which you have a distinct horizon.

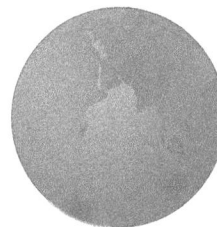

Sunrise/Sunset	
Civil	6°
Nautical	12°
Astronomical	18°

21 (C).

22 (B).

23 (D).

24 (C).

25 (A).

26 (D). See Q 20.

27 (A).

28 (B).

Time	From	To	FL/ Alt	Safety Alt	TAS	W/V	Track T	Drift	Hdg T	Var	Hdg M	G/S	Dist	Time	ETA
1200	GOW	INS	4500	4300	90	180/15	007	+ 1	008	+ 5.5	013	105	104	60	1300
Alternate											Totals →				

29 (A).

30 (B).

31 (B).

32 (A).

33 (B).

34 (B).

35 (A).

36 (C).

37 (A).

38 (B).

39 (A).

40 (C).

41 (B).

42 (A).

43 (C).

44 (B).

45 (B).

The Flight Plan
See overleaf.

1 (A).

2 (D).

3 (B).

4 (B).

5 (B).

6 (C).

7 (B).

8 (C).

9 (B).

10 (C).

11 (C).

12 (A).

13 (C).

14 (B).

15 (A).

16 (B).

17 (C). See above for completed plan.

Time	From	To	FL/Alt	Safety Alt	TAS	W/V	Track T	Drift	Hdg T	Var	Hdg M	G/S	Dist	Time	ETA
11:00	BEAULIEU	PTSFLD	3000	1200	90	180/15	062	8L	070	5W	075	96	24.5	15	11:15
11:15	PTSFLD	TANGMERE	3500	1200	90	180/15	138	6L	144	5W	149	86	13.5	10	11:25
											Totals →		2	2	
Alternate															
	TANGMERE	EGHR	2000	1200	90	180/15	288	8R	280	5W	285	94	2	2	

Radio Navigation

1 (D). VHF reception is line-of-sight and as such will not curve to follow the Earth's surface, so you have to be high enough to receive your selected station at a particular distance. As an example, when crossing the Irish Sea, you must be above 3000 feet to hear either Shannon or London Information. The calculation is 1.23 x the sq root of the height, which in this case ends up as 38.89 nm.

2 (B). Distance Measuring Equipment is secondary radar, but in reverse. It measures the time difference between pulses being sent from an aircraft, and received back (on different frequencies). Then the distance is calculated.

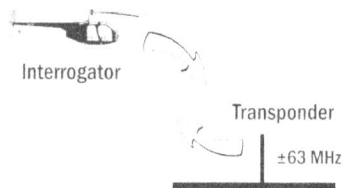

Interrogator

Transponder

±63 MHz

In other words, the aircraft is the first to transmit on UHF, then the DME transponder on the ground returns the signal (with the same pulse spacing), ±63 MHz, after a 50 microsecond delay.

Instruments in the cockpit will not only show your distance to a station, but will calculate the rate of movement and display the groundspeed (just multiply the distance flown in 6 minutes by 10 if yours doesn't). The reason it's not completely accurate is because the distance measured is the *slant range* from the station, and not from your equivalent position on the ground, although at long distances and lower altitudes, this will be minimised. In practical terms, the difference is insignificant when more than 10 miles from the station, and the *maximum error occurs overhead* - at 12,000 ft, the instrument would read 2 nm, and 4 nm at 24,000 ft, and so on.

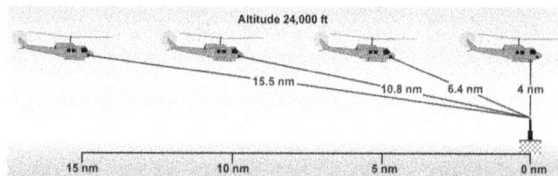

Altitude 24,000 ft

15.5 nm   10.8 nm   6.4 nm   4 nm

15 nm   10 nm   5 nm   0 nm

3 (B). In the bowels of the aircraft will be a large black box, connected to a *remote indicator* in the cockpit, that might also double as an ILS display.

This one is a 5-dot display, using 4 dots plus a circle, so each one is 2°, for an overall width of 10°. For 3 dots plus a circle, each is 2.5°.

4 (C). See Q 3.

5 (C). Secondary Surveillance Radar (SSR) improves on primary radar by using double-pulse secondary equipment to provide more information, hence the name. Participating aircraft carry a *transponder* (for *transmitter/responder*) that receives the interrogation pulse from the transmitter (1030 MHz ±0.2 MHz), superimposes information on it and sends it right back on another paired frequency (1090 MHz). This means, first of all, that the range of operation can be doubled immediately, and, secondly, that the blip on the screen can be made much smaller, together with information that makes it more easily identifiable to ATC, because the pulses can be coded. As well, there is no storm clutter, as the principle of echo return is not used. Computer trickery can provide predicted tracks and collision warnings, amongst other things.

6 (B).

7 (D).

8 (B). See Q 1.

9 (D).

10 (C). See Q 1.

11 (B). See Q 1.

12 (D). Limitations of the system include:

- **static**, including local thunderstorm activity, which is likely to cause the greatest inaccuracy and make the needle point towards a storm.

- **night effect,** where the needle swings erratically, at its strongest just after sunset and before sunrise. The loop is designed to receive surface waves - any sky waves will be out of phase and distorted, because they energise the horizontal parts of the loop (waves change their polarisation when

reflecting off the ionosphere). If the ionosphere is not parallel with the Earth's surface, they will also arrive from different directions. Low power beacons are virtually unaffected by this as they can only produce a ground wave. Check for an unsteady needle and a fading audio signal.

- **station overlap**, when NDBs have the same frequency. Because this is more pronounced at night, it can easily be confused with *night effect*, below (promulgated ranges are not valid at night for this reason). This will have the greatest effect on ADF accuracy, particularly at night.

- **mountain effect**, or variations caused by reflections from high ground, where two signals might be received at once from different paths.

- **quadrantal error**, or variations from the aircraft itself, in the same way as it might affect a compass. The signal is reradiated by the airframe and the receiver gets an additional (much weaker) signal to contend with. The greatest error lies at 45° to the fore and aft axis, hence the term *quadrantal*. Modern systems have corrector boxes for this.

- **coastal refraction**, from radio waves in transit from land to sea, because they travel slightly faster over water, which makes you aircraft appear closer to the shore. This effect is most noticeable at less than 30° to the coastline (i.e. an acute angle), and at lower frequencies, so expect errors if you are using an NDB inland directly in front of or behind you. With two NDBs, one 20 nm, and the other 50 nm inland from the coast, and if the coastal error is the same for both, the error seen by an aircraft will be greater from the beacon that is further away.

Picture: NDB Coastal Effect

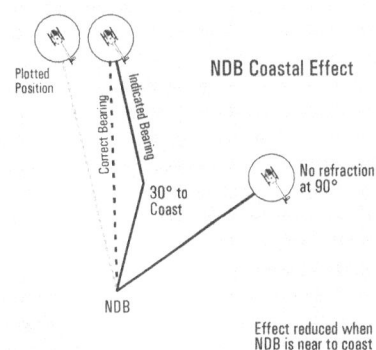

- **Identification**. As there is no flag indication of failure, as there is with the VOR, you should continuously monitor the station ID when relying on the instrument. Aside from that, the only way of knowing about problems is seeing the needle rotate to the right if the signal is not received.

This is useful knowledge if you want to do an NDB approach to a coastal aerodrome in mountains just as the sun is setting!

13 (C). See Q 2.

14 (B). See Q 12.

15 (C). Never use any navaid if you can't identify it!

16 (D). VDF is VHF and therefore line-of-sight.

17 (B).

18 (C).

19 (C). A radial is always from the VOR.

20 (A).

21 (B). See *Communications*, Q 11.

22 (B). The equipment electronically measures an angle. A 30 MHz *omniphase signal* is received by all stations at the same phase, and a *variphase* signal rotates clockwise at the same frequency, being received at different phases according to its azimuth angle. Both signals are in phase when the rotating signal passes Magnetic North, but they get more out of phase by the amount of degrees you go round the circle. Thus, your receiver picks up the all-directional signal first and the maximum point of the rotating signal a little bit later. The time difference is indicated in degrees as your magnetic bearing from the VOR (actually called a *radial*).

23 (B). See Q 2.

24 (C). See Q 5.

25 (A). The signals are line of sight, so any obstructions degrade it.

26 (D).

27 (D).

28 (B).

29 (B).

30 (B).

31 (A).

32 (A).

33 (C). Accuracy comes in these classes, in relation to bearing or position, and will be included in the transmission:

Class	Bearing	Position
A	±2°	5 nm
B	±5°	20 nm
C	±10°	50 nm
D	<C	<C

Flight Computer Practice

1. A
2. D
3. B
4. D
5. A
6. B
7. C
8. C
9. B
10. D
11. C
12. A
13. A
14. B
15. D
16. D. Temp is ISA +1.
17. C
18. C
19. D
20. D
21. B
22. B
23. A
24. C
25. C
26. B
27. C
28. B

29. B

30. D

31. B

32. C

No	G/S	Time	Distance
33	120 kts	1:15	150 nm
34	105 kts	0:52	91 nm
35	145 kts	1:33	225 nm
36	168 kts	1:40	280 nm
37	152 kts	0:35	88.5 nm
38	110 mph	1:22	150 sm
39	133 mph	2:15	300 sm
40	108 mph	2:02	220 sm
41	210 mph	0:48	168 sm
42	183 mph	1:25	260 sm
43	184 kts	0;20.3	62 nm
44	108 kts	2:29	268 nm
45	165 kts	0:36.5	100 nm
46	198 kts	1:01	202 nm
47	87 kts	1:27.5	127 nm
48	208 mph	0:30	104 sm
49	122 mph	4:48	583 sm
50	346 mph	0:37	213 sm
51	56 mph	5:20	298 sm
52	100 mph	2:30	250 sm
53	85 mph	0:48	68 sm
54	113 mph	1:48	204 sm
55	197 mph	2:02	400 sm
56	68 mph	1:35	108 sm
57	206 mph	0:28	96 sm
58	120 kt	0:13	26 nm
59	200 kts	1:47	356 nm
60	223 kts	2:03	457 nm
61	190 kt	1:04	203 nm
62	112 kts	0:58	108 nm
63	116 mph	1:04	123.5 sm
64	156 mph	0:53	138 sm
65	209 mph	1:56	404 sm
66	98 mph	2:54	284 sm

No	G/S	Time	Distance
67	358 mph	4:59	1780 sm
68	122 kts	0:47	95 nm
69	330 kts	1:13	401 nm
70	98 kts	2:56	287 nm
71	106 kts	3:26	364 nm
72	208 kts	1:37	336 nm
73	129 mph	0:13	28 sm
74	116 mph	0:07	13.5 sm
75	220 mph	0:18	66 sm
76	192 mph	0:05	16 sm
77	157 mph	0:08	21 sm
78	175 kts	2:51	500 nm
79	149 kts	0:58	144 nm
80	118 kts	1:03	124 nm
81	137 kts	1:20	183 nm
82	102 kts	0:4.5	7.64 nm
83	362 mph	2:34	930 sm
84	222 mph	0:5.6	20 sm
85	149 mph	1:40	248 sm
86	100 mph	0:48	80 sm
87	109 mph	1:17	140 sm
88	100 kts	10:00	1000 nm
89	278 kts	1:23	385 nm
90	188 kts	0:40	125.5 nm
91	99 kts	6:40	660 nm
92	85 kts	0:1.1	1.56 nm
93	15	13	24
94	210	182	337
95	14.5	12.6	23.2
96	178	154	285.5
97	57	49.5	91.5
98	820	710	1315
99	95	82.5	152
100	127	110	204
101	265	230	425
102	38	33	61
103	51	44.5	82
104	750	650	1202
105	4.5	3.9	7.2

No	G/S	Time	Distance
106	921	800	1480
107	0.145	0.126	0.232
108	180	156	289
109	23	20	37
110	30.5	26.5	49
111	1.92	1.67	308
112	470	409	751
113	36	31.2	57.6
114	84	73	135
115	9.7	8.4	15.5
116	75	65	120.5
117	115	100	184.5
118	10	8.7	16
119	13 000	11 300	20 840
120	950	823	1521
121	6	5.2	9.6
122	69	60	111
123	62	54	99
124	137	119	220
125	356	310	570
126	20.3	17.6	32.5
127	122	106	196
128	115	100	184.5
129	1.36	1.18	2.18
130	57.6	50	92.5
131	2100	1820	3370
132	0.138	0.12	0.221
133	353	306	565
134	27.4	23.7	43.8
135	189	164	303
136	780	678	1250
137	15 400	13 340	24 620
138	19	16.5	30.5
139	132.5	115	212.5
140	276	239	441
141	4240	3 670	6780
142	109.5	95	176
143	33	28.7	53
144	424	367	678

No	G/S	Time	Distance
145	72	62	115
146	28.5	24.7	45.6
147	38	33	61
148	3300	2860	5280
149	8.32	7.23	13.4
150	1.04	0.9	1.67
151	560	485	897
152	85	73.7	136

No	PA Ft	Temp C	IAS mph	TAS mph
153	10 000	0	178	210
154	15 000	-20	160	200
155	12 000	-25	180	210
156	8 000	10	164	189
157	30 000	10	192	350
158	28 000	-40	190	300
159	1 000	5	85	85
160	4 000	-20	190	192
161	5 500	15	135	150
162	7 200	22	158	184
163	4 000	40	89	100
164	3 000	10	77	81
165	12 500	-10	103	125
166	9 000	-3	120	138
167	18 000	-15	134	180
168	23 500	-35	174	252
169	8 000	5	85	97
170	9 500	0	117	137
171	3 000	-22	174	172
172	30 000	-45	350	574
173	1 500	38	122	131
174	3 750	22	116	126
175	22 500	-34	248	353
176	17 000	-24	186	240
177	13 500	-3.5	154	195
178	11 000	0	122	147
179	8 000	1	117	133
180	16 400	-11	157	206
181	10 000	10	142	170

No	PA Ft	Temp C	IAS mph	TAS mph
182	6 300	11	178	199
183	15 500	-32	280	346
184	13 000	-20	113	136
185	10 500	-10	115	134
186	11 450	-2	147	178
187	8 000	-9	111	124
188	4 500	22	131.5	145
189	5 000	30	97.5	110
190	2 500	40	110	120
191	3 000	35	141	154
192	5 500	20	111	124
193	22 000	-33	182	256
194	30 000	-45	258	422
195	19 000	-23	164	222
196	11 500	-12	171	203
197	10 000	0	139	164
198	12 000	-9	99.5	120
199	7 500	16	144.5	167
200	4 000	15	134	145
201	2 000	20	190	200
202	1 670	16	130	135
203	28 000	-38	175	278
204	16 000	-27	166	210
205	12 500	-14	152	184
206	16 000	-16	124	160
207	1 000	40	130	138
208	2 750	38	100.5	110
209	30 000	-40	276	456
210	13 500	-28	159	190
211	4 500	0	148	157
212	2 000	20	190	200

No	TH	TAS	TC	GS	W/V
213	162	132 kts	160	147 kts	320/16
214	36	168 kts	29	173 kts	135/23
215	347	128 kts	336	149 kts	110/34
216	122	100 kts	142	104 kts	35/35

No	TH	TAS	TC	GS	W/V
217	236	137 kts	227	148 kts	345/26
218	122	139 kts	122.5	118 kts	119/21
219	189	214 kts	189.5	225 kts	16/11
220	122	316 kts	118	341 kts	256/34
221	56	114 kts	33	100 kts	116/46
222	108	108 kts	99	104 kts	180/18
223	189	146 kts	188	167 kts	360/21
224	356	213 kts	353	217 kts	101/13
225	89	103 kts	89	129 kts	267/26
226	112	235 kts	112	222 kts	116/13
227	167	126 kts	167	150 kts	346/24
228	162.5	123 mph	153	113 mph	222/22
229	185	221 mph	189	214 mph	124/17
230	242	154 mph	239	187 mph	46/34
231	157	109 mph	162	102 mph	111/11
232	350	153.5 mph	347	168 mph	137/17
233	000	141 mph	002	118 mph	352/23
234	058	150 mph	046	137 mph	119/33
235	316.5	123 mph	305	129 mph	54/26
236	116	149 mph	107	43 mph	187/25
237	165.5	69 mph	167	102 mph	349/33
238	207	200 mph	216	202 mph	121/30
239	122	105.5 mph	111	97 mph	183/22
240	265	179 mph	271	174 mph	192/19
241	008.5	189 mph	001	203 mph	122/29
242	091	160 mph	083	143 mph	138/27
243	163	136 mph	163	112 mph	165/24
244	215	199 mph	222	211 mph	104/29
245	169	208 mph	161	186 mph	218/36
246	296	309 mph	298	354 mph	132/46
247	016	122 mph	009	118.5 mph	090/15
248	031	239 mph	036	255 mph	267/27
249	162	162 mph	162	146 mph	162/16
250	132	119 mph	137	134 mph	351/19
251	304	139 mph	317	138 mph	221/30
252	205	183 mph	213	185 mph	114/26
253	225	171 mph	227	142.5 mph	213/29
254	309	196 mph	305	220 mph	098/28
255	299.5	209 mph	300	232 mph	123/22

No	TH	TAS	TC	GS	W/V		No	Dist	Time	G/S
256	115	163 mph	122	181 mph	347/27		8	36.7	:25	88
257	265	356 mph	267	374 mph	119/21		9	93	1:30	62
258	100	122 mph	104	116 mph	049/10		10	9.1	:07	78

Find the groundspeeds:

No	Dist	Time	G/S
1	90	:50	108
2	75	2:00	37.5
3	60	:40	90
4	35	:16	133
5	110	:120	55
6	65	:30	130
7	12	:10	72
8	120	1:55	62.5
9	115	:50.5	137
10	90	1:40	54

Find the times:

No	Dist	Time	G/S
1	80	1:09	70
2	120	2:00	60
3	150	2:08	70
4	90	:41.5	130
5	95	:30	190
6	110	:30	220
7	170	2:07	80
8	115	1:17	90
9	300	2:37	115
10	45	:32.5	83

Find the distances:

No	Dist	Time	G/S
1	53.5	:80	40
2	45	:30	90
3	170	2:00	85
4	240	:120	120
5	90	:37	146
6	266	2:10	123
7	320	1:50	175

Fill in the missing boxes:

No	Dist	Time	G/S
1	120	2:00	60
2	156	:120	78
3	104	:42	149
4	75	:36	125
5	36	:18	120
6	42	:17.5	143
7	180	3:00	60
8	89	1:10	76
9	181	1:37	112
10	166	1:32	108
11	82	:43	115
12	84.5	:46	111
13	81	:45	107
14	113	:80	85
15	11	:04.1	117
16	12.8	:07	110
17	120	1:40	72
18	80	:43	112
19	125	1:12	104
20	150	1:06	137

Find the fuel consumption:

No	Fuel	Time	Gals/Hr
1	42	3:00	14
2	36	3:30	10.3
3	33	2:45	12
4	6	:26	13.9
5	30	3:15	9.3

Find the flying time:

No	Fuel	Time	Gals/Hr
1	40	5:00	8
2	38	3:24	11

No	Fuel	Time	Gals/Hr
3	37	5:42	6.5
4	26	2:10	12
5	40	2:40	15

Find the fuel used:

No	Fuel	Time	Gals/Hr
1	12	2:00	6
2	25.6	2:20	11
3	47	3:46	12.5
4	13.7	1:50	7.5
5	9.1	1:18	7

Fill in the missing boxes:

No	Fuel	Time	Gals/Hr
1	39	4:00	9.8
2	27	3:30	7.7
3	16.5	2:04	8
4	25.3	3:12	8
5	21	3:00	7
6	37.5	4:10	9
7	42	3:00	14
8	37	2:18	16.1
9	22.7	2:30	9.1
10	32.3	3:14	10
11	18	3:00	6.0
12	25	3:01	8.3
13	80	6:10	13
14	11	:35	18.8
15	58	3:44	15.5
16	70	5:15	13.4
17	21	3:30	6
18	19	2:15	8.4
19	23.5	3:12	7.4
20	62	:41	9.1

Find the true altitude:

No	Ind Alt	Temp	True
1	20,000	-15	20,800
2	13,000	-10	13,000

No	Ind Alt	Temp	True
3	30,000	-30	31,800
4	10,000	10	10,550
5	6,000	20	6,250
6	14,000	5	14,950
7	8,000	-20	7,400
8	18,000	-5	19,100
9	8,000	10	8,300
10	15,000	0	15,800

Find the temperatures:

No	Ind Alt	Temp	True
1	20,000	0	22,000
2	25,000	-25	26,000
3	18,000	-14	18,500
4	10,000	-26	9,200
5	11,500	3	12,000
6	10,000	-18	9,500

Find the indicated altitudes:

No	True	Temp	PA	Ind
1	20,000	-25	21,000	19,900
2	10,000	-10	9,800	10,200
3	19,000	-30	18,000	19,700
4	25,500	10	26,000	21,350
5	4,900	25	5,000	4,560
6	5,500	25	6,000	5,100

Find the TAS:

No	IAS	Ind Alt	Temp	TAS
1	190	10,000	-15	217
2	200	20,000	-30	272
3	150	5,000	-20	154
4	180	12,000	-10	216
5	140	3,000	5	143
6	140	4,000	-5	146
7	120	4,000	-30	119
8	210	7,000	-15	226
9	165	15,000	-20	206
10	190	12,000	15	238

Find the IAS:

No	IAS	Ind Alt	Temp	TAS
1	125	12,000	-10	150
2	138	20,000	5	200
3	115	18,000	10	165
4	119	6,000	-20	125
5	122	5,000	20	135
6	98	7,000	-5	107

Find the Indicated Altitude:

No	IAS	Ind Alt	Temp	TAS
1	175	10,000	-15	200
2	230	4,000	-35	225
3	180	4,000	-10	185
4	145	2,000	15	150
5	118	3,000	15	125
6	110	9,500	10	130

Fill in the empty spaces:

No	IAS	Ind Alt	Temp	TAS
1	140	5,000	23	156
2	178	12,000	-20	210
3	235	12,500	-35	270
4	207	16,000	-25	260
5	116	6,000	-5	125
6	115	17,000	16	160
7	158	12,000	-20	186
8	123	18,300	-18	165
9	165	18,500	-45	211
10	190	3,500	-45	180

WIND TRIANGLES

Find the course, groundspeed and drift:

No	W/V	Hdg	A/S	Cs	G/S	Dft
1	090/30	350	120	337	129	13L
2	050/20	260	140	256	158	4L
3	270/25	180	125	169	127	11L
4	300/22	360	110	011	101	11R
5	225/25	045	170	045	195	0
6	360/30	100	135	112	143	12R

No	W/V	Hdg	A/S	Cs	G/S	Dft
7	315/26	041	117	054	118	13R
8	180/27	090	128	078	131	12L
9	360/12	299	130	294	125	5L
10	360/11	080	90	087	89	7R

Find the wind speed, direction and drift:

No	W/V	Dft	Hdg	A/S	Cs	G/S
1	Calm	0	090	120	090	120
2	292/13	5R	355	135	360	130
3	165/18	7L	045	118	038	128
4	235/27	9L	192	140	183	120
5	350/41	13R	090	165	103	178
6	035/12	8L	271	65	263	72
7	338/10	0	158	68	158	78
8	085/18	0	085	78	085	60
9	028/25	16L	285	85	270	94
10	308/10	3L	183	155	180	161

Find the heading and groundspeed:

No	W/V	Hdg	A/S	Cs	G/S
1	320/30	271	140	260	123
2	050/25	230	120	230	140
3	045/20	276	130	270	143
4	090/32	153	110	170	100
5	180/28	103	125	090	122
6	260/15	185	160	180	157
7	050/30	325	174	315	174
8	050/11	004	110	360	103
9	180/32	059	92	045	112
10	270/32	193	140	180	136

Fill in the missing spaces:

No	W/V	Hdg	A/S	Cs	G/S	Dft
1	270/32	278	115	120	142	8L
2	240/20	243	140	080	159	3L
3	090/22	183	135	192	137	9R
4	184/18	350	105	352	123	2R
5	270/20	270	160	270	140	0
6	147/19	180	90	188	75	8R

No	W/V	Hdg	A/S	Cs	G/S	Dft
7	120/20	163	130	170	115	7R
8	175/20	180	125	181	105	1R
9	206/20	255	100	265	88	10R
10	186/25	158	140	152	115	6L
11	180/25	262	192	270	190	8R
12	350/18	090	125	098	129	8R
13	270/26	180	150	170	152	11L
14	250/20	339	108	350	110	11R
15	045/20	077	187	080	157	3R

AIR LAW

1 (A). You are overtaking when approaching another aircraft from behind at less than 70° from the longitudinal axis, which means that, at night, you should not be able to see its port or starboard navigation lights. **Aircraft being overtaken have right of way**, and the overtaking aircraft, whether climbing, descending or in horizontal flight, must keep out of the way by altering course to the right (*well clear* on the ground) until well past and clear. Gliders in UK may go right or left.

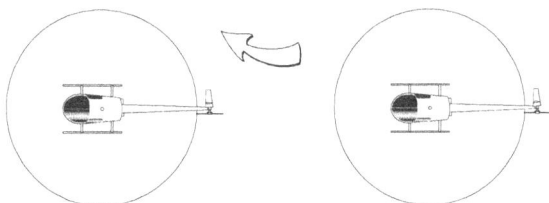

2 (B). Cruising levels are expressed in terms of:

- **Flight Levels**, at or above the lowest usable flight level, or above the transition altitude. Flight Levels are based on QNE, or 1013.25. Flight Level Zero starts at that setting, and carries on through 500 feet increments. Usually, the *lowest usable FL* is that which corresponds to, or is immediately above, the established minimum flight altitude

- **Altitudes**, below the lowest usable flight level, or at or below the transition altitude, based on QNH

- **Heights** are used within the traffic pattern and are based on QFE. Vertical positions are normally from the airfield elevation, but the threshold elevation is used for instrument runways if there is more than a 2 m difference, and precision approach runways.

3 (A). A transition altitude is normally specified for an aerodrome by the State in which it is located. It is as low as possible, but normally at least 3000 feet, rounded up to the nearest 1000. Below the Transition Altitude, vertical position is controlled by reference to altitude.

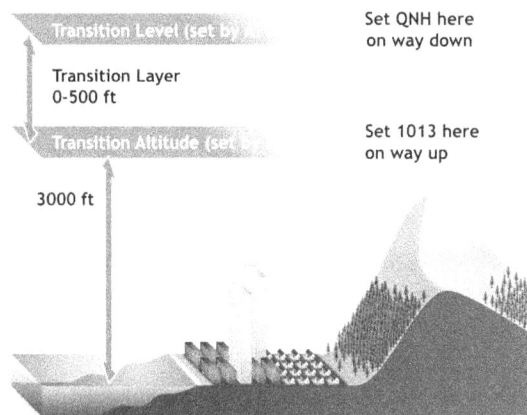

The *Transition Level* is the lowest available flight level above the Transition Altitude when the altimeter is set to 1013.2 hPa, so it would normally be FL 30 in UK, including when the QNH is more than standard. However, if the QNH is less than standard, the transition level will be higher than that. The Transition Level is determined by the ATS unit concerned, since it varies with pressure from day to day, and it is always *higher* than the Transition Altitude. The difference between transition altitude and transition level is the *Transition Layer*, which will be *more than zero and less than 500 feet*.

The change in reference between flight levels and altitudes is made, when climbing, at the Transition Altitude, and, when descending, at the Transition Level.

4 (B). Class D airspace consists of control zones and areas of lesser importance, so IFR and VFR traffic is allowed, but separation is provided only between IFR aircraft. However, they are informed about VFR flights (VFR traffic details are also given to VFR flights). The maximum speed is 250 kts IAS for IFR and VFR up to 10,000 feet. For VFR flights, visibility must be 8 km above 10,000 feet and 5 km below that, 1500 m horizontally and 300 m vertically from cloud.

Two-way radio communication is required, as is clearance to enter, so *minimum radio equipment* is *VHF comms*.

5 (C). Although the airspace you fly in comes in several varieties, it is, essentially, controlled or uncontrolled, although it's fair to say that, in Europe, once you are above

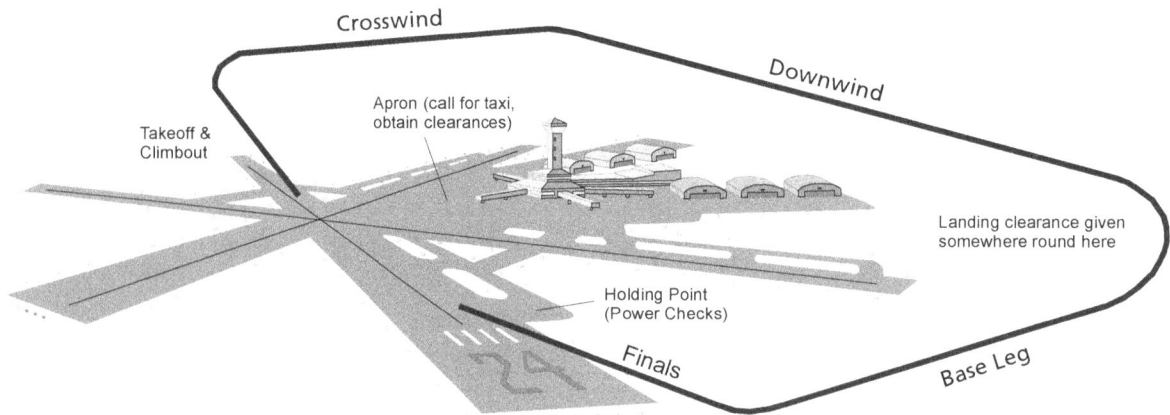

3000 feet, most airspace is controlled in one form or another. As the names imply, in the first you do as you're told (by ATC), and, in the second, **you, as pilot, are responsible for the safe conduct of the flight**, which means avoiding obstacles and other aircraft, which you can only do if you can see them. The official definition of a flight under VFR is "one conducted under Visual Flight Rules", conveniently leaving out what the Rules are.

The Visual Flight Rules govern flight in *Visual Meteorological Conditions* (VMC). A flight may only be conducted under VFR if the conditions exist all the way along the route. When the weather gets so bad that you can't see where you are going, *Instrument Meteorological Conditions* (IMC) apply, and you must fly under *Instrument Flight Rules* (IFR), although you can fly IFR at any time, even in VMC (you just have to obey tighter rules for obstacle clearance, etc., since you're not supposed to be looking out of the window).

6 (B). A Flight Information Region is a large area (London & Scottish) extending up to but not including FL 245.

7 (A). **Control Zones** are areas around busy airspace in which IFR traffic is controlled (VFR traffic may or may not be, depending on airspace notification*). They start at the surface and go up to specified levels of controlled airspace above, or the height on the map (or in the AIP). Lateral limits extend to at least 5 nm (9.3 km) from the centre of the aerodrome(s) where approaches are made.

*A CTZ may be Class A (IFR only) or B, C or D if VFR aircraft become involved.

In a CTZ, ATC provides separation between Special VFR and IFR flights.

8 (B). A Control Area, as it does not start at the ground.

9. An instrument approach with all or part of it completed by visual reference to terrain.

10 (D).

11 (C).

12 (B).

13 (A). In the UK, you normally make all turns to the left (but check the signals square), arriving overhead the landing point at 2000' AGL and at 90° to it, in a position to make a descending 180° turn over the *dead side* to arrive at circuit height over the other end of the runway, going the other way, tight crosswind. Then you join the downwind leg in the normal way, all the while looking for other traffic.

14 (C). The white lights are tail lights (and you can't see the port and starboard lights), so you are overtaking. You should therefore pass the other aircraft on the right.

15 (B).

16 (B). Overtaking on the left means you can be seen by the pilot in the other aircraft, if it is an aeroplane. You should also keep well clear.

17 (A). If a steady relative bearing is kept between two aircraft at the same altitude, they will eventually collide.

When two aircraft are converging in this way, **the one coming from the right has the right-of-way**, except:

- power-driven, heavier-than-air aircraft (flying machines) give way to airships, gliders and balloons

- airships give way to gliders and balloons

- gliders give way to balloons

- power-driven aircraft give way to aircraft that are seen to be towing or carrying loads

When two balloons converge at different altitudes, the higher one must give way.

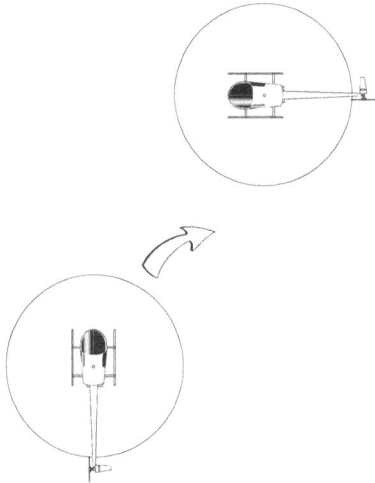

18 (C).

19 (A).

20 (B). See Q 26.

21 (D).

22 (C). Except where ATC dictate otherwise, or in emergency, aircraft landing or on finals have right of way over others in flight or on the ground or water. Where several are involved in landing, *the lowest has right of way*, as long as it does not cut in front of another on finals, or overtake it. However, power driven heavier-than-air aircraft must give way to gliders. *An aircraft whose pilot is aware that another is compelled to land shall give way to it.*

23 (A).

24 (B).

25 (D).

26 (B). Lights & Pyrotechnic Signals sent from the Tower to an aircraft are listed below. Acknowledge by rocking the wings or flashing the landing lights once.

Signal	To Air	To Ground
Steady Red	Give way to others, keep circling	Stop
Red Flashes	Airport unsafe do not land	Clear landing area
Green Flashes	Return for landing	Cleared to taxi
Steady Green	You may land	Cleared to take off
White Flashes	Land after continuous green. After green flashes, go to apron	Return to start point
Bursting Red/ Green Stars	You are in or near a danger area; push off	
Blinking Runway Lights		Ground staff clear areas

A red pyrotechnic means - *Regardless of previous instructions, do not land for the time being.* Refer to *CAP 637 - Visual Aids Handbook* for full details.

27 (A). See Q 17.

28 (B). See Q 1.

29 (C). See Q 1.

30 (A).

31 (C).

32 (A).

33 (A). See Q 105.

34 (A).

35 (C). An airway does not start at the surface, but at some specified altitude.

36 (B).

37 *C).

38 (A). An aerodrome traffic zone is an airspace of defined dimensions established around an aerodrome for the protection of aerodrome traffic. A control zone is a controlled airspace **extending upwards from the surface of the earth to a specified upper limit**.

39 (D). Position reports (at compulsory reporting points) require the time and level and usually the ETA of the next position. They shall similarly be made in relation to additional points when requested. If there are no designated reporting points, position reports shall be made at intervals prescribed by ATC.

The standard position report contains the:

- aircraft identification
- position
- time
- flight level/altitude
- next position and time over
- ensuing significant point

in that order.

40 (A). See *Navigation*, Q 20. In the UK, it lasts from 30 minutes after sunset until 30 minutes before sunrise.

41 (C). *Radar Contact* means "your aircraft has been identified and you will receive separation from all aircraft while in contact with this facility"

42 (A).

43 (B).

44 (A). Survivors can communicate with SAR aircraft visually by making signals on the ground. They should be at least 8 feet high (or as large as possible) with as large a contrast as possible between the materials used and the background.

Need Assistance	V
Need Medical Help	X
No	N
Yes	Y
Going This Way	←

Rescue units can use these (mostly double symbols):

Operation Complete	LLL
Found All Personnel	LL
All Well	LL
Found some personnel	++
Cannot continue - going home	XX
Split into different groups in directions indicated	← →
Aircraft in this direction	→ →
Nothing found but continuing	NN

45 (C). If you need to direct another craft to the scene, circle it at least once, fly low just in front and rock the fuselage, then fly off in the direction you want them to go.

In theory, they should hoist the *Code Pennant*, which is a flag with vertical red and white stripes, close up, or flash a series of *T*s in Morse Code with a lamp. On the other hand, they could just turn in the direction requested. A blue and white chequered flag means *Much Regret, Unable* (i.e. *NO*), as does a series of *N*s in Morse.

46 (C). A reportable accident occurs when:

- anyone is killed or seriously injured from contact with the aircraft (or any bits falling off), including jet blast or rotor downwash
- the aircraft sustains damage or structural failure
- The aircraft is missing or inaccessible

between the time any person boards it **with the intention of flight**, and all persons have disembarked (ICAO). This does not include injuries from natural causes, which are self-inflicted or inflicted by other people, or to stowaways hiding in places not normally accessible to passengers and crew. So if someone is seriously injured by walking into the back of a wing during disembarkation, that is an accident.

Significant or *Substantial Damage* in this context essentially means anything that may involve an insurance claim, but officially is damage or failure affecting structure or performance, normally meaning major repairs.

47. (B).

48 (A).

49 (A).

50 (D). Under ICAO, *investigation* of accidents or incidents is instituted by the State of *Occurrence*, who must forward notification of accidents or serious incidents by the quickest and most suitable means to the States of *Registry*, the *Operator*, of *Design*, of *Manufacture*, and ICAO when the aircraft weighs more than 2250 kg.

51 (D). See Q 45.

52 (B).

53 (B). See Q 45.

54 (B).

55 (A).

56 (A).

57 (B).

58 (D).

59 (A). See Q 42.

60 (D).

61 (B). For further information on marshalling signals, refer to CAP 637.

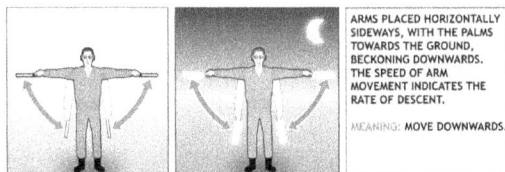

ARMS PLACED HORIZONTALLY SIDEWAYS, WITH THE PALMS TOWARDS THE GROUND, BECKONING DOWNWARDS. THE SPEED OF ARM MOVEMENT INDICATES THE RATE OF DESCENT.

MEANING: MOVE DOWNWARDS.

62 (B).

15-33

63 (C).

A→

64 (D). A beacon is required if aircraft navigate mostly visually, or reduced visibility is frequent, or it is hard to see the aerodrome, especially at night.

- **Identification beacons** (*pundits*) are green for civil aerodromes, and yellow for those on water, used where many other aerodromes are nearby and identification could be difficult. Military aerodromes have a flashing red one. All show a two-letter Morse group

- **Aerodrome location beacons** are for smaller, more remote, aerodromes, with no problem as to identification. They are white and flashing, if they are well away from background lighting, or white & green where there is a lot of background lighting, like near a city (again, yellow for water)

65 (C). From CAP 637: Paved taxiway markings are yellow in colour and consist of Centreline, Runway Taxi-Holding Position, Intermediate Taxi-Holding Position, Edge and Information markings.

66 (B). A non-instrument runway will have a yellow single solid and a single dashed line across the taxiway (the dashed line is on the runway side). An instrument runway has a double set of each (an *A Pattern*) going to the runway (on the way back, they tell you when you are clear, when *all parts* of the aircraft have crossed the line).

67 (D).

68 (B). See Q 3.

69 (B). From CAP 637: Runway end lighting is red and marks the extremity of the runway that is available for

manoeuvring. Pilots must NOT land before the green threshold lighting nor continue a landing roll or taxi beyond the red runway end lights.

70 (B). See Q 69.

71 (A). See Q 69.

72 (C). From CAP 637: Runway Edge Lighting is normally located along the edges of the area declared for use as the runway. However, where a paved surface is wider than the declared runway width, the lights may be located at the edge of the pavement and the declared width delineated by white edge markings.

73 (A).

74 (C).

75 (C). Under Article 1 of the Chicago Convention, States have complete and exclusive sovereignty* over airspace above their territory, although this was actually established in 1919 at the Paris Peace Conference. *Scheduled services* may not operate over or into the territory of a Contracting State without first obtaining permission, although this is hardly ever refused, as the States concerned need it for their own aircraft to land in others.

*Sovereignty means having supreme, independent authority over a territory.

76 (B). Under Article 29 of the Chicago Convention, before entering the sovereign airspace of a foreign State with the intention of landing there, an aircraft must be airworthy, with all relevant documents on board:

- Certificate of Registration
- Certificate of Airworthiness
- Flight Crew Licences
- Journey Log Book
- Aircraft Radio Station Licence
- Passenger List
- Cargo Manifest and declarations of the cargo

77 (B). Under Article 17 of the Chicago Convention, the State of Registry is the State in whose Register an aircraft is entered.

78 (D). Under Article 24 of the Chicago Convention, subject to Customs regulations, aircraft on flights to, from or across the territory of another State are admitted temporarily free of duty. Fuel, oil, stores and spares, etc. on board and destined to be leaving again are exempt from duties, inspection fees or similar charges, but this does not apply to any quantities or articles unloaded,

except under customs regulations, which may require that they be kept under customs supervision. Spares and equipment imported for aircraft of other States engaged in international air navigation shall be admitted free of duty, but they may need to be kept under supervision.

79 (D). The Aeronautical Information Publication is a summary of the rules and regulations that affect aviation or, in other words, a publication containing aeronautical information of a *lasting character essential to air navigation*. As such, it is not the final authority for the rules you have to obey, but the law that backs it up is. A clue as to what is or isn't supported by law is given by the word "shall". The AIP should be easy to use in flight, and comes in 3 parts:

PART 1 - GENERAL (GEN)

- **GEN 1** - *National Regulations & Requirements*. Entry, transit and departure of aircraft and cargo, Aircraft instruments, Summary of national regulations and differences from ICAO SARPS

- **GEN 2** - *Tables & Codes*. Measurements, Aircraft markings, Holidays, Abbreviations, Chart symbols, Navaids, Conversions, Sunrise & sunset tables

- **GEN 3** - *Services*. AIS, Charts, ATC, Met, SAR

PART 2 - EN-ROUTE (ENR)

- **ENR 1** - *General Rules & Procedures*. VFR, IFR, Airspace Classes, Procedures, radar services, Flight Planning ATC flow management, Interception, Unlawful interference, ATC incidents

- **ENR 2** - *ATS Airspace*. FIR, UIR, TMA, etc.

- **ENR 3** - *ATS Routes*

- **ENR 4** - *Radio Navigation Aids & Systems*.

- **ENR 5** - *Navigation Warnings*. Danger areas, Military stuff, Obstacles, Bird migration, Sports

- **ENR 6** - *En-Route Charts*

PART 3 - AERODROMES (AD)

- **AD 1** - *Aerodromes/Heliports*. Index, Availability, Services

- **AD 2** - *Aerodromes*. Location indicators, Names, Hours, Facilities, Markings, Obstacles, Runways and distances, Communications, Noise abatement

- **AD 3** - *Heliports*. As above

Note: The above sections should be the same from country to country so you can find the information easier. When airspace is *notified*, its details are published in the

AIP so you can take notice of them. Charts relating to aerodromes must be included in a specific order.

Permanent changes are issued as *AIP Amendments*. Temporary changes of long duration (3 months) and those of short duration containing extensive text or graphics are issued as *AIP Supplements*. Supplement pages are coloured, so they stand out, preferably in yellow.

80 (C). A *NOTice to AirMen* is a warning or notice about anything that might affect a flight that is either temporary or happened too late to be in charts, etc., such as changes to frequencies or serviceability of navaids. They are in the list of items to be checked before flight and can be obtained by telephone, from ATC or over the Internet.

NOTAMs do not amend the AIP, but they may affect the information it contains - for example, a permanent danger area will have its hours of operation published in the AIP, and variations published by NOTAM. A temporary danger area, on the other hand, may be *activated* by NOTAM (where a permanent danger area has two upper limits, the higher one is raised by NOTAM). In fact, a NOTAM is generated and issued when its information is:

- *Temporary* and of *short duration*, or of *long duration* made at *short notice*. If it contains *extensive text and/or graphics*, it becomes an *AIP Supplement*

- *Permanent*, but operationally significant

Operationally significant means the establishment, closure or significant changes in the operation of aerodromes or runways, or the operation of aeronautical services, electronics, aids to navigation (frequencies, ID, etc), visual aids, fuel, SAR facilities, fire fighting, hazards to air navigation (obstacles), and the like.

These items are *not* covered by NOTAM:

- routine maintenance work on aprons and taxiways which does not affect safe movement of aircraft

- runway marking, when operations can safely be conducted on other available runways, or the equipment can be removed when necessary

- temporary obstructions near aerodromes that do not affect the safe operation of aircraft

- partial failure of lighting where it does not directly affect aircraft operations

- partial temporary failure of air-ground communications when suitable alternative frequencies are known to be available and working

- the lack of apron marshalling services and road traffic control

- the unserviceability of location, destination or other instruction signs on the aerodrome movement area

- parachuting in uncontrolled airspace under VFR, when controlled, at promulgated sites or within danger or prohibited areas

- other information of a similar temporary nature

DISTRIBUTION

NOTAMs are issued in three categories to addressees for whom the information has direct operational significance, if they would not otherwise have 7 days prior notification (exam question). The categories are:

- *NOTAMN* - one with new information

- *NOTAMR* - one replacing a previous NOTAM

- *NOTAMC* - one cancelling a previous NOTAM

Temporary NOTAMS must include an expiry date, which may be estimated (with an EST suffix).

A checklist of valid NOTAMs is distributed over the AFTN at regular intervals of up to a month, to the same distribution list as the NOTAMs themselves.

81 (A). See Q 79.

82 (A). Annex 17 requires each ICAO State to designate an appropriate authority within its administration to be responsible for the development, implementation and maintenance of a national aviation security program, which should apply to all international civil air transport, including cargo aircraft, and to domestic flights at the discretion of the State.

83 (A).

84 (B). Annex 2 Table A2-1 refers. Here are some pertinent phrases:

Phrase	Meaning
Callsign	My callsign is....
Can Not	Sorry, can't do that.....
Am Lost	Where the hell am I?
Wilco	Your instructions will be complied with
Mayday	Help!
Hijack	Have been hijacked
Land	I would like to land at....
Descend	I require descent

Phrase	Meaning
Repeat	Say that again
Callsign	What is your callsign?
Recleared	Ignore last clearance, receive a new one
Descend	Descend for landing
You land	Land here
Proceed	You may proceed
Follow	Follow me

85 (A).

86 (D). See Qs 79 & 80.

87 (C). The AIP is amended regularly, and you should always make sure yours is up to date. Operationally significant changes are published through the AIRAC system, in Parts 1 and 2, which is aimed at advanced notification based on common effective dates of circumstances that necessitate significant changes in operational practices. So there. AIRAC information must be distributed at least 42 days ahead of the effective date, so the recipients get it 28 days ahead. The information should not change for another 28 days, unless it is of a (very) temporary nature.

In fact, AIRAC happens at 0001 every fourth Thursday, so that changes to navigation databases, FMS and charts can be done at the same time. Every country issues a circular with AIRAC changes, which are usually new waypoints on airways and updates to SIDs and STARs. If there is nothing new, they "no AIRAC changes".

The initials stand for *Aeronautical Information Regulation And Control.*

88 (C). Permanent changes to the AIP are issued as *AIP Amendments.* Temporary changes of long duration (3 months) and those of short duration containing extensive text or graphics are issued as *AIP Supplements.* Supplement pages are coloured, so they stand out, preferably in yellow.

89 (B). See Q 84.

90 (A). See Q 79.

91 (C). Under Article 9 of the Chicago Convention, contracting states reserve the right to stop aircraft from other states flying over their territory. As a result, aircraft may need to be led away from an area or be required to land at a particular aerodrome. A copy of the interception procedures must be carried on international flights.

If an aircraft assumes a position slightly above and ahead of you (normally on the left), rocks its wings, then turns slowly to the left in a level turn, you have officially been intercepted. Your response should be to rock your own wings and follow (the intercepter will normally be faster than you, so expect it to fly a racetrack pattern and rock its wings each time it passes). After interception, try to inform ATC and make contact with the intercepting aircraft on 121.5 or 243 MHz. You should also squawk 7700 with Mode C, unless otherwise instructed. If the intercepting aircraft's instructions conflict with those from ATC, you should obey the interceptor.

If the aircraft performs an abrupt breakaway manoeuvre, such as a climbing turn of 90° or more without interfering with your line of flight, you have been released. If it lowers its gear and descends to a runway (or helipad), you are expected to land there (the accepted phrase is *Descend*). However, you can make an approach to check the area, then proceed to land. Lowering your gear or showing a steady landing light means you acknowledge the instruction. Flashing the landing light means the area is unsuitable, as does overflight with the gear up somewhere between 1000-2000 feet.

At night, the substitute for rocking wings is irregular flashing of navigation lights.

92 (B). AICs contain operational and safety information that does not qualify for the AIP or NOTAMs. They contain amendments to the AIP, but not officially (this is done by replacing complete pages occasionally). *Pink* AICs concern safety matters which should be brought to everyone's attention (they are Very Important).

The others are:

- *White* - Admin
- *Yellow* - Operational
- *Mauve* - Airspace restrictions
- *Green* - Maps and Charts

AICs have serial numbers, based on the year and number, such a 27/2003, but they will also be called something like *Pink 27* or *Yellow 42*, in brackets afterwards. A checklist of valid AICs is issued once a year.

93 (B). See Q 79.

94 (B). See Q 79.

95 (C).

96 (A). State assistance to aircraft subjected to unlawful seizure include the *provision of navaids, air traffic services* and *landing permission*, as may be required under the circumstances.

Measures must be taken, as far as practicable, to detain such aircraft on the ground, unless there is an overriding duty to protect human life, with due consultation between the State of the incident and the State of the operator. The State must take adequate measures for the safety of the passengers and crew until their journey can be continued.

97 (B). See Q 80.

98 (C). See Q 80.

99 (C).

100 (C).

101 (D). See 115.

102 (A).

103 (B).

104 (A). Annexes contain *Standards and Recommended Practices* (SARPs), which the various countries adopt as the framework (i.e. source documents) for their legislation. There are 18:

- *Annex 1* - Personnel Licensing
- *Annex 2* - Rules of the Air
- *Annex 3* - Meteorological Services for International Air Navigation
- *Annex 4* - Aeronautical Charts
- *Annex 5* - Measurement (Dimensional) Units
- *Annex 6* - Aircraft Operation
- *Annex 7* - Nationality and Registration Marks
- *Annex 8* - Airworthiness
- *Annex 9* - Facilitation (entry and departure for passengers and baggage)
- *Annex 10* - Aeronautical Telecommunications
- *Annex 11* - Air Traffic Services
- *Annex 12* - Search and Rescue
- *Annex 13* - Investigation of Accidents
- *Annex 14* - Aerodromes
- *Annex 15* - Aeronautical Information Services
- *Annex 16* - Environmental Protection 1 - Noise
- *Annex 17* - Security, for a program at each airport serving international civil aviation, by each contracting state
- *Annex 18* - Dangerous Goods

105 (B). The legal responsibility for notification of an accident (or incident) lies with the pilot, then the operator if the pilot cannot do so. If it happens near an aerodrome, the aerodrome authority must also report it. However, in practice, the AAIB usually get told by the police, since they must also be informed by the people mentioned above. Normally, accidents to gliders, hang gliders, paragliders and parachutists are investigated by the relevant Associations, who have their own safety organisations, which are supervised by the AAIB, who will not attend unless the circumstances are weird enough. As for microlights, balloons or airships, the AAIB will only investigate if there is a fatality.

106 (B). It must be done on the 21st day.

107 (C).

108 (A).

109 (B).

110 (D). Type ratings apply to any aircraft needing 2 pilots, any helicopter, and *any considered necessary*. To obtain one, you must pass a *skill test*.

Your licence will be issued with one type on it. Subsequent type ratings will theoretically need 5 hours each, but Part FCL allows this to be reduced to 3 hours by the TRTO, if the TRTO considers you to have enough time on a similar enough type, *and* if this discretion is written into their training manual. A first turbine type will need 5 hours. Type ratings are valid for 1 year *from the date of issue.*

111 (A). Part–FCL 2.320G FI(H) – Revalidation & Renewal refers - for revalidation of a FI(H) rating the holder shall fulfil two of the following three requirements:

* give at least 50 hours of flight instruction in helicopters as FI(H), TRI(H), IRI(H), or Examiner during the period of validity of the rating, of which at least 15 hours shall be within the 12 months preceding the expiry date of the FI rating;
* attend an instructor refresher seminar (see AMC FCL 2.320G(a)(2)), as approved by the Authority, within the validity period of the FI rating;
* pass, as a proficiency check, the skill test in Appendices 1 and 2 to Part FCL 2.320E in the 12 months preceding the expiry date of the FI rating.

112 (C).

113 (A).

114 (C).

115 (D). EASA medicals are only issued for professional and private pilot licences for aeroplanes and helicopters. Flight Engineers have different arrangements.

CLASS 1

Although intended for professional licences, a PPL holder may hold one of these at any time. It is valid for 12 months if you are under 40 and 6 months if you are over (but 12 months when multi-crew). When a license holder with a Class 1 Medical certificate passes 40 years of age, the validation period changes from 12 to 6 months.

CLASS 2

Required for the PPL. The initial issue can be done by any aviation medical examiner. If your national licence does not meet Class 2 standards, you can still exercise the privileges of that licence. The validity is 60 months until you are 40.

116 (C).

117 (B). Under Part FCL 2.025, licences are not valid without the signature of the holder in ink.

118 (A).

119 (C).

120 (A).

121 (D).

122 (C).

123 (A). Under Article 10 of the Chicago Convention, except when crossing without landing, aircraft entering State territory must, if required, land at customs airports and depart from them. Contracting states shall accept an oral declaration of baggage from pax and crew.

124 (C).

125 (A).

126 (D).

127 (B).

128 (C). ICAO Annex 2, Chapter 2, para 2.3.2 Pre-flight action - Before beginning a flight, the pilot-in-command of an aircraft shall become familiar with all available information appropriate to the intended operation. Pre-flight action for flights away from the vicinity of an aerodrome, and for all IFR flights, shall include a careful study of available current weather reports and forecasts, taking into consideration fuel requirements and an alternative course of action if the flight cannot be completed as planned.

129 (B). ICAO Annex 2, Chapter 2, para 2.4 - The pilot-in-command of an aircraft shall have final authority as to the disposition of the aircraft while in command.

130 (C). Under ICAO Annex 7, marks must be in Roman characters, displayed to their best advantage, after the features of the aircraft, and be clean and visible. They must also be on a fireproof metal plate in a prominent position on the fuselage, wing (microlight), or basket or envelope (balloon).

131 (B).

132 (C). Anywhere at any time, in theory, but the local rules always take precedence under ICAO. Under UK Rule 2, however, the Rules Of The Air, insofar as they apply to aircraft, shall apply:

(a) to all aircraft within the United Kingdom

(b) for the purposes of rule 5, to all aircraft in the neighbourhood of an offshore installation; and

(c) to all aircraft registered in the United Kingdom, wherever they may be.

Under Article 2 of the Chicago Convention, aircraft inside a State's territory or carrying its nationality mark (wherever they may be), must obey its regulations, which will be uniform, as far as possible, with ICAO rules. However, over the high seas, this convention applies. Each State also undertakes to ensure the prosecution of anyone violating regulations. State rules take precedence over ICAO where they conflict, but the Authority in the State of registration will most likely require to be informed.

133 (A). These are just two of a long list in the ANO.

134 (A).

135 (A). See Q 76.

136 (A).

137 (A).

138 (C). Under Article 16 of the Chicago Convention, the appropriate authorities of each State may, without unreasonable delay, search aircraft of other States when landing or departing, and to inspect documentation, which must be produced within a reasonable time.

139 (D). Under Article 5 of the Chicago Convention, aircraft of other contracting States not on scheduled international air services (i.e. general aviation aircraft) may, subject to the Convention, make flights into or non-stop in transit, and to stop for non-traffic purposes (refuel, emergency) without prior permission from the State concerned. However, they may have to follow prescribed routes for safety or security reasons. Assuming they are engaged in such services, they may also take on or discharge passengers, cargo or mail, subject to State regulations (see Article 7, *Cabotage*).

140 (B).

141 (C).

142 (B).

143 (D).

144 (B). Rule 5 (b) (The 500 feet rule) states: Except with the written permission of the CAA, an aircraft shall not be flown closer than 500 feet to any person, vessel, vehicle or structure.

145 (A). See Q 17.

146 (B).

147 (C). See Q 17.

148 (B).

149 (B).

150 (D). See Q 4.

151 (C).

152 (C).

153 (D).

154 (D).

155 (D).

156 (A).

157 (C). Above 3000 ft AMSL, or above the appropriate transition altitude, whichever is higher, you must fly at a level appropriate to your magnetic track (see table below), using 1013.2 hPa or 29.92", or whatever the competent authority dictates wherever you are, unless otherwise instructed by ATC or in an established traffic pattern.

Below 24 500 Feet (UK)

Magnetic Track	Cruising Level (ft)
000° - 089°	Odd thousands to FL 230
90° - 179°	Odd thousands + 500 to FL 235
180° - 269°	Even thousands to FL 240
270° - 359°	Even thousands + 500 to FL 225

158 (C).

159 (A).

160 (B). See Q 2.

161 (B).

162 (A).

163 (C).

164 (A).

165 (D).

166 (D).

167 (C).

168 (C). See Q 46.

169 (D).

170 (B).

171 (C). See Q 109.

172 (B).

173 (B).

174 (A).

175 (B).

176 (B).

177 (B). See Q 128.

178 (B)

179 (C). See Q 17.

180 (A).

181 (A). See Q 17.

182 (B).

183 (C).

184 (B). See Q 1.

185 (C).

186 (B). See Q 4.

187 (C).

188 (C).

189 (D).

190 (C).

191 (B). In addition, under the UN Convention of the High Seas, *territorial waters* are coastal waters of a State which may go out to 12 nm.

192 (D).

193 (A). ICAO does not split the Medium category nor do they recognise Small as a category.

194 (C).

195 (D).

196 (D).

197 (A).

198 (C).

199 (D).

200 (B).

201 (B).

202 (C).

203 (D). A VFR flight must be operated in conditions of visibility and distance from clouds equal to or greater than those given in the table below.

OVERWATER

Flight shall not be conducted overwater out of sight of land when the flight visibility is less than that for the appropriate airspace, and in any case when it is less than 1500 m. The minimum cloudbase shall be 600 feet.

CLASS A AIRSPACE

This is the most restrictive, requiring the most experienced pilots. Except for gliders, all flights are IFR - you may not convert to VFR.

CLASS B AIRSPACE

You must be clear of cloud, with visibility at least 8 km (5 km below 10,000' AMSL). In UK, Class B airspace only exists above FL 245.

CLASS C, D OR E AIRSPACE

You must be at least 1500 m horizontally and 1000 feet vertically from cloud in visibility of at least 8 km (5 km below 10,000' AMSL). Class C airspace does not as yet exist in UK.

CLASS F & G AIRSPACE

Above 3,000 ft AMSL, or 1,000 AGL, whichever is higher, you must be at least 1500 m horizontally and 1000 feet vertically from cloud in visibility at least 8 km (5 km below 10,000' AMSL). **Helicopters** may operate down to 1500 m by day, if ATC allows the use of visibility below 5 km, and the probability of encounters with other traffic is low, at 140 kts or less. As well, ATC permitting, helicopters may operate down to 800 m by day, with the surface in sight, at a speed that allows other traffic and obstacles to be seen and avoided. When visibility is less than 5 km, the forward visibility should be at least the distance travelled in 30 seconds.

Advisory speeds are:

Visibility (m)	Speed (Kts)
800	50
1500	100
2000	120

204 (D).

205 (D).

206 (D).

207 (A).

208 (D).

209 (B).

210 (B).

211 (C).

212 (A).

213 (D).

214 (A).

215 (C).

216 (C).

217 (A).

218 (A).

219 (B).

220 (A).

221 (B).

222 (C).

AIRSPACE CLASSIFICATION IN GERMANY FOR VFR

A	B	C	D	E	F	G	
	SEPARATION ALL AIRCRAFT	SEPARATION VFR FROM IFR	SEPARATION NOT PROVIDED	SEPARATION NOT PROVIDED	SEPARATION NOT PROVIDED	SEPARATION NOT PROVIDED	
	ATC CLEARANCE REQUIRED	ATC CLEARANCE REQUIRED	ATC CLEARANCE REQUIRED	ATC CLEARANCE NOT REQUIRED	ATC CLEARANCE NOT REQUIRED	ATC CLEARANCE NOT REQUIRED	
	RADIO CONTINUOUS TWO-WAY	RADIO CONTINUOUS TWO-WAY	RADIO CONTINUOUS TWO-WAY	RADIO NOT REQUIRED	RADIO NOT REQUIRED	RADIO NOT REQUIRED	
	SERVICES AIR TRAFFIC CONTROL SERVICE	SERVICES AIR TRAFFIC CONTROL SERVICE FOR SEPARATION FROM IFR, VFR TRAFFIC INFORMATION & TRAFFIC AVOIDANCE ON REQUEST	SERVICES TRAFFIC INFORMATION BETWEEN VFR AND IFR FLIGHTS & TRAFFIC AVOIDANCE ON REQUEST	SERVICES TRAFFIC INFORMATION AS FAR AS PRACTICAL	SERVICES FLIGHT INFORMATION SERVICE	SERVICES FLIGHT INFORMATION SERVICE	
	SPEED LIMITATIONS NOT APPLICABLE	SPEED LIMITATIONS 250kt IAS BELOW FL100	SPEED LIMITATIONS 250kt IAS BELOW FL100	SPEED LIMITATIONS 250kt IAS BELOW FL100	SPEED LIMITATIONS 250kt IAS BELOW FL100	SPEED LIMITATIONS 250kt IAS BELOW FL100	

VFR PROHIBITED (column A)

VMC MINIMA
8KM
— FL 100 —
5KM

CLEAR OF CLOUD
CLEAR OF CLOUD
CLEAR OF CLOUD

(column C) VMC MINIMA 8KM — FL 100 — 5KM 300M 1500 M 300M

(column D) VMC MINIMA 8KM — FL 100 — 5KM 300M 1500 M 300M
WITHIN CTR: GROUND VISIBILITY 5KM CEILING 1500 CLEAR OF CLOUDS

(column E) VMC MINIMA 8KM 300M 1500 M 300M

(column F) VMC MINIMA 8KM — FL 100 — 5KM 300M 1500 M 300M

(column G) VMC MINIMA FLIGHT VISIBILITY 1.4KM 800M FOR ROTORCRAFT, AIRSHIPS AND BALLOONS

ADDITIONALLY, DUE RECOGNITION OF OBSTACLES MUST BE POSSIBLE

PERMANENT VISUAL CONTACT TO THE GROUND

CLEAR OF CLOUDS

ONLY CLASSES C, D, E, F AND G ARE USED IN GERMANY

223 (C).

224 (C).

225 (B). Certain distances are "declared" by the Airport Authority (to the nearest foot or metre for runways used by international commercial air transport) and published in the AIP, although they can be found in many other publications, such as Jeppesen. These include:

- **TORA** - Takeoff Run Available

- **TODA*** - Takeoff Distance Available

- **ASDA** - Accelerate-Stop Distance Available

- **LDA** - Landing Distance Available

*Any areas at the end of a runway unsuitable to run on, but still clear of obstacles, are called *Clearways*, which start at the end of the TORA, for up to half the length of the TORA. Clearways should extend to at least 75 m either side of the centre line.

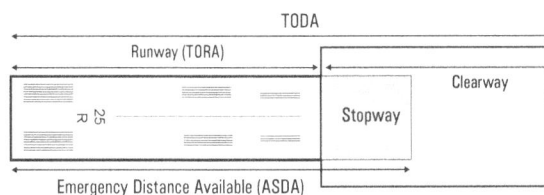

The TODA is TORA + Clearway.

Part of the Clearway that can support an aircraft while stopping, although not under takeoff conditions, is declared as *Stopway* which may be added to the TORA to form the *Emergency Distance Available* (EDA), which is marked with yellow chevrons. This is the ground run distance available for an aircraft to abort a takeoff and come to rest safely - the essential point is that Stopway is ground-based and clearways are not, but they can be included in performance calculations. Stopways are the same width as the runway, and are included in the ASDA.

If a runway does not have a stopway or clearway (meaning that the threshold is right at the end), the declared distances above would normally equal the runway length.

226 (D). *Flight time* is the total time from when an aircraft first moves under its own power with the intention of taking off until it comes to rest after the flight, so it includes taxi time (for helicopters, the flight time starts and stops when the rotors do). This is what goes in your log book and on customer invoices. *Air time*, on the other hand, is between wheels or skids off and when they touch the Earth again. This is what goes in the Tech Log.

A number of flights on the same day, returning to the same departure point, with intervals between them of less than 30 minutes, are counted as one flight.

227 (A).

228 (A). An unavoidable landing or ditching with a *reasonable expectancy* of *no injuries* to persons *in the aircraft* or *on the surface*. This is an ICAO concept that has been adopted in EU (Part) OPS.

229 (D).

230 (A).

231 (B).

232 (C).

233 (A).

234 (C).

235 (A).

236 (A).

237 (C).

238 (C).

239 (C).

240 (A).

241 (B).

242 (D).

243 (C).

244 (B).

245 (D).

246 (D).

247 (D).

248 (D).

249 (A).

250 (A). There are three types of flying, *Commercial Air Transport*, *Aerial Work* and *Private*:

- **Commercial Air Transport** exists where payment is given for the use of an aircraft, which in this context means like a taxi or a bus, as opposed to self-drive car hire (but single seats cannot be sold on charter flights without special arrangements).

- **Aerial Work** covers other situations where payment is still given, but in specialised roles not involving the usual passenger or freight carrying. Specialised operations include, but are not limited to: helicopter external load operations, helicopter survey operations, human external cargo operations, parachute operations, agricultural flights, aerial photography operations, aerial mapping operations, glider towing, aerial advertising, calibration flights, oil spill work, stringing power line operations, pollution control activity, survey operations, news media flights, flying displays, aerial entertainment, competition flights, clearing saw operations, animal herding and rescue, maritime funeral operations, veterinary vaccine dropping flights, scientific research flights, avalanche mining operations, construction work flights, television and movie flights. Thus, the Part OPS definition of aerial work is pretty wide-ranging. You can also take up to 6 "essential persons" in the machine to, during and from a job. The problem with UK is that its legislation only defines *passengers* or *flight crew*, so you can't carry passengers on aerial work.

Private flying speaks for itself, its most distinguishing feature being that no payment exists, other than by the pilot, for the right to use the aircraft in the first place (but you can take money for some 'private flights').

251 (C). See Q 225.

252 (C).

PERFORMANCE, M & B

General

1 (B).

2 (C). The total moment is 218400. The moment of the fuel burn is 16200. The landing moment is therefore 202200. The landing weight is 2220. Divide the landing moment by the landing weight to get the landing C of G of 91.08.

3 (A). If air density reduces, the engine develops less power and accelerates less because the power developed depends on the weight of the fuel/air mixture that is burned. In addition, looking at the lift formula, TAS will automatically decrease as density does, so it needs to be increased to compensate.

$$\text{Lift} = C_L(\tfrac{1}{2}\,\rho\,V^2)S$$

Coefficient Of Lift — C_L
Air Density (rho) (same as mass) — ρ
Surface Area Of Aerofoil — S
Average — $\tfrac{1}{2}$
True Airspeed — V

In short, reduced air density lowers the effectiveness of the engine(s) and the lift producing surfaces, so it will take a longer time and distance to get airborne.

Picture: Example of Station Numbers. They correspond with distances from the datum.

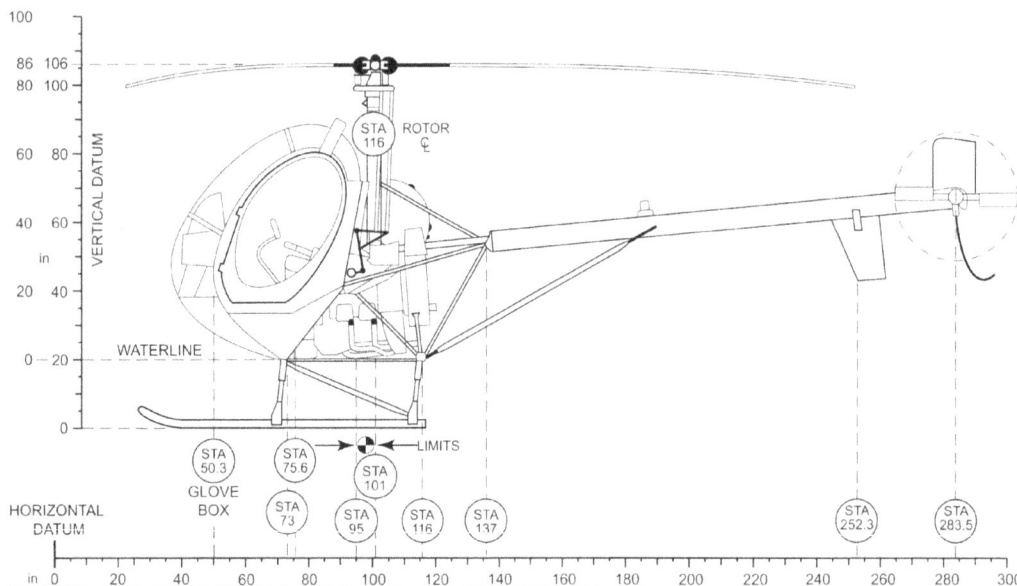

4 (A).

5 (C). Carb heat reduces air density.

6 (D).

7 (D). 100 x 80 = 8000 + the original 160,000 = 168,000.

8 (D). You will only be able to carry full fuel if the maximum weight of the aircraft allows it (check the flight manual). Very few aircraft can carry full passengers, baggage and fuel anyway, so you will have to adjust one of them. As the point of the trip is to carry the passengers and baggage somewhere, the fuel must be adjusted to keep within limits.

9 (B). The oil weighs 17 lbs (8.5 x 2) x 10 = 170 lb/ins.

10 (B). The falling pressure outside relaxes the pressure on the capsule in the altimeter, which expends - this is the same effect as if you had increased altitude, so the needle increases its reading.

11. (C).

12 (C). The *reference datum* is an imaginary point placed in a convenient location by the manufacturer from which all measurements and calculations start and where some C of G ranges are expressed (for example, *106 inches aft of datum*). Mostly, it is forward of the nose, so that all moments are positive, but it depends on the manufacturer.

13 (B). A *station* is a location (on the fuselage) identified by a number designating its distance from the datum. To get the longitudinal C of G of an aircraft, you multiply the weight of each item in it by the *lever arm* of the location it occupies to get the *moment*, or the amount of leverage that item contributes. For example, a 200 lb load 6 feet behind the datum would have the same downwards force as a 100 lb load 12 feet from it - the moment is the mass of an item multiplied by its distance from the datum, which can be represented by a station number. See the picture on the previous page.

14 (B). The **Disposable Load** (or *Useful Load*) includes freight, passengers and usable fuel and oil (e.g. *Traffic Load* and *fuel*). If the aircraft gets heavier, useful load decreases.

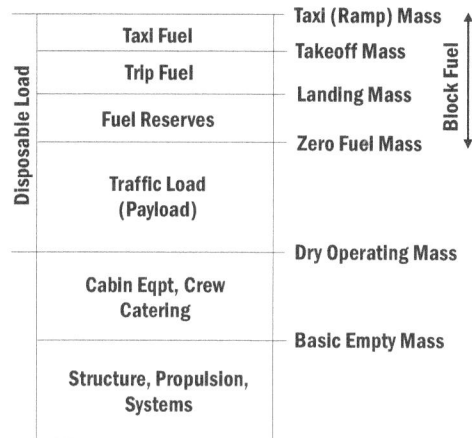

15 (A). Density altitude is the altitude in the Standard Atmosphere at which the prevailing density occurs, meaning your real altitude from the effects of pressure (height), temperature and humidity, and is used to establish performance, as it is a figure that expresses where your machine thinks it is, as opposed to where it actually is - see *Performance*. For now, it is *pressure altitude corrected for non-standard temperature*, or the true air temperature at a given level. Thus, density altitude has the same value as pressure altitude at standard temperature

16 (A). Clockwise motion of a seesaw is regarded as positive, and anticlockwise is negative. Any stations to the right of the fulcrum (or datum point) will incur clockwise rotation and are therefore positive. Easier to add up!

17 (B). In an aeroplane, this concerns the wing bending moment at the root with no fuel in the tanks, when they are in the wings. In a helicopter, it concerns the range of control movement without fuel on board.

18 (A). The C of G of an aircraft is an average figure derived from dividing the total moments by the total weight, normally along the longitudinal axis. The aircraft is considered to be on balance when the average moment arm falls within its C of G range, which can be allowed to move within defined limits.

19 (A). See Q 16.

20 (B). See Q 18.

21 (A). See Q 18.

22 (A). See Q 16.

23 (D). See Q 18.

24 (A). See Q 16.

25 (B).

26 (B). If the static port becomes blocked, the altimeter's capsule does not expand or contract, and the readings will stay the same as when it became blocked. A partial blockage would cause a significant time delay. In the ASI, the pressure inside the instrument (but outside the capsule) remains the same. The ASI will still read correctly in the cruise as long as the OAT doesn't change but, in the descent, it will over-read because the static element of pitot pressure increases inside the capsule - you will be closer to the stall than you think. In the climb, the static element of pitot pressure decreases, which causes a partial collapse of the capsule, so the instrument will under-read.

As for the VSI, the pressure differentials disappear and the instrument reads zero.

27 (B). Climbing requires more power, so if the power remains constant, something has to give - in this case it is the rate of climb.

28. (B). 698 feet. 2600 lbs is 28.5% of the difference between 2500 and 2850 lbs. 10°C is halfway between -5°C and 15°C. 637 is halfway between 614 and 660, and 902.5 is halfway between 876 and 929. 28.5% of the difference between 902.5 and 637 (265.5) is 61, which, added to 637 is 698.

29 (A). The weight of the aircraft is artificially increased in a turn, which is overcome with more lift. This is done with more power and a larger angle of attack.

30 (D).

31 (C). The air becomes less dense and less power is available.

32 (B). The configuration includes the weight, and the relative airflow determines the angle of attack.

33 (C).

34 (A). Less mass requires less power, meaning more is available for climbing.

35 (D). A lower pressure altitude means that the air is more dense, therefore more power is available and takeoff speed can be attained more quickly.

36 (A). **True Air Speed** (TAS) is the CAS corrected for altitude and temperature, or density (remember its original calibration is based on the standard atmosphere). *It is the only speed* and the only figure used for navigation - the others are pressures and are to do with aircraft behaviour! The slide rule part of the flight computer is used to calculate these. On average, the TAS increases by 2% over the IAS for every 1,000 feet. Refer to the *Performance* chapter for a discussion on the effects of air density on TAS.

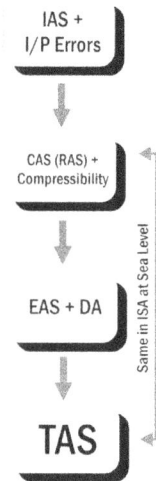

37 (A). Endurance does not depend on your position over the ground, only your time in the air mass. Therefore it does not matter where the wind is coming from.

38 (A). More altitude means the air is less dense, so there is less power available.

39 (B).

40 (A). The aircraft will be heavier so, assuming the same power, it will be harder to climb.

41 (B). That is, you get a steeper approach.

42 (B). Density altitude is the pressure altitude corrected for non-standard temperature, so is where your machine thinks it is.

43 (B). At 4500 feet, the ISA temperature should be 6° (15 - 9), but it is 20, so it is ISA plus 14. Multiply that by 120 to get 1680 feet. Add that to 4500 to get 6180. If the ISA deviation was minus you would subtract.

44 (A). The difference between 1013 and 995 is 18 hPa. Multiplied by 30 feet, this gives 540 feet to be added to 6000 feet for 6540 feet. The closest answer is 6,500. If you draw a diagram with the highest pressures to the bottom, you will see it has to be added.

For example, what would happen if you departed the spot in the diagram above and returned several hours later to find the 1020 QNH below had reduced to 995 Mb? The altimeter would be over-reading by 675 feet and you would only be 325 feet off the ground (1020 - 995 x 27 = 675,

1500 - 675 = 825 AMSL = 325 AGL). The altimeter needs constant updating as you fly.

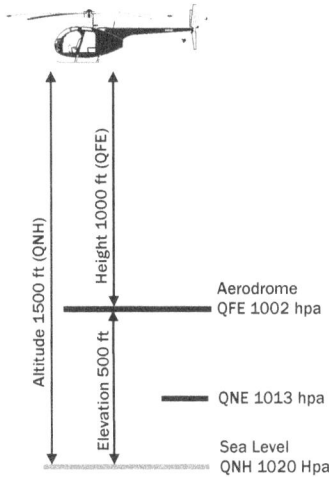

45 (C).

46 (B). Water is 5/8 of the weight of air, so dry air is denser.

47 (B).

48 (B). Cooler air is more dense and allows the engine to produce more power and the wings to produce more lift.

49 (A). The temperature in the carburettor will be considerably less than 10°C, due to the venturi, certainly lower than the dewpoint.

50 (A). Both conditions make the air less dense, so less power will be available.

51 (A). 61°F is 16°C, so 50°F will be +10°C. At 12,000 feet it should be -9°C (15-24), so it is ISA +19°C. Multiply by 120 to get 2280 and add to 12,000 to get 14,280. 14,130 is the nearest answer.

52 (B).

53 (B). Higher pressure makes the air more dense and allows the engine to produce more power and the wings to produce more lift.

54 (C). 8,500 feet. The temperature should be 1.1 degrees (15-13.9, or 7 x 1.98), but it is 15, so it is 13.9 degrees above ISA. 13.9 x 120 = 1668, plus 7000 is 8668.

55 (A). 10°C x 2°C = 20°C. From 15, this is -5°C

56 (D). An inversion is an *increase* of temperature with height (it normally decreases).

57 (C).

58 (B). The fuel arm should be in inches!

59 (B).

60 (A).

61 (D).

62 (B).

63 (B).

Fixed Wing

1 (B). See *Law*, Q 225.

2 (C). In the power required curve, the best speed for range occurs where the Power/Speed ratio is smallest, shown by the tangent from the origin. This is where the combined values of induced and parasite drag are smallest, or minimum drag speed. It is faster than the lowest point on the curve, which is the minimum flight speed, but it doesn't require that much more power, because induced drag reduces at a greater rate than parasite drag increases. Thus, it will provide the greatest distance for the least amount of fuel. However, in a tailwind, a slower airspeed is used because of the tradeoff between ground speed and specific fuel consumption.

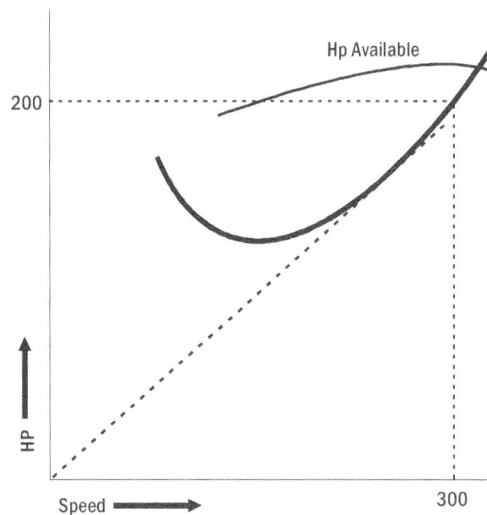

3 (C).

4 (A). For the same power, an upslope will slow the aircraft down, so a longer takeoff run will be needed to compensate, but the landing run will be shorter.

5 (A). The best lift/drag ratio is achieved at a speed that produces the most lift for the least drag, which occurs at a relatively low angle of attack.

6 (D). In the glide, a component of weight replaces propeller thrust. When the aircraft is heavy, the glidepath

must be steepened to allow the speed, and therefore lift, to be increased.

7 (A). Wind does not affect your path through the air, but it does affect its path over the ground.

8 (D). Increased weight requires more speed over the wings to create the equivalent lift. More speed requires longer distances.

9 (B). The flaps change the shape of the wing so that the angle of attack is increased, so you can have more lift for the same speed, or have the same lift with less speed. The extra drag also helps reduce speed - this is overcome with engine power.

10 (C). Going faster needs more space in which to stop.

11 (C). See Q 2.

12 (A). The downslope means it is easier to gain takeoff speed. On takeoff, this is useful because it reduces your ground run, but it will increase it on landing. At the very least it will require more use of brakes.

13 (C). As you go higher, you need more lift to compensate for the reduction in air density. This is achieved with more speed, i.e. TAS.

14 (D). It also reduces the stopping distance required and leaves more runway for an aborted takeoff.

15 (C). The aircraft will be nose-up, so it will suffer from increased drag, which needs more power and uses fuel up faster.

16 (D).

17 (A). The coefficient of drag will be increased, and more power will be needed to maintain the cruise, so less will be available for the climb.

18 (A). On average, the TAS increases by 2% over the IAS for every 1,000 feet for the same lift, so if the TAS remains constant, there has to be compensation somewhere - in this case, the lift reduces if the TAS remains constant.

19 (A).

20 (B).

21 (C). As density decreases, so does the lift created, according to the lift formula.

22 (A).

23 (A).

24 (C).

25 (C). Takeoff flap is usually between 0-20° to provide extra lift with a relatively small amount of drag. Landing flap, on the other hand, is set between 20-40° to provide large amounts of drag with relatively small amounts of lift

26 (C).

27 (A).

28 (B).

29 (B).

30 (A).

31 (C).

32 (A).

33 (C).

34 (D).

35 (A). An aeroplane's rated strength is a measure of the load the wings can carry without being damaged. Light aircraft can take total loads in three categories:

- *Normal*, 3.8 x gross weight

- *Utility*, 4.4 x gross weight

- *Acrobatic*, 6 x gross weight

Naturally, there is a safety factor involved, but the above should not be exceeded. Normal or utility categories do not allow manoeuvres with high positive and negative load factors. Bank angles would normally be inside 60°.

36 (C).

37 (D).

38 (B).

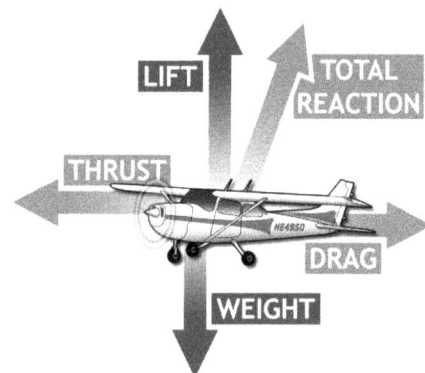

A couple is a combination of two equal, *parallel* and opposite forces that produces a rotation. In the picture, the couple formed by Thrust and Drag will cause the nose to change its position when thrust is altered.

39 (C).

40 (C).

41 (A).

42 (C). From the CAA Safety Sense Leaflet:

Landing on a wet surface, or snow, can result in increased ground roll, despite increased rolling resistance. Tyre friction reduces, as does the amount of braking possible. Very short wet grass with a firm subsoil will be slippery and can give a **60% distance increase (1.6 factor)**. When landing on grass the pilot cannot see or always know whether the grass is wet or covered in dew. Landing distances quoted in the Pilot's Operating Handbook/Flight Manual assume the correct approach speed and technique is flown, a higher speed will add significantly to the distance required whilst a lower speed will erode stall margins.

43 (C). See CAA Safety Sense Leaflet 7.

44 (C).

45 (B). See CAA Safety Sense Leaflet 7.

46 (A).

47 (A).

48 (C).

49 (C).

50 (B).

51 (D)

52 (D).

53 (A).

54 (C).

55 (C).

56 (C).

57 (D).

58 (C).

59 (A).

Helicopters

1 (C).

2 (C).

3 (C).

4 (C). The high grass dissipates the downwash and reduces ground effect.

5 (B).

6 (B). Yes. A hostile environment exists where a safe forced landing cannot be made because:

- the surface is inadequate

- the occupants of a helicopter cannot be adequately protected from the elements

- SAR response or capability is not consistent with anticipated exposure, or

- there is an unacceptable risk of endangering people or property on the ground

7 (C).

8 (A).

9 (B).

10 (C).

11 (C).

12 (B).

13 (C).

14 (B).

15 (A).

16 (D).

17 (B).

Item	Wt	Arm	Mom
Aircraft	1400	89	124600
Pilot	210	83.2	17472
Pax C	150	80	12000
Pax R		83.2	
Zero Fuel	1760	87.54	154072
Fuel	200	108.5	21700
Total	1960	**89.68**	175772

18 (A).

Item	Wt	Arm	Moment
Aircraft	1881	116.5	219136.5
Front pax	400	65	26000
Rear Pax		104	
Baggage	50	147.50	7375
Zero Fuel CG	2331	108.33	252511.5
Fuel	240	110.7	26568
Total	**2571**	108.55	**279079.5**

19 (A).

20 (C).

21 (B). As 1 US gallon is around 4 litres, there really is only one answer. 96 - 28 = 68 gallons to be converted.

22 (A).

23 (C).

24 (C).

25 (D).

Turbine Engines

1 (A).

2 (C).

3 (C).

4 (B).

5 (D).

6 (C).

7 (C).

8 (B).

9 (A).

10 (D).

11 (C).

12 (D).

13 (A).

14 (A).

15 (A).

16 (A).

17 (C).

18 (C).

19 (B).

20 (D).

METEOROLOGY

1 (B). During the day, the pressure is measured at many hundreds of weather stations, converted to sea level pressure (using ISA) and marked on a map, with the points that have equal pressure being connected up. The lines that join the dots are called *isobars* (*iso* is Greek for *same*), and will be 4 hectopascals apart, counting up and down from 1000. The closer they are together, the more the pressure drops per mile and the more severe the pressure gradient will be, for stronger winds (air moves from high to low pressure).

Isobars are like contours, and make common patterns, two of which are the *low* or *high*, other names for *cyclone* and *anti-cyclone*, respectively (nothing to do with the cyclones that seem to damage trailer parks). Another name for a low is a *depression*. The exact position of a system will be marked by an X.

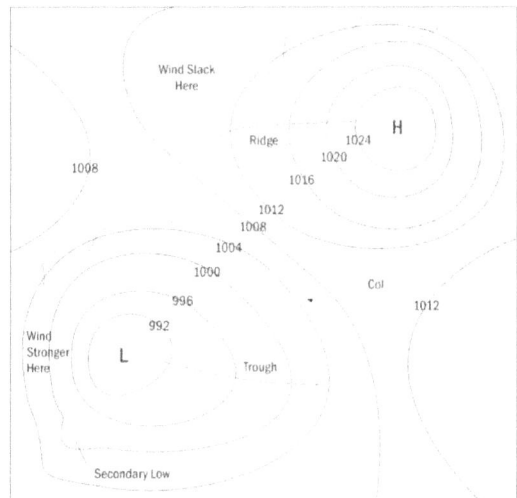

In the diagram above, the air is going into the High at the top, twisting to the right, and coming out of the low at the bottom, twisting left (air moves clockwise round a high, and anticlockwise round a low). Thus, if you were flying from East to West, it would be best going South of a High and North of a Low, in the Northern Hemisphere.

2 (D). Temperature normally decreases with height. Where it remains constant, there is an *isothermal layer*. Where it *increases* (typical in anticyclonic conditions), you have an *inversion*. The end result is that cold air is

underneath warmer air, which can happen during the passage of a cold front, or a cooler onshore breeze might be flowing over warm sea water. Cool air that is rising will lose its buoyancy and be stopped from rising further upon reaching its equilibrium level. In a thunderstorm, this happens just above the tropopause, where the cloud material settles into a layer that causes the anvil shape. Thus, conditions in an inversion are stable, because lifted air is always cooler than the environment.

However, aircraft performance is affected by variations in temperature, and inversions will make things worse. Large ones encountered shortly after takeoff can seriously degrade your climb performance, particularly when you're heavy. Even a small one in the upper levels can prevent you reaching a preferred cruising altitude. At lower levels, expect deteriorating visibility, as an inversion can prevent fog clearance for prolonged periods until it is blown away by horizontal movement of air. Below a low level inversion, visibility is often moderate or poor because there is no vertical exchange to carry pollutants and haze into the free atmosphere (industrial pollutants, especially incinerated pesticides during the stubble burning season, collect at the base of an inversion).

3 (A). A large body of air will have the characteristics of its origin (the *source region*), particularly with regard to moisture and temperature, in that, a mass of air can originate from Tropical or Polar regions (i.e. be warm or cold) or be Maritime or Polar (wet or dry). The effects might be spread throughout the air mass by conduction, convection or turbulence.

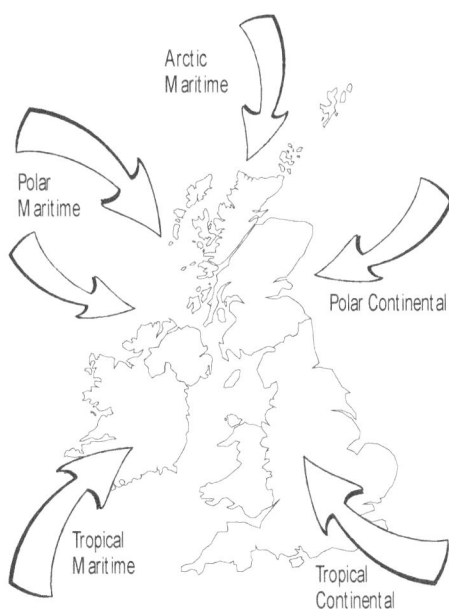

To acquire the characteristics to meet the classification, a mass of air has to stay in one more or less uniform place for several days, so one definition of an air mass could be *a huge body of air with uniform properties of temperature and moisture*. For the necessary stagnation for air to acquire such characteristics, light winds are needed, so a source region is likely to be subject to high pressure. Air masses are basically *Arctic* or *Polar*, *Tropical* or *Equatorial*, *Maritime* (sea-based) or *Continental* (land-based). Arctic and Polar only really differ at the upper levels, otherwise they are much the same, especially at the surface.

4 (B). Advection is a lateral or horizontal transfer of mass, heat, or other property.

5 (C). Backing is an anticlockwise movement.

6 (D). Air converging (coming together) at ground level is forced upwards.

7 (D).

- **Condensation** occurs when moist air become saturated

- **Evaporation** is the process of liquid water turning into vapour

- **Deposition** occurs when water vapour goes directly to the solid state (i.e. ice) without a liquid stage, but it can be referred to as sublimation.

- **Sublimation** occurs when ice is converted directly to water vapour

- **Freezing** is the process of turning water into a solid. Zero degrees is when water becomes *capable* of freezing. A Supercooled Water Droplet is one below freezing, but not frozen, because of the absence of hygroscopic nuclei* to bind on to.

- **Melting** (or fusion) is the change of state of water from a solid to a liquid state.

8 (C). See Q 7.

9 (B).

10 (C). *Gusts* are rapid changes of speed and direction that don't last long, while *squalls* do. They are sudden increases by at least 16 kts lasting at least 1 minute, reaching a top speed of 22 kts.

11 (C). A lapse rate is the rate at which an air sample cools as it rises, which varies according to whether the air is dry or saturated. The change of temperature with height is usually a decrease, which is positive - a negative lapse rate is a temperature *increase*, or an inversion. A layer of air which does not change with height is isothermal.

12 (A). Air may be lifted by:

- convection

- convergence

- mechanical turbulence

- orographic means (i.e. over geographic barriers, like a mountain range)

- frontal means

13 (D).

14 (B). See Q 11.

15 (C). The atmosphere is split into four concentric(ish) gaseous areas, according to the mean variation of temperature with height.

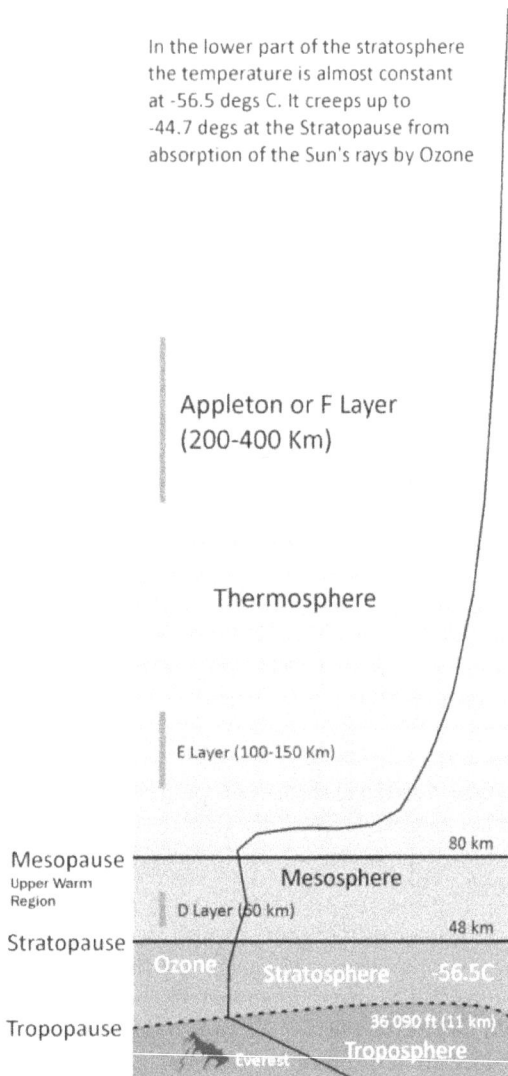

In the lower part of the stratosphere the temperature is almost constant at -56.5 degs C. It creeps up to -44.7 degs at the Stratopause from absorption of the Sun's rays by Ozone

Appleton or F Layer (200-400 Km)

Thermosphere

E Layer (100-150 Km)

80 km

Mesopause
Upper Warm
Region

Mesosphere

D Layer (60 km)

48 km

Stratopause

Ozone   Stratosphere   -56.5C

Tropopause

36 090 ft (11 km)

Troposphere

Everest

Starting from the bottom, these are the *troposphere*, *stratosphere*, *mesosphere* and *thermosphere*, although the last two are not of much concern to the average pilot. The first two are, however, and the boundary (or transition zone) between them is the *tropopause*, where any clouds are made of ice crystals.

Almost all weather happens in the troposphere, because it contains more than 75% of the mass of the atmosphere, which is drawn to the Earth by gravity. About half of that mass is below 18 000 feet, with no clear cut upper limit.

16 (D). As pressure decreases, so does the temperature, resulting in *adiabatic cooling*. *Adiabatic* means that the air gets hot, or cold, all by itself, according to whether it is being compressed or expanded - no energy is added or taken away, or exchanged with the outside world. In other words, as air expands, the molecules have more room to move around in, so they slow down, which has the effect of reducing the temperature. Similarly in reverse. Thus, as a parcel of air rises (into a region of lower pressure, which makes it expand), it cools adiabatically, through its own expansion, in the short term. Conduction between different sources of air takes quite a long time.

17 (C). Over the Equator, the tropopause lies between 16-18 km, higher than at the Poles (8 km), because the air is warmer and has expanded, taking the tropopause with it.

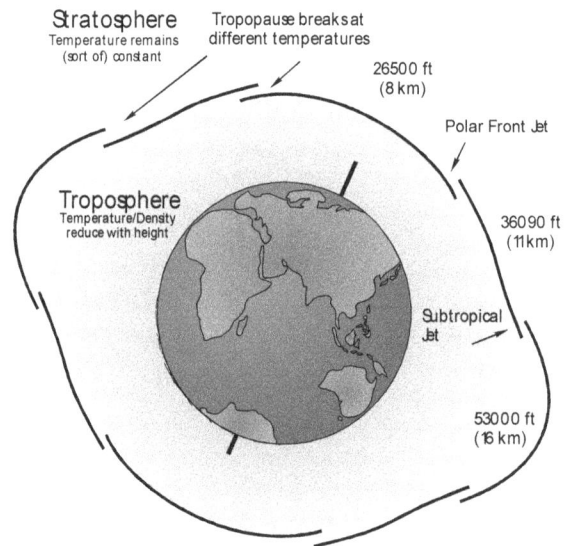

Stratosphere
Temperature remains
(sort of) constant

Tropopause breaks at
different temperatures

26500 ft
(8 km)

Polar Front Jet

Troposphere
Temperature/Density
reduce with height

36090 ft
(11km)

Subtropical
Jet

53000 ft
(16 km)

North of 60°N in Winter, the tropopause will be found at about 29 000 ft. At 50°N, at around 36 090 feet (average 11 km). However, the height of the tropopause can be locally affected by the movement of various airmasses, so there can be sudden variations.

At 40°N, 55°N and between 60-70°N, it changes height quite abruptly, and can fold over, or even break, which is an instrumental factor in the formation of jetstreams which can affect the weather at lower levels.

18 (A). As air descends in a high pressure system, it gets warmed by adiabatic compression. This also leads to low relative humidities, and the absence of cloud.

19 (D). Although oxygen may be important to pilots and engines, the proportion of gases making up the atmosphere has no relevance to meteorology, except that it holds water as:

• a gas (water vapour)

• a liquid (clouds or rain)

• a solid (ice)

Water vapour is important because it is invisible, and affects the humidity ratio of the air. Because it weighs five-eighths of an equivalent amount of dry air, water vapour will also reduce the density of the air and your engine's punch, but that's the subject of the *Performance* chapter. The water vapour content on average is around 1%, but can get as high as 4%. The troposphere (the lower part of the atmosphere) contains more than 90% of all water vapour, but the correction is small and generally negligible.The presence of water is expressed as *relative humidity*, and its importance lies in the energy that is released and consumed as it changes from gas to liquid to ice and back.

20 (A). The standard reduction of temperature with height (lapse rate) is 1.98°C per thousand feet, although 2° is often used for convenience.

21 (A). True altitude is your (geometric) elevation above mean sea level. It would be the distance you could normally find with a tape measure, but this is impractical, so we use instruments such as the altimeter instead, to show an *indicated* altitude.

The only time an altimeter will indicate true altitude is in ISA conditions. As such conditions are rare, indications are almost always in error due to temperature.

The difference between true and standard (ISA) altitude is 4 feet per thousand feet per degree of deviation from ISA. That is, true altitude changes by 4% for every 10°C deviation from ISA conditions, or 2% for every 5.5°C*.

*4% is correct for the stratosphere, but more like 3.5% for lower altitudes. 4% for every 11°C is more accurate.

One source of error can occur when the temperature at a level might be close to ISA, when the lapse rate is not.

Note: All calculations should be rounded to the nearest lower hPa. The barometric lapse rate near mean sea level is 27 ft (8m) per hPa. Also, the airport elevation must be taken into account - that is, *only use the layer between the ground and the position of the aircraft.*

In practice, true altitude is obtained from knowing the outside air temperature (OAT) at the level you are flying at, and using a computer. This will be reasonably accurate when the actual lapse rate is, or is near, that of ISA, i.e., 2°C per 1 000 feet, but if it's very hot, or very cold, you need further adjustments.

22 (C).

23 (C). Turbulence can be found in cloud and clear air (that is, *Clear Air Turbulence*, or CAT), and usually comes from friction when air currents mix, from various sources, such as *convective, orographic, windshear* and *mechanical*, and is reported as:

• *Light*, with small changes in height or attitude, near stratocumulus

• *Moderate*, more severe, but you are still in control. ICAO definition: *There may be moderate changes in aircraft attitude and/or altitude but the aircraft remains in positive control at all times. Usually, small variations in air speed. Changes in accelerometer readings of 0.5 to 1.0 g at the aircraft's center of gravity. Occupants feel strain against seat belts. Loose objects move about. Food service and walking are difficult.* Good indicators are Cumulus-type clouds, which may also warn you about....

• *Severe*, with abrupt changes, and being temporarily out of control, indicated by Cumulonimbus and lenticular clouds, if there are many stacked on top of each other. Expect the latter when winds across mountain ranges are more than 40 kts

• *Extreme*, impossible to control

If turbulence is likely, use turbulence speed, which will be less than normal. Advise the passengers to securely fasten their seat belts/harnesses. Catering and other loose equipment should be stowed and secured.

24 (C). Isobars are like contours, and make common patterns, two of which are the *low* or *high*, other names for *cyclone* and *anti-cyclone*, respectively (nothing to do with the cyclones that seem to damage trailer parks). Another name for a low is a *depression*.

25 (B). See Q 24.

26 (A). When flying from high to low pressure, your altimeter will also over-read (from HIGH to LOW, it is

HIGH), so you would be lower than planned and liable for a nasty surprise. It's therefore much safer to be going the other way (that is, from LOW to HIGH, where your instrument is LOW).

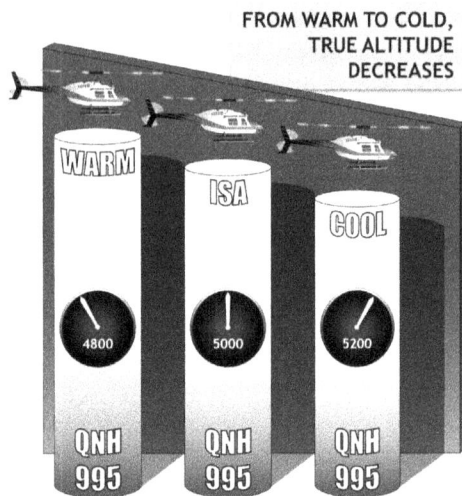

FROM WARM TO COLD, TRUE ALTITUDE DECREASES

An *increase* in pressure equals a *decrease* in altitude, so if you start with 29.92, then go to where it is 30.92, the altimeter reading would be 1,000 feet less, even though the figures themselves increase.

27 (C). Density Altitude is the altitude in the Standard Atmosphere at which the prevailing density occurs, meaning your real altitude from the effects of height, temperature and humidity, and is used to establish performance, as it is a figure that expresses where your machine thinks it is, as opposed to where it actually is - see *Performance*. For now, it is *pressure altitude corrected for non-standard temperature*, or the true air temperature at a given level. Thus, density altitude has the same value as pressure altitude at standard temperature.

To find DA on the flight computer, set the aerodrome elevation or Pressure Altitude against the temperature in the *airspeed* window (see right).

In the picture, the temperature is -21°C at 10 100 feet (follow the red line about midway). The indicated airspeed is 177 kts, and the TAS is 200. The Density Altitude (bottom right) is 8100 feet - that's quite a difference!

If you want a formula:

        PA ± (118.8 x ISA Dev)

(Multiplying the ISA Dev by 120 is usually good enough).

Picture: Density Altitude calculation

28 (D). Wind is the *horizontal* movement of air from high to low pressure, just like the air from a pricked balloon - the larger the pressure difference, the faster the wind will flow. Where isobars are closer together, there is a greater rate of change over a short distance.

Wind is expressed as a velocity, so it needs direction and speed to fit the definition. The wind always comes *from* somewhere, expressed as a *true bearing* in weather reports (*magnetic* from the Tower), so a *Southerly* wind is *from* 180°. The speed is mostly in knots, or nautical miles per hour, as if you didn't know already, measured at 10 metres over open terrain as a ten-minute average.

29 (C). According to Professor *Buys Ballot's Law* (a Dutch meteorologist who lived in Utrecht in 1857), if you stand with your back to the wind in the Northern hemisphere, the low pressure is on your left (on the right in the Southern hemisphere), so if you fly towards lower pressure, you will drift to starboard as the wind is coming from the left.

30 (C). Land & sea breezes arise out of a temperature difference between land and sea areas. Air over land warms up and cools down faster than that over the sea, because land has a lower specific heat than water does and needs less heat to warm it up. Thus, temperature changes over land will occur a lot more frequently than they do over the sea. When the land is warmer than the sea, the air over it becomes less dense and the space left by the rising air is filled with an extra component coming from over the water to produce a *sea breeze* which is added to any existing wind (in fact, a relatively high pressure is created at about 1000 feet over land, to produce a pressure gradient aloft).

With lower pressure at the same height over the water, there will be air movement towards the sea, at the upper levels (because the column of warm air is taller, and the relative pressure is higher), which will subside to come back towards the land. At night, the process is reversed to get a land breeze. However, land areas are poor conductors of heat and will only be affected through a shallow layer. As a result, land breezes are weaker because the temperature differences are smaller and so is the local pressure gradient.

A prevailing wind can oppose a sea-breeze and delay its development, or go with it and increase its speed, although, at latitudes greater than about 20°, Coriolis can change the direction of a sea breeze by itself.

If a convergence is created, sea breezes can be strong enough to create their own cold fronts, well inland*, and even trigger thunderstorms, as the colder sea air undercuts the land air. Here are possible examples for the UK.

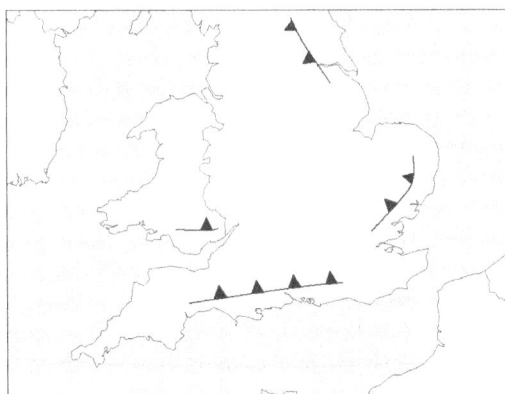

*In Australia, for example, sea breezes have been encountered 400 km away from the sea.

Knowing this is useful when you're going to a destination near the sea, and the wind (and landing direction) could be different than what you might expect, or you might be offshore and know that a tailwind will be around to help

bring you home. Fishing fleets time their movements in and out of port around these winds.

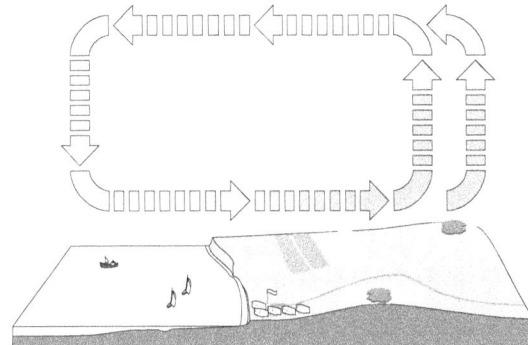

31 (B). As you descend, friction with trees, rocks, etc. will slow the wind down by just over 50%, which lessens the geostrophic effect and gives you an effective change of wind direction to the left. Over the sea, the geostrophic effect will be less, giving about 10° difference in direction, as opposed to the 30° you can expect over land (the speed reduces to about 70% over water, and 50% over land).

32 (A). *Pressure altitude* is the height in the standard atmosphere that you may find a given pressure, usually 29.92" or 1013 Mb, but actually whatever you set on the altimeter - if you set 1013 on the subscale and the needles read 6,000 feet, the PA *for that setting* is 6,000 feet. PA is a starting point for any calculations for performance, TAS, etc., and is the altimeter setting used above the transition altitude, where all altimeters must be set to 1013 hPa so that everybody is using the same standard (every country has a different transition altitude). Below the transition altitude, local altimeter settings are used.

If an altimeter is set to 1013, it is measuring Pressure Altitude with respect to Mean Sea Level. In ISA conditions, Pressure Altitude is the same as True Altitude.

33 (C). The cold front occurs when cold dense air moves towards the Equator (from the Poles) and undercuts warm air to force it aloft. A cold front has a much steeper slope (1:50) than a warm front, and brisker activity, with more of a likelihood of thunderstorms, because the convergence is typically stronger, providing a greater forcing mechanism. The rain becomes more showery and the wind veers more, to the West or Northwest. Pressure gets higher, and temperature and humidity decrease. In temperate climates,

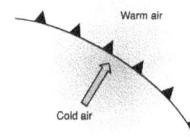

large amounts of Cu-nim are unusual at this point, but they are not over continental land areas. The rain belt is relatively small compared to the warm front, and visibility will improve markedly.

A cold front moves at about the speed of the wind perpendicular to it just above the friction level (about 2,000 feet, for 15-25 kts), but they are faster in Winter because the air is colder and exerts greater pressure. However, friction with the ground will slow the lower levels, so there is a bulge effect along the leading edge. The friction, coupled with strong heating from below as the cold air crosses warmer ground, often creates gusty wind conditions. The weather is generally colder after its passage, and with less cloud, because pressure is greater to the West and less to the East, limiting the inflow of air.

34 (B). Warm air moving over cold ground tends to stable and smooth air.

35 (B). In simple terms, when the surface temperature is well *below* ISA (starting at -16°C), correct your altitudes by:

Surface Temp (ISA)	Correction
-16°C to -30°C	+ 10%
-31°C to -50°C	+ 20%
-51°C or below	+ 25%

For example, at -20°C at 500 feet, your altimeter should be reading 570 ft to ensure a height above ground of 500 ft. Just remember that, when temperatures are *less* than ISA, you will be lower than the altimeter reading, so *add* any values in tables to published altitudes or heights,

36 (A). Whatever radiation gets through from the Sun heats the Earth's surface by insolation. **Radiation** involves the flow of heat from one material to another without affecting the temperature of the space between them. The atmosphere gains little or no heat from direct radiation.

The air in contact with the surface is heated by **conduction**, where heat can pass from a warmer to a colder body without the transfer of matter. As air is a poor conductor of heat, the air close to the ground usually ends up warmer than that above it, although the opposite can happen with an **inversion**.

Convection exists where the body carrying the heat itself moves, usually vertically*, which is how warmth is spread through the rest of the atmosphere, until the temperature equalises with the surrounding air. Turbulence has a similar effect, and there is also latent heat transfer, which occurs when heat absorbed during evaporation at the

surface is released when condensation occurs. Finally, some direct transfer of heat is done when short wave radiation is absorbed by the ozone layer.

37 (B). The DALR is the (constant, fixed) *decrease in temperature of unsaturated air with height* at around 3°C per 1,000 feet or 9.8°C (10°C) per 1,000 m (*Dry* just means a relative humidity of less than 100%).

38 (A).

39 (D).

40 (B). Radiation fog forms over land, preferably low-lying, when temperatures approach the dewpoint with very slight winds (2-8 kts), with moisture present, so high relative humidity, long cooling periods and clear skies are relevant. It doesn't form over the sea, because the diurnal temperature variation is less. It is often found in the early morning after a clear night, since it likes high relative humidity, light winds and clear skies (and long cooling periods). Its vertical extent is typically 500 feet, and it usually clears quickly, once the Sun's heat gets to work, often getting worse before it gets better. If the winds are just enough to stir things up, fog will form. If there is no wind, you will get dew on the ground, and if the wind is too strong you will get low level stratus. Radiation fog disperses with wind, heat, or a drier air mass. You can expect the densest type the night after an afternoon of heavy rains, in low lying areas, which, naturally, is where you will find most airfields.

Picture: Radiation Fog In The Rockies

41 (C).

42 (A).

43 (B). See picture below.

44 (C). Advection fog arises from warm air flowing over a cold surface, and it can be encountered immediately after

the passage of a cold front. Advection simply means the sideways movement of air in bulk - warm advection means warm air replacing colder air, and *vice versa*, as you would find with fronts. It is not the same as radiation fog because air movement is involved, and the coolness does not arise from diurnal variations, but longer periods, as with the sea, where this type of fog is commonly found. It is the type of fog that rolls in to cover the San Francisco bridge.

Winds over 15 kts will lift advection fog into a layer of low stratus or stratocumulus.

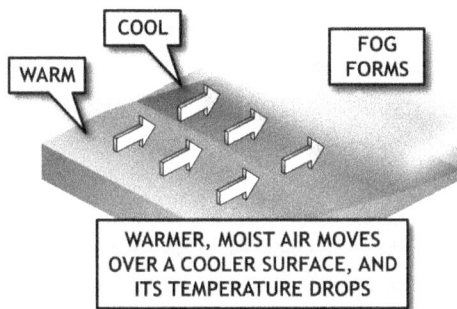

45 (D).

46 (C). For example, at -20°C at 500 feet, your altimeter should be reading 570 ft to ensure a height above ground of 500 ft. Just remember that, when temperatures are less than ISA, you will be lower than the altimeter reading.

47 (A).

48 (B).

49 (A).

50 (D). Nimbostratus (Ns) is thick, dark, low rain cloud, typically found in warm fronts. It may be found through all layers, but at least starts in the alto range. Moderate to heavy continual rain or snow.

51 (D).

52 (C). A warm front exists where warm air overtakes a colder air mass and is forced upwards over it, meaning clouds. Its symbol on a weather map, resembling beads of sweat, is shown on the left. The frontal slope has a gradient in the order of 1:150, although the clouds themselves will be about 5 miles high, starting with Nimbostratus at more or less ground level, through alto-stratus to cirrostratus. When flying towards it, you would see the clouds the other way round, of course, so once you start seeing cirrus clouds, you know that a warm front is somewhere ahead, anywhere between 300-600 miles away, or nearly 24 hours at a typical speed of about 25 kts, so have an overnight kit if you have to wait it out (rain will typically be 200 miles ahead). You can use the typical slope figure to work out the cloud base in front of the system. At 100 miles, it will be 2,640 feet, which comes from 1/200*100, making half a mile, multiplied by 5280 (feet).

Clouds will therefore appear in this order as you fly towards a warm front - cirrus, cirrostratus, altostratus, stratus and nimbostratus (see picture at bottom of page). The extensive cloud layers are caused by unstable warm air overrunning retreating cold air, with a high moisture content. Thus, the precipitation will change from steady rain to heavy showers.

Picture below: Side view of frontal system

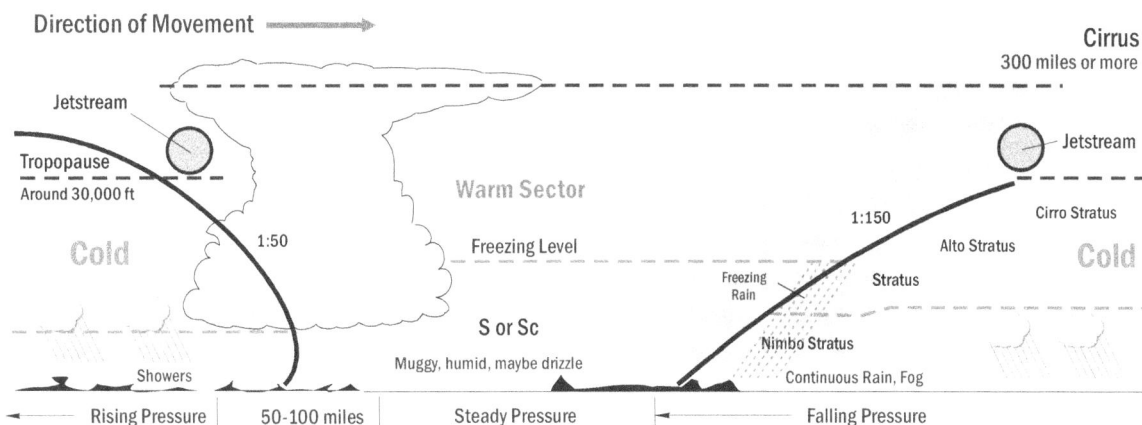

53 (B). Virga is like a fine mist that evaporates before reaching the ground, which looks like streamers just below the cloud base. It should be avoided because it is turbulent**, and may be coming from a microburst.

**As rain changes from liquid to vapour, it removes heat from the air. The colder air can descend rapidly, creating a dry microburst.

54 (A). The shallow slope of a warm front ensures that whatever is coming will last some time, and you can expect the pressure to fall, the cloud to get lower, the wind to back and increase in speed, rising humidity, bad visibility, drizzle and rain, though not necessarily in that order. The freezing level will be lower in front than behind, and the slope means that freezing rain will be falling on anything underneath (see diagram below), so if you are flying towards a warm front, or towards the rear of a cold front, in between their freezing levels and that in the warm sector, watch out! Supercooled water droplets from above will freeze onto your cold airframe. Once you see ice pellets, expect freezing rain next.

55 (C). See Q 106.

56 (B). Water vapour is important because it is invisible, and affects the humidity ratio of the air. Because it weighs five-eighths of an equivalent amount of dry air, water vapour will also reduce the density of the air and your engine's punch. The water vapour content on average is around 1%, but can get as high as 4%. The troposphere (the lower part of the atmosphere) contains more than 90% of all water vapour, but the correction is small and generally negligible. The presence of water is expressed as relative humidity, and its importance lies in the energy that is released and consumed as it changes from gas to liquid to ice and back. Warmer air holds more water vapour.

57 (C). Identical clouds, well isolated, dense, with well defined contours, developing vertically in a cauliflower shape, with the sides lit by the sun being bright white and

their essentially horizontal bases, relatively dark, are *towering cumulus*, which are typically found between FL 30 and FL 150.

58 (B). Cirrus (Ci) is a high and fibrous filament indicating that a warm front is around 200 nm away. Otherwise known as *Horse tails*, or *Mares' tails*, they can produce precipitation that evaporates well before reaching ground level - the falling ice streaks form the distinctive filaments.

59 (A). Hail forms from large water droplets forced above the freezing level, although there is an accretion and growth process as well. Raindrops in this situation can turn into small pieces of ice which may collide with supercooled water droplets and get larger, until they get so large that they fall out of the sky at some speed and cause damage to people or property. Hail is typically found coming out of thunderstorms (CB).

60 (D). East of Greenland. The air will be cold (Polar) and wet (Maritime).

61 (B). See Q 54.

62 (B) Typically found underneath the slope of a warm front in winter.

63 (B).

64 (B).

65 (B).

66 (C). See Q 40.

67 (A).

68 (A).

69 (C).

70 CU, CB.

71 (C).

72 (A).

73 (D).

74 (A).

75 (A).

76 (A).

77 (B).

78 (B).

79 (B).

80 (D).

81 (D).

82 (B).

83 (C).

84 (A) No.

- EGLL - The airfield concerned, in this case London Heathrow

- 0550 - The time, 0550 UTC

- 21008 - surface wind 210°T, at 80 kts

- 0600 - visibility 600 m

- R0560 - RVR 560 m

- 45 FG - Fog

- 9///// - sky obscured

- Temperature 18°C, dewpoint 17°C

- QNH 1020 hPa

- GRADU - gradually changing to become....

- 3000 - 3 km visibility

- 7ST006 - seven oktas of stratus, base 600 ft agl

85 (A).

86 (B).

87 (D).

88 (A).

89 (A).

90 (A).

91 (A).

92 (D).

93 (A).

94 (D).

95 (A).

96 (B).

97 (A).

98 (C). There is no cloud reported, so there will be a clear sky. The wind is light, and the temperature and dewpoint are very close, and the pressure is high. As the visibility is already poor, radiation fog is the best answer, although CAVOK would be better later on in the morning.

99 (D). When an obstruction such as a mountain range has stable air flowing over it at the 10,000 foot level at about 20 knots (depends on the size of the range), blowing broadside on (within about 30°), you can get standing waves for some miles downwind. These occur

because the wind has enough momentum to bounce off the ground behind the mountain and push the air already there out of the way. That air will fall again when it reaches a peak. The Fohn, Mistral and Bora behave in a similar way.

Being standing waves, they do not move (although the air flowing through them does), and the distance between them is constant. They are easily identified by the types of cloud associated with them, which also do not move, such as the lenticular shown below that can be found at the peak of each wave.

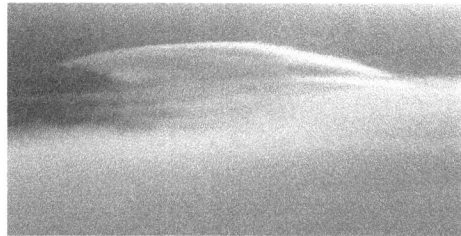

Although the waves as a whole can reach up several thousand feet, the air oscillates up and down about a central mean as it moves downwind.

The flowing air can be deceptively smooth, and only the VSI will tell you if you are going up or down. If you are flying parallel to a ridge on the downwind side in a smooth downdraught, as a result of the local drop in pressure associated with the wave, the VSI and the altimeter will not indicate a descent until you pass through a layer equal to the error caused by the mountain wave (they may indicate a climb for a short while), so you may not recognise that you are in a downdraught until you pass through the original pressure level which is closer to the ground than before you entered the wave.

Thus, in cloud, or at night, you could be in some danger*. There could also be turbulence with accelerations up to 20 G in extreme cases.

*This does not just apply to light aircraft! 747s have lost complete engines in mountain wave downdraughts, but the most common problems are severe reductions in rates of climb and excessive rates of sink.

The trapped lee waves are associated with marked adverse pressure gradients as they go up and down, sometimes dropping over 5 hPa through just a few kilometres. There could also be large vertical increases of temperature (inversions) in the order of 10°C over 200 metres.

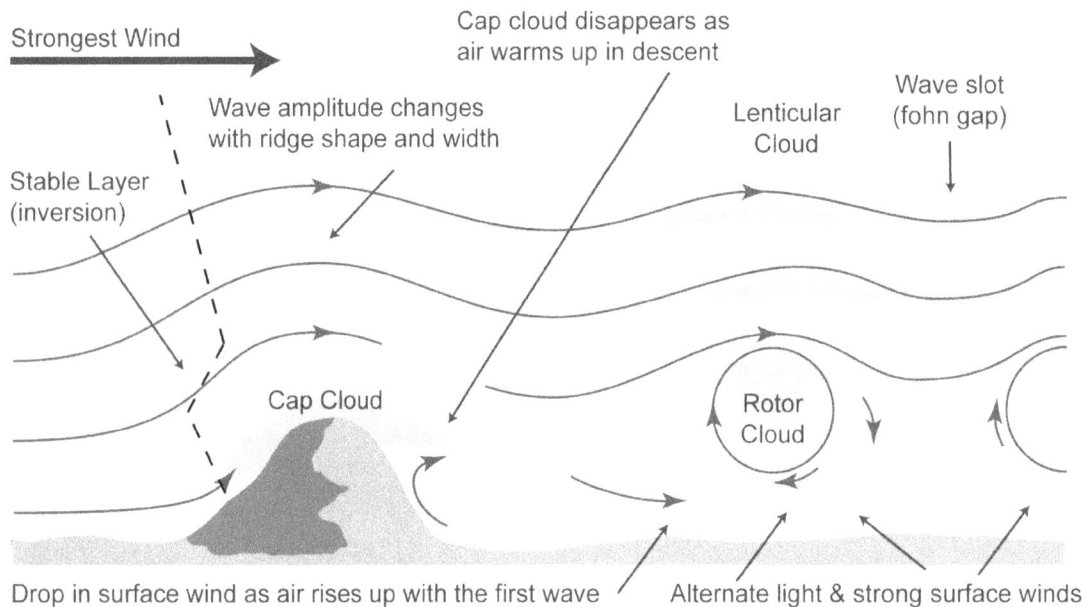

Strongest Wind

Cap cloud disappears as air warms up in descent

Wave amplitude changes with ridge shape and width

Lenticular Cloud

Wave slot (fohn gap)

Stable Layer (inversion)

Cap Cloud

Rotor Cloud

Drop in surface wind as air rises up with the first wave

Alternate light & strong surface winds

The combination of mountain waves and non-standard temperature may result in your altimeter over-reading by as much as 3 000 feet!

An aircraft affected by mountain waves can expect severe turbulence below any rotors, downdraughts that may be stronger than the rate of climb and greater than normal icing in associated clouds.

Downdraughts can be particularly dangerous when flying towards a range into a headwind, as the airflow follows the general shape of the surface, and you will experience a strong downdraught just before the ridge:

In other words, when into wind, height variations are out of phase with the waves. They are usually in phase when you are flying downwind.

Note: The wind speed and direction should be more or less constant up to about 18,000 feet, although it doesn't have to be particularly fast over the peaks. However, it must increase with height.

As the wind needs to be fairly straight in direction, warm sector winds and jetstreams can be very conducive to the formation of waves. They will be more dangerous in Winter simply because the wind speeds are stronger, and there will be a longer wavelength. There can be several miles between their peaks and troughs, which can extend between 10,000-20,000 feet above the range and up to 200 or 300 miles downwind:

Watch for long-term variations in speed and pitch attitude in level cruise (the variations may be large). Near the ground in a mountain wave area, severe turbulence and windshear may be encountered, especially at the bottom of a rotor where you may get a performance decreasing shear if you are going in the same direction as the wind.

The potential loss of altitude is 500 feet if the wind is between 30-40 kts, 1000 feet between 40-50, 1500 feet between 50-60 kts and 2000 feet over 60 kts.

ROTORS

Rotors are ares of rotating turbulence found under the lenticular clouds that are a clue to the position of the peak of a wave. They are always in circular motion, constantly forming and dissipating as water vapour is added and taken away. They are dangerous, and the most turbulence will be found in them, or between them and the ground. Rotor clouds are formed in the same way as lenticular clouds, that is, from air forced upwards and condensing, then dissipating as they proceed downwards in the wave.

Rotor streaming is a phenomenon that occurs when air flowing across a mountain is enough to create waves, but decreases in effect with altitude above the mountain - that is, they are only strong in the lower levels. The air downstream of the mountain still breaks up and becomes turbulent, similar to a rotor, but there are no lee waves, so the rotors travel downwind rather than stay in one place as they normally would. Watch for ragged cumuliform cloud.

If the rotor forms in an inversion, warm air from above is rotated downward and heated further as it is compressed. On the other way up, cold air is expanding to cool further. Thus, very cold air ends up lying over warm air and conditions are extremely unstable.

OTHER CLOUDS

You will see a *cap cloud* over the top of the range, creeping down the *lee side* (downwind), from the downdraught.

It disappears as air descends and warms adiabatically.

100 (D). See Q 99.

101 (D).

102 (C).

103 (D). The CAA might want answer a).

104 (B).

105 (C). **Frontal fog** may simply be low cloud touching high ground, or come from rain falling through unsaturated air beneath:

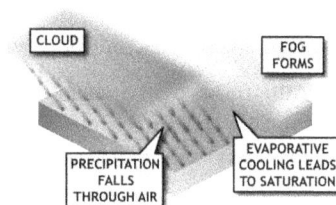

106 (C). There are three classifications of clouds based on the height of the cloud base.

- **Low** (Strato) - from SL to about 6500 ft, mainly water:

  - **Stratus** (St), thin, uniform, low, boring, associated with relatively stable air. Not much precipitation, but may give drizzle or snow grains. At ground level, stratus is called fog or mist. It is caused by large areas cooling, rather than individual pockets of air, as with cumulus. When the sun is visible through the cloud, the outline is clearly discernible. Sometimes it appears as ragged patches. A layer of stratus is most likely to be dispersed by insolation resulting in the lifting of the mixing condensation level

  - **Stratocumulus** (Sc). Like stratus, but cumulus-like, with small globules popping up here and there, and well-defined bases. Often formed in eddy currents which cause stratus to clump up, because the stratus tops will be cool from reflecting the Sun's rays and the bases warm from absorbing the Earth's infrared radiation. These can also form from cumulus joining up under an inversion. Sc can produce light rain or snow - any heavy showers will come from embedded cumulus. You might see clouds in patches, sheets or grey or whitish layers made up of elements resembling large pebbles or rollers, together or not, and clear of the ground

  - **Nimbostratus** (Ns). Thick, dark, low rain cloud, typical in warm fronts, which may be found through all layers, but at least starts in the *alto* range. Moderate to heavy continual rain or snow

- **Middle** (Alto) - between 6 500-23 000 feet, made of water, ice, or supercooled water droplets, depending on temperature:

  - **Altocumulus** (Ac) is similar to Sc (above), but higher. Size of cloudlets is between one and three finger-widths, with noticeable shading (not dark and gloomy, like stratus)

  - **Altostratus** (As), similar to stratus, but higher, medium sheet greyish or bluish cloud, any thickness up to 10-12,000'. No ground shadow

- **High** (Cirro) - between 16 500-45 000 feet, made of ice crystals, so they have some transparency:

  - **Cirrocumulus** (Cc) is high sheet cloud, made of small cloudlets (for want of a better word) which do not cast shadows, looking like a mackerel sky

  - **Cirrostratus** (Cs) translucent high cloud, very delicate, made up of ice crystals. When in front of the Sun, you may see a halo round it

  - **Cirrus** (Ci) is a high and fibrous filament indicating that a warm front is around 200 nm away. Otherwise known as *Horse tails*, or *Mares' tails*, they can produce precipitation which evaporates well before reaching ground level - falling ice streaks form distinctive filaments

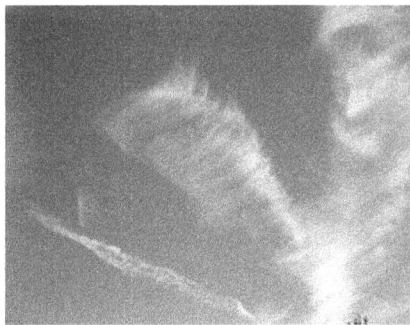

- **Other - Heap clouds** (i.e. marked vertical extent):

  - **Cumulus** (Cu), are small amounts of heap cloud at low and medium levels, looking a bit like small balls of cotton wool with flat bases.

It's actually *convection cloud*, which gives you a clue as to how it is made, and glider pilots seek out the thermals underneath them for lift (when a cumulus cloud is removed from its thermal, it can still grow from the latent heat that is released inside it, making it warmer than its surroundings to cause it to float upwards). In strong winds, you might see them in long lines called *cloud streets*.

So-called "fair weather cumulus", as seen on a nice Summer's day, normally forms directly as such, but (less commonly) can develop from stratus or strato-cu that has broken up with morning heating (they can also spread out into strato-cu or alto-cu in the presence of an inversion). Fair weather cumulus is often an indication of turbulence at and below the cloud level. It is known as fair weather cloud because it produces no precipitation.

Over land, fair weather cu usually forms in the morning and reaches its maximum in terms of number and size by mid afternoon. It dissipates rapidly in the evening once the ground cools and convection currents die out.

Over the sea, this is less marked and tends to be the reverse because the sea temperature stays the same while the air aloft cools.

Characteristics of cumuliform cloud include large water droplets, instability, turbulence, showers, and mainly clear ice. *Cumulus Congestus* has a large vertical extent. *Cumulus Castellanus* looks like the side of a castle. *Mediocris* are as tall as they are wide, and *Humilis* are the smallest, being wider than they are tall. *Cumulus Fractus* clouds are decaying, and appear ragged and woolly.

- **Cumulonimbus** is towering storm cloud. "Towering" means up to as much as 60,000 feet, and the anvil shape at the top is due to it meeting the tropopause, where temperature starts to remain constant, stopping the cloud's ascent. CBs are mostly found around late afternoon, and can project into the stratosphere. They are cumulus congestus until the upper regions turn into ice crystals. See also *Thunderstorms*

107 (D).

108 (C).

109 (D).

110 (B).

111 (D).

112 (B).

113 (D).

114 (C).

115 (C).

116 (D).

117 (B).

118 (A).

119 (D).

120 (C).

121 (D).

122 (C).

123 (D).

124 (A).

125 (C).

126 (C).

127 (D).

128 (A).

129 (C).

130 (A).

131 (A).

132 (B).

133 (D).

134 (A).

135 (A).

136 (C).

137 (C).

138 (D).

139 (C).

140 (C).

141 (D).

142 (B).

143 (A).

144 (B).

145 (B).

146 (C).

147 (C).

148 (C).

149 (B).

150 (A). The DALR is modified by the dewpoint lapse rate of 5°C, to become 2.5°C per thousand feet. Subtract the dewpoint temperature from the surface temperature and divide by 2.5.

151 (D).

152 (D).

153 (D).

154 (D).

155 (C).

156 (B).

157 (B).

158 (C).

159 (C).

160 (B).

161 (B). Trick question! 59°F is 15°C.

162 (B).

163 (A).

164 (A).

165 (A).

166 (C).

167 (A).

168 (C).

169 (C).

170 (D).

171 (D).

172 (A).

173 (A).

174 (B).

175 (C).

176 (A).

177 (D).

178 (D).

179 (B).

180 (C).

181 (C).

182 (B).

183 (B)

184 (B)

IMC RATING

1. (D). The validity runs for 25 months from the beginning of the day of the successful test.

2 (A). An IMC rated pilot may fly out of sight of the surface in visibility less than 3 km outside controlled airspace (which is the whole point of the exercise). Otherwise, you can only go IFR in Class D or E airspace (A, B, or C requires a full Instrument Rating).

Special VFR requires sight of the surface. The minimum visibility for takeoff or landing is 1800m (1.8km).

3 (B). 4 is wrong. Even if an approach needs only 600 m visibility, an IMC rated pilot may not descend to below 1000 feet above the aerodrome elevation below cloud unless the visibility is at least 1800 m.

4 (C). The OBS has no effect on instrument indications when in ILS mode.

5 (A).

6 (A).

7 (C).

8 (D).

9 (B)

10 (A).

11 (A).

12 (C).

13 (B)

www.ingramcontent.com/pod-product-compliance
Lightning Source LLC
Chambersburg PA
CBHW080419270326
41929CB00018B/3081

9 781926 833187